# THE GERMAN STAGE,
## *1767–1890*

# THE GERMAN STAGE, 1767–1890

## A Directory of Playwrights and Plays

Compiled by
Veronica C. Richel

Bibliographies and Indexes in the Performing Arts, Number 7

**Greenwood Press**
New York • Westport, Connecticut • London

Library of Congress Cataloging-in-Publication Data

Richel, Veronica C.
  The German stage, 1767-1890.

  (Bibliographies and indexes in the performing
arts, ISSN 0742-6933 ; no. 7)
  Bibliography: p.
  Includes index.
  1. German drama—18th century—Bio-bibliography.
  2. German drama—19th century—Bio-bibliography.
  3. Theater—Germany—History—18th century—Sources.
  4. Theater—Germany—History—19th century—Sources.
  I. Title.  II. Series.
  PT641.R5  1987      016.832'008        87-25155
  ISBN 0-313-24990-3 (lib. bdg. : alk. paper)

British Library Cataloguing in Publication Data is available.

Library of Congress Catalog Card Number: 87-25155
ISBN: 0-313-24990-3
ISSN: 0742-6933

First published in 1988

Greenwood Press, Inc.
88 Post Road West, Westport, Connecticut 06881

Printed in the United States of America

10 9 8 7 6 5 4 3 2 1

# Contents

# Introduction

Much of what has been written about German drama of the eighteenth and nineteenth centuries emanates from literary historians and critics who judge the success or failure of a play according to its literary merits. However, it is well known that many "good" plays had little impact on the theatre, while countless long-forgotten works comprised the regular entertainment of the theatre-going public. The authors of these plays are themselves often equally obscure. Although some playwrights, such as August von Kotzebue, August Wilhelm Iffland, Charlotte Birch-Pfeiffer and Ernst Raupach, are frequently cited--and sometimes studied--as prolific writers of popular plays, most authors fail to earn even brief mention. But the purpose of this book is neither to resurrect neglected playwrights nor to revise opinions of their works. Rather, it is to facilitate investigation of the working repertory of German theatres between 1767 and 1890 by recording the production of more than four thousand plays in ten selected cities. The data presented here in a systematic way have been extracted from a variety of sources, many of which are difficult to obtain and inconveniently arranged. By including the works of both dilettantes and literary giants, such a compilation provides insight into the practical theatre of the period in question and should also prove useful for research on German "Trivialliteratur" of the eighteenth and nineteenth centuries, a subject of recent scholarly interest.

The historical scope of the compilation will be apparent to students of German drama. 1767 marked the inauguration of the ill-fated "Hamburg enterprise," the first attempt to establish a German national theatre, as well as the publication of G. E. Lessing's Hamburg Dramaturgy, the first serious critical essays to concern themselves (at least initially) with contemporary theatrical performance. Despite the fact that both endeavors were short-lived, they gave impetus, on the one hand, to the rise of popular theatre in Germany and, on the other, to a host of theatre journals which chronicled and criticized the productions of the day. Throughout most of the nineteenth century the enormous public appetite for "Novitäten" was satisfied by the staging of a prodigious number of

new works.  Although many of them were never published and few
of them outlived their creators on the stages of Germany,
these were the plays which captured the imagination of
audiences and succeeded at the box office.  While the taste
for popular neo-romantic fare did not end abruptly in 1890,
the final decades of the century are commonly regarded as a
turning point in German drama, as attention shifted to modern
realism under the influence of Henrik Ibsen and Gerhart
Hauptmann.  An additional reason for terminating the present
documentation with the year 1890 is the appearance in that
year of the first volume of the Neuer Theater-Almanach (published since 1915 as the Deutsches Bühnen-Jahrbuch).  Its sur-
vival since 1890 is indicative of the improved record-keeping
and accessibility of information which benefit scholars of
twentieth-century drama.

Indeed, the inaccessibility of sources and the lack of
consistent records presented often insurmountable problems in
the compilation of this book.  It must be emphasized here that
the performance data were taken only from the sources listed
below, all of which were obtained through the inter-library
loan system from libraries in the United States.  Thus, ar-
chives such as the Fambach collection in Bonn and printed
sources not owned by American libraries were not consulted.
Also, it should be stressed that the available sources provide
only incomplete data.  Most chronicles cover a relatively
short period in the history of one particular theatre in a
given location.  As one might expect, there are gaps in
chronology and many theatres are not represented at all.  Be
that as it may, the sources at hand were plumbed as thoroughly
as possible.  One exception must be noted, namely Vol. 11 of
Goedeke's Grundriß, which is devoted to theatre and drama in
Germany (Pt. I) and Austria (Pt. II) from 1815 to 1830.  This
indispensible volume was used to corroborate information found
elsewhere, such as titles, publication dates or dates and
locations of performances.  However, performance data which
appear only in Goedeke are not repeated.  In several cases,
most of them involving Viennese playwrights, the user of this
book is referred to Goedeke 11 for additional listings.  A
typical example is Josef Alois Gleich, for whom there are 222
entries consisting primarily of plays written when he was
employed as "Theaterdichter" for the Theater in der Josefstadt
and the Theater in der Leopoldstadt and usually performed only
in Vienna.  Since performance calendars for these theatres are
not among the sources consulted, most of Gleich's plays are
not included here.  A similar case is that of Louis Angely,
whose works were written for and produced at the Königstädti-
sches Theater in Berlin.  Also, because Vol. 11 of the Grundriß is readily available and considerably more "user friendly"
than the remaining volumes, a re-listing of such accessible
material would be redundant.

## SOURCES OF PERFORMANCE DATA

Bartels, Adolf.  Chronik des Weimarischen Hoftheaters 1817-1907.  Weimar, 1908.

Bing, Anton.  Rückblicke auf die Geschichte des Frankfurter Stadttheaters von dessen Selbständigkeit (1792) bis zur Gegenwart.  2 Bde.  Frankfurt/M., 1892-96.

Blümner, Heinrich.  Geschichte des Theaters in Leipzig.  Leipzig, 1818.  Reprint: Leipzig, 1979.

Brachvogel, Albert Emil.  Geschichte des Königlichen Theaters zu Berlin.  Bd.I: Das alte Berliner Theaterwesen bis zur ersten Blüthe des deutschen Dramas.  Berlin, 1877.

Burckhardt, Carl August Hugo.  Das Repertoire des Weimarischen Theaters unter Goethes Leitung 1791-1817.  Hamburg und Leipzig, 1891.  Reprint: Nendeln/Liechtenstein, 1977.

Fambach, Oscar.  Das Repertorium des Hof- und Nationaltheaters in Mannhein 1804-1832.  Bonn, 1980.

Fambach, Oscar.  Das Repertorium des Stadttheaters zu Leipzig 1817-1828.  Bonn, 1980.

Grandauer, Franz.  Chronik des königlichen Hof- und Nationaltheaters in München.  Zur Feier seines hundertjährigen Bestehens.  München, 1878.

Hadamowsky, Franz.  Die Wiener Hoftheater (Staatstheater) 1776-1966.  Verzeichnis der aufgeführten Stücke mit Bestandsnachweis und täglichem Spielplan.  Teil I, 1776-1810.  Wien, 1966.

Knispel, Hermann.  Das Großherzogliche Hoftheater zu Darmstadt von 1810-1890.  Darmstadt und Leipzig, 1891.

Legband, Paul.  Münchener Bühne und Litteratur im 18. Jahrhundert.  München, 1901-02.

Mentzel, Elisabeth.  Das alte Frankfurter Schauspielhaus und seine Vorgeschichte.  Frankfurt/M., 1902.

Mentzel, Elisabeth.  Geschichte der Schauspielkunst in Frankfurt a.M. von ihren Anfängen bis zur Eröffnung des städtischen Komödienhauses.  Leipzig, 1882.  Reprint: Leipzig, 1975.

Meyer, Reinhart, ed.  Bibliographia dramatica et dramaticorum.  Kommentierte Bibliographie der im ehemaligen Reichsgebiet gedruckten und gespielten Dramen des 18. Jahrhunderts.  3 Bde.  Tübingen, 1986.

Möhring, Paul.  Von Ackermann bis Ziegel.  Theater in Hamburg.  Hamburg, 1970.

Müller, Georg Hermann.   Das Stadt-Theater zu Leipzig vom 1. Januar 1862 bis 1. September 1887.   Nach amtlichen Quellen bearbeitet.   Leipzig, 1887.

Oven, Anton Heinrich Emil von.   Das erste städtische Theater zu Frankfurt a. M.   Ein Beitrag zur äusseren Geschichte des Frankfurter Theaters 1751-1872.   Frankfurt/M., 1872.

Perfall, Karl von.   Ein Beitrag zur Geschichte der königlichen Theater in München 25. November 1867 - 25. November 1892.   München, 1894.

Pichler, Anton.   Chronik des Großherzoglichen Hof- und Nationaltheaters in Mannheim.   Mannheim, 1879.

Prölss, Robert.   Geschichte des Hoftheaters zu Dresden.   Von seinen Anfängen bis zum Jahre 1862.   Dresden, 1878.

Richard, Paul.   Chronik sämmtlicher Gastspiele des Herzogl. Sachs.-Meiningen'schen Hoftheaters während der Jahre 1874-1890.   Leipzig, 1891.

Rub, Otto.   Das Burgtheater.   Statistischer Rückblick auf die Tätigkeit und die Personalverhältnisse während der Zeit vom 8. April 1776 bis 1. Januar 1913.   Wien, 1913.

Schäffer, C. and C. Hartmann.   Die Königlichen Theater in Berlin.   Statistischer Rückblick auf die künstlerische Tätigkeit und die Personal-Verhältnisse während des Zeitraums vom 5. Dez. 1786 bis 31. Dez. 1885.   Berlin, 1886.

Schanze, Helmut.   Drama im Bürgerlichen Realismus (1850-1890).   Theorie und Praxis.   Frankfurt/M., 1973.

Schlösser, Rudolf.   Vom Hamburger Nationaltheater zur Gothaer Hofbühne 1767-1779.   Dreizehn Jahre aus der Entwicklung eines deutschen Theaterspielplans.   Hamburg und Leipzig, 1895.   Reprint: Nendeln/Liechtenstein, 1978.

Schönwald, Alfred and Hermann Peist.   Geschichte des Thalia-Theaters in Hamburg von seiner Gründung bis zum 25jährigen Jubiläum desselben (1843-68).   Hamburg, 1868.

Schulz, Ursula.   Lessing auf der Bühne.   Chronik der Aufführungen 1748-1789.   Bremen, 1977.

Schütze, Johann Friedrich.   Hamburgische Theater-Geschichte.   Hamburg, 1794.   Reprint: Leipzig, 1975.

Tyrolt, Rudolf.   Chronik des Wiener Stadttheaters 1872-1884.   Ein Beitrag zur deutschen Theatergeschichte.   Wien, 1889.

Uhde, Hermann.   Das Stadttheater in Hamburg 1827-1877.   Ein Beitrag zur deutschen Culturgeschichte.   Stuttgart, 1879.

Wagner, Hans.   200 Jahre Münchner Theaterchronik 1750-1950.   München, 1958.

Walter, Friedrich, ed.    Archiv und Bibliothek des Großherzoglichen Hof- und Nationaltheaters in Mannheim 1779-1839.    Leipzig, 1899.

Winkler, Karl Theodor.    Tagebuch der deutschen Bühnen.    Dresden, 1816-35. [Unavailable: 1817-20; 1825, 1826]

Wlassack, Eduard.    Chronik des k.k. Hof-Burgtheaters.    Zu dessen Säcular-Feier im Februar 1876.    Wien, 1876.

Wollrabe, Ludwig.    Chronologie sämmtlicher Hamburger Bühnen
nebst Angabe der meisten Schauspieler, Sänger, Tänzer und
Musiker, welche seit 1230 [1630] bis 1846 an denselben enga-
girt gewesen und gastirt haben.    Hamburg, 1847.

## ARRANGEMENT OF CITATIONS

**1**  ALVENSLEBEN, KARL LUDWIG
      [Pseud.: Gustav Sellen]
**2**  Berlin 1800-1868 Vienna
**3**  Ref.: Brüm 19, Goe 10, Ko 2,
      NDB

**4**  Die Gevatterschaften [Die
      Kameradschaften] - C5 - Fr  **5, 6**
**7**  (1842)
**8**      Dr:1838   Wm:1839

    (1)    A playwright is entered under the name most freqent-
ly used.    This may be either the real name or the pseudonym.
All names and pseudonyms are cross-referenced.
    (2)    Place and date of birth are followed by date and
place of death.
    (3)    Additional biographical information about the play-
wright can be found in the sources cited.  (See table of abbreviations.)
    (4)    Variants of the title or subtitle are given in
square brackets.
    (5)    Letters of the alphabet refer to genre (see table of
abbreviations); numerals refer to the number of acts.
    (6)    The abbreviations (see table below) refer to the
language of the original play from which the German play was
adapted.    Many plays which are referred to as adaptations
(i. e. "nach dem Englischen") were probably in fact translations, but it was not possible to check the accuracy of the
designation.    Plays acknowledged to be translations (i. e.
"aus dem Englischen") were excluded.
    (7)    The date in parentheses is a date of publication; it
is not necessarily the date of first publication.
    (8)    The letters of the alphabet are abbreviations for
the ten cities used in this compilation (see table below).
The date refers to a year in which the play was known to have
been performed in a given city.    Every effort was made to

determine the year of first performance, but this was not always possible. Unspecific dates, such as "in the 1820s," were not included.

Clearly, this book is intended as a reference tool and, as such, does not constitute an end in itself. Perhaps its publication will encourage others to continue the work begun here. In any case, the compiler hopes that the assembled material answers many questions, but leads to interesting new ones as well.

The completion of this lengthy project would have been very difficult, if not impossible, without the assistance of colleagues and friends. Sandra Gavett and Elizabeth Hoose in the Inter-Library Loan Department of the Bailey-Howe Library, University of Vermont, deserve special mention for their expertise and good will. To Professors George B. Bryan, Wolfgang Mieder, Janet Whatley and Malcolm Whatley, all of the University of Vermont, I am deeply grateful for technical advice, encouragement and, above all, for their friendship.

# Abbreviations

Biographical references:

Brüm 18 - Brümmer, Franz. Lexikon der deutschen Dichter und Prosaisten von den ältesten Zeiten bis zum Ende des 18. Jahrhunderts. Leipzig, 1884.

Brüm 19 - Brümmer, Franz. Lexikon der deutschen Dichter und Prosaisten vom Beginn des 19. Jahrhunderts bis zur Gegenwart. 6. Auflage. Leipzig, 1913. Reprint: Nendeln/Liechtenstein, 1975.

Goe - Goedeke, Karl. Grundriß zur Geschichte der deutschen Dichtung. 2. Auflage (Bd. 4 in 3. Auflage). Dresden, Berlin und Düsseldorf, 1884-1966.

Goe NF - Goedekes Grundriß zur Geschichte der deutschen Dichtung. Neue Folge, 1. Band. Hrsg. von Georg Minde-Poet und Eva Rothe. Berlin, 1962.

Ko Th - Kosch, Wilhelm. Deutsches Theater-Lexikon. Klagenfurt und Wien, 1953-.

Ko 2 - Kosch, Wilhelm. Deutsches Literatur-Lexikon. 2. Auflage. Bern, 1949-58.

Ko 3 - Kosch, Wilhelm. Deutsches Literatur-Lexikon. 3. Auflage. Bern und München, 1968-.

ADB - Allgemeine Deutsche Biographie. Leipzig, 1875-1912.

NDB - Neue Deutsche Biographie. Berlin, 1953-.

OC - Garland, Henry and Mary Garland, eds. The Oxford Companion to German Literature. Second edition. Oxford and New York, 1986.

Genre codes:

C  - comedy: includes Humoreske, Lustspiel, Komödie and
     Scherz;
D  - drama: includes Characterbild, Drama, dramatische Anek-
     dote, dramatische Aufgabe, dramatisches Gedicht, Fami-
     liengemälde, Festspiel, Märchen, Melodrama, Schauspiel
     and Sittengemälde;
F  - farce: includes Posse and Schwank;
FP - folk play;
T  - tragedy: includes Tragödie and Trauerspiel;
TC - tragicomedy;
Vv - vaudeville;
Z  - includes Zaubermärchen, Zauberposse and Zauberspiel.

N.B. Liederspiele and Singspiele are not included.

Language of original play in        City codes:
cases of adaptation:

Eng - English                        Bn - Berlin
Fr  - French                         Da - Darmstadt
It  - Italian                        Dr - Dresden
Lat - Latin                          Fr - Frankfurt
Rus - Russian                        Ha - Hamburg
Sp  - Spanish                        Lg - Leipzig
                                     Mh - Mannheim
                                     Mu - Munich
                                     Va - Vienna
                                     Wm - Weimar

# THE GERMAN STAGE,
## *1767–1890*

# Directory

**ADAM, PAUL**
Ref: Goe NF

Im Feuer - C3 (1862)
  Fr:1865

**ADAMI** see Frohberg, Paul

**ADEL, W.** [Pseud. of Johann Krueger]
Ref: Goe NF

Eines Hochzeitstages Fatali-
täten - C2
  Bn:1845  Ha:1845

**ADOLPHI** see Winterfeld, Adolf Wilhelm Ernst von

**ADOLPHI, FELIX** see Schack, Adolf Friedrich, Graf von

**AHRBECK**

Die Gemahlin pro forma - C2
  Bn:1835  Ha:1835

**ALBERT** (ALBRECHT?)
Ref: Goe 11

Männertreue o. So sind sie
alle - C1
  Bn:1831  Dr:1814  Lg:1817
  Mh:1817  Mu:1834  Va:1815

**ALBERT, ANNY** [Pseud. of Anna Kistner]
Celle 1834-1911 Hanover
Ref: Brüm 19, Ko Th

Hut ab! - C1 (1883)
  Fr:1876

**ALBERT, KARL** [Pseud. of Friedrich Groch]
Kottbus 1827-after 1906
Ref: Brüm 19, Ko 3

Ein Aprilscherz - C1
  Va:1884

**ALBINI** [Pseud. of Albin Johann Baptist von Meddlhammer]
Marburg, Styria 1777-1838 Berlin
Ref: Brüm 18, Goe 11, Ko Th

Die Bekehrten o. Der tür-
kische Edukationsrat - F2 (1827)
  Bn:1826
Das Crimen plagii o. Die
Gleichen haben sich gefunden
- C1 (1835)
  Bn:1834
Endlich hat er es doch gut
gemacht - C3 (1836)
  Bn:1835  Da:1837  Dr:1835
  Fr:1843  Ha:1835  Mh:1837
  Va:1848  Wm:1846
Die Flucht nach Afrika - F1 (1836)
  Bn:1831  Va:1833
Frauenliebe - D4 (1832)
  Bn:1831  Mh:1832  Wm:1831
Die gefährliche Tante - C4 (1838)
  Bn:1836  Da:1838  Dr:1837
  Fr:1837  Ha:1836  Lg:1836
  Mh:1839  Mu:1873  Va:1837
  Wm:1857

Der Generalhofschneider - F2
(1837)
   Wm:1836
Der kleine Proteus - C1
(1827)
   Va:1814
Kunst und Natur - C4 (1828)
   Da:1852  Dr:1826  Fr:1827
   Ha:1824  Lg:1831  Mh:1833
   Mu:1832  Va:1830  Wm:1831
Die Menagerie - C3 (1837)
   Bn:1829
Mir gelingt alles - C4 (1839)
   Wm:1836
Seltsame Ehen - F2 (1832)
   Bn:1831  Mh:1832  Mu:1832
Studentenabenteuer o. Eine
Helene des 19. Jahrhunderts -
F2 (1834)
   Lg:1832
Was den Einen tötet, gibt dem
Andern das Leben - C1 (1839)
   Bn:1838  Dr:1838
Zu zahm und zu wild - C3
(1827)
   Bn:1825  Da:1827  Dr:1826
   Lg:1832  Wm:1828

**ALBRECHT, FRIEDRICH JOHANN**
[Pseud.: Friedrich Siegmund]
Glatz 1818-1890 Wiesbaden
Ref: Brüm 19, Goe NF, Ko Th,
NDB

Feldkaplan und Lieutenant -
D3 (1862)
   Fr:1860  Mu:1858

**ALBRECHT, JOHANN FRIEDRICH
ERNST** [Pseud.: J.F.A. Stade]
Stade 1752-1814 Altona
Ref: Brüm 18, Goe 5, Ko Th,
ADB, NDB, OC

Brüder in allen Ecken - C5
   Dr:1787
Das Donnerwetter - C3
   Dr:1792
Die Engländer in Amerika - D4
(1790)
   Dr:1788  Wm:1791
Die Kolonie - C4 (1792)
   Dr:1790
Masaniello - T5 (1789)
   Dr:1789
Zieh' aus, Herr Bruder! - C3
(1790)
   Dr:1790

**ALEXIS, WILLIBALD** [Pseud.
of Georg Wilhelm Häring]
Breslau 1798-1871 Arnstadt
Ref: Brüm 18, Goe 9, Ko Th,
ADB, NDB, OC

Aennchen von Tharau - D3
(1829)
   Bn:1828
Der Prinz von Pisa - C5
(1843)
   Bn:1825
Der Salzdirektor - C3 - with
G. Putlitz (1851)
   Bn:1849  Da:1849  Fr:1851
   Ha:1862  Va:1854
Der verwunschene Schneider-
gesell - F5 (1841)
   Bn:1827  Lg:1827  Wm:1827

**ALGARDI, FRIEDRICH**  see
Wacht, Gustav

**ALKIES, Z.**

Die Adoptivtochter - D3
   Da:1851
Barbara, Königin von Polen -
T5
   Da:1859

**ALTMANN, FRIEDRICH**
Ref: Goe NF

Zwei Häuser voll Eifersucht -
C3 (ca. 1860)
   Da:1857  Fr:1853

**ALVENSLEBEN, KARL LUDWIG**
[Pseud.: Gustav Sellen]
Berlin 1800-1868 Vienna
Ref: Brüm 19, Goe 10, Ko 2,
NDB

Forte Spada, der Abenteurer -
D5 - Fr
   Va:1845
Die Gevatterschaften [Die
Kameradschaften] - C5 - Fr
(1842)
   Dr:1838  Wm:1839
Rücksichten - C3 - Fr (1843)
   Mu:1839  Va:1839  Wm:1839

**AMALIE LOUISE**  see Liebhaber,
Amalie Louise

AMALIE MARIE FRIEDERIKE,
Princess of Saxony [Pseud.:
Amalie Heiter, A. Serena]
Dresden 1794-1870 Pillnitz
Ref: Brüm 18, Goe NF, Ko Th,
ADB, NDB

Die Abenteuer der Thoren-
burg - D5
　　Dr:1817
Der alte Herr - C2 (1844)
　　Bn:1841　Dr:1842　Va:1842
　　Wm:1843
Die Braut aus der Residenz -
C2 (1836)
　　Bn:1834　Da:1838　Dr:1834
　　Fr:1836　Ha:1836　Lg:1835
　　Mh:1837　Mu:1834　Va:1841
　　Wm:1835
Der Brief aus der Schweiz -
D5
　　Bn:1845　Dr:1845　Ha:1845
　　Va:1846
Fräulein Sibylle - C2
　　Dr:1847
Das Fräulein vom Lande - C5
(1839)
　　Bn:1836　Dr:1836　Ha:1837
　　Wm:1836
Die Fürstenbraut - D5 (1837)
　　Bn:1836　Dr:1835　Ha:1836
　　Va:1841　Wm:1838
Die Heimkehr des Sohnes - D4
(1842)
　　Bn:1841　Dr:1841　Wm:1841
Kapitän Firnewald - C4 (1842)
　　Bn:1840　Dr:1840　Wm:1840
Der Krönungstag - D5 (1873)
　　Dr:1829
Der Landwirt - D4 (1837)
　　Bn:1836　Da:1838　Dr:1836
　　Fr:1837　Ha:1836　Mu:1868
　　Va:1837　Wm:1836
Lüge und Wahrheit - D4 (1836)
　　Bn:1834　Da:1837　Dr:1834
　　Fr:1836　Ha:1834　Mh:1837
　　Mu:1834　Va:1834　Wm:1835
Der Majoratserbe - C4 (1839)
　　Bn:1838　Da:1852　Dr:1838
　　Fr:1840　Ha:1840　Mu:1839
　　Va:1845　Wm:1838
Mesru, König von Bactriana -
D2 (1847)
　　Dr:1829
Der Mörder - C4
　　Dr:1844　Ha:1844
Der Oheim - C5 (1836)
　　Bn:1835　Da:1837　Dr:1835
　　Fr:1836　Ha:1836　Mh:1836
　　Va:1836　Wm:1835

Ottfelds Erben - D5
　　Dr:1848
Der Pflegevater - C4 (1839)
　　Bn:1837　Fr:1840　Ha:1839
　　Va:1839　Wm:1837
Pflicht und Liebe - D2 (1841)
　　Dr:1839　Mu:1839　Wm:1839
Regine - C5 (1844)
　　Bn:1843　Dr:1843
Der Siegelring - D4 (1844)
　　Bn:1843　Dr:1843　Va:1843
　　Wm:1844
Die Stieftochter - C4 (1841)
　　Bn:1839　Fr:1841　Ha:1844
　　Va:1840　Wm:1839
Die Unbelesene - C4 (1841)
　　Bn:1838　Dr:1839　Wm:1838
Der Unentschlossene - C4
　　Bn:1837　Wm:1837
Der Verlobungsring - C4
(1837)
　　Bn:1835　Dr:1836　Wm:1835
Vetter Heinrich - D5 (1838)
　　Bn:1837　Fr:1843　Ha:1838
　　Wm:1837
Der Zögling - D4 (1838)
　　Bn:1836　Dr:1838　Fr:1839
　　Ha:1837　Wm:1836

**AMMER, THEODOR von der**　see
Perfall, Karl

**ANGELY, LOUIS**
Leipzig 1787-1835 Berlin
Ref: Brüm 18, Goe 11, Ko Th,
ADB, NDB, OC

Die beiden Eifersüchtigen -
C1 - Fr (1830)
　　Da:1830　Ha:1820　Va:1814
Die beiden Hofmeister o.
Asinus asinum fricat - Vv1 -
Fr (1828)
　　Bn:1824　Dr:1835　Ha:1825
　　Lg:1825
Der Brandstifter - D3 - Fr
　　Bn:1832　Ha:1838
Die Braut aus Pommern - C1
　　Bn:1828　Ha:1834　Wm:1844
Der Dachdecker - C5 - Fr
(1834)
　　Bn:1834　Da:1836　Dr:1838
　　Ha:1837　Lg:1833　Wm:1832
Drei Tage aus dem Leben eines
Spielers - D4 - Fr
　　Bn:1827　Da:1853　Fr:1829
　　Ha:1828

Das Duell [Der Zweikampf im
dritten Stock; Ein Zweikampf]
- C1 - Fr
    Bn:1832    Dr:1836    Ha:1845
    Va:1856
Das Ehepaar aus der alten
Zeit - Vv1 (1828)
    Bn:1825    Dr:1827    Ha:1850
    Lg:1825    Wm:1831
Das erste Debüt - C3
    Bn:1829    Ha:1830    Lg:1835
Das Fest der Handwerker - C1
(1830)
    Bn:1828    Da:1835    Dr:1832
    Fr:1829    Ha:1858    Mu:1833
    Wm:1829
Der Freiball - Vv2
    Ha:1842
Der Geizige und seine
Tochter - D2 - Fr (1840)
    Lg:1835
Herr Blaubart o. das geheim-
nisvolle Kabinett - F1 - Fr
(1828)
    Bn:1825    Lg:1834    Mh:1828
Der hundertjährige Greis - C1
(1834)
    Bn:1828    Fr:1830    Ha:1830
    Mu:1833    Wm:1830
Jugend muß austoben - C1
(1836-41)
    Bn:1835    Dr:1848
Klatschereien - Vv1 (1867)
    Bn:1826    Ha:1857
Ein kleiner Irrtum - C1
(1836-41)
    Bn:1834    Ha:1853
Leontine - D3 - Fr
    Bn:1833    Fr:1834
List und Pflegma - Vv1 - Fr
(1830)
    Bn:1827    Da:1835    Dr:1835
    Fr:1835    Ha:1848    Mu:1833
    Wm:1829
Ein Mädchen, nicht ein Knabe
- C1
    Dr:1848
Nach Sonnenuntergang - C1 -
Fr
    Da:1835
Onkel Brand - C3 - Fr
    Bn:1830    Dr:1832    Fr:1831
    Ha:1830    Va:1833    Wm:1831
Paris in Pommern - Vv1 (1840)
    Bn:1826    Da:1835    Dr:1850
    Ha:1844    Wm:1846

Die Reise auf gemeinschaft-
liche Kosten - C1 - Fr (1836-
41)
    Bn:1834    Da:1838    Dr:1834
    Fr:1835    Ha:1845    Lg:1834
    Mu:1875    Wm:1834
Schlafrock und Uniform - C1 -
Fr (1828)
    Bn:1825    Dr:1827    Lg:1834
Die Schneidermamsells - Vv1 -
Fr (1834)
    Bn:1824    Mh:1829
Schülerschwänke o. Die
kleinen Wilddiebe - Vv1 - Fr
(1828)
    Bn:1825    Da:1837    Dr:1826
    Fr:1851    Ha:1847    Lg:1826
    Mh:1828    Wm:1827
Die Schwestern - C1 - Fr
(1836-41)
    Bn:1835    Dr:1836    Fr:1840
    Ha:1849    Va:1841
Sieben Mädchen in Uniform -
Vv1 - Fr (1830)
    Bn:1825    Da:1836    Dr:1825
    Fr:1825    Ha:1834    Lg:1825
    Mu:1833    Va:1825    Wm:1825
Der Stellvertreter - C1 - Fr
(1834)
    Bn:1831    Da:1841    Dr:1835
Trübsäle einer Postwagenreise
- F2 - Fr (1836-41)
    Bn:1829    Dr:1835    Mh:1830
Der Unglücksgefährte - C1 -
Fr (1834)
    Bn:1831    Lg:1834
Von sieben die Häßlichste -
C3 (1836)
    Bn:1834    Da:1840    Dr:1834
    Fr:1835    Ha:1834    Lg:1834
    Mh:1836    Mu:1835    Va:1843
    Wm:1834
Die Wahnsinnige [Sie ist
wahnsinnig] - D2 - Fr
    Bn:1835    Da:1840    Fr:1835
    Lg:1835    Wm:1835
Warum? - C1 - Fr
    Bn:1833    Wm:1835
Die Weihnachts-Präsente - C1
(1842)
    Bn:1834    Fr:1833
Wohnungen zu vermieten - D5 -
Fr (1836-41)
    Bn:1832    Dr:1840    Ha:1845
Die Zwillingsbrüder - C1
(1836-41)
    Bn:1834    Dr:1836    Lg:1834
    Wm:1834
See Goedeke 11 for additional
listings.

**ANNO, ANTON JOSEPH HUBERT**
Aachen 1838-1893 Berlin
Ref: Brüm 18, Goe NF, Ko Th

Die beiden Reichenmüller -
FP4 (1882)
  Ha:1879  Mu:1879

**ANSCHÜTZ, RODERICH**
Breslau 1818-1888 Mödling
Ref: Brüm 19, Goe NF, Ko Th

Brutus und sein Haus - T5 -
(1857)
  Va:1857
Die Familie Wetter o. Die
Ehestifter - C4 (1892)
  Va:1879
Johanna Gray - T5 (1860)
  Bn:1861  Va:1861
Kunz von Kaufung - D5 (1863)
  Va:1863

**ANTHONY, WILHELM** [Pseud. of
Wilhelm Asmus]
Lübeck 1837-1902 Weimar
Ref: Brüm 19, Ko Th

Im Traum - C2 (1875)
  Lg:1876

**ANTON, JOHANN DANIEL**
Darmstadt 1801-1853 Darmstadt
Ref: Goe NF

Herz und Verstand - C3
  Da:1831
Die häßliche Fremde - F1
  Da:1838
Der Zweikampf unter dem Kar-
dinal Richelieu - D3 - Fr
  Da:1840  Fr:1838

**ANZENGRUBER, LUDWIG** [Pseud.:
Ludwig Gruber]
Vienna 1839-1889 Vienna
Ref: Brüm 19, Goe NF, Ko Th,
ADB, NDB, OC

Alte Wiener - FP4 (1879)
  Va:1878
Aus'm gewohnten G'leis - F5
(1880)
  Va:1879
Doppelselbstmord - C3 (1876)
  Va:1876
Elfriede - D3 (1873)
  Dr:1877  Va:1873
Ein Faustschlag - D3 (1878)
  Va:1879

Der Fleck auf der Ehr - FP3
(1889)
  Fr:1890  Lg:1889  Mu:1889
  Va:1889  Wm:1889
Der G'wissenswurm - C3 (1874)
  Bn:1887  Da:1887  Lg:1882
  Mu:1874  Va:1874
Hand und Herz - T4 (1875)
  Bn:1875  Va:1874
Heimg'funden - C3 (1885)
  Bn:1888  Dr:1889  Lg:1888
  Va:1889
's Jungferngift - C5 (1878)
  Bn:1878  Va:1878
Die Kreuzelschreiber - C3
(1872)
  Bn:1877  Fr:1890  Va:1872
Der ledige Hof - D4 (1877)
  Bn:1877  Dr:1877  Lg:1878
  Mu:1877  Va:1877
Der Meineidbauer - FP3 (1872)
  Bn:1878  Fr:1882  Mh:1879
  Mu:1872  Va:1871  Wm:1889
Der Pfarrer von Kirchfeld -
FP4 (1871)
  Bn:1871  Da:1881  Fr:1871
  Lg:1871  Mh:1871  Mu:1870
  Va:1870  Wm:1879
Stahl und Stein - FP3 (1887)
  Bn:1887  Va:1887
Ein Telegraphist im Nacht-
dienst - C1
  Va:1866
Die Tochter des Wucherers -
D5 (1873)
  Va:1873
Die Trutzige - C3 (1879)
  Bn:1879  Va:1878
Die umkehrte Freit' - D1
(1879)
  Va:1879
Das vierte Gebot - FP4 (1878)
  Bn:1890  Fr:1890  Mu:1878
  Va:1877

**APEL, GUIDO THEODOR**
Leipzig 1811-1867 Leipzig
Ref: Brüm 19, Goe NF, Ko Th,
ADB

Ein Abenteuer Ludwig Dev-
rients - C1 (1856)
  Ha:1863  Wm:1863
Columbus - D5
  Lg:1835
Günther von Schwarzburg,
erwählter deutscher König -
T5 (1856)
  Wm:1858

Nähkätchen - D3 (1856)
    Da:1853  Dr:1852  Fr:1853
    Ha:1852
Die verzauberte Rose o. Ist
sie treu? - C1 (1856)
    Dr:1854

**APELL, JOHANN DAVID**
Kassel 1754-1833
Ref: Goe 6

Der Blasbalgmacher - C (1806)
    Fr:1802

**d'ARIEN, BERNHARD CHRISTOPH**
Hamburg 1754-1793 Hamburg
Ref: Brüm 18, Goe 5, Ko Th

Der Blinde und der Taube - C1
(1794)
    Dr:1795
Klaus Storzenbecher - T5
(1783)
    Ha:1783
Das Landmädchen - C4 (1794)
    Dr:1778  Fr:1794  Ha:1786
    Wm:1794
Marie von Wahlburg - T5
(1776)
    Bn:1777
Natur und Liebe im Streit -
D5 (1783)
    Bn:1783  Dr:1783  Ha:1780
    Lg:1783  Va:1780
Olinth und Sophronie - D5 -
Fr (1788)
    Va:1788
Die Rückkehr o. Liebe läßt
von Liebe nicht - D5 (1783)
    Bn:1783

**ARND [-KÜRENBERG], FRIEDRICH
HELWIG**
St. Petersburg 1839-1911
Munich
Ref: Goe NF, Ko 3

Kriemhild - T5 (1874)
    Wm:1874

**ARNSTEIN, BENEDIKT DAVID**
Vienna 1765 [1761?]-1841
Vienna
Ref: Brüm 18, Goe 5, Ko Th

Das Billet - C1 (1800)
    Va:1800
Die Maske - C1 - Fr (1791)
    Va:1788

Die Nachschrift - C1 (1787)
    Fr:1793  Va:1785

**ARRESTO, CHRISTLIEB GEORG
HEINRICH** [also known as Bur-
chardi]
Schwerin 1768-1817 Doberan
Ref: Brüm 18, Goe 5, Ko Th,
ADB

Der feindliche Sohn - D5
    Ha:1839
Der Indienfahrer - D4 (1803)
    Da:1824  Mh:1826  Mu:1813
Der Plan - C1
    Fr:1804
Die Soldaten - D5 (1804)
    Dr:1803  Fr:1804  Ha:1803
    Mh:1804  Mu:1815  Wm:1822

**ARTER, EMIL** [Pseud. of Mar-
zellin Adalbert Reitler]
Prague 1838-?
Ref: Brüm 19

Duelle - D3 (1880)
    Fr:1880  Lg:1880  Va:1880
Pikante Enthüllungen - D4
(1877)
    Va:1879

**ASCHER, ANTON** [Pseud.: Anton
Roger]
Dresden 1820-1884 Meran
Ref: Goe NF, Ko Th

Ein delikater Auftrag - C1 -
Fr (1873)
    Fr:1868  Va:1883
Dir wie mir - C1 (1863)
    Da:1864  Dr:1861  Fr:1865
    Lg:1864  Wm:1864
Zwei Ehen - C1 - Fr (1872)
    Fr:1866

**ASMUS, WILHELM**  see Anthony,
Wilhelm

**AUERBACH, BERTHOLD** [Pseud.
of Moses Baruch Auerbacher]
Nordstetten 1812-1882 Cannes
Ref: Brüm 19, Goe NF, Ko Th,
ADB, NDB, OC

Andree Hofer - T5 (1850)
    Bn:1879
Das erlösende Wort - C1
(1877)
    Bn:1878  Mu:1878  Va:1878

Eine seltene Frau - C1 (1878)
    Bn:1878
Der Wahrspruch - FP5 (1859)
    Wm:1859

**AUFFENBERG, JOSEF von**
Freiburg/Br 1798-1857
Freiburg/Br
Ref: Brüm 18, Goe 11, Ko Th,
ADB, NDB, OC

Das böse Haus - D5 (1834)
    Bn:1835    Ha:1835
Die Flibustier o. Die
Eroberung von Panama - T4
(1819)
    Va:1833
Der Löwe von Kurdistan - D5
(1828)
    Bn:1831    Dr:1827    Fr:1828
    Ha:1828    Lg:1827    Mh:1827
    Wm:1834
Ludwig der Elfte in Peronne -
D5 (1827)
    Bn:1828    Fr:1827    Lg:1833
    Mh:1827
Das Nordlicht von Kasan - T5
(1838)
    Lg:1830
Das Opfer des Themistokles -
T5 (1821)
    Wm:1822
Die Verbannten - D4 (1821)
    Mu:1821
Wallas - T5 (1819)
    Fr:1823

**AUGUSTSOHN, WILHELM** [Pseud.
of Wilhelm Kotzebue]
Reval 1813-1887 Reval
Ref: Brüm 19, Ko 3

Die orientalische Frage - F
    Mu:1869
Ein unbarmherziger Freund -
D1
    Mu:1872    Va:1867
Zwei Sünderinnen - D
    Mu:1869

**AUZINGER, PETER**
Athens 1836-1914 Munich
Ref: Brüm 19, Goe NF, Ko 3,
NDB

Der Büchsenfranzl - D4
    Mu:1878

**AYRENHOFF, CORNELIUS HERMANN
von**
Vienna 1733-1819 Vienna
Ref: Brüm 18, Goe 4/1, Ko Th,
ADB, NDB, OC

Alte Liebe rostet wohl - C5
(1789)
    Dr:1786    Va:1780
Antiope - T4 (1789)
    Va:1772
Aurelius o. Wettstreit der
Großmut - T5 (1789)
    Va:1766
Erziehung macht den Menschen
- C5 (1789)
    Bn:1788    Dr:1785    Mh:1786
    Va:1785
Die Freundschaft der Weiber -
C2 (1784)
    Va:1782
Die gelehrte Frau - C5 (1789)
    Va:1775
Die große Batterie - C1
(1789)
    Bn:1771    Dr:1777    Fr:1780
    Lg:1779    Va:1770
Hermanns Tod - T5 (1803)
    Va:1768
Hermann und Thusnelde - T5
(1772)
    Ha:1768    Va:1768
Irene - T3 (1789)
    Va:1781
Kleopatra und Antonius - T4
(1784)
    Va:1783
Der Postzug - C2 (1772)
    Bn:1771    Ha:1784    Lg:1775
    Mh:1780    Mu:1771    Va:1769
    Wm:1772
Virginia o. Das abgeschaffte
Decemvirat - T4 (1803)
    Va:1790

**BABO, JOSEF MARIUS**
Ehrenbreitstein 1756-1822
Munich
Ref: Brüm 18, Goe 5, Ko Th,
ADB, NDB, OC

Arno - D2 (1772)
    Va:1777
Bürgerglück - C3 (1793)
    Bn:1792    Da:1812    Dr:1792
    Fr:1792    Ha:1792    Mh:1791
    Mu:1791    Va:1791    Wm:1792

Dagobert, König der Franken -
T5 (1779)
    Bn:1782
Genua und Rache - T5 (1804)
    Bn:1803   Mh:1804   Mu:1801
Das Lustlager - D1
    Va:1779
Die Maler - C1 (1783)
    Bn:1783   Da:1813   Dr:1788
    Fr:1793   Ha:1785   Lg:1799
    Mh:1783   Mu:1782   Va:1801
Mittel und Wege - C5 - Eng
    Va:1811
Oda, die Frau von zwei
Männern - T5 - Eng (1782)
    Bn:1783   Dr:1782   Ha:1783
    Mh:1785   Mu:1780
Otto von Wittelsbach - T5
(1782)
    Bn:1782   Da:1812   Dr:1782
    Fr:1794   Ha:1783   Lg:1814
    Mh:1802   Mu:1781   Wm:1791
Der Puls - C2 (1804)
    Bn:1802   Da:1810   Dr:1803
    Lg:1805   Mh:1803   Mu:1829
    Va:1803   Wm:1804
Die Römer in Deutschland - D5
(1780)
    Ha:1780   Mh:1779   Mu:1779
Standesproben - C3
    Da:1818   Dr:1817   Fr:1831
    Ha:1827   Va:1811
Die Strelitzen - D4 (1793)
    Bn:1790   Da:1814   Dr:1796
    Fr:1793   Ha:1790   Lg:1790
    Mh:1789   Mu:1789   Va:1790
    Wm:1791
Das Winterquartier in Amerika
- C1 (1778)
    Bn:1784   Va:1778

**BACHER, JULIUS**
Ragnit 1810-?
Ref: Brüm 19, Ko Th

Aus dem Leben - D5 (1858)
    Bn:1857
Die Brautschau Friedrichs des
Großen - C4 (1857)
    Dr:1860

**BAHRDT, JOHANN FRIEDRICH**
[Pseud.: Faverius Barba]
Dargun 1789-1847 Neustrelitz
Ref: Brüm 18, Goe 14, Ko Th,
NDB

Die Grabesbraut - D5 (1834)
    Bn:1832   Lg:1832

Johann von Braganza - D
    Ha:1840
Die Lichtensteiner o. Die
Macht des Wahns - D5 (1834)
    Bn:1831   Lg:1832   Mh:1832

**BAISON, JEAN BAPTIST**
Haltersdorf/Mainz 1812-1849
Ref: Ko Th, ADB

Eine Gastrolle
    Ha:1847
Ein Gerichtstag auf Helgoland
    Ha:1847
Die öffentliche Meinung - C4
(1845)
    Bn:1845   Ha:1845

**BARBA, FAVERIUS**   see Bahrdt,
Johann Friedrich

**BÄRMANN, GEORG NIKOLAUS**
Hamburg 1785-1850 Hamburg
Ref: Brüm 18, Goe 9, Ko Th,
ADB, NDB

Alexander von Soltwedel o.
Der Hansa Begründung - D4
(1817)
    Ha:1817
Alte Sünden - F1 - Fr (1838)
    Bn:1847   Ha:1846
Bürgertreue - D3 (1828)
    Ha:1828
Claus Störtebecker - T5
(1822)
    Ha:1819
Don Juan von Österreich - D5
(1836)
    Bn:1839   Ha:1841
Frauenehre - D5 - Sp
    Fr:1844   Ha:1839
Die glücklichen Bettler - D5
It (1819)
    Ha:1818
Der Graf von Bazan - C5 - Fr
    Da:1853
Die Herzogin von La Valière -
D
    Ha:1838
Die Höhle auf Lampedusa - T1
(1826)
    Ha:1825
König Kanut - D4 (1829)
    Ha:1832
Der König und der Künstler -
D1 (1824)
    Ha:1821   Mu:1824

Der Oberrock - D1 (1825)
    Bn:1826   Fr:1825   Ha:1824
    Wm:1827
Ritter und Zitherschlägerin -
D5
    Ha:1844   Va:1845
Die schöne Lyoneserin - C
    Ha:1838
Die Schule der Armen - D
(1843)
    Ha:1843
Die Schwiegermutter - D3 - Fr
(1838)
    Ha:1831
Die Sklavin in goldenen Ket-
ten - D
    Ha:1841
Der Sohn der Wellen - D5
(1842)
    Dr:1842   Ha:1841   Va:1842
Der Staatsminister - D5 - Eng
(1838)
    Dr:1840   Ha:1839
Staatspapiere - C1 (1827)
    Ha:1826
Welcher ist mein Vetter? - C1
Fr (1822)
    Ha:1812
Zum Benefiz - C1 (1838)
    Ha:1831

**BARNEKOW, GUSTAV FRIEDRICH
WILHELM**
Bergen/Rügen 1779-1838 Berlin
Ref: Goe 11

Der bestrafte Verläumder - D3
    Bn:1811
Die Einquartierung - C3
    Bn:1837
Haß allen Männern - C1
    Bn:1811
Der Nebenbuhler - F1
    Bn:1818
Nein! - C1
    Bn:1815   Dr:1821   Fr:1824
    Ha:1823
Ein Tag auf dem Lande
[Freuden des Landlebens] - C4
    Bn:1821

**BARTHEL, GUSTAV EMIL**   see
Haller, Gustav

**BAUDISSIN, ULRICH von**
Greifswald 1816-1893 Wies-
baden
Ref: Brüm 19, Ko Th

Am Scheidewege - D4
    Fr:1881
Fünfundzwanzigtausend Taler -
C1
    Bn:1879

**BAUDISSIN, WOLF von**
Rantzau 1789-1878 Dresden
Ref: Ko Th, ADB, NDB, OC

Regen und Sonnenschein - C1 -
Fr
    Wm:1862

**BAUER, EMIL**   see Peschkau,
Emil

**BAUERLE, ADOLF**   [Pseud.: Otto
Horn]
Vienna 1786-1859 Basel
Ref: Brüm 18, Goe 11, Ko Th,
ADB, NDB, OC

Aline, Königin von Golconda -
C3 (1826)
    Bn:1826   Dr:1834   Mh:1824
    Va:1822
Die falsche Primadonna [Die
falsche Primadonna in Kräh-
winkel; Die falsche Catalani]
F3 (1818)
    Bn:1820   Ha:1820   Lg:1819
    Mh:1820   Va:1818
Der Freund in der Not - C1
(1820)
    Da:1852   Dr:1835   Ha:1845
    Wm:1822
Der Kurier in Wien o.
Staberls Hochzeit - F3 (1820)
    Bn:1822   Fr:1815   Va:1814
    Wm:1822
Der Leopoldstag o. Kein Men-
schenhaß und keine Reue - F3
(1820)
    Bn:1824   Mu:1834   Va:1814
Lindane o. Die Fee und der
Haarbeutelschneider - Z3
(1937)
    Bn:1831   Ha:1836   Va:1824
Der Parapluimacher o. Die
Bürger in Wien - F3 (1820)
    Bn:1818   Fr:1815   Ha:1822
    Lg:1823   Mh:1815   Va:1813
    Wm:1822
See Goedeke 11 for additional
listings.

**BAUERMEISTER, MAX**
Berlin 1841-1917 Berlin
Ref: Brüm 19, Ko Th

Eine komische Alte - C1
(1873)
    Fr:1873
Werbeoffiziere - C1
    Fr:1881

**BAUERNFELD, EDUARD**
Vienna 1802-1890 Döbling
Ref: Brüm 19, Ko Th, ADB,
NDB, OC

Des Alcibiades Ausgang - C5
(1882)
    Va:1883
Der Alte vom Berge - D1
(1873)
    Fr:1883  Mu:1873  Va:1873
Ein altes Recht - C1
    Va:1876
Aus der Gesellschaft - D4
(1865)
    Fr:1868  Ha:1867  Mh:1868
    Mu:1868  Va:1867  Wm:1867
Das Beispiel - D1 (1865)
    Va:1859
Die Bekenntnisse - C3 (1834)
    Bn:1834  Da:1837  Dr:1834
    Fr:1834  Ha:1834  Lg:1834
    Mh:1835  Mu:1834  Va:1834
    Wm:1834
Der Brautwerber - C5 (1828)
    Va:1828
Bürgerlich und romantisch -
C4 (1834)
    Bn:1836  Da:1839  Dr:1836
    Fr:1836  Ha:1835  Lg:1865
    Mh:1838  Mu:1868  Va:1835
    Wm:1836
Ein deutscher Krieger - D3
(1844)
    Bn:1845  Da:1850  Dr:1846
    Fr:1845  Ha:1845  Mh:1845
    Mu:1845  Va:1844  Wm:1848
Ernst und Humor - C4
    Bn:1841  Va:1840
Ewige Liebe - C1
    Bn:1832
Excellenz o. Der Backfisch -
C1
    Va:1865
Fata Morgana - C4 (1855)
    Dr:1855  Fr:1862  Ha:1859
    Va:1855
Franz von Sickingen - D4
(1850)
    Fr:1850  Va:1850
Franz Walter - D4 (1834)
    Bn:1835  Va:1834

Frauenfreundschaft - C1
(1865)
    Va:1865
Die Gebesserten - C3 (1841)
    Bn:1842  Va:1841
Die Geschwister von Nürnberg
- C4 (1840)
    Va:1840
Großjährig - C2 (1846)
    Bn:1847  Da:1849  Dr:1847
    Fr:1847  Ha:1847  Mu:1847
    Va:1846  Wm:1848
Helene - D4 (1834)
    Bn:1834  Fr:1835  Mu:1834
    Va:1833
Im Alter - D1 - Fr
    Bn:1876  Da:1859  Lg:1876
    Va:1853
Im Dienste des Königs - F3
    Va:1875
Industrie und Herz - C4
(1842)
    Bn:1842  Da:1847  Ha:1842
    Va:1842
Der kategorische Imperativ -
C3 (1851)
    Bn:1852  Fr:1862  Lg:1876
    Mu:1871  Va:1850
Krisen - D4 (1852)
    Bn:1853  Da:1855  Dr:1854
    Fr:1857  Ha:1859  Mh:1855
    Mu:1874  Va:1852  Wm:1853
Die Kunstjünger - D1
    Va:1836
Landfrieden - C3 (1869)
    Bn:1870  Mu:1871  Va:1870
Leichtsinn aus Liebe o. Täu-
schungen - C4 (1831)
    Bn:1831  Da:1831  Dr:1832
    Mu:1832  Va:1831  Wm:1833
Das letzte Abenteuer - C5
(1834)
    Bn:1834  Dr:1832  Fr:1833
    Ha:1832  Lg:1834  Mu:1833
    Va:1832  Wm:1833
Das Liebesprotokoll - C3
(1871-73)
    Bn:1832  Da:1851  Dr:1832
    Fr:1849  Ha:1832  Lg:1834
    Va:1831
Der literarische Salon - C4
(1836)
    Bn:1836  Va:1836
Die Löwen von ehedem - D4
    Va:1854
Mädchenrache o. Die Studenten
von Salamanca - C2 (1881)
    Mu:1885  Va:1882

Moderne Jugend - C3 (1869)
    Bn:1870  Mh:1870  Va:1869
    Wm:1888
Der Musikus von Augsburg - C3
(1832)
    Bn:1832  Ha:1832  Va:1832
    Wm:1837
Ein neuer Mensch - C
    Va:1849
Ohne Leidenschaft - D1
    Va:1871
Die reiche Erbin - C2 (1876)
    Va:1876
Die Ritter vom Stegreif - C1
    Va:1847
Selbständig - C3
    Va:1874
Der Selbstquäler - D3 (1840)
    Bn:1839  Fr:1838  Va:1837
    Wm:1840
Soldatenliebchen - D4
    Va:1863
Das Tagebuch - C2 (1836)
    Bn:1837  Da:1839  Dr:1837
    Fr:1837  Ha:1838  Mu:1869
    Va:1836  Wm:1862
Unter der Regentschaft - C3
    Va:1856
Untertänig - C1
    Va:1847
Der Vater - C4 (1840)
    Bn:1837  Da:1841  Dr:1837
    Ha:1838  Va:1837
Die Verlassenen - C1 (1878)
    Bn:1878
Das Versprechen - D1
    Bn:1847  Dr:1847  Fr:1847
    Ha:1847  Va:1846
Die Virtuosen - C2 (1865)
    Dr:1858  Fr:1856  Ha:1855
    Va:1855
Welt und Theater - C2
    Va:1859
Der Zauberdrache - C5
    Ha:1838  Va:1833
Die Zugvögel - C1 (1852)
    Ha:1856  Va:1855
Zu Hause - D1 (1852)
    Bn:1853  Da:1854  Dr:1852
    Fr:1852  Mu:1871  Va:1852
    Wm:1852
Zwei Familien - D4 (1840)
    Va:1838

**BAUMANN, ALEXANDER**
Vienna 1814-1857 Graz
Ref: Brüm 19, Ko Th

Die beiden Ärzte - C3 (1849)
    Bn:1841  Ha:1841  Va:1840

Die Engländerin - C1
    Va:1850
Eine Liebschaft in Briefen -
C2
    Bn:1851  Dr:1852  Fr:1858
    Va:1851
Die unnötigen Intriguen - C4
    Va:1850

**BAYER, KARL EMMERICH ROBERT
von** see Byr, Robert

**BECK, HEINRICH**
Gotha 1760-1803 Mannheim
Ref: Brüm 18, Goe 5, Ko Th,
ADB, NDB, OC

Alles aus Eigennutz o. Die
Erbin - C5 - Eng (1807)
    Dr:1792  Fr:1798  Lg:1812
    Mh:1789  Va:1803  Wm:1794
Das Chamäleon - C5 (1803)
    Bn:1800  Da:1811  Dr:1801
    Fr:1804  Ha:1820  Mh:1801
    Mu:1801  Va:1801  Wm:1807
Echter Adel und echte Liebe -
C3
    Va:1796
Das Herz behält seine Rechte
- D5 - Eng (1788)
    Dr:1788  Mh:1787  Va:1788
Die Quälgeister - C5 - Eng
(1801)
    Bn:1796  Da:1811  Dr:1793
    Fr:1793  Ha:1820  Lg:1801
    Mh:1792  Mu:1793  Va:1793
    Wm:1796
Rettung für Rettung - D5
(1803)
    Da:1811  Dr:1799  Fr:1799
    Mh:1799  Va:1799  Wm:1807
Die Schachmaschine - C4
(1798)
    Bn:1797  Da:1810  Dr:1795
    Fr:1795  Lg:1817  Mh:1795
    Mu:1796  Va:1795  Wm:1798
Verirrung ohne Laster [Natur
und Heuchelei] - D5 - Eng
(1793)
    Bn:1790  Fr:1791  Dr:1790
    Ha:1790  Mh:1790  Va:1790

**BECK, LUISE** [Pseud.: Ludwig
Becker]
Mannheim 1789-1857 Stuttgart
Ref: Goe 11, Ko Th

Morgen gewiss! - D1 (1829)
    Bn:1826  Mh:1825

Das Opfer [Opfertreue] - D3
    Mh:1825

**BECK, S.**

Nachbar Specht o. Ihm entgeht
nichts! - C
    Fr:1832

**BECKER, LUDWIG**   see Beck,
Luise

**BEER, MICHAEL**
Berlin 1800-1833 Munich
Ref: Brüm 19, Goe 8, Ko Th,
ADB, NDB, OC

Klytämnestra - T4 (1823)
    Bn:1819   Va:1820
Der Paria - T1 (1829)
    Bn:1823   Da:1826   Dr:1836
    Fr:1835   Lg:1824   Mh:1826
    Mu:1827   Va:1827   Wm:1824
Schwert und Hand - T5 (1835)
    Bn:1832
Struensee - T5 (1829)
    Bn:1846   Da:1854   Dr:1847
    Fr:1847   Mh:1867   Mu:1828
    Va:1881   Wm:1847

**BEIL, JOHANN DAVID**
Chemnitz 1754-1794 Mannheim
Ref: Brüm 18, Goe 5, Ko Th,
ADB, NDB

Armut und Hoffart - C5 (1789)
    Bn:1789   Ha:1788   Mh:1788
Die Familie Spaden - D4
(1794)
    Mh:1793   Wm:1794
Curt von Spartau - D4 (1794)
    Ha:1789   Mh:1789
Die Schauspielerschule - C3
(1785)
    Ha:1785   Lg:1787   Mh:1785
    Wm:1791
Schonung bessert o. Die
Spieler - D5 (1785)
    Lg:1785   Mh:1785   Wm:1792

**BEIL, KARL THEODOR**
Mannheim 1788-1867 Mannheim
Ref: Brüm 18, Goe 7, Ko Th

Alexander - D4 (1821)
    Mh:1825
Raphael von Aquillas - T4
(1819)
    Mh:1819

**BELLY, GEORG FRIEDRICH**
Stolp 1836-1875 Berlin
Ref: Brüm 19, Ko Th

Bädecker - F1
    Da:1863   Fr:1863   Ha:1863
    Wm:1863
Bis in den Urwald - D1
    Fr:1870
Hohe Gäste - F1 - with
P. Henrion (1869)
    Fr:1867   Ha:1865
Monsieur Herkules - F1 (1863)
    Da:1863   Fr:1863   Ha:1862
    Mu:1866   Wm:1864

**BENEDIX, RODERICH**
Leipzig 1811-1873 Leipzig
Ref: Brüm 19, Ko Th, ADB,
NDB, OC

Abenteuer in Rom - C (1846-
74)
    Fr:1869
Der achtundachtzigste Ge-
burtstag - D3 (1846-74)
    Fr:1868   Ha:1868   Lg:1869
Die alte Jungfer - D4 (1846-
74)
    Da:1854   Dr:1854   Fr:1854
    Ha:1854
Der alte Magister - D4 (1846-
74)
    Bn:1846   Da:1852   Dr:1845
    Fr:1846   Ha:1846   Lg:1871
    Mu:1847   Va:1846   Wm:1848
Ein altes Sprichwort - C
(1846-74)
    Fr:1873   Mu:1870
Angela - D1 (1846-74)
    Bn:1853   Fr:1854   Va:1851
Das Armband - C1 (1846-74)
    Lg:1866   Va:1865
Aschenbrödel - D4 (1868)
    Bn:1867   Da:1868   Fr:1867
    Ha:1867   Mh:1867   Mu:1883
    Wm:1869
Auf dem Lande - C4 (1846-74)
    Da:1856   Fr:1856   Va:1855
    Wm:1855
Ausreden lassen - C1 (1846-
74)
    Bn:1864   Fr:1865   Lg:1864
Die Banditen o. Abenteuer
einer Ballnacht - C4 (1846-
74)
    Bn:1847   Da:1849   Dr:1847
    Fr:1849
Der Barrikadenbauer - C1
    Fr:1849

Das bemooste Haupt o. Der
lange Israel - D4 (1841)
    Da:1841  Fr:1840  Ha:1848
    Mh:1840  Lg:1868  Mu:1847
    Wm:1841
Die Crinolinenverschwörung -
C3 (1846-74)
    Da:1861  Wm:1862
Die Dienstboten - C1 (1865)
    Bn:1857  Da:1859  Dr:1855
    Fr:1854  Ha:1864  Mu:1871
    Va:1864  Wm:1855
Doktor Treuwald - C5 (1846-
74)
    Da:1878  Ha:1864  Lg:1865
    Mu:1880  Va:1865
Doktor Wespe - C5 (1843)
    Bn:1842  Da:1843  Dr:1843
    Fr:1843  Ha:1842  Mh:1843
    Mu:1843  Va:1843  Wm:1843
Die Eifersüchtigen - C1
(1846-74)
    Bn:1852  Da:1851  Dr:1851
    Fr:1850  Ha:1850  Mu:1870
    Va:1851  Wm:1851
Eigensinn - C1 (1846-74)
    Bn:1847  Da:1857  Dr:1848
    Fr:1853  Ha:1864  Mu:1847
    Va:1850  Wm:1847
Die Epigramme - C3 (1846-74)
    Bn:1866  Fr:1866  Wm:1867
Die Fremden - C3
    Bn:1862  Ha:1862  Wm:1862
Das Gefängnis - C4 (1859)
    Bn:1851  Da:1852  Dr:1851
    Fr:1851  Ha:1851  Mh:1853
    Mu:1851  Va:1851  Wm:1851
Gegenüber - C3 (1846-74)
    Bn:1863  Da:1882  Fr:1872
    Mh:1865  Mu:1876  Va:1862
Der geheimnisvolle Brief - C1
(1846-74)
    Fr:1866  Lg:1865  Va:1865
Die Gesellschafterin - D3
(1846-74)
    Fr:1857
Die Großmutter - D1 (1846-74)
    Va:1861
Günstige Vorzeichen - C1
(1846-74)
    Fr:1868  Va:1862
Herrschsucht - C3 (1846-74)
    Lg:1866
Die Hochzeitsreise - C2
(1859)
    Bn:1850  Dr:1868  Dr:1850
    Fr:1850  Ha:1850  Mu:1868
    Va:1865  Wm:1850

Isidor und Athanasia - C1
(1846-74)
    Mu:1873  Va:1873
Junker Otto - C4 (1846-74)
    Ha:1859  Lg:1870
Der Kassenschlüssel - C1
(1846-74)
    Fr:1866  Lg:1864
Der Kaufmann - D5 (1846-74)
    Da:1868  Dr:1850  Fr:1850
    Ha:1850  Mu:1868  Va:1865
    Wm:1852
Das Konzert - C4 (1846-74)
    Fr:1855  Va:1855  Wm:1855
Landwehrmanns Christfest - D1
(1846-74)
    Bn:1870  Da:1870  Fr:1871
    Lg:1871
Der Liebesbrief - C3 (1846-
74)
    Bn:1851  Da:1851  Dr:1851
    Fr:1851  Ha:1851  Va:1851
    Wm:1851
Der Liebestrank - F (1846-74)
    Ha:1844
Das Lügen - C3 (1846-74)
    Bn:1852  Da:1852  Dr:1853
    Fr:1852  Ha:1852  Mu:1852
    Va:1852  Wm:1853
Ein Lustspiel - C4 (1846-74)
    Bn:1853  Da:1853  Dr:1853
    Fr:1853  Ha:1867  Mh:1853
    Mu:1853  Va:1854  Wm:1853
Mathilde - D4 (1846-74)
    Bn:1853  Da:1853  Dr:1853
    Fr:1853  Ha:1853  Mh:1855
    Mu:1853  Va:1854  Wm:1853
Die Mode - C3 (1846-74)
    Dr:1843  Fr:1858  Wm:1843
Moritz Schnörche o. Die
Bürgermeisterwahl - F1 - with
G. Moser (1862)
    Da:1874  Dr:1861  Fr:1863
Muttersöhnchen - C3 (1846-74)
    Lg:1867  Va:1867
Die Neujahrsnacht - D1 (1846-
74)
    Bn:1868  Da:1870  Fr:1869
    Ha:1868  Lg:1869
Die Pasquillanten - C3 (1846-
74)
    Da:1868  Ha:1860
Der Pflegmaticus - C1 (1846-
74)
    Fr:1871  Lg:1870
Die Phrenologen - C1 (1846-
74)
    Fr:1854  Va:1852

Der Prozeß - C1 (1846-74)
    Da:1850  Dr:1849  Fr:1849
    Va:1849  Wm:1848
Reden muß man - C3 (1846-74)
    Fr:1870  Lg:1870  Mu:1871
    Va:1871
Die relegierten Studenten -
C4 (1846-74)
    Bn:1868  Da:1870  Fr:1869
    Lg:1868  Mh:1869  Mu:1871
    Va:1869  Wm:1868
Der Ruf - C (1846-74)
    Ha:1845
Sammelwut - D4 (1846-74)
    Bn:1863  Da:1867  Fr:1863
Die Schuldbewußten - C3
(1846-74)
    Bn:1858  Dr:1857  Fr:1858
Der Sohn der Gärtnerin - C4
(1846-74)
    Lg:1881  Va:1872
Die Sonntagsjäger - C1 (1846-
74)
    Wm:1846
Der Steckbrief - C3 (1846-74)
    Bn:1844  Dr:1849  Fr:1843
    Ha:1843  Va:1844
Die Stiefmutter - D3 (1846-
74)
    Dr:1860  Ha:1863  Va:1860
Der Störenfried - C3 (1846-
74)
    Bn:1861  Da:1862  Dr:1861
    Fr:1863  Ha:1861  Mh:1862
    Mu:1861  Va:1862  Wm:1863
Der Strauß - D1 (1846-74)
    Fr:1869
Die Sündenböcke - C3 (1846-
74)
    Bn:1848  Fr:1849  Wm:1850
Unerschütterlich - C1
    Fr:1857
Versalzen - C1 (1846-74)
    Da:1868  Fr:1867  Ha:1868
    Lg:1867
Der Vetter - C3 (1846-74)
    Bn:1846  Da:1847  Dr:1847
    Fr:1846  Ha:1846  Mu:1846
    Va:1847  Wm:1846
Weibererziehung - C4 (1846-
74)
    Lg:1872  Va:1872
Der Weiberfeind - C1 (1846-
74)
    Bn:1843  Da:1846  Dr:1847
    Fr:1844  Ha:1846  Mu:1868
Weihnachten - D1 (1846-74)
    Lg:1869

Eine Whistpartie unter Frauen
- C1 (1846-74)
    Fr:1865
Die zärtlichen Verwandten -
C3 (1866)
    Bn:1866  Da:1866  Fr:1866
    Ha:1865  Lg:1865  Mh:1866
    Mu:1866  Va:1866  Wm:1866
Zwei Pflegetöchter - C3
(1846-74)
    Va:1864
Zwischenträgerei - C4 (1846-
74)
    Bn:1867  Lg:1867
1813 - D1 (1846-74)
    Lg:1870

**BERG, O. F.** [Pseud. of Otto
Franz Ebersberg]
Vienna 1833-1886 Döbling
Ref: Brüm 19, Ko Th, ADB, NDB

Berlin [Das Volk], wie es
weint und lacht - FP3 - with
D. Kalisch
    Fr:1859  Wm:1859
Einer von unsre Leut - F3 -
with D. Kalisch (1859)
    Da:1861  Dr:1860  Fr:1860
    Ha:1860  Mu:1863  Wm:1866
Das neue Kleid - F5
    Va:1878
Unter dem Siegel der Ver-
schwiegenheit - C5
    Mu:1871  Va:1874

**BERGE, RUDOLF vom**
Herrendorf 1775-1821 Breslau
Ref: Goe 7

Caspar von Coligny - T5
    Bn:1811
Das Haus Barcellona - T5
    Va:1816

**BERGEN, ALEXANDER** [Pseud. of
Marie Gordon-Saphir]
Vienna 1812-1863 Trieste
Ref: Brüm 19, Ko Th

Der arme Marquis - D2 - Fr
    Va:1861
Ein Autograph - C1 - Fr
    Da:1860  Fr:1860  Ha:1861
    Va:1860
Der Gesandtschaftsattaché -
C3
    Da:1863

Eine Jugendschuld - C1 - Fr
    Va:1863
Kleine Mißverständnisse - F1
Eng (1868)
    Bn:1882    Fr:1871
Ein liebenswürdiger Jüngling
- D1 - Fr
    Va:1868
Regen und Sonnenschein - C1 -
Fr
    Fr:1862    Va:1862
Sand in die Augen - C2 - Fr
    Da:1863    Fr:1862    Va:1861
Ein ungeschliffener Diamant -
F1 - Eng (1864)
    Fr:1870
Zwei Witwen - C1 -Fr
    Fr:1862    Va:1862

**BERGER, ALFRED MARIA JULIUS**
**von**
Vienna 1853-1912 Vienna
Ref: Brüm 19, Ko Th, NDB

Oenone - T1 (1873)
    Va:1873

**BERGER, KARL PHILIPP**
Altötting 1793-1853 Altötting
Ref: Ref: Brüm 18, Ko Th

Die Bastille o. Wer Andern
eine Grube gräbt, fällt
selbst hinein - C3 (1836)
    Da:1838    Dr:1837    Ha:1836
    Mh:1839    Mu:1869    Va:1868
    Wm:1836
Bruder und Schwester - C2 -
(1836)
    Bn:1836
Jean Bart am Hofe - C4
    Dr:1847    Ha:1847    Mu:1872
Die Körbe - C5
    Va:1844
Marie von Medicis - C4 (1836)
    Bn:1839    Da:1841    Dr:1837
    Fr:1837    Ha:1837    Mu:1872
    Va:1841    Wm:1853

**BERGER, L. H.**

Alexandra - D5
    Va:1877

**BERGER, TRAUGOTT BENJAMIN**
Wehlen 1754-1810 Dresden
Ref: Brüm 18, Goe 4/1, Ko Th

Galora von Venedig - T5
(1778)
    Bn:1779

**BERGOPZOOMER, JOHANN BAPTIST**
Vienna 1742-1804 Vienna
Ref: Brüm 18, Goe 5, Ko Th,
ADB

Alle irren sich - C5 - Eng
    Va:1777
Die drei Zwillingsbrüder von
Venedig - C4 - It (1778)
    Va:1778
In der Not lernt man die
Freunde kennen  - C5 (1776)
    Bn:1782    Va:1777
Der Zerstreute - C5 - Fr -
(1775)
    Va:1764

**BERLA, ALOIS**
Vienna 1826-1896 Vienna
Ref: Brüm 19, NDB

Durchgegangene Weiber - F
    Fr:1888
Das große Kind - F1
    Fr:1862
Der Narr von Untersberg - F3
(1854)
    Fr:1854    Ha:1852
Ein russischer Beamter - D5
    Fr:1878
Der Zigeuner - D1 (1862)
    Da:1867    Fr:1862    Ha:1860
    Va:1877

**BERN, MAXIMILIAN**
Cherson 1849-1923 Berlin
Ref: Brüm 19, Ko 3

Meine geschiedene Frau - C
(1878)
    Mu:1879

**BERNBRUNN, KARL ANDREAS**
[Pseud.: Karl Carl]
Cracow 1789-1854 Ischl
Ref: Goe 11, Ko Th, ADB, NDB,
OC

Staberls Reiseabenteuer - F2
    Bn:1822    Da:1842    Fr:1819
    Ha:1844    Lg:1823    Mh:1820
    Mu:1816    Va:1817    Wm:1826
See Goedeke 11 for additional
listings.

**BERNBRUNN, MARGARETE** see
Prix, Adalbert

**BERNHARD, J. C.**

Der erste Kranke - C1 - Fr
   Bn:1851
Eine Liebe mit Dampf - F1
   Fr:1862
Zwei Tassen - C1
   Fr:1874

**BERNSTEIN, KARL HUGO** see
Hugo, Karl

**BERNSTEIN, MAX**
Fürth 1854-1925 Munich
Ref: Brüm 19, Ko Th, NDB

Coeur-Dame - C1 (1888)
   Da:1889
Mein neuer Hut - D1 (1881)
   Da:1889  Fr:1887  Mu:1881
   Va:1882

**BERTRAM, MARTIN** see
Schleich, Martin

**BERTUCH, FRIEDRICH JUSTIN von**
Weimar 1747-1822 Weimar
Ref: Goe 4/1, Ko Th, ADB,
NDB, OC

Elfride - T3 - Eng (1775)
   Bn:1788  Da:1822  Dr:1782
   Fr:1780  Ha:1785  Lg:1777
   Mh:1782  Mu:1776  Va:1776
   Wm:1773
Ines de Castro - T5 - Fr
(1773)
   Wm:1773

**BIEDENFELD, FERDINAND LEOPOLD von**
Karlsruhe 1788-1862 Karlsruhe
Ref: Brüm 18, Goe 10, Ko Th

Baron Martin - C2 - Fr (1822)
   Fr:1830  Mh:1825  Lg:1825
   Mu:1823  Va:1821
Die Einsiedler im Walde o.
Der unsichtbare Zeuge - D3 -
Fr (1822)
   Va:1819
Johann Vernot - D3 - Fr
(1822)
   Va:1821
Die Parias - T5 - Fr (1824)
   Bn:1824

Der Schiffskapitän - C1 - Fr
(1822)
   Dr:1818
So macht man sein Glück - C1
Fr (1835)
   Va:1839
Vetter Wunderlich - C3 - Fr
(1835)
   Wm:1835

**BIEDERMANN, FRIEDRICH KARL**
Leipzig 1812-1901 Leipzig
Ref: Brüm 19, Ko Th, NDB

Kaiser Heinrich der Vierte -
T5 (1861)
   Wm:1861
Kaiser Otto der Dritte - T5
(1863)
   Wm:1862
Der letzte Bürgermeister von
Straßburg - D5 (1870)
   Lg:1871

**BILDERBECK, LUDWIG FRANZ von**
Weißenburg 1764-1833
Ref: Goe 5

Die Liebe in Spanien - C3
(1806)
   Va:1804
Männertugend und Weiberliebe
- D4 (1801)
   Fr:1800

**BINZER, EMILIE** see Ritter,
Ernst

**BIRCH-PFEIFFER, CHARLOTTE**
[Pseud.: Franz Fels]
Stuttgart 1800-1868 Berlin
Ref: Brüm 18, Goe 11, Ko Th,
ADB, NDB

Alles für andere - C1 (1848)
   Bn:1848  Dr:1849
Auf dem Oberhof o. Kaiser
Karls Schwert - D5
   Bn:1872
Ein alter Musikant - D1
(1852)
   Bn:1852  Da:1852  Dr:1853
   Fr:1852  Ha:1852  Va:1852
Anna von Österreich - D4
(1845)
   Bn:1846  Da:1849  Dr:1846
   Fr:1847  Ha:1845  Wm:1849
Die beiden Meister - D5
   Lg:1829

Der beste Arzt - D4 (1838)
Bn:1839  Dr:1840
Ein Brief [Ein Billet] - D5 (1847)
Bn:1847  Dr:1843  Ha:1843
Va:1850  Wm:1845
Dorf und Stadt - D5 (1847)
Bn:1847  Da:1848  Dr:1847
Fr:1848  Ha:1847  Mh:1848
Mu:1848  Va:1847  Wm:1848
Elisabeth von England - D5 (1841)
Bn:1843  Dr:1841  Va:1842
Die Engländer in Paris - F4
Bn:1834  Ha:1845  Mu:1833
Eine Familie - D5 (1846)
Bn:1846  Da:1847  Fr:1847
Ha:1848  Mh:1849  Va:1848
Wm:1848
Ferdinand Avelli, der Flücht-
ling - D3
Bn:1830
Das Forsthaus - D4 (1850)
Bn:1850  Da:1851  Dr:1851
Ha:1850  Wm:1850
Fra Bartolomeo der Maler - D5
Lg:1829
Francis Johnston - C5
Bn:1849
Die Frau in Weiß - D5 (1866)
Bn:1866  Da:1867  Fr:1867
Ha:1866  Lg:1866  Va:1866
Fräulein Höckerchen - C3 (1858)
Bn:1858  Va:1858
Die Fräulein von St. Cyr - C5
- Fr
Dr:1844
Der Glöckner von Notre Dame -
D6 (1837)
Da:1849  Dr:1836 Fr:1844
Ha:1835
Der Goldbauer - D4 (1860)
Bn:1861  Da:1861  Dr:1861
Fr:1861  Ha:1861  Mh:1861
Va:1861  Wm:1861
Graf von Falkenberg - F1
Bn:1860
Graf Waltron - D4
Dr:1846  Ha:1845
Die Grille - D1 (1866)
Bn:1856  Da:1857  Dr:1858
Fr:1857  Ha:1856  Mh:1858
Mu:1857  Va:1857  Wm:1857
Gunst und Liebe - D5
Dr:1836

Die Günstlinge [Katharina II.
und ihr Hof] - D5 (1839)
Bn:1834  Da:1844  Dr:1834
Fr:1836  Ha:1834  Lg:1834
Mu:1834
Herma o. Die Söhne der Rache
- D5
Va:1828
Der Herr Cassationsrat - C1 (1864)
Fr:1870
Der Herr Studiosus - D1 (1866)
Bn:1866  Fr:1867  Ha:1867
Va:1867  Wm:1867
Hinko - D5 (1834)
Bn:1834  Fr:1834  Ha:1833
Lg:1833  Mh:1835  Mu:1834
Wm:1837
Iffland - D5 (1858)
Bn:1858  Dr:1859
Im Walde - D4 (1849)
Bn:1850  Dr:1849  Fr:1849
Ha:1849
In der Heimat - D5 (1865)
Bn:1865  Va:1865
Johannes Gutenberg - D5 (1834)
Bn:1835  Dr:1835  Fr:1836
Ha:1835  Lg:1835  Wm:1836
Ein Kind des Glücks - D5 (1860)
Bn:1860  Da:1860  Dr:1860
Fr:1860  Ha:1860  Mu:1868
Va:1860  Wm:1860
König und Freiknecht - D
Lg:1834
Königin Bell - D5 (1863)
Bn:1864  Ha:1863
Die Lady von Worsley Hall -
D5 (1855)
Bn:1856  Dr:1856  Va:1856
Der Leiermann und sein
Pflegekind - D4 (1859)
Dr:1859  Fr:1860  Ha:1859
Magdala - D4 (1851)
Bn:1851  Ha:1851
Marguerite o. Die Macht des
Zufalls - D6 (1855)
Fr:1855
Die Marquise von Vilette - D5 (1844)
Bn:1845  Da:1848  Dr:1845
Fr:1845  Ha:1845  Mu:1870
Va:1846  Wm:1846
Mazarin - D4 (1849)
Bn:1849  Dr:1850  Fr:1850

Mutter und Sohn - D2 (1843)
    Bn:1844    Da:1844    Dr:1843
    Fr:1845    Ha:1843    Mh:1845
    Mu:1867    Va:1846    Wm:1845
Mutter und Tochter - D (1844)
    Ha:1844
Nacht und Morgen - D6 (1842)
    Da:1843    Dr:1843    Fr:1842
    Ha:1843    Wm:1844
Natalie - D5
    Va:1862
Onkel und Nichte - C5 (1836)
    Bn:1838    Dr:1836    Ha:1838
    Va:1836    Wm:1835
Peter von Scapar - D5
    Bn:1834
Der Pfarrherr - D5 (1848)
    Bn:1848    Da:1849    Dr:1848
    Fr:1848    Ha:1848    Wm:1848
Pfeffer-Rösel o. Die Frank-
furter Messe im Jahre 1297 -
D5 (1829)
    Bn:1829    Da:1831    Dr:1830
    Fr:1829    Ha:1829    Lg:1830
    Mh:1837    Mu:1830    Wm:1833
Revanche - C2 (1865)
    Bn:1866    Da:1867    Fr:1869
    Lg:1866    Mu:1872    Wm:1867
Ein Ring - D5 (1851)
    Bn:1855    Da:1866    Dr:1852
    Fr:1866    Ha:1851    Va:1861
    Wm:1856
Rose und Röschen - C4 (1853)
    Bn:1853    Da:1857    Dr:1853
    Fr:1853    Ha:1853    Va:1854
    Wm:1857
Die Rose von Avignon - D4
(1850)
    Dr:1850    Fr:1850    Ha:1850
Rubens in Madrid - D5 (1836)
    Bn:1838    Da:1840    Dr:1837
    Fr:1837    Ha:1837    Mh:1839
    Va:1838    Wm:1837
Der Schatz des Webers - D5
    Ha:1862
Scheibentoni, der Tyroler
Schütz - D5 (1834)
    Dr:1840    Fr:1855    Ha:1840
    Mu:1839    Wm:1842
Schloß Greifenstein o. Der
Samtschuh - D6 (1833)
    Bn:1830    Dr:1829    Fr:1830
    Ha:1835    Lg:1829    Mu:1831
Schön Clärchen - D4
    Bn:1831    Va:1830
Steffen Langer aus Glogau -
C5 (1841)
    Da:1843    Dr:1842    Fr:1842
    Ha:1842    Mh:1843    Wm:1858

Die Taube von Cerdrons - D4
    Bn:1830
Das Testament eines Sonder-
lings - D5 (1867)
    Bn:1867    Ha:1867    Va:1868
Thomas Thyrnau - D5 (1844)
    Bn:1844    Da:1845    Dr:1844
    Fr:1844
Eine Tochter des Südens - D5
(1862)
    Ha:1862    Wm:1863
Ein Trauschein - D5
    Va:1855
Trudchen - D3
    Mu:1831
Die Waise von Lowood - D4
(1853)
    Bn:1853    Da:1854    Dr:1853
    Fr:1853    Ha:1853    Lg:1865
    Mh:1854    Mu:1854    Va:1853
    Wm:1854
Der Wartturm - D
    Va:1829
Wer ist sie? - D4 (1868)
    Bn:1868
Wie man Häuser baut - D4
(1851)
    Bn:1851    Da:1864    Dr:1853
    Fr:1852    Ha:1852    Va:1851
    Wm:1852
Die Witwe - D4
    Bn:1836

**BIRON, LUDWIG**  see Siegert,
Georg

**BITTNER, ANTON**
Melk 1820-1880 Vienna
Ref: Brüm 19, Ko Th

Domestikenstreiche - F1
(1862)
    Fr:1871

**BITTONG, FRANZ**  [Pseud.:
Oskar Stern]
Mainz 1842-1904 Altona
Ref: Brüm 19, Ko Th

Des Königs Schwert - C2
(1877)
    Bn:1878    Fr:1879    Lg:1878
Der Lügner - C4 - Sp (1884)
    Lg:1886

**BLITTERSBERG, GUSTAV von**

Crescentia - D4
    Va:1860

**BLUM, CARL**
Berlin 1786-1844 Berlin
Ref: Brüm 18, Goe 11, Ko Th,
ADB, NDB

André - C1 - Fr (1824)
    Bn:1822    Da:1824    Fr:1823
    Ha:1822
Der Ball zu Ellerbrunn - C3 -
It (1839-44)
    Bn:1835    Da:1840    Dr:1836
    Fr:1836    Ha:1837    Mh:1838
    Mu:1868    Va:1836    Wm:1836
Der Bär und der Bassa - Vv1 -
Fr (1821)
    Bn:1821    Da:1826    Dr:1822
    Fr:1823    Ha:1822    Lg:1822
    Mh:1823    Mu:1840    Va:1820
    Wm:1823
Die beiden Briten - C3 - Fr
(1827)
    Bn:1824    Da:1826    Dr:1825
    Fr:1825    Ha:1825    Lg:1825
    Mh:1828    Mu:1834    Va:1825
    Wm:1825
Die beiden Waisen - Vv
    Ha:1844
Bruno und Balthasar - C3 - It
(1838)
    Bn:1838    Dr:1838    Ha:1839
    Wm:1839
Capricciosa - C3 - It (1835)
    Bn:1834    Da:1844    Dr:1835
    Fr:1839    Ha:1835    Lg:1835
Christoph und Renate - D2 -
Fr
    Bn:1844    Dr:1844    Fr:1844
    Ha:1855    Lg:1844    Va:1844
    Wm:1844
Erziehungsresulte o. Guter
und schlechter Ton - C2 - Fr
(1839-44)
    Bn:1840    Da:1846    Dr:1840
    Fr:1845    Lg:1840    Mh:1840
    Va:1852    Wm:1840
Der Fächer - C3 - It (1832)
    Bn:1831    Fr:1832    Ha:1831
    Wm:1832
Friedrich August in Madrid -
D5 (1832)
    Bn:1831    Ha:1831
Gänserich und Gänschen - Vv1
Fr (1824)
    Bn:1822    Da:1826    Fr:1823
    Ha:1823
Die Geheimnisse von Paris -
D5 - Fr (1844)
    Lg:1844

Des Goldschmieds Töchterlein
- C2 (1835)
    Bn:1833    Da:1836    Dr:1833
    Fr:1834    Ha:1855    Lg:1833
    Mh:1835    Mu:1834    Va:1833
    Wm:1834
Ein Herr und eine Dame - C1 -
Fr (1842)
    Bn:1841    Dr:1843    Ha:1845
    Va:1845
Herr von Ich - C1 - Fr (1826)
    Bn:1826    Dr:1828    Lg:1827
    Wm:1827
Die Herrin von der Else - D5
Eng (1839-44)
    Bn:1837    Da:1843    Dr:1837
    Fr:1838    Ha:1845
Der Hirsch - C2 - It (1835)
    Bn:1834    Da:1843    Dr:1834
    Fr:1840    Ha:1838    Lg:1835
    Va:1835
Ich bleibe ledig - C3 - It
(1839-44)
    Bn:1835    Da:1840    Dr:1840
    Fr:1836    Ha:1846    Mh:1842
    Mu:1868    Va:1839    Wm:1836
Der Invalide - C
    Ha:1844
John Bull - D3 - Eng
    Bn:1825    Ha:1830
Die Kunst zu gefallen [Der
Vicomte von Letorières] - C3
Fr (1839-44)
    Bn:1842    Da:1844    Dr:1850
    Fr:1843    Ha:1844    Lg:1842
    Wm:1843
Lisette - C1 (1835)
    Bn:1835    Da:1843    Ha:1838
    Va:1843
Lord Davenant - D4 - Fr
    Bn:1826    Ha:1827
Magister Quadrat - C1 - Fr
    Bn:1823    Ha:1824
Die Mäntel o. Der Schneider
in Lissabon - C2 - Fr (1828)
    Bn:1826    Da:1828    Dr:1827
    Fr:1827    Ha:1827    Lg:1827
    Mh:1828    Mu:1829    Wm:1826
Marie, die Tochter des Regi-
ments - Vv4 - Fr
    Ha:1845
Mirandolina - C3 - It (1828)
    Bn:1833    Da:1828    Dr:1828
    Fr:1829    Ha:1827    Lg:1831
    Mh:1831    Mu:1830    Va:1830
    Wm:1829
Die Novize - C1 (1836)
    Bn:1831    Lg:1836

Der Oberst - C1 - Fr (1826)
    Bn:1821   Da:1828   Dr:1821
    Fr:1822   Ha:1822   Wm:1823
Pietro Metastasio - C4 - It
(1835)
    Bn:1834   Ha:1835   Lg:1835
    Wm:1835
Die Reise nach Dieppe - C3 -
Fr (1827)
    Bn:1821   Mh:1827   Wm:1827
Der Schiffskapitän o. Die Un-
befangenen - Vv1 - Fr (1824)
    Bn:1817   Da:1821   Fr:1831
    Ha:1820   Lg:1818
Die Schule der Verliebten -
C5 - Eng
    Bn:1845   Da:1859   Dr:1845
    Fr:1849   Ha:1845   Lg:1844
    Va:1857
Schwärmerei nach der Mode -
D4 (1840)
    Bn:1839   Dr:1840   Fr:1840
    Ha:1840   Lg:1840
Der Sekretär und der Koch -
C1 - Fr (1826)
    Bn:1821   Da:1827   Fr:1821
    Ha:1821   Lg:1822   Mh:1826
    Mu:1829   Va:1821
Der Spiegel des Tausendschön
- Vv1
    Bn:1831   Ha:1846   Lg:1833
    Wm:1833
Stadt und Land - D5 - Eng
(1828)
    Bn:1826   Fr:1827
Ein Stündchen [Abend] vor dem
Potsdamer Tor - Vv1 (1830)
    Bn:1823   Ha:1846   Lg:1832
    Va:1833
Tempora mutantur o. Die
gestrengen Herren - C3 - It
(1839-44)
    Bn:1840   Dr:1840   Fr:1842
    Ha:1841   Lg:1840
Die ungleichen Brüder [Die
Brüder Philibert] - C3 - Fr
(1827)
    Bn:1817   Da:1818   Dr:1818
    Mh:1817   Va:1817
Die Verlobung in Genf - C2
    Bn:1837   Fr:1844   Mu:1839
    Wm:1837
Wer trägt die Schuld? - C1
(1843)
    Bn:1830   Fr:1831
Die zweite Frau - C2
    Bn:1838   Ha:1839
See Goedeke 11 for additional
listings.

**BLUM, HANS**
Leipzig 1841-1910 Rheinfelden
Ref: Brüm 19, Ko Th

York - D5 (1884)
    Lg:1884

**BLUMAUER, JOHANN ALOIS**
Steier 1755-1798 Vienna
Ref: Brüm 18, Goe 4/1, ADB,
NDB, OC

Erwine von Steinheim - T5
(1802)
    Dr:1792   Fr:1801   Lg:1789
    Mu:1781   Va:1780

**BLUMENHAGEN, PHILIPP WILHELM**
Hanover 1781-1839 Hanover
Ref: Brüm 18, Goe 10, Ko Th,
ADB

Die Schlacht bei Thermopylae
- T4 (1814)
    Bn:1815
Simson - D5 (1816)
    Dr:1819   Fr:1820

**BLUMENTHAL, OSKAR**
Berlin 1852-1917 Berlin
Ref: Brüm 19, Ko Th, NDB, OC

Anton Antony - C
    Fr:1888
Betrogene Betrüger - C4 - Fr
    Bn:1877   Mh:1878
Die große Glocke - C4 (1885)
    Da:1885   Fr:1884   Mu:1885
    Wm:1884
Ich bitte um's Wort - F4
    Va:1881
Die Philosophie des Unbe-
wußten - C1 (1876)
    Va:1876
Der Probepfeil - C4 (1884)
    Da:1884   Fr:1884   Lg:1885
    Mu:1884   Va:1884
Der schwarze Schleier - C4
(1887)
    Da:1887   Fr:1886   Lg:1887
    Mu:1887
Die Teufelsfelsen - F4 (1881)
    Lg:1881   Mu:1881   Va:1880
Tollköpfchen - C3 - Fr
    Da:1882
Ein Tropfen Gift - D4 (1886)
    Da:1886   Fr:1885   Lg:1886
    Mu:1886   Va:1886   Wm:1885

Um ein nichts - C4 - with
O. Girndt
  Da:1884  Mu:1882  Va:1882
Der Zaungast - C4 (1889)
  Da:1890  Va:1890

**BLUMHOFER, MAXIMILIAN**
[i.e. Blaimhofer]
Munich 1759-?
Ref: Goe 5, Ko 3

Die Schweden in Bayern o. Die
Bürgertreue - D (1783)
  Mu:1783

**BLÜMNER, HEINRICH**
Leipzig 1765-1839 Leipzig
Ref: Brüm 18, Goe 6, Ko Th

Der Alcade von Molidoro - C5
  Wm:1811
Eitle Mühe der Verliebten -
C1 - Fr (1808-09)
  Lg:1821  Wm:1807
Haß den Frauen - C1 - Fr
(1808-09)
  Lg:1819  Wm:1809
Herr Temperlein o. Wie die
Zeit vergeht! - C1 - Fr
(1808-09)
  Lg:1818  Mh:1820
Die seltsame Wette - C1 - Fr
  Lg:1819  Mh:1820  Wm:1810
Die spanische Wand - C1 - Fr
(1808-09)
  Wm:1809

**BOAS, EDUARD**
Landsberg 1815-1853 Landsberg
Ref: Brüm 19, Ko Th, ADB

Der alte Fritz und die
Jesuiten - C5 (1848)
  Ha:1853
Shakespeare o. Gaukeleien der
Liebe - C3 (1848)
  Dr:1852

**BOCK, JOHANN CHRISTIAN**
Dresden 1724 [1750?]-1785
Dresden
Ref: Brüm 18, Goe 4/1, Ko Th

Achmet - T3 - It
  Bn:1781  Dr:1780
Der Adel des Herzens o. Die
ausgeschlagene Erbschaft - D1
  Va:1771

Athelstan - T3 - Eng
  Bn:1779  Dr:1778  Ha:1776
  Mh:1780
Die beiden Freunde o. Der
Kaufmann in Lyon - D5 - Fr
  Bn:1809  Dr:1779  Ha:1771
  Mh:1791  Wm:1792
Der beste Mann - D4 - Eng
(1778-81)
  Dr:1779  Ha:1774
Der Bettler - C1 - It (1771)
  Bn:1774  Dr:1778  Ha:1772
  Va:1773
Elvira - T5 - Fr (1779)
  Dr:1778  Ha:1773
Der flatterhafte Ehemann o.
Wie man eine Hand umkehrt -
C5 - Eng (1784)
  Bn:1784  Dr:1780  Fr:1792
  Ha:1777  Mh:1779  Va:1778
Geschwind, eh' es jemand
erfährt - C3 - It (1784)
  Bn:1778  Dr:1777  Fr:1780
  Ha:1775  Mh:1778  Mu:1782
  Va:1777
Gustav Wasa - T5 - Eng (1779)
  Da:1779
Hanno, Fürst im Norden - D3 -
It (1781)
  Bn:1780  Dr:1780  Fr:1782
Die Holländer o. Was vermag
ein vernünftiges Frauenzimmer
nicht! - C3 - It (1778)
  Bn:1779  Dr:1778  Fr:1780
  Ha:1777  Mh:1780  Va:1778
  Wm:1792
Das Mädchen im Eichtal - C5 -
Eng (1785)
  Bn:1784  Dr:1778  Ha:1776
Die Nebenbuhler - C5 - Eng -
with J. Engelbrecht (1775)
  Ha:1775  Va:1777  Wm:1792
Paridom Wrantpott o. Wer
schilt, wird wieder gut - C3
- It (1779)
  Bn:1786  Dr:1778  Ha:1772
Die Reise nach Ostindien o.
Wie die Arbeit, so der Lohn -
C
  Ha:1774
Der Verschlag o. Hier wird
Versteckens gespielt - C3 -
Sp (1781)
  Dr:1780  Wm:1797
Was sein soll, schickt sich
wohl o. Die Schwester - C5
Eng (1778)
  Bn:1795  Dr:1781  Ha:1773
  Va:1776

Wissenschaft geht vor Schönheit - C3 - It (1778)
    Bn:1786   Dr:1786   Fr:1778
    Ha:1773  Mh:1781

**BÖCKER, EWALD**
Solingen 1844-1901 Bad Kösen
Ref: Brüm 19, Ko 3

Lalage - C3 (1879)
    Fr:1879  Wm:1879

**BODE, HEINRICH**

Mazarins letzte Rechnung - C3
    Da:1854

**BODENSTEDT, FRIEDRICH**
Peine 1819-1892 Wiesbaden
Ref: Brüm 19, Ko Th, ADB,
NDB, OC

Alexander in Korinth - D
(1876)
    Bn:1883  Fr:1876  Mu:1883
Demetrius - T (1856)
    Mu:1856
König Autharis Brautfahrt - D
(1860)
    Mu:1859

**BOHL, OTTO ERNST** [Pseud. of
August Gottlieb Hornbostel]
Vienna 1786-1838 Vienna
Ref: Goe 10, Ko Th

Die Heimberufenen - T5
    Va:1835
Maria o. Die Pest zu Leon -
T3
    Va:1833

**BÖHM, GOTTFRIED**
Nördlingen 1845-1927 Munich
Ref: Brüm 19, Ko Th

Art läßt nicht von Art - C
(1873)
    Mu:1872
Frühlingsschauer - D (1880)
    Mu:1882
Herodias - D (1883)
    Mu:1887

**BÖHM, JULIUS**

Ein Walzer von Chopin - C
    Mu:1879

**BOHRMANN, HEINRICH**
Saarbrücken 1840-1908 Vienna
Ref: Brüm 19, Ko Th

Ein Löwenritt - C4 (1880)
    Va:1881
Verlorene Ehre - D3 (1876)
    Lg:1876

**BOLZ, RICHARD**

Johann von Werth - D5
    Fr:1878

**BONIN, CHRISTIAN FRIEDRICH
FERDINAND**
Magdeburg 1755-1813 Neu-
strelitz
Ref: Goe 5, Ko Th, ADB

Blanfurt und Wilhelmine - C3
(1779)
    Bn:1779
Die Drillinge - C4 - Fr
(1781)
    Bn:1778  Da:1813  Dr:1779
    Fr:1781  Ha:1781  Lg:1817
    Mh:1820  Wm:1787
Ernest o. Die unglücklichen
Folgen der Liebe - D3 - Fr
(1776)
    Bn:1776
Haß und Liebe - D4 (1786)
    Dr:1787  Mh:1786  Va:1786
Hofmeister Amor - F2 - Fr
    Bn:1784
Der Postmeister - C4 (1792)
    Va:1790
Der weibliche Kammerdiener -
C1 (1780)
    Bn:1779

**BONN, FERDINAND**
Donauwörth 1861-1933 Bernau
Ref: Brüm 19, Ko Th

Gundl vom Königssee - FP4
    Mu:1878  Wm:1888
Das Haus Turnhill - T
    Mu:1888

**BÖRNSTEIN, HEINRICH**
Hamburg 1805-1892 Vienna
Ref: Ko Th

Ein Beschützer - D2 - Fr
    Bn:1847

Eine Frau, die sich zum
Fenster hinausstürzt - C2 -
Fr
    Da:1847
Das Fräulein von St. Cyr - C5
- Fr
    Bn:1843  Da:1855  Fr:1860
Hohe Brücke und tiefer Graben
- C1 - Fr
    Dr:1843
Der Lumpensammler von Paris -
D - Fr
    Fr:1847
Mein Mann geht aus - C2 - Fr
    Bn:1846  Da:1846  Fr:1876
Michel Bremond - D5 - Fr
    Bn:1846
Der Puff - C - Fr
    Fr:1847
Reich an Liebe - C1 - Fr
    Fr:1846
Die Tochter des Regenten - C5
- Fr
    Wm:1846
Die unsichtbare Beschützerin
- C4 - Fr
    Va:1843
Vater Hiob - D2 - Fr
    Dr:1843  Ha:1843

**BÖSENBERG, JOHANN HEINRICH**
Hanover 1745-1828 Dresden
Ref: Brüm 18, Goe 5, Ko Th

Die Lieblinge - C1
    Dr:1789
Ritterschwur und Treue - D5
    Dr:1790
Die verschlossene Tür - C3
(1792)
    Dr:1791

**BOTH, L. W.**  see Schneider,
Louis

**BRACHVOGEL, ALBERT EMIL**
Breslau 1824-1878 Lichter-
felde
Ref: Brüm 19, Ko Th, ADB,
NDB, OC

Adalbert vom Babenberge - T5
(1858)
    Bn:1856  Ha:1856  Wm:1856
Alte Schweden - D5 (1875)
    Bn:1874
Die Harfenschule - D3 (1874)
    Bn:1869  Da:1870  Fr:1869
    Lg:1869  Mh:1869  Mu:1869

Mondecaus - T5 (1858)
    Bn:1858  Ha:1858
Narciß - T5 (1857)
    Bn:1856  Da:1856  Dr:1856
    Fr:1856  Ha:1856  Mh:1858
    Mu:1855  Va:1864  Wm:1856
Prinzessin Montpensier - D5
(1865)
    Bn:1865  Da:1869  Ha:1865
    Lg:1865  Va:1865  Wm:1865
Der Trödler - D5 (1865)
    Ha:1862
Der Usupator - T5 (1860)
    Bn:1860

**BRAHM, MORITZ**
Ehrenbreitstein 1744-1822
Vienna
Ref: Goe 5, Ko 3

Der Deserteur - C3 - Fr
(1770)
    Dr:1778  Va:1770
Der Schubkarren des Essig-
händlers - C3 - Fr (1775)
    Lg:1817  Va:1775
Der Sklavenhändler von Smyrna
- C1 - Fr (1770)
    Va:1770
Die Stimme der Natur o. Die
schöne Lüge - C1 - Fr (1775)
    Va:1775
Der ungegründete Verdacht -
C1 (1771)
    Bn:1794  Dr:1778

**BRANDES, JOHANN CHRISTIAN**
Stettin 1735-1799 Berlin
Ref: Brüm 18, Goe 4/1, Ko Th,
ADB, NDB, OC

Alderson - T4 (1790)
    Dr:1790  Ha:1788  Mh:1788
    Mu:1790
Ariadne auf Naxos - D1 (1790)
    Bn:1791  Da:1812  Fr:1780
    Ha:1776  Lg:1775  Mh:1779
    Mu:1779  Va:1780  Wm:1793
Belohnte Wohltat - C3
    Dr:1791
Die Erbschaft o. Der junge
Geizige - C4 (1790)
    Ha:1781  Va:1796
Graf von Olsbach o. Die
Belohnung der Rechtschaf-
fenheit - C5 (1774)
    Bn:1772  Dr:1778  Fr:1778
    Ha:1769  Mh:1781  Va:1769

Gutherzigkeit und Eitelkeit -
C5
    Dr:1792
Der Hagestolze o. Wie mans
treibt, so gehts - C5 (1774)
    Ha:1772
Hans von Zanor o. Der Land-
junker in Berlin
    Ha:1785
Die Hochzeitsfeier o. Ist's
ein Mann oder ein Mädchen?
C5 (1790)
    Bn:1782  Fr:1777  Wm:1791
Die Irrtümer - C1 (1791)
    Va:1796  Wm:1791
Die Komödianten in Quirle-
quitsch - C3 (1791)
    Ha:1786
Der Landesvater - D5 (1790)
    Bn:1787  Ha:1786
Die Mediceer - T5 (1776)
    Bn:1776  Dr:1783  Ha:1776
    Mh:1779  Mu:1776  Va:1776
Die Meierei - C5
    Dr:1794
Miß Fanny o. Der Schiffbruch
T5 (1765)
    Ha:1782  Mh:1781
Miß Sara Salisbury - D4
    Bn:1790  Dr:1794  Ha:1788
Der Namenstag [Der geadelte
Kaufmann] - C5 (1790)
    Bn:1773  Fr:1777  Ha:1771
    Mh:1779
Die neugierigen Frauenzimmer
- C3 - It
    Dr:1793
Olivie - T5 (1790)
    Ha:1774  Lg:1775  Mh:1779
    Va:1776  Wm:1774
Ottilie - T5 (1791)
    Bn:1780  Va:1780
Der Schein betrügt o. Der
liebreiche Ehemann - C5
(1776)
    Dr:1778  Ha:1768  Lg:1774
    Mh:1777  Mu:1772  Va:1768
    Wm:1772
Die Schwiegermütter - C5
    Bn:1809  Fr:1792  Ha:1781
    Mh:1780
Trau, schau, wem o. Der
Gasthof - C5 (1776)
    Dr:1778  Fr:1780  Lg:1775
    Mu:1778  Va:1769  Wm:1772
Die ungleichen Schwestern -
C4
    Dr:1782

Was dem Einen recht ist, ist
dem Andern billig - C3 (1790)
    Dr:1791
Der Weg zum Verderben - D5
    Dr:1793

BRAUN von BRAUNTHAL, KARL
JOHANN [Pseud.: Jean
Charles]
Eger 1802-1866 Vienna
Ref: Brüm 19, Ko Th, ADB, NDB

Die Engländer am Rhein - C4
    Dr:1842
Erinnerungen der Marquise von
Verrières - C1 - Fr
    Va:1846
Die Großtante - C1 - Fr
    Va:1837
Molly - D2 - Fr
    Va:1840
Nach Mitternacht - D1 - Fr
    Va:1840
Ritter Shakespeare - D3
(1836)
    Dr:1843
Schleife und Blume - C3 - Sp
    Va:1847

BRAUNAU, FRANZ von  see
Fritsch, Franz Xaver

BREE, MORITZ
Proßnitz 1842-1916 Vienna
Ref: Brüm 19, Ko 3

Zwischen zwei Stühlen - C2
    Va:1879

BREITENSTEIN   see Holbein,
Franz Ignaz

BRENTANO, FRITZ
Mannheim 1840-1914 Berlin
Ref: Brüm 19, Ko Th

Alfreds Briefe - F4 - with
A. Klaußmann (1886)
    Fr:1886  Lg:1886  Wm:1886
Durchlaucht haben geruht -
C4 (1885)
    Fr:1884  Lg:1886

BRETZNER, CHRISTOPH FRIEDRICH
Leipzig 1748-1807 Leipzig
Ref: Brüm 18, Goe 4/1, Ko Th,
ADB, NDB, OC

Der argwöhnische [miß-
trauische] Liebhaber - C5
(1790)
    Bn:1783   Da:1812   Dr:1782
    Fr:1802   Ha:1782   Lg:1782
    Mh:1893   Wm:1800
Der Eheprokurator - C5 (1790)
    Bn:1781   Fr:1797   Ha:1781
    Mh:1782   Wm:1796
Die Erbschaft aus Ostindien -
C4 (1796)
    Dr:1798   Wm:1797
Felix und Hannchen - (1791)
    Mu:1792   Wm:1791
Heimburg und Maria - C5
(1796)
    Bn:1799   Fr:1797   Lg:1797
    Mu:1815
Die Pastete - F2 (1808)
    Wm:1798
Die Physiognomie o. Karl und
Sophie - C5 (1784)
    Bn:1780   Dr:1780   Mh:1784
    Wm:1792
Das Räuschchen - C4 (1786)
    Bn:1786   Da:1811   Dr:1785
    Fr:1787   Ha:1785   Lg:1785
    Mh:1786   Mu:1787   Va:1789
    Wm:1786
Die verstorbene Ehefrau - C5
(1771)
    Bn:1774   Dr:1780

**BROCKMANN, JOHANN FRANZ
HIERONYMOUS**
Graz 1745-1812
Ref: Goe 5, Ko Th, ADB, NDB

Der Diener zweier Herren - C3
It
    Va:1788
Das Familien-Souper - D2 - Fr
(1802)
    Va:1805
Hattya Ilona o. Die Witwe von
Kecskemét - C2 (1791)
    Va:1788
Das Schloß Limburg o. Die
beiden Gefangenen - C2 - Fr
    Va:1802

**BRÖMEL, WILHELM HEINRICH**
Loburg 1754-1808 Berlin
Ref: Brüm 18, Goe 5, Ko Th,
ADB

Der Adjutant - C3 (1780)
    Bn:1789   Dr:1780   Ha:1779
    Mh:1780   Va:1779

Die buchstäbliche Auslegung
der Gesetze o. Wie machen sie
es in der Komödie - C1 (1785)
    Bn:1784   Da:1814   Fr:1799
    Ha:1784   Mh:1785   Va:1784
    Wm:1792
Die Fallbrücke - C5
    Bn:1797
Gerechtigkeit und Rache - D4
Eng (1785)
    Bn:1784   Dr:1784   Fr:1798
    Ha:1784   Mh:1785   Mu:1785
    Va:1783   Wm:1794
Die Rückkehr - C3
    Va:1799
Der Tabuletkrämer - C1
    Dr:1797
Die Verlobung - C1 (1780)
    Dr:1789   Lg:1783   Mh:1793
    Va:1780
Wilmot und Agnes - T (1784)
    Ha:1781

**BRÜHL, ALOIS FRIEDRICH von**
Dresden 1739-1793 Berlin
Ref: Brüm 18, Goe 5, Ko Th,
ADB, OC

Der Bürgermeister - C5 (1786)
    Bn:1786   Mh:1785   Mu:1785
    Va:1785
Die Brandschatzung - C5
(1785)
    Dr:1780   Ha:1783
Edelmut stärker als Liebe -
C1 (1790)
    Dr:1790   Va:1796
Der eiserne Mann - C1 (1786)
    Va:1785
Das entschlossene Mädchen -
D1 (1785)
    Dr:1789
Die Erbschaft o. Das seltsame
Testament - C5 (1788)
    Dr:1788
Das Findelkind - C5 (1785)
    Bn:1783   Dr:1778   Fr:1802
    Va:1781
Der ganze Kram und das
Mädchen dazu - C1 (1785)
    Va:1787   Wm:1794
Der Harfner - D3 (1786)
    Dr:1792
Jeder reitet sein Stecken-
pferd - C5 (1785)
    Dr:1786
Nancy o. Die Schule der
Eheleute - D5
    Va:1778

So zieht man dem Betrüger die
Larve ab - C5 (1788)
   Dr:1788
Verständnis und Mißverständ-
nis - C5
   Dr:1789   Va:1788
Die würdige Mutter - D5 - Fr
(1790)
   Dr:1790

**BRUMMER, ANDREAS**

Tasso - D4
   Mh:1833

**BRUNNER, ANTON**

Das Souvenir - D5
   Va:1790

**BULTHAUPT, HEINRICH ALFRED**
Bremen 1849-1905 Bremen
Ref: Brüm 19, Ko Th, NDB, OC

Die Copisten - C1 (1875)
   Bn:1890   Wm:1876
Gerold Wendel - T5 (1884)
   Lg:1885
Lebende Bilder - C1 (1880)
   Wm:1880
Die Maltheser - T (1884)
   Mu:1889
Marguerite - D5
   Lg:1885
Eine neue Welt - D4
   Bn:1890

**BULWER, E. L.**   see Gutzkow,
Karl

**BUNGE, RUDOLF**   [Pseud.:
B. Rudolf]
Köthen 1836-1907 Halle
Ref: Brüm 19, Ko Th

Der Herzog von Kurland - T5
(1872)
   Lg:1871   Wm:1874

**BUNSEN, PHILIPP LUDWIG**
Arolsen -1809 Arolsen
Ref: Goe 5, Ko 3

Der Emigrant - D5 (1793)
   Mh:1794   Wm:1793
Siegfried von Lindenberg - D5
   Ha:1813
Zwei Augen für eins - D2
(1807)
   Fr:1807   Mh:1807

**BURCHARD, FRIEDRICH GOTTLIEB
JULIUS**
see Roller, Max

**BURCHARDI**   see Arresto,
Christlieb Georg Heinrich

**BURCKHARDT, E.**

Lucretia - T5
   Lg:1865

**BÜRGER, ELISE**, née Hahn
[Pseud.: Theodora]
Stuttgart 1769-1833 Frank-
furt/M
Ref: Goe 5, Ko Th

Das Bouquet - D2 (1801)
   Mh:1802
Klara von Montalban - D5 - Fr
   Da:1820   Fr:1820   Mh:1814
Die schwäbische Bäuerin - D1
   Mh:1814

**BÜRGER, HUGO**   see Lubliner,
Hugo

**BURI, ERNST KARL LUDWIG
YSENBURG von**
Bierstein 1747-1806 Gießen
Ref: Goe 5, Ko Th

Das Intelligenzblatt - D3
(1787)
   Va:1778

**BÜRKNER, ROBERT EMANUEL
HEINRICH** [Pseud.: Vesper-
tinus]
Breslau 1818-1886 Steglitz
Ref: Brüm 19, Ko Th

Alle spekulieren - C5 - with
M. Ring
   Bn:1851   Wm:1851

**BUSCH, BERNHARD**

Aus dem Urwalde - C1
   Bn:1880
In einer Stunde - C1
   Bn:1880   Da:1881
Ein Portemonnaie - C1
   Bn:1873   Va:1875

**BÜSCHEL, JOHANN GABRIEL
BERNHARD**
Leipzig 1758-1813
Ref: Goe 5, Ko 3

Der Graf von Warwick - T5
(1780)
   Dr:1789    Lg:1789

**BYR, ROBERT** [Pseud. of Karl
Emmerich Robert von Bayer]
Bregenz 1835-1902 Baden/
Vienna
Ref: Brüm 19, Ko Th

Lady Gloster - T5 (1872)
   Va:1869
Der wunde Fleck - C4 (1885)
   Va:1872


**CACHE, JOSEF**
Vienna 1770-1841 Vienna
Ref: Goe 11, Ko 3

Das Hauptquartier - D4 (1807)
   Va:1803
Herrmanns Enkel o. Echter
deutscher Sinn - D4
   Va:1813
Das Küchenregiment
   Va:1833
Die Probe - C1
   Va:1805
Seelenadel - D2 (1805)
   Va:1805
Sie sind verheiratet! - C1
   Va:1808
Die Wette um die Braut - F3
   Va:1824

**CALMBERG, ADOLF**
Lauterbach 1837-1887 Küßnacht
Ref: Brüm 19, Ko Th

Der Sohn des Pastors - D1
(1874)
   Da:1874
Wer ist der Herr Pfarrer? -
C1 (1869)
   Da:1872

**CAMPO, H.**   see Laube, Heinrich

**CARL, KARL**   see Bernbrunn,
Karl

**CARO, KARL**
Breslau 1850-1884 Vienna
Ref: Brüm 19, Ko Th

Am Herzogshof - T2 (1885)
   Va:1884
Die Burgruine - C1 (1883)
   Da:1885    Fr:1882    Lg:1883
   Mu:1885

**CASTELLI, IGNAZ FRANZ**
Vienna 1781-1862 Vienna
Ref: Brüm 18, Goe 11, Ko Th,
ADB, NDB, OC

Abraham - D4 (1818)
   Fr:1820   Ha:1845   Va:1817
Der alte Jüngling - C1 - Fr
(1817)
   Bn:1815
Das Anekdotenbüchlein - C1 -
Fr (1828)
   Da:1830    Dr:1833    Fr:1839
   Mu:1834    Va:1827    Wm:1834
Artaxerxes, Kronprinz von
Persien - T5 - Fr
   Bn:1812
Aurelie, Prinzessin von
Amalfi - C5 - Fr (1845)
   Dr:1829    Fr:1832    Lg:1829
Die beiden Duennen - D1 - Fr
(1822)
   Dr:1822
Der bucklige Liebhaber - C1 -
Fr (1823)
   Bn:1822    Da:1823    Dr:1822
   Lg:1822    Va:1822
Czar Ivan - D2 (1820)
   Da:1825    Dr:1819    Fr:1819
   Ha:1820    Va:1819
Diana von Poitiers [Der König
und der Narr] - C2 (1821)
   Bn:1811    Va:1818
Domestikenstreiche - C1 - Fr
(1805)
   Bn:1817    Lg:1821    Va:1804
   Wm:1808
Die Ehemänner als Junggesel-
len - C1 - Fr (1809)
   Bn:1809    Da:1815    Mu:1808
   Wm:1812
Eine für die Andere - C3 - Fr
(1830)
   Dr:1817    Mh:1830
Der Einsiedler im Lerchen-
walde - C1 Fr (1821OC
   Ha:1821    Mu:1822    Va:1820
Die Familie Rickeburg - C1 -
Fr (1832)
   Dr:1833    Mu:1834    Va:1832

Das Fläschchen Kölnerwasser
o. Die Denkschrift eines
Husaren-Offiziers C1 - Fr
(1823)
    Da:1823
Folgen einer Mißheirat - C4 -
Fr (1835)
    Dr:1836  Ha:1835  Va:1834
Das Frühstück - C1 - Fr
(1807)
    Mu:1807  Va:1807
Gabriele - D3 - Fr (1824)
    Bn:1823  Da:1823  Fr:1825
    Mu:1823  Va:1823
Gleiche Schuld, gleiche
Strafe - C3 - Fr (1822)
    Bn:1822  Da:1824
Der Großpapa - C1 - Fr (1825)
    Bn:1824  Lg:1825  Mu:1833
    Va:1823
Gustav von Dalekarlien o. Die
Minengräber in Schweden - D5
Fr (1805)
    Da:1811  Dr:1810  Lg:1809
    Va:1805
Gutes Beispiel - C1 - Fr
(1826)
    Bn:1825  Va:1825
Haß allen Weibern - C1 - Fr
(1809)
    Bn:1809  Da:1810  Dr:1810
    Fr:1811  Ha:1822  Lg:1811
    Mh:1810  Mu:1809  Va:1808
Der Haustyrann - D3 - Fr
(1828)
    Dr:1819  Va:1819
Johann von Calais - D3
    Bn:1828  Da:1812  Fr:1812
Die junge Tante - C1 - Fr
(1824)
    Bn:1823  Da:1823  Ha:1824
    Va:1823
Klimpern gehört zum Handwerk
- C1 - Fr (1826)
    Mh:1826  Va:1826
Der Kuß durch einen Wechsel -
F1 - Fr (1826)
    Da:1826  Mh:1826  Mu:1829
    Va:1824
Der Liebe Listgewebe - F3
(1832)
    Bn:1830  Va:1836
Liebeszunder - C1 - Fr (1825)
    Da:1827  Dr:1826  Lg:1826
Lully und Quinault - C1 - Fr
(1829)
    Da:1820  Dr:1819  Mu:1832
    Va:1813

Der Marschall von Luxemburg -
D3 - Fr (1820)
    Mu:1820
Die Papageie - C1 - Fr (1820)
    Bn:1827  Va:1819
Peter und Paul - C3 -Fr
(1818)
    Bn:1818  Da:1818  Dr:1817
    Fr:1819  Ha:1821  Mh:1824
    Mu:1822  Va:1816
Die pisanischen Brüder - D3 -
It (1827)
    Da:1828  Va:1825
Der Prinz kommt - C1 - Fr
(1821)
    Bn:1826  Va:1820
Die Puppe o. Das kluge Kind -
C1 - Fr (1822)
    Bn:1823  Ha:1824  Va:1821
Raphael - D1 (1810)
    Bn:1811  Da:1812  Dr:1814
    Fr:1817  Lg:1816  Mh:1812
    Va:1810  Wm:1820
Der Rasttag - C1 - Fr (1818)
    Bn:1828  Dr:1818
Roderich und Kunigunde - C2 -
Fr (1807)
    Bn:1827  Da:1828  Fr:1850
    Ha:1830  Mh:1821  Mu:1823
    Va:1807
Der Schicksalsstrumpf - TC2 -
Fr (1818)
    Mu:1823
Die Schwäbin - C1 (1834)
    Bn:1834  Da:1843  Dr:1838
    Fr:1839  Ha:1839  Va:1835
    Wm:1849
Der Sie - C1 (1818)
    Fr:1818  Va:1827
Der Student und die Dame - C2
Fr (1841)
    Dr:1850  Va:1838  Wm:1840
Ein Tag Carls des V. - D2
(1827)
    Dr:1827  Ha:1826  Va:1830
Das Testament des Onkels - D3
Fr (1808)
    Da:1822  Fr:1821  Lg:1810
    Mh:1807  Va:1808
Die Waise aus Genf - D3 - Fr
(1822)
    Da:1824  Dr:1821  Fr:1822
    Lg:1822  Va:1821
Die Waise und der Mörder - D3
Fr (1819)
    Bn:1819  Da:1822  Dr:1817
    Fr:1818  Ha:1822  Lg:1818
    Mh:1819  Mu:1817  Va:1817
    Wm:1819

Der Weibertausch - C1 - Fr
(1821)
   Bn:1825  Dr:1822  Ha:1821
   Mu:1822  Va:1820
Die Zeche o. Gastwirt und
Bürgermeister in einer Person
F1 (1819)
   Bn:1819  Da:1820  Va:1819
Zwei Freunde und ein Rock -
C1 - Fr (1827)
   Bn:1827  Da:1827  Va:1826
   Wm:1827
See Goedeke 11 for additional
listings.

**CHRISTERN, JOHANN WILHELM**
[Pseud.: Felix Rose]
Karolinenhof 1809-1877 Ham-
burg
Ref: Brüm 19, Ko Th

Sesenheim - C (1846)
   Ha:1845

**CLAAR, EMIL**
Lemberg 1842-1930 Frankfurt/M
Ref: Brüm 19, Ko Th

Nach Leipzig zur Messe - C1
   Lg:1867
Simson und Delila - C1 (1873)
   Fr:1881  Wm:1870

**CLAUDIUS, GEORG KARL**
[Pseud.: Franz Ehrenberg]
Zschopau 1757-1815 Leipzig
Ref: Brüm 18, Goe 5, Ko Th,
ADB

Die Grafen Guiscardi - T5
(1787)
   Bn:1790  Dr:1795  Wm:1787

**CLAUREN, HEINRICH** [Pseud. of
Carl Gottlieb Samuel Heun]
Dobrilugk 1771-1854 Berlin
Ref: Brüm 18, Goe 10, Ko Th,
ADB, NDB, OC

Der Abend im Posthause - C5
(1817)
   Bn:1816  Dr:1816  Fr:1816
   Mh:1818
Der Bräutigam aus Mexiko - C5
(1824)
   Bn:1822  Da:1822  Dr:1823
   Fr:1822  Ha:1823  Lg:1822
   Mh:1824  Mu:1822  Va:1823
   Wm:1824

Der Brauttanz o. Der
Schwiegersohn von ungefähr -
C5 (1817)
   Bn:1815  Dr:1815  Fr:1815
   Ha:1817  Lg:1816  Va:1815
   Wm:1818
Das Doppelduell - C5 (1817)
   Bn:1826  Da:1817  Dr:1816
   Fr:1816  Lg:1816  Wm:1821
Die Folgen eines Maskenballs
- C1 - Fr (1817)
   Bn:1815  Fr:1815
Das Gasthaus zur Goldenen
Sonne - C4 (1823)
   Bn:1822  Da:1822  Fr:1822
   Ha:1822  Va:1822
Das Vogelschießen - C5 (1822)
   Bn:1819  Da:1823  Dr:1819
   Fr:1819  Ha:1819  Lg:1820
   Mh:1822  Va:1819  Wm:1820
Der Vorposten - D5 (1821)
   Bn:1817  Da:1823  Dr:1817
   Fr:1817  Ha:1817  Mh:1817
   Va:1817  Wm:1821
Der Wollmarkt o. Das Hotel de
Wibourg - C4 (1826)
   Bn:1824  Da:1824  Dr:1824
   Fr:1824  Ha:1823  Lg:1824
   Mh:1825  Mu:1831  Va:1823
   Wm:1824

**CLEMENS, FRIEDRICH**  see
Gerke, Friedrich

**CLEMENT, LOTHAR**  [Pseud. of
F. Woldemar Ortleb]

Anonyme Briefe - C1
   Bn:1890
Ludwig der Elfte - T5 (1881)
   Wm:1882
Die Prüfung - C1 (1888)
   Bn:1888  Wm:1888
Die vier Temperamente - C4
(1883)
   Bn:1885  Wm:1884

**CLODIUS, CHRISTIAN AUGUST**
Annaberg 1738-1784 Leipzig
Ref: Brüm 18, Goe 3, Ko Th,
ADB, NDB

Medon o. Die Rache des Weisen
C3 (1767)
   Bn:1771  Dr:1778  Va:1770

**COHN, MARTIN**  see Mels,
August

COHN, OSKAR JUSTINUS  see
Justinus, Oskar

COLLIN, HEINRICH JOSEF von
Vienna 1771-1811 Vienna
Ref: Brüm 18, Goe 6, Ko Th,
ADB, NDB, OC

Balboa - T4 (1806)
    Bn:1805   Da:1819   Dr:1833
    Mh:1807   Mu:1821   Va:1805
Bianca della Porta - T5
(1808)
    Da:1826   Fr:1808   Mh:1820
    Mu:1809   Va:1807   Wm:1810
Coriolan - T5 (1804)
    Bn:1803   Va:1802
Die Horatier und Curiatier -
T5 (1812)
    Va:1817
Mäon - T5 (1809)
    Fr:1813   Lg:1819   Mu:1820
    Va:1807
Polyxena - T5 (1804)
    Va:1803
Regulus - T5 (1802)
    Bn:1802   Da:1811   Dr:1805
    Fr:1802   Lg:1805   Mh:1803
    Mu:1804   Va:1801   Wm:1805

COLLIN, MATTHÄUS von
Vienna 1779-1824 Vienna
Ref: Brüm 18, Goe 6, Ko Th,
ADB, NDB, OC

Der Cid - T5 - Fr (1813-17)
    Lg:1823   Va:1822
Essex - T5 - Eng (1827)
    Da:1828   Dr:1830   Mu:1830
    Va:1823

CONRAD, G.  see Georg von
Preußen, Prince

CONRAD, GUIDO  see Mosing,
Guido Konrad

CONTESSA [SALICE-CONTESSA],
KARL WILHELM von
Hirschberg 1777-1825 Berlin
Ref: Brüm 18, Goe 6, Ko Th,
ADB, NDB, OC

Der Findling o. Die moderne
Kunstapotheose - C3 (1810)
    Bn:1810   Da:1813   Dr:1814
    Fr:1818   Lg:1811   Wm:1810

Ich bin mein Bruder - C1
(1819)
    Bn:1819   Da:1819   Dr:1821
    Fr:1819   Fr:1830   Lg:1819
    Mh:1819   Va:1818   Wm:1819
Ich bin meine Schwester - C1
(1821)
    Lg:1820
Das Quartettchen im Hause -
C1 (1826)
    Da:1826   Dr:1829   Fr:1825
    Lg:1830   Va:1823
Das Rätsel - C1 (1808)
    Bn:1807   Da:1810   Dr:1808
    Fr:1808   Lg:1811   Mh:1808
    Va:1807   Wm:1805
Der Schatz - C1 (1818)
    Bn:1817   Da:1818   Dr:1818
    Fr:1817   Va:1817
Der Talisman - C1 (1810)
    Bn:1815   Da:1810   Dr:1809
    Fr:1810   Mh:1810   Va:1809
    Wm:1809
Der unterbrochene Schwätzer -
C1 - Fr (1808)
    Dr:1818   Va:1808   Wm:1825
Der Weiberfeind - C1 (1826)
    Da:1812

COSMAR, ALEXANDER  [Pseud.:
Max Larceso]
Berlin 1805-1842 Berlin
Ref: Brüm 19, Goe 11, Ko Th,
ADB

Das Abenteuer an der Stras-
senecke - F1
    Ha:1839
Der Bekehrte - C1 - Fr (1837)
    Fr:1840
Charlotte Mardyn - C2 - Fr
(1842)
    Bn:1839   Lg:1839
Drei Ehen und eine Liebe - C3
Fr (1839)
    Bn:1838   Ha:1838
Drei Frauen auf einmal - C1 -
Fr (1836)
    Bn:1834   Dr:1835   Fr:1838
    Ha:1835   Lg:1836
Drei Portraits unter einer
Nummer - F1
    Ha:1841
Die Ehe nach der Mode - C4 -
Fr
    Lg:1841
Die Ehrendame - C1 - Fr
(1839)
    Bn:1835   Dr:1836

Frauenwert - D2 - Fr (1839)
    Bn:1838   Wm:1838
Gasthofabenteuer - C1 - Fr
(1841)
    Bn:1838   Lg:1839
Gatte und Junggeselle - C3 -
Fr
    Bn:1823   Dr:1823
Der Gemahl an der Wand - F1
(1841)
    Bn:1838   Lg:1838   Va:1842
Die Getrennten - C1 - Fr
(1841)
    Bn:1839   Ha:1839
Hummer und Compagnie - C1 -
Fr (1837)
    Bn:1836   Lg:1837
Die Husaren in der Klemme -
C1 - Fr (1842)
    Bn:1840   Lg:1841
Ein junger Weiberhasser - C1
Fr
    Lg:1835
Die Liebe im Eckhause - C2 -
Sp (1839)
    Bn:1836   Da:1846   Dr:1837
    Fr:1837   Ha:1847   Lg:1836
    Va:1854   Wm:1852
Mädchen und Frau - C2 - Fr
(1841)
    Bn:1839   Ha:1839
Der Maler - D - Fr
    Mu:1838
Der Meuchelmörder o. Der
Fluch der bösen Tat - F1 - Fr
(1835)
    Bn:1833   Va:1841
Miß Fragoletta - C2
    Ha:1840
Molière als Liebhaber - C2 -
Fr (1841)
    Bn:1839   Ha:1839
Onkel und Neffe - C1 - Fr
(1839)
    Bn:1837   Da:1838   Dr:1838
    Ha:1837
Der Räuber Sobri - C1 (1840)
    Bn:1837   Ha:1837
Riquiqui o. Die seltsame
Heirat - C3 - Fr (1842)
    Bn:1837   Da:1846
Die Seeräuber - Vv2 - Fr
    Bn:1839   Dr:1839   Ha:1839
Die Tochter Cromwells - D1 -
Fr (1840)
    Bn:1836   Dr:1837
Eine Treppe höher - F1 - Fr
(1840)
    Bn:1837   Fr:1865   Lg:1838

Vater und Sohn - D1
    Bn:1838   Ha:1837
Die Zwillingsgeschwister - C2
Fr (1839)
    Bn:1837   Ha:1837   Lg:1838
See Goedeke 11 for additional
listings.

**COSTA, KARL**  [Pseud. of Karl
Kostia]
Vienna 1832-1907 Vienna
Ref: Ko Th

Ein Blitzmädel - F (1878)
    Fr:1887   Mu:1877
Ihr Corporal - F
    Fr:1890

**COSTENOBLE, CARL LUDWIG**
Herford 1769-1837 Prague
Ref: Brüm 18, Goe 11, Ko Th,
ADB, NDB

Der Alte muß! [Gleiche Wahl]
- C2 - Fr (1825)
    Bn:1825   Dr:1822   Fr:1821
    Va:1835
Drei Erben und keiner - L1
(1824)
    Da:1823   Va:1823
Die Drillinge - F
    Fr:1812   Ha:1812
Die Einquartierung - C1
    Fr:1821
Erdbeeren und Küsse - C1
(1825)
    Bn:1829
Fehlgeschossen - C1 (1811)
    Bn:1827   Da:1815   Dr:1835
    Fr:1815   Ha:1806   Mh:1815
    Va:1812
Die Gefallsucht - C3 - It
    Bn:1823   Va:1821
Graf Niemand - C1 (1811)
    Dr:1832   Ha:1810
Die Kapitulation - C1 (1816)
    Mu:1816
Ländliche Stille - C5
    Bn:1824   Fr:1825   Mu:1824
Der Mann im Feuer o. Der
Bräutigam auf der Probe - C3
    Fr:1809   Lg:1829
Die Milchbrüder - C2 - Fr
    Ha:1816   Va:1821
Der Schiffbruch - D1 (1830)
    Bn:1828   Ha:1816
Die Steckenpferde - C1 (1809)
    Ha:1810

Die Testamentsklausel - C1 -
Fr (1830)
    Bn:1827  Wm:1826
Der tote Onkel - F1 (1830)
    Ha:1800
Die Wunderkur - C4 - Fr
    Ha:1809  Va:1812
Die Zauberflöte - C1 (1809)
    Ha:1810

**CRAMM [-BURGDORF], C.F. BURG-
HARD von** [Pseud.: C. von
Horst]
Lesse 1837-1913 Blankenburg
Ref: Brüm 19, Ko Th

Schlittenrecht - C1 (1872)
    Lg:1873  Wm:1873

**CRONEGK, JOHANN FRIEDRICH von**
Ansbach 1731-1758 Nuremberg
Ref: Brüm 18, Goe 4/1, Ko Th,
ADB, NDB, OC

Codrus o. Muster der Vater-
landsliebe - T5 (1760)
    Bn:1771  Dr:1784  Ha:1769
    Mu:1784  Va:1771
Olinth und Sophronia - T5
(1760)
    Ha:1767  Mh:1780  Mu:1787

**CUNO, HEINRICH**
Pommerania-1829 Karlsbad
Ref: Goe 11, Ko Th

Alles schriftlich o. Der
Schlaukopf - C4 - It (1813)
    Va:1820
Die Brautkrone - D5 (1811)
    Bn:1822  Dr:1813  Ha:1813
    Lg:1816  Va:1817
Dankbarkeit - D5
    Da:1814
Das Diadem o. Die Ruinen von
Engelhaus - D5 (1821)
    Mu:1821  Va:1828
Die Geistermühle bei Saaz -
D5
    Va:1834
Die Räuber auf Maria-Kulm o.
Die Kraft des Glaubens - D5
(1816)
    Da:1818  Fr:1833  Ha:1815
    Mh:1829  Mu:1822  Va:1815
Die Schreckensnacht im
Schlosse Paluzzi - D3 - Fr
    Va:1818

Vetter Benjamin aus Polen -
C5 (1822)
    Bn:1820  Da:1822  Dr:1819
    Ha:1818  Mh:1821  Va:1819
    Wm:1821

**CZECHTITZKY, KARL**
Trautenau/Bohemia 1759-1813
Prague
Ref: Goe 5, Ko Th, ADB

Graf Treuberg - T (1785)
    Mu:1778

**DAHN, FELIX**
Hamburg 1834-1912 Breslau
Ref: Brüm 19, Ko Th, NDB, OC

Deutsche Treue - D5 (1871)
    Bn:1876  Mu:1876
König Roderich - T5 (1875)
    Lg:1875  Mh:1876
Markgraf Rüdeger von Beche-
laren - T (1875)
    Mu:1875
Skalden-Kunst - D3 (1882)
    Bn:1882
Die Staatskunst der Frauen -
C3 (1877)
    Bn:1877  Mu:18777

**DALBERG, WOLFGANG HERIBERT
von**
Schloß Herrnsheim 1750-1806
Mannheim
Ref: Goe 5, Ko Th, ADB, NDB

Der Einsiedler [Der Mönch;
Der Pilger] von Carmel - T5
- Eng (1787)
    Bn:1788  Dr:1787  Fr:1807
    Ha:1786  Mh:1786  Mu:1787
    Va:1787
Die eheliche Probe - C1 - Eng
    Dr:1791  Fr:1792  Ha:1788
    Lg:1794  Mh:1788  Wm:1793
Die eheliche Vergeltung - C1
- Eng
    Fr:1792  Ha:1789  Mh:1792
Die eheliche Versöhnung - C1
- Eng
    Mh:1793
Das Incognito - D5 - It
    Ha:1804  Mh:1796

Montesquieu o. Die unbekannte
Wohltat - D3 - Fr (1787)
    Dr:1787   Mh:1787   Va:1787
Walwais und Adelaide - D5
(1778)
    Bn:1780   Dr:1787   Mh:1778
    Mu:1779
Der weibliche Ehescheue - D2
(1787)
    Mh:1780

**DALLMANN**

Sophie van der Daalen - C5
    Dr:1800

**DECKER, KARL von**   see Thale,
Adalbert vom

**DEINHARDSTEIN, JOHANN LUDWIG**
[Pseud.: Dr. Römer]
Vienna 1794-1859 Vienna
Ref: Brüm 18, Goe 9, Ko Th,
ADB, NDB, OC

Das Bild der Danae - C2
(1823)
    Bn:1826   Da:1822   Ha:1828
    Mh:1831   Mu:1822   Va:1822
Boccaccio - D2 (1816)
    Va:1816   Wm:1820
Brautstand und Ehestand - C4
(1837)
    Va:1835   Wm:1838
Deutscher Sinn - D
    Va:1813
Das diamantene Kreuz - C2
(1826)
    Bn:1828   Da:1826   Fr:1842
    Va:1827   Wm:1826
Der Egoist - D5 (1848)
    Va:1831
Ehestandsqualen - C1 (1820)
    Va:1820
Erzherzog Maximilians Braut-
zug - D5 (1832)
    Dr:1833   Fr:1830   Ha:1832
    Lg:1832   Mh:1832   Mu:1830
    Va:1829
Fürst und Dichter - D4 (1851)
    Va:1847
Garrick in Bristol - C4
(1834)
    Bn:1832   Da:1837   Dr:1832
    Fr:1833   Ha:1832   Lg:1833
    Mh:1835   Mu:1833   Va:1832
    Wm:1833
Der Gast - D2 (1827)
    Va:1824

Die Gönnerschaften - C5 - Fr
(1838)
    Bn:1861   Ha:1839   Va:1837
Hans Sachs - D4 (1829)
    Bn:1828   Da:1828   Dr:1828
    Fr:1828   Ha:1827   Lg:1828
    Mh:1829   Mu:1830   Va:1827
Irrtum und Liebe - C4 (1850)
    Va:1821
Leichtsinn und seine Folgen -
D5 - Fr (1841)
    Va:1840   Wm:1841
Liebe und Liebelei - C4
(1837)
    Bn:1834   Dr:1834   Ha:1834
    Mu:1834   Va:1833   Wm:1839
Louise von Lignerolles - D5 -
Fr (1841)
    Va:1839
Ludovico - T5 - Fr
    Va:1848
Mädchenlist - C1 (1816)
    Va:1816
Modestus - C4 (1848)
    Dr:1845   Va:1844
Peter und der Ring - D1
    Va:1826
Pigault Lebrun - C5 (1845)
    Dr:1844   Va:1843   Wm:1845
Der Rosenstock - D1 (1816)
    Bn:1815   Va:1815
Die rote Schleife - C4 (1851)
    Dr:1847   Fr:1847   Mu:1870
    Va:1845
Die seltene Liebschaft - C1 -
Fr (1838)
    Ha:1839   Va:1837
Das Sonnett - D1 (1816)
    Va:1813
Verirrungen der Liebe - C4
(1849)
    Va:1846
Viola - C5 - Eng (1841)
    Fr:1858   Ha:1841   Mh:1846
    Va:1839
Der Witwer - C1 (1816)
    Bn:1830   Da:1818   Dr:1850
    Fr:1818   Ha:1816   Lg:1819
    Mh:1818   Mu:1829   Va:1814
Zwei Tage aus dem Leben eines
Fürsten - C4 (1849)
    Bn:1845   Da:1857   Dr:1846
    Fr:1845   Ha:1845   Mu:1869
    Va:1845   Wm:1852

**DENECKE, F.**

Eine Partie Piquet - C1 - Fr
    Bn:1865   Da:1866

Zum goldenen Lachs - C1
  Fr:1856

**DEVRIENT, EDUARD PHILIPP**
Berlin 1801-1877 Karlsruhe
Ref: Brüm 19, Ko Th, ADB,
NDB, OC

Der Fabrikant - D3 - Fr
(1839)
  Bn:1840   Da:1842   Dr:1840
  Fr:1840   Ha:1840   Mh:1840
  Mu:1872   Va:1840   Wm:1849
Das graue Männlein - D5
(1833)
  Bn:1834   Dr:1833   Ha:1834
Die Gunst des Augenblicks -
C3 (1835)
  Bn:1836   Da:1839   Dr:1836
  Fr:1842   Va:1836   Wm:1836
Herr Baron - C5
  Bn:1843
Treue Liebe - D5 (1841)
  Bn:1844   Da:1843   Dr:1843
  Fr:1842   Mh:1843   Va:1842
Die Verirrungen - D5 (1837)
  Bn:1838   Da:1848   Dr:1838
  Fr:1845   Ha:1838   Mh:1839
  Va:1841   Wm:1874

**DEVRIENT, OTTO**
Berlin 1838-1894 Stettin
Ref: Brüm 19, Ko Th, ADB

Zehn Minuten Aufenthalt - F1
(1866)
  Fr:1867

**DIERICKE, FRIEDRICH OTTO**
Potsdam 1743-1819 Neu-
Schöneberg
Ref: Goe 5, Ko 2

Eduard Montrose - T5 (1776)
  Bn:1786   Dr:1780   Fr:1778
  Mh:1779   Mu:1778   Va:1776

**DIETRICHSTEIN, MORITZ von**
Vienna 1775-1864 Vienna
Ref: Goe 11, Ko 3, ADB, NDB

Auf und ab - C1 - Fr (1807)
  Va:1807

**DILG, MATTHIAS**
Haimbach 1778-1830 Vienna
Ref: Goe 11, Ko 3

Alles mit Anstand - C4
  Va:1811

Die Einquartierung - C1
  Va:1805
Der Ehekontrakt - C1
  Va:1811
Die güldene Gans - F2
  Va:1812
Der Korb - D2 (1820)
  Bn:1830   Da:1812   Dr:1805
  Fr:1805   Ha:1832   Lg:1816
  Mh:1810   Mu:1816   Va:1805
Das Mädchen aus Siberien - D3
  Va:1805
Soldatentreue - C2
  Va:1816
Theaternachrichten o. Die
Dorfkomödie - F1
  Va:1811
Der Verdacht - C2
  Va:1808
Der Vetter aus Indien - C2
  Va:1814

**DINGELSTEDT, FRANZ von**
Halsdorf 1814-1881 Vienna
Ref: Brüm 19, Ko Th, ADB,
NDB, OC

Das Haus der Barneveldt - T5
(1850)
  Da:1853   Dr:1850   Fr:1850
  Ha:1854   Mh:1850   Wm:1851
Ein toller Tag - C5 - Fr
  Bn:1862   Ha:1865

**DOCZY, LUDWIG**
Oldenburg 1845-1919
Ref: Brüm 19, Ko 3

Der Kuß - C4 (1877)
  Fr:1881   Mu:1877   Va:1875
Letzte Liebe - C5 (1887)
  Bn:1888   Mu:1888   Va:1885

**DOHM, HEDWIG**, née Schleh
Berlin 1833-1919 Berlin
Ref: Brüm 19, Ko Th, NDB

Ihr Retter - F1
  Ha:1866
Der Ritter vom goldenen Kalb
- C1 (1879)
  Bn:1879
Der Seelenretter - C1 (1876)
  Bn:1875   Va:1876
Vom Stamme der Asra - C1
(1876)
  Bn:1874   Da:1876   Fr:1875
  Va:1875

**DOLCE, CARLO**   see Groß, Karl

DÖRING, C.

Die verhängnisvolle Cor-
respondenz - C1
    Fr:1885

DÖRING, GEORG CHRISTIAN
WILHELM
Kassel 1789-1833 Frankfurt/M
Ref: Brüm 18, Goe 9, Ko Th,
ADB

Cervantes - D3 (1819)
    Wm:1823
Gellert - C1 (1825)
    Da:1844  Fr:1832  Lg:1834
    Wm:1829

DÖRING, MORITZ WILHELM
Dresden 1798-1856 Freiberg
Ref: Goe 13, Ko 2, ADB

Markgraf Friedrich - D3
(1846)
    Dr:1837

DORNAU, JULIUS   [Pseud. of A.
Julius Naundorff]
Dresden 1821-?
Ref: Brüm 19

Georg Washington - D5 (1862)
    Dr:1847

DRAXLER-MANFRED, KARL
Lemberg 1806-1879 Darmstadt
Ref: Brüm 19, Goe 12, Ko Th,
ADB

Marie-Anne o. Ein Weib aus
dem Volke - D5 - Fr (1846)
    Fr:1846  Ha:1846  Mu:1846
    Wm:1846

DREHER, HEINRICH

Hochzeit oder Festung? - C3
    Da:1860
Theodor Körner - D1
    Dr:1860  Ha:1860

DREYEN, GEORG

Das kritische Alter - C4
    Lg:1887

DROST, WILHELM ELIAS
Hamburg 1821-1897 Hamburg
Ref: Ko Th

Eine kranke Familie - F3 -
with G. Moser (1883)
    Fr:1863  Wm:1875
Ein Königreich für zwei
Kinder - F1
    Fr:1864

DUNCKER, DORA
Berlin 1855-1916 Berlin
Ref: Brüm 19, Ko Th

Nelly - C3 (1884)
    Lg:1885

DUNGERN, JULIE
Augsburg 1822-1886 Mannheim
Ref: Brüm 19, Ko 3

Er kann nicht dividieren - C1
    Fr:1864

DUNKLAND, FRITZ

Sympathie - C1
    Bn:1886  Fr:1883

DYK [DYCK], JOHANN GOTTFRIED
Leipzig 1750-1813 Leipzig
Ref: Goe 5, Ko Th, ADB

Ehrsucht und Schwatzhaftig-
keit - D5 - Fr (1781)
    Bn:1780  Dr:1779
Graf von Essex [Die Gunst der
Fürsten] - T5 - Eng (1786)
    Bn:1787  Da:1813  Dr:1777
    Fr:1793  Ha:1773  Lg:1777
    Mh:1781  Mu:1778  Wm:1786
Jack Spleen o. Ich erschieße
mich nicht - C1 - Fr (1786)
    Bn:1786  Dr:1785  Mh:1786
Der liebenswürdige Alte - C5
- Fr (1786)
    Bn:1782
Sechs Wagen mit Contrebande
o. Großtun und Knickerei - C5
- Eng (1786)
    Mh:1787
Thomas More - T5 - Eng (1786)
    Bn:1787  Mh:1788

EBERSBERG, OTTO FRANZ   see
Berg, O. F.

**EBERT, KARL EGON**
Prague 1801-1882 Prague
Ref: Brüm 19, Goe 10, Ko Th,
ADB, NDB, OC

Bretislaw und Jutta - D5
(1835)
   Mu:1829  Va:1829

**EBNER-ESCHENBACH, MARIE von**
Zdislavic 1830-1916 Vienna
Ref: Brüm 19, Ko Th, NDB, OC

Doctor Ritter - D1 (1872)
   Va:1869
Marie Roland - T5 (1867)
   Wm:1868
Die Veilchen - C1 (1874)
   Bn:1862  Fr:1874  Mu:1873
   Va:1863  Wm:1872
Das Waldfräulein - C4 (1872)
   Va:1873

**ECKARDT, FRIEDRICH SAMUEL
LUKAS von**
Berlin 1759-1806 Riga
Ref: Brüm 18, Goe 7, Ko Th

Die Abgebrannten - D2 (1782)
   Va:1782
Die Ehebrecher - D1
   Bn:1776
Der fleißige Schuster - D1
   Bn:1778
Die Schwätzer - T5 (1780)
   Va:1781
Wer wird sie kriegen? - C1 -
(1780)
   Dr:1784  Lg:1793  Mh:1781
   Va:1781

**ECKARDT, LUDWIG**
Vienna 1827-1871 Tetschen/
Bohemia
Ref: Brüm 19, Ko Th, NDB

Schiller - D (1859)
   Ha:1860
Sokrates - T5 (1858)
   Bn:1862

**ECKSTEIN, ERNST**
Gießen 1845-1900 Dresden
Ref: Brüm 19, NDB, OC

Der Besuch im Karzer - C1
(1875)
   Bn:1876  Fr:1876

Ein Pessimist - C4 (1877OC
   Bn:1877

**EGBERT, W.** see Grieben,
Ferdinand

**EHRENBERG, FRANZ** see
Claudius, Georg Karl

**EIDEX, SAMSON** see Sessa,
Karl Boromäus

**EINSIEDEL, FRIEDRICH
HILDEBRAND von**
Lumpzig 1750-1828 Weimar
Ref: Brüm 18, Goe 4/1, Ko Th,
ADB, NDB, OC

Die Abenteuer auf Reisen - C5
   Va:1787
Die Brüder - C4 - Lat (1802)
   Bn:1815  Da:1825  Lg:1807
   Mu:1852  Va:1841  Wm:1801
Cervantes' Portrait - C3 - Fr
   Wm:1803
Der Fremde aus Andros - D5
   Wm:1803
Die Gefangenen - C5 - Lat
   Bn:1816
Der Geheimniskrämer - C4
   Wm:1806
Das Gespenst - C5 - Lat
   Wm:1807
Der Heautontimorumenos - C5 -
Lat
   Wm:1804
Die Mohrin - C5 - Lat
   Wm:1803
Die Verbannung des Grafen
Rochester o. Die Taberne - C1
   Wm:1812

**EIRICH, OSKAR FRIEDRICH**
Peterwardein 1845-1921 Vienna
Ref: Ko 3

Taub muß er sein - F1 - Fr
   Lg:1867

**ELIMAR, DUKE OF OLDENBURG**
see Günther, Anton

**ELISABETH, QUEEN OF RUMANIA**
see Sylva, Carmen

ELLMENREICH, FRIEDERIKE, née
Brandl
Köthen 1775-1845 Schwerin
Ref: Brüm 18, Goe 11, Ko Th,
ADB

Die beiden Witwen o. Der
Kontrast - C1 - Fr (1827)
    Fr:1822
Der entführte Offizier - C1 -
Fr (1827)
    Mu:1827
Der Großpapa - C1 - Fr (1827)
    Dr:1833  Fr:1824  Lg:1833
Heirat vor hundert Jahren -
C1
    Lg:1852
Die Männerlotterie - C1 - Fr
(1827)
    Fr:1829
Die Nachtwandlerin - C - Fr
(1827)
    Fr:1825
Röschens Aussteuer o. Das
Duell - C3 - Fr (1827)
    Bn:1824  Da:1827  Dr:1826
    Fr:1823  Lg:1826  Mh:1824
    Va:1849  Wm:1830
Der Vampyr - F1 - Fr (1827)
    Ha:1839

ELMAR, KARL  [Pseud. of Karl
Swiedack]
Vienna 1815-1888 Vienna
Ref: Brüm 19, Ko 3

Der Fabrikjunge - F3
    Ha:1853
Städtische Krankheit und
ländliche Kur - F3
    Ha:1848
Unter der Erde - F3 (1856)
    Fr:1852  Ha:1848
Die Weltreise eines
Kapitalisten - Z5
    Ha:1849

d'ELPONS, FRIEDRICH WILHELM
von  [Pseud. of Carl Hanisch]
Silesia ca. 1780-1831 Berlin?
Ref: Goe 10, Ko 3

Die Einquartierung - C1
(1822)
    Bn:1816  Da:1815  Ha:1816
    Va:1814
Jonas Prellhammer - C3
    Bn:1818  Dr:1818

ELSHOLTZ, FRANZ von
Berlin 1791-1872 Munich
Ref: Goe 8, Ko Th, ADB

Erziehungsmethoden o. Wie
schwer, ein Mann zu sein - F4
(1849)
    Bn:1849
Die Hofdame - C5 (1830)
    Fr:1828  Mu:1839
Hymens Bild - D1
    Mu:1836  Wm:1834
Jugendstreiche - F4
    Wm:1847
Komm her - D1 (1830)
    Bn:1825  Da:1838  Dr:1826
    Fr:1826  Ha:1857  Lg:1827
    Mh:1827  Mu:1834  Va:1826
    Wm:1829
König Harald - T5 (1853)
    Bn:1834

ELSNER, OSKAR  [Pseud.: Ernst
Leonhard]
Neustadt 1845-1909 Lichten-
berg
Ref: Brüm 19, Ko Th

Gute Zeugnisse - C3 (1878)
    Lg:1880
Wenn man im Dunkeln küßt - F
(1876)
    Fr:1877

ELTON, V.

Schach und matt - C5
    Dr:1851

ELZ, ALEXANDER  [Pseud. of
Friedrich Adolf Stein]

Eine Maskerade vor der Mas-
kerade - C1
    Da:1855
Er ist nicht eifersüchtig -
C1 - Fr
    Da:1854  Dr:1852  Fr:1853
    Ha:1852  Mu:1868  Va:1852
    Wm:1853
Müller und Miller - F2
    Da:1857  Fr:1859  Ha:1845
    Mu:1868
Die schöne Müllerin - C1 - Fr
    Fr:1860

ENGEL, JOHANN JAKOB
Parchim 1741-1802 Parchim
Ref: Brüm 18, Goe 5, Ko Th,
ADB, NDB, OC

Der dankbare Sohn - C1 (1783)
 Bn:1771 Da:1812 Dr:1778
 Fr:1796 Ha:1771 Lg:1772
 Mh:1779 Mu:1780 Va:1771
 Wm:1772
Der Diamant - C1 - Fr (1783)
 Dr:1778 Fr:1780 Mu:1778
Der Edelknabe - C1 (1783)
 Bn:1775 Da:1814 Dr:1778
 Fr:1778 Ha:1775 Lg:1774
 Ha:1778 Mu:1778 Va:1774
Der Eid - T5 (1803)
 Va:1796
Der Philosoph
 Mh:1778
Die sanfte Frau - C3 - It
(1779)
 Bn:1781 Fr:1780 Ha:1779
 Va:1779

ENGEL, KARL CHRISTIAN
Parchim 1752-1801 Schwerin
Ref: Brüm 18, Goe 5, Ko Th

Der Dienstfertige - C
 Fr:1799
Der Geburtstag [Namenstag] o.
Die überraschungen - C1
(1796)
 Bn:1793 Dr:1797 Ha:1811
 Va:1794 Wm:1797
Der Geburtstag auf dem Lande
- C2
 Va:1791
Das Mutterpferd - C2 (1799)
 Bn:1797 Dr:1797 Fr:1799
 Mu:1801 Va:1797

ENGELBRECHT, JOHANN ANDREAS
Hamburg 1733-1803 Bremen
Ref: Brüm 18, Ko Th

Die Nebenbuhler - C5 - Eng -
with J. Bock (1775)
 Ha:1775 Va:1777 Wm:1792
So muß man mir nicht kommen!
o. Der Schläger - C5 - Eng
(1778)
 Va:1778

ENGELHARDT, EUGENIE  see
Heiden, Eugenie

ENGELKEN, FRIEDRICH
Oberneuland ca. 1804-1879
Munich
Ref: Ko Th

Latude - D
 Ha:1835

EPHEU, F. L.  [Pseud. of
Garlieb Hanker]
Hamburg 1758-1807 Hamburg
Ref: Goe 5, Ko Th, ADB

Sophonisbe - T4 (1782)
 Va:1784

EPSTEIN, MORITZ
Trebitsch 1844-1915 Vienna
Ref: Brüm 19, Ko Th

Im Tanzsaal - D1 (1875)
 Va:1879

ERICH, M. L.

M.T.F. [T.F.] o. Der
Enthusiast - F1
 Da:1856 Dr:1851 Ha:1844

ERNEST, MARIE von  see
Vaselli, Marie von

ERNST, FERDINAND VALENTIN
Mainz ca. 1800-1852 Prague
Ref: Goe 11, Ko 3

Jung und alt - C3
 Va:1848

ERNST, KARL  see Tempeltey,
Karl Ernst Eduard

ERNST, W.

Castor und Pollux - C1
 Bn:1883

ESCHENBACH

Die Veilchen - C1
 Bn:1862 Fr:1874

EULENBURG-HERTEFELD, PHILIPP
von [Pseud.: Iwan Svenson]
Königsberg 1847-1921 Schloß
Liebenberg
Ref: Ko Th, NDB

Margot - D (1885)
 Mu:1885

Seestern - D3
    Wm:1890

**EWALD**

Mutterherz und Gattenliebe -
D5
    Ha:1845


**FABER, HERMANN** [Pseud. of
Hermann Goldschmidt]
Frankfurt/M 1860-?
Ref: Brüm 19, Ko Th

Fortuna - D (1890)
    Fr:1889

**FALK, JOHANN DANIEL** [Pseud.:
Johannes von der Ostsee]
Danzig 1768-1826 Weimar
Ref: Brüm 18, Goe 5, Ko Th,
ADB, NDB, OC

Das Gedicht o. Die junge
Schweizerin - C2
    Va:1800

**FELDMANN, LEOPOLD**
Munich 1802-1882 Vienna
Ref: Brüm 19, Ko Th, ADB

Drei Kandidaten - C3 (1845-
52)
    Da:1847
Der dreißigste November - F1
(1845-52)
    Da:1860  Fr:1857  Ha:1857
    Va:1858
Die freie Wahl - C1 (1845-52)
    Da:1842
Ein Freundschafts-Bündnis -
C3 (1845-52)
    Ha:1845  Va:1846
Ein höflicher Mann - C3
(1845-52)
    Bn:1848  Da:1850  Dr:1850
    Fr:1852  Ha:1848  Va:1847
    Wm:1847
Immer zu vorschnell - C3
(1845-52)
    Da:1854
Ein Mädchen vom Theater - C4
(1845-52)
    Da:1846  Wm:1846

Das Portrait der Geliebten -
C3 (1845-52)
    Bn:1843  Da:1845  Dr:1843
    Fr:1843  Ha:1842  Mu:1869
    Va:1843  Wm:1844
Ein Prozeß zwischen Eheleuten
- C3 (1845-52)
    Bn:1854
Der Rechnungsrat und seine
Töchter - C3 (1845-52)
    Bn:1847  Da:1850  Dr:1851
    Fr:1847  Mu:1847  Va:1849
    Wm:1848
Die Schicksalsbrüder - C4
(1845-52)
    Bn:1851  Da:1871  Fr:1853
    Lg:1871  Va:1867  Wm:1851
Die schöne Athenienserin - C4
(1845-52)
    Da:1845  Fr:1844  Va:1843
    Wm:1844
Der Sohn auf Reisen - C2
(1845-52)
    Bn:1842  Da:1842  Dr:1841
    Fr:1842  Ha:1847  Mu:1835
    Va:1842  Wm:1843
Ein Steckenpferd - C1
    Va:1859

**FELS, FRANZ**  see Birch-
Pfeiffer, Charlotte

**FERO, KARL**  see Klähr, Karl

**FINDEISEN, JULIUS**
Leipzig 1809-1879 Vienna
Ref: Ko Th

Herr von Perlacher - F3
    Fr:1884
Unsere Nachbarin - F1
    Fr:1877  Va:1864

**FIRMENREICH-RICHARTZ, JOHANN
MATTHIAS**
Cologne 1808-1889 Potsdam
Ref: Brüm 19, Ko 3, ADB

Klothilde Montalvi - T5
(1840)
    Bn:1840

**FISCHER, FRANZ JOSEF**
ca. 1745-after 1799
Ref: Goe 5, Ko Th

Alles aus Freundschaft - C5
    Va:1778

FISCHER, JOHANN GEORG
Groß-Süßen 1816-1897
Stuttgart
Ref: Brüm 19, Ko Th, ADB, NDB

Friedrich II. von
Hohenstaufen - T5 (1863)
    Wm:1862

FISCHER, LOUISE
Vienna 1782-?
Ref: Ko Th

Revanche - C1
    Bn:1839

FITGER, ARTHUR
Delmenhorst 1840-1909 Horn
Ref: Brüm 19, Ko Th, NDB

Die Hexe - T5 (1876)
    Bn:1884   Dr:1883   Fr:1880
    Lg:1879   Wm:1884
Die Rosen von Tyburn - T5
(1888)
    Lg:1889   Mu:1888

FLOTO, WILHELM
Tangermünde 1812-1869 Braun-
schweig
Ref: Brüm 19, Ko Th, ADB

Der grüne Mann - C4
    Dr:1846
Das Sonntagsräuschchen - C1
(1846)
    Dr:1847   Fr:1853

FÖRG, KARL
Fürstenfeld 1755-1799 Munich
Ref: Goe 5, Ko Th

Helena und Paris - D3
    Mh:1805   Mu:1782

FÖRSTER, AUGUST
Lauchstädt 1828-1889 Vienna
Ref: Ko Th, ADB, NDB

Ein Attaché [Der Gesandt-
schaftsattaché] - C4 - Fr
    Fr:1865   Va:1863
Ein Bräutigam um jeden Preis
- C2 - Fr
    Bn:1867
Feuer in der Mädchenschule -
C1 - Fr
    Bn:1862   Da:1863   Fr:1861
    Ha:1860   Va:1860

Flattersucht - C3 - Fr
    Fr:1866   Va:1865
Der Freund der Frauen - C1 -
Fr
    Lg:1867
Ein hoher Gast - D1 - Fr
    Va:1874
Die lachende Anna und die
weinende Anna [Die Eine
weint, die Andere lacht] - D4
- Fr
    Bn:1863   Da:1863   Ha:1862
    Mh:1863   Wm:1864
Man muß Rücksicht nehmen - C2
- Fr
    Va:1861
Miß Susanne - C4 - Fr
    Va:1868
Nicht Fluchen - C1 - Fr
    Lg:1868
Schwager Spürnas - F1 - Fr
    Lg:1869
So muß man's machen - C1 - Fr
    Fr:1868
Eine Tasse Tee o. Morgens
zwei Uhr - F1 - Fr
    Da:1865   Va:1860
Die Toilette meiner Frau - C1
- Fr
    Da:1868   Ha:1868
Umkehr - D4 - Fr
    Fr:1871   Va:1869
Wenn man allein ausgeht - C3
- Fr
    Va:1866
Zwei Väter - D4 - Fr
    Va:1870

FÖRSTER, FRIEDRICH
Münchengosserstädt 1791-1868
Berlin
Ref: Brüm 18, Goe 7, Ko Th,
ADB, NDB, OC

List und Liebe - C5 - Eng
(1828)
    Bn:1828   Mu:1829   Va:1828
Der Sylvesterabend - C1
(1818)
    Bn:1815

FOUQUE, FRIEDRICH HEINRICH DE
LA MOTTE
Brandenburg 1777-1843 Berlin
Ref: Goe 6, Ko Th, ADB, NDB,
OC

Die Heimkehr des großen
Kurfürsten - D3 (1813)
    Bn:1815

**FRANKE, EDUARD**

Karls XII. einzige Liebe - C3
    Fr:1853    Ha:1853
Quid pro quo - C3
    Dr:1850

**FRANZ, OTTO**    see Gensichen,
Otto Franz

**FRESENIUS, AUGUST**
Frankfurt/M 1834-1911 Munich
Ref: Brüm 19, Ko Th

Ein gefährlicher Freund - C1
- Fr (1870)
    Fr:1873
Eine Heirat unter Ludwig XV.
- C5 - Fr (1871)
    Lg:1874
Ich verspeise meine Tante -
F1
    Va:1881
Die Lebensretter - F4 - Fr
(1873)
    Lg:1873

**FREY**

Die Tochter ihres Mannes - C1
    Va:1883

**FREY, FRIEDRICH HERMANN**    see
Greif, Martin

**FREYTAG, GUSTAV**
Kreuzburg 1816-1895 Wiesbaden
Ref: Brüm 19, Ko Th, ADB,
NDB, OC

Die Brautfahrt o. Kunz von
der Rose - C5 (1844)
    Fr:1889    Ha:1842    Va:1843
    Wm:1843
Die Fabier - T5 (1859)
    Bn:1861    Dr:1860    Mh:1863
    Mu:1879    Va:1861
Graf Waldemar - D5 (1850)
    Bn:1848    Da:1858    Dr:1849
    Fr:1848    Ha:1848    Lg:1864
    Mh:1858    Mu:1848    Va:1859
    Wm:1848
Die Journalisten - C4 (1854)
    Bn:1857    Da:1861    Dr:1853
    Fr:1854    Ha:1854    Mh:1854
    Mu:1853    Va:1853    Wm:1853
Die Valentine - D5 (1845)
    Bn:1847    Da:1848    Dr:1848
    Fr:1847    Ha:1847    Mh:1846
    Mu:1848    Va:1848    Wm:1847

**FRIEDEL, JOHANN**
Temesvar/Hungary 1755-1789
Klagenfurt
Ref: Brüm 18, Goe 5, Ko Th,
ADB

Christel und Gretchen - C3
(1785)
    Va:1784
Der Fremde - C4 (1785)
    Bn:1785

**FRIEDMANN, ALFRED**
Frankfurt/M 1845-1923 Berlin
Ref: Brüm 19, Ko Th

Geben ist seliger denn nehmen
- D1 (1878)
    Bn:1878    Fr:1880

**FRIEDRICH, W.**  [Pseud. of
Friedrich Wilhelm Riese]
Berlin ca. 1805-1879 Naples
Ref: Ko 3

Ein bengalischer Tiger - F1
    Fr:1854
Die Blutrache - F1 - Fr
(1847-52)
    Fr:1843    Ha:1858    Va:1855
Der Confusionsrat - C3 - Fr
(1849-50)
    Dr:1845    Ha:1852
Der Corporal - F (1855-56)
    Ha:1843
Ein Damenkampf - C3 - Fr
    Ha:1857
Doktor Robin - C1 - Fr (1849-
50)
    Bn:1844    Da:1848    Dr:1846
    Fr:1845    Ha:1845    Va:1849
    Wm:1848
Dornen und Lorbeer o. Das un-
bekannte Meisterwerk - D2 -
Fr (1847-52)
    Bn:1844    Da:1850    Fr:1843
    Ha:1842
Drei Farben - C3 (1852)
    Fr:1852
Drei Feen - C3 - Fr (1847)
    Fr:1843    Va:1843
Eduard aus der Vorstadt - D5
Fr
    Ha:1845
Er muß aufs Land - C3 - Fr
(1848)
    Bn:1844    Da:1845    Fr:1845
    Ha:1844    Mh:1845    Va:1845
    Wm:1845

Farinelli - D3
  Ha:1842
Fräulein Gattin - C1 - Fr
(1847-52)
  Bn:1847  Fr:1847
Gänschen von Buchenau - C1 -
Fr (1850-52)
  Da:1861  Fr:1857  Ha:1852
  Va:1856  Wm:1863
Die Gefangenen der Czarin -
C2 - Fr (1847-52)
  Da:1850  Dr:1851  Fr:1846
  Ha:1845
Graf Irun - D5 - Fr
  Dr:1846  Fr:1845  Ha:1844
Guten Morgen, Herr Fischer -
Vv1 - Fr (1852)
  Da:1853  Fr:1852  Ha:1852
  Wm:1852
Die Handwerker - D
  Ha:1842
Hans und Hanne - F1 (1852)
  Fr:1853
Der Häßliche - F1 - Fr (1847-
52)
  Bn:1851
Helene von Seiglière - D4 -
Fr
  Bn:1852  Fr:1852  Ha:1852
  Wm:1852
Herr Dunst - Vv2 - Fr (1849-
50)
  Ha:1861
Jacquard - D
  Ha:1843
Köck und Guste - Vv1
  Fr:1846  Ha:1843
Lady Harriet - Vv5
  Ha:1845
Major Haudegen - C1 - Fr
  Dr:1847
Mariette und Jeanetton - Vv3
- Fr (1852)
  Ha:1843
Die Schauspielerin - C1 - Fr
(1847-52)
  Dr:1849  Ha:1846  Wm:1850
Der Schierlingstrank - C
  Ha:1845
Sie will gebieten - C2 - Fr
  Va:1847
Ein Stündchen in der Schule -
F1 - Fr (1847-52)
  Da:1867  Ha:1846
Die Tochter - D
  Ha:1843
Die Tochter Lucifers - F5
(1849-50)
  Ha:1846

Überraschungen - C1 - Fr
(1852)
  Bn:1845
Der unbekannte Beschützer -
C1 - Fr
  Ha:1847  Va:1847
Der Weg durchs Fenster - C1 -
Fr (1847-52)
  Bn:1847  Fr:1847  Ha:1848
  Va:1847  Wm:1847
Die weibliche Schildwache -
D1 (1849-50)
  Ha:1844
Ein weißer Othello - F1 - Fr
(1850-52)
  Da:1857  Dr:1850  Ha:1849
  Wm:1851
Wer ißt mit? - F1 - Fr (1847-
52)
  Da:1851  Dr:1847  Fr:1848
  Ha:1845  Wm:1864
Zwei Herren und ein Diener -
Vv1 - It (1849-50)
  Ha:1848

**FRIESE, EUGEN**
Königsberg 1845-1915
Ref: Brüm 19, Ko Th

Die Andreasnacht - D5 (1882)
  Lg:1885

**FRITSCH, FRANZ XAVER**
[Pseud.: Franz von Braunau]
Braunau/Bohemia 1779-1870
Vienna
Ref: Ko Th

Beruf und Liebe - C5 (1842)
  Va:1842
Jadest - C1
  Dr:1842  Va:1840  Wm:1841
Querstreiche - C3 (1852)
  Va:1852
Waldemar - D5 (1845)
  Va:1845
Wer die Liebe hat, führt die
Braut heim - D5 (1840)
  Bn:1842  Ha:1841  Va:1840
  Wm:1841

**FROHBERG, PAUL** [Pseud. of
Friedrich Adami]
Suhl 1816-1893 Berlin
Ref: Brüm 19, Goe NF, Ko Th

Die Auferstandene - D3 - Fr
(1847)
  Bn:1843

Barcelonas Aufstand o. Das
Gelübde - D3 - Fr (1843)
    Bn:1843
Ein deutscher Leinweber - D4
    Bn:1847
Eine Dorf-Familie in Berlin -
C3 - Fr (ca. 1850)
    Bn:1847
Feurige Kohlen o. Ein
ehrlicher Mann - D3 (1850)
    Bn:1845   Va:1848
Freund und Feind - D1 (1870)
    Bn:1866
Die Geheimnisse der Kapelle -
F3
    Bn:1844
Grillen der Zeit o. Tausend
Ängste um nichts - C4
    Bn:1846
Der Hollandgänger - D3 (1870)
    Bn:1868   Lg:1868
Kleine Leiden des mensch-
lichen Lebens - F1 - Fr (ca.
1850)
    Bn:1844
Königin Margot und die
Hugenotten - D5 - Fr (1855)
    Bn:1848
Lord und Räuber o. Des Meeres
und des Lebens Wogen - TC4 -
Fr
    Bn:1842
Prinz und Apotheker o. Der
letzte Stuart - C4 (1842)
    Bn:1842
Provinzial-Unruhen - F3
(1871)
    Bn:1848
Seeleute o. Deutsch und
Dänisch - D3 (1870)
    Bn:1869
Die zwölfte Stunde - D3
(1851)
    Bn:1850

**FROHBERG, REGINA**, née Salomo
Berlin 1783-1850 [1858?]
Ref: Brüm 18, Goe 10, ADB

Der Jüngling von sechzig
Jahren - C1 - Fr
    Mh:1826
Der Page und das Pasquill -
D1
    Mh:1814

**FRONHOFER, LUDWIG**
Ingolstadt 1746-1800 Munich
Ref: Goe 4/1, Ko 3

Mathilde - D3 (1774)
    Mu:1774

**FULDA, LUDWIG**
Frankfurt/M 1862-1939 Berlin
Ref: Brüm 19, Ko Th

Die Aufrichtigen - C1 (1863)
    Fr:1883
Frühling im Winter - C1
(1889)
    Fr:1888
Ein Meteor - C (1884)
    Fr:1888   Mu:1887
Das Recht der Frau - C3
(1888)
    Fr:1886   Lg:1887
Unter vier Augen - C1 (1887)
    Fr:1886   Mu:1886   Va:1887
Das verlorene Paradies - D
(1892)
    Fr:1890
Die wilde Jagd - C4 (1893)
    Da:1889   Fr:1889   Mu:1889
    Va:1889   Wm:1889

**FUSS, FRANZ**
Beraun/Bohemia 1747-1805
Beraun
Ref: Ko 3

Der Schneider und sein Sohn -
C2 (1775)
    Fr:1780   Va:1773
Die Schwiegermutter - C3
(1776)
    Va:1776

**GADERMANN, RICHARD**
Tirschenreuth 1839-?
Ref: Ko 3

C. Krüger - C (1878)
    Mu:1877

**GALL, LUISE von** [i.e. Luise
von Schücking, née Gall]
Darmstadt 1815-1855 Augsburg
Ref: Ko 3, ADB

Ein schlechtes Gewissen - C1
(1842)
    Wm:1853

## GANGHOFER, LUDWIG
Kaufbeuren 1855-1920
Tegernsee
Ref: Brüm 19, Ko Th, NDB, OC

Der Geigenmacher von Mit-
tenwald - FP3 - with
H. Neuert (1884)
    Fr:1885  Mu:1884  Wm:1886
Der Herrgottschnitzer von Am-
mergau - FP5 - with H. Neuert
(1880)
    Dr:1884  Fr:1884  Mu:1880
    Wm:1885
Die Hochzeit zu Valeni - D
(1891)
    Mu:1889
Der Prozeßhandel - FP4 - with
H. Neuert (1881)
    Fr:1884  Mu:1881  Wm:1885
Die Schwester des Oberst-
lieutenants - C
    Mu:1881

## GASSMANN, THEODOR
Braunschweig 1828-1871 Ham-
burg
Ref: Brüm 19, Ko Th

Ein Blatt Papier - C3 - Fr
(1865)
    Da:1861
Blumengeister - C5 (1871)
    Fr:1857  Ha:1856  Lg:1871
Die Feenhände - C5 - Fr
    Dr:1861  Fr:1865  Va:1859
    Wm:1868
Homöopatisch - C1 - Fr (1869)
    Dr:1855
Der letzte Brief - C3 - Fr
    Bn:1873
Plauderstunden - C1 - Fr
(1856)
    Da:1858  Dr:1857  Fr:1866
    Ha:1856  Wm:1863
Schwabenstreiche - C5 (1871)
    Va:1872
Zur Miete beim Bedienten - F1
(1863)
    Fr:1856

## GATSCHENBERGER

Altes und neues Wissen - C
    Mu:1870

## GEBLER, TOBIAS PHILIPP von
Zeulenroda 1726-1786 Vienna
Ref: Brüm 18, Goe 4/1, Ko Th,
ADB, NDB, OC

Die abgenötigte Einwilligung
- C1 - Fr (1772)
    Va:1771
Adelheid von Siegmar - T5
(1774)
    Bn:1776
Der Adelsbrief o. Das
Prädikat - C3 (1772)
    Va:1770
Darf man seine Frau lieben? -
C5 - Fr (1772)
    Va:1772  Wm:1773
Klementine o. Das Testament -
D5 - (1772)
    Dr:1779  Va:1771  Wm:1773
Leichtsinn und gutes Herz -
C5 (1773)
    Va:1772  Wm:1773
Der Minister - D5 (1772)
    Dr:1783  Lg:1775  Va:1771
    Wm:1772
Die Osmonde - D5 (1773)
    Va:1772  Wm:1772
Der Terno o. Das Lottoglück -
C1
    Va:1770
Das unruhige Namensfest o.
Der Weiberstreit - C5
    Va:1771
Die Versöhnung - C5 (1773)
    Bn:1774  Va:1772

## GEHE, EDUARD
Dresden 1793-1850 Dresden
Ref: Brüm 18, Goe 11, Ko Th,
ADB

Anna Boleyn - T4
    Dr:1823  Mu:1822
Das Gastmahl zu Rudolstadt -
D1 (1837)
    Dr:1836
Gustav Adolf in Deutschland -
T4 (1818)
    Ha:1832
Kampf und Friede - D
    Fr:1819
Die Maltheser - D5 (1836)
    Dr:1827  Mu:1826
Peter der Große und Alexis -
T4
    Dr:1821  Fr:1821  Ha:1821
    Lg:1821

Der Tod Heinrichs IV. von
Frankreich - T5 (1820)
    Dr:1818   Fr:1818   Ha:1820

GEIBEL, EMANUEL
Lübeck 1815-1884 Lübeck
Ref: Brüm 19, Ko Th, ADB,
NDB, OC

Brunhild - T5 (1857)
    Bn:1872   Lg:1881   Mu:1861
Echtes Gold wird klar im
Feuer - D1 (1882)
    Bn:1883   Mu:1883   Wm:1877
König Roderich - T5 (1844)
    Wm:1846
Meister Andrea - (1855)
    Bn:1855   Mu:1855
Sophonisbe - T5 (1868)
    Bn:1869   Mh:1875   Va:1868

GELLERT, CHRISTIAN
FÜRCHTEGOTT
Mainichen 1715-1769 Leipzig
Ref: Brüm 18, Goe 4/1, Ko Th,
ADB, NDB, OC

Das Los in der Lotterie - C5
(1747)
    Bn:1771
Die kranke Frau - C1 (1747)
    Bn:1773   Ha:1767

GEMMINGEN-HORNBERG, OTTO
HEINRICH von
Heilbronn 1755-1836 Heidel-
berg
Ref: Brüm 18, Goe 4/1, Ko Th,
ADB, NDB, OC

Die Erbschaft - C1 (1779)
    Dr:1782
Die Familie o. Der deutsche
Hausvater - D5 (1780)
    Bn:1781   Da:1812   Dr:1780
    Fr:1792   Ha:1780   Lg:1799
    Mh:1780   Mu:1823   Va:1781
    Wm:1796

GENAST, KARL ALBERT WILHELM
Leipzig 1822-1887 Weimar
Ref: Brüm 19, Ko Th

Bernhard von Weimar - T5
(1855)
    Wm:1855
Florian Geyer - T5 (1857)
    Wm:1858

GENEE, FRIEDRICH
Königsberg 1795 [1796?]-1856
Danzig
Ref: Ko Th

Der Advokat und sein Sohn o.
Der erste Prozeß - C1 - Fr
    Bn:1834
Italienische Rache o. Der
Franzose in Florenz - C2 - FR
    Lg:1833
Das Kloster von Tonnington o.
Die Pensionärin - D3 - Fr
    Bn:1830
Das Königreich der Weiber o.
Die verkehrte Welt - F2 - Fr
    Bn:1834   Lg:1835
Philipp - D1
    Bn:1831
Der Reiche und der Arme - D5
- Fr
    Da:1839   Fr:1837
Der Reisewagen des Emigranten
- D - Fr
    Fr:1837
Wilhelm Kolmann - D
    Ha:1838

GENEE, RUDOLF
Berlin 1824-1914 Berlin
Ref: Brüm 19, Ko Th

Diavolina von Kreuzwetter-
grund o. Vierundzwanzig Jahre
- C3 - It
    Da:1859
Durch - C1 (1855)
    Dr:1853   Fr:1853
Ehestandsexercitien - C1
(1855)
    Dr:1856
Gastrecht - D1 (1884)
    Bn:1885   Mu:1886
Die Klausnerin - D4 (1885)
    Wm:1885
Die Konzertprobe - F1
    Fr:1872
Ein neuer Timon - C5 (1857)
    Dr:1857   Fr:1857
Schleicher und Genossen - C4
- Eng (1875)
    Bn:1869   Mu:1869
Ein seltsamer Richter - D2 -
Fr
    Dr:1853   Wm:1853
Stephi Girard - D1 (1879)
    Va:1878   Fr:1861
Das Vermächtnis o. Sein böser
Damon - C3
    Da:1856

Vor den Kanonen - C3 (1857)
    Bn:1867
Das Wunder - C4 (1854)
    Bn:1854

**GENSICHEN, OTTO FRANZ**
[Pseud.: Otto Franz]
Driesen 1847-1933 Berlin
Ref: Brüm 19, Ko Th

Der Blitzableiter - C1 (1872)
    Fr:1878   Wm:1872
Euphrosyne - D1 (1878)
    Bn:1877   Fr:1880
Frau Aspasia - C4 (1883)
    Bn:1883   Fr:1885
Lydia - D1 (1885)
    Bn:1885   Da:1887   Dr:1884
Die Märchentante - C4 (1881)
    Bn:1881   Fr:1881   Mu:1880
    Wm:1881
Minnewerben - C1 (1871)
    Bn:1871   Da:1877   Mu:1871
Was ist eine Plauderei? - D1
(1874)
    Bn:1875

**GEORG von PREUSSEN, PRINCE**
[Pseud.: G. Conrad]
Düsseldorf 1826-1902
Düsseldorf
Ref: Brüm 19, Ko 3

Cleopatra - T1 (1877)
    Bn:1871
Katharina Voisin - T5
    Bn:1869
Phädra - T5 (1877)
    Bn:1867   Lg:1868

**GERHARD, WILHELM CHRISTOPH
LEONHARD**
Weimar 1780-1858 Heidelberg
Ref: Brüm 18, Goe 13, Ko Th

Die Flitterwochen - C1 - Fr
    Bn:1813
Sophronia - D4 (1822)
    Lg:1820

**GERKE, FRIEDRICH** [Pseud.:
Friedrich Clemens]
Osnabrück 1801-1888
Eimsbüttel
Ref: Ko Th

Die Auswanderer am Ohio - C
(1838)
    Ha:1837

**GERLACH**

Der erste April - C3
    Dr:1809

**GERLE, WOLFGANG ADOLF**
Prague 1783-1846 Prague
Ref: Brüm 18, Goe 9, Ko Th,
ADB

Der falsche Prinz - C4
    Lg:1833
Der Familienvertrag - D1
    Bn:1832
Häusliche Wirren - C3 - with
J. Lederer (1837)
    Bn:1852   Dr:1851   Fr:1852
    Ha:1852   Mu:1883   Va:1850
Die kranken Doctoren - C3 -
with J. Lederer (1842)
    Va:1842
Der letzte April - F1 (1832)
    Bn:1831
Das Liebhabertheater - C5
    Bn:1832   Mu:1830
Der Naturmensch - C4 - with
U. Horn (1838)
    Ha:1839   Va:1840
Die Vormundschaft - C2 - with
U. Horn (1836)
    Bn:1837   Dr:1839   Va:1837
    Wm:1837

**GERSTÄCKER, FRIEDRICH**
Hamburg 1816-1872 Braun-
schweig
Ref: Brüm 19, ADB, NDB, OC

Der Wilderer und seine Braut
- D5 (1864)
    Fr:1864   Mu:1873

**GERSTEL, GUSTAV**
Wiesbaden 1844-1889
Nordhausen
Ref: Brüm 19, Ko Th

Abgemacht - C4 (1874)
    Lg:1875
Feder und Schwert - C3
    Va:1874

**GERSTENBERG, HEINRICH WILHELM**
Tondern 1737-1823 Altona
Ref: Brüm 18, Goe 4/1, Ko Th,
ADB, NDB, OC

Ugolino - T5 (1768)
    Bn:1769

**GESSNER, SALOMON**
Zurich 1730-1788 Zurich
Ref: Brüm 18, Goe 4/1, ADB,
NDB, OC

Erast - C1 (1762)
   Bn:1771   Ha:1769

**GEWEY, FRANZ XAVER KARL**
Vienna 1774-1819 Vienna
Ref: Brüm 18, Goe 11, Ko Th,
NDB

Fernando von Kastilien - D5
   Va:1802
Der höfliche Grobian - C3
   Va:1810
Die Hüttenkomödie am Graben -
F2
   Va:1816
Die Modesitten - C5 (1801)
   Va:1800
Der seltene Prozeß - D3
(1802)
   Bn:1826  Mh:1808  Va:1801
Der seltene Prozeß, 2. Teil -
D4 (1809)
   Va:1809
Der Totenansager seiner
selbst - F1 - Fr
   Va:1807
Die vergrabene Kiste - D1
   Va:1813
Der Vetter von Mistelbach -
F1 - Fr
   Va:1814

**GEYER, LUDWIG HEINRICH**
[Pseud.: E. Willig]
Eisleben 1779-1821 Dresden
Ref: Brüm 18, Goe 11, Ko Th

Der Bethlehemitische
Kindermord - C2 (1823)
   Bn:1823  Da:1822  Dr:1821
   Fr:1822  Ha:1821  Lg:1824
   Mh:1826  Wm:1822
Das Erntefest - D1 (1822)
   Dr:1818
Das Mädchen aus der Fremde -
C2
   Dr:1817

**GIRNDT, OTTO**
Landsberg 1835-1911 Sterzing
Ref: Brüm 19, Ko Th

Am andern Tage - C3 (1887)
   Ha:1868

Dankelmann - T (1882)
   Mu:1880
Die Ephraimiten - C4
   Ha:1867
Erich Brahe - T5 (1889)
   Bn:1890
Die Hofmeisterin - C
   Mu:1889
In einem Garten vor dem Tor -
C3
   Wm:1872
Letzte Liebe - D1 (1876)
   Bn:1861
Die Maus - F4
   Bn:1887
Die Menschenfreunde - C
   Mu:1874
Mit Vergnügen - F4 - with
G. Moser
   Da:1886  Fr:1886  Lg:1884
   Va:1883
Politische Grundsätze - C4
(1867-74)
   Bn:1867  Ha:1868
Der Soldatenfreund - F5 -
with G. Moser
   Lg:1887
Die Sternschnuppe - F4 - with
G. Moser
   Fr:1887  Lg:1886
Strafrecht [Deutsches Straf-
recht] - F3
   Bn:1870  Da:1872  Fr:1873
Touristen - F4
   Bn:1876
Um ein nichts - C4 - with
O. Blumenthal
   Da:1884  Mu:1882  Va:1882
Und - C4
   Bn:1866  Ha:1866
Unter der Linde von Steinheim
- C
   Mu:1871
Y.1. o. Das Heiratsgesuch -
C3
   Bn:1865  Da:1867  Fr:1864
   Ha:1866  Va:1866

**GISEKE, ROBERT**
Marienburg 1827-1890 Leubus
Ref: Ko Th, ADB, OC

Johann Rathenow, ein Bürgermeister von Berlin - T5
(1855)
   Bn:1854

**GLASER, ADOLF** [Pseud.:
Reinald Reimar]
Wiesbaden 1829-1916 Frei-
burg/Br
Ref: Brüm 19, Ko Th

Galileo Galilei - T5 (1861)
    Wm:1861
Johanna von Flandern - D5
    Da:1864
Der Weg zum Ruhme - D4
    Fr:1864

**GLEICH, JOSEF ALOIS**
Vienna 1772-1841 Vienna
Ref: Brüm 18, Goe 11, Ko Th,
ADB, NDB, OC

Der alte Geist in der mo-
dernen Welt - Z2 (1822)
    Bn:1831  Va:1821
Der Berggeist - Z3 (1820)
    Mu:1821  Va:1819
Die Brüder Liederlich - Z2
(1820)
    Mu:1822  Va:1820
Doktor Stakelbein [Fünf
Bräutigame und eine Braut] -
F2 (1820)
    Bn:1832  Ha:1824  Lg:1823
    Mh:1823  Mu:1831  Va:1816
Der Eheteufel auf Reisen - Z2
(1822)
    Bn:1831  Mu:1831  Va:1821
Der Hungerturm - D3 (1805)
    Dr:1812  Va:1805
Den Keller oder die Braut? -
C3 (1822)
    Mu:1822  Va:1819
Der Wolfsbrunnen - Z2
    Bn:1827  Va:1823
See Goedeke 11 for additional
listings.

**GÖBEL, A.**

Sylvester-Abend - C1
    Fr:1864
Zwei Logenbillets - C1
    Fr:1864

**GOETHE, JOHANN WOLFGANG von**
Frankfurt/M 1749-1832 Weimar
Ref: Brüm 18, Goe 4/2-5,
Ko Th, ADB, NDB, OC

Der Bürgergeneral - C1 (1793)
    Wm:1793

Clavigo - T5 (1774)
    Bn:1774  Da:1814  Dr:1774
    Fr:1778  Ha:1774  Lg:1780
    Mh:1779  Mu:1777  Va:1786
    Wm:1792
Egmont - T3 (1788)
    Bn:1801  Da:1814  Dr:1814
    Fr:1821  Ha:1815  Lg:1807
    Mh:1806  Mu:1812  Va:1810
    Wm:1796
Faust, 1. Teil - T (1808)
    Bn:1838  Da:1838  Dr:1829
    Ha:1831  Mh:1835  Mu:1830
    Va:1839  Wm:1829
Faust, 2. Teil - T (1832)
    Fr:1858  Ha:1854  Lg:1873
    Va:1883
Die Geschwister - D1 (1787)
    Bn:1788  Da:1812  Dr:1788
    Fr:1793  Ha:1790  Lg:1822
    Mh:1788  Mu:1805  Va:1787
    Wm:1776
Götz von Berlichingen mit der
eisernen Hand - D5 (1773)
    Bn:1774  Da:1817  Dr:1815
    Fr:1778  Ha:1774  Lg:1807
    Mh:1786  Mu:1825  Va:1830
    Wm:1804
Der Groß-Cophta - C5 (1792)
    Lg:1792  Wm:1791
Iphigenie auf Tauris - D5
(1787)
    Bn:1802  Da:1830  Dr:1821
    Fr:1831  Ha:1831  Lg:1807
    Mh:1820  Mu:1825  Va:1800
    Wm:1802
Mahomet - T5 - Fr (1802)
    Bn:1810  Da:1815  Fr:1804
    Mu:1803  Wm:1800
Die Laune des Verliebten - D1
(1806)
    Bn:1813  Da:1827  Dr:1819
    Fr:1816  Ha:1812  Lg:1816
    Va:1821  Wm:1805
Die Mitschuldigen - C3 (1787)
    Bn:1846  Da:1815  Fr:1830
    Ha:1798  Lg:1825  Wm:1776
Die natürliche Tochter - T5
(1804)
    Bn:1803  Lg:1807  Wm:1803
Paläophron und Neoterpe - C1
(1801)
    Wm:1803
Stella - T5 (1776)
    Bn:1776  Fr:1809  Ha:1776
    Lg:1807  Mu:1777  Wm:1806
Tancred - T5 - Fr (1802)
    Bn:1801  Dr:1804  Fr:1807
    Mh:1807  Mu:1807  Va:1803
    Wm:1801

Torquato Tasso - D5 (1790)
   Bn:1811  Da:1819  Dr:1827
   Fr:1819  Ha:1819  Lg:1807
   Mh:1840  Mu:1822  Va:1816
   Wm:1807

**GÖLER, LOUIS**
1819-1868
Ref: Koh Th

Doctor Robin - C - Fr (1843)
   Ha:1845

**GOIER, K.**

Vetter Raoul - C4
   Bn:1853  Fr:1852  Va:1852

**GOLDSCHMIDT, HERMANN** see
Faber, Hermann

**GOLDSCHMIDT, KARL** [Pseud.:
J. E. Mand]
Berlin 1792-1857 Berlin
Ref: Goe 11, Ko Th

Demoiselle Bock - C1 (1832)
   Bn:1831  Dr:1831  Fr:1832
   Ha:1831  Lg:1833  Mu:1831
   Va:1832
Ein gescheiter Hausvater - C1
   Bn:1853
Das Heiratsgesuch - F2 (1831)
   Bn:1827
Die Lokalposse - F1 (1830)
   Bn:1828
Das Rätsel - C5 (1834)
   Bn:1829
Sein Onkel und ihre Tante -
C1 (1834)
   Bn:1832

**GOLLMICK, KARL**
Dessau 1796-1866 Frankfurt/M
Ref: Goe 11, Ko Th, ADB

Malchen und Milchen - C1
(1854)
   Da:1855  Fr:1855
Eine Mutter des Hauses - F1
   Fr:1847
Eine Räubergeschichte - F1
   Da:1859
Tantchen Rosmarin - C2
   Fr:1856
Tischrücken - F3
   Fr:1853
Die weibliche Waffe - D3
   Fr:1859

**GORDON-SAPHIR, MARIE** see
Bergen, Alexander

**GÖRLITZ, KARL**
Stettin 1830-1890 Berlin
Ref: Brüm 19, Ko Th

Drei Paar Schuhe - C3 (1872)
   Fr:1886
Das erste Mittagessen - C1
(1869)
   Bn:1869  Da:1873  Fr:1870
   Wm:1886
Eine Jugendfreundin - F1
(1872)
   Fr:1883
Madame Flott - C1 (1875)
   Fr:1883  Wm:1886
Eine vollkommene Frau - C1
(1870)
   Fr:1881  Lg:1870  Va:1884

**GÖRNER, IDA**
Ludwigslust 1830-1888 Hamburg
Ref: Ko Th

Die Großmutter - D5 - Fr
   Ha:1864
Unsere Alliirten - C3 - Fr
   Bn:1864

**GÖRNER, KARL AUGUST**
Berlin 1806-1884 Hamburg
Ref: Brüm 19, Goe 11, Ko Th,
ADB

Amerikanisch - C5
   Fr:1884
Aufgeschoben nicht aufgehoben
- C2 (1851-68)
   Dr:1854  Ha:1852
Auf Rosen o. Füchse, lauter
Füchse - C4
   Da:1870  Lg:1867
Denk an Pfingsten - F1 (1851-
68)
   Fr:1858
Englisch - C1 - (1851-68)
   Da:1853  Dr:1852  Fr:1853
   Ha:1852  Mh:1853  Mu:1872
   Va:1853  Wm:1856
En passant - F1
   Fr:1867
Die erste Gastrolle des Frl.
Aurora Veilchenduft - C1
(1851-68)
   Fr:1856
Erziehung macht den Menschen
- C4 (1851-68)
   Da:1870  Lg:1866

Eine freudige Überraschung -
D1 (1851-68)
    Da:1861  Fr:1874
Ein geadelter Kaufmann - C5
(1851-68)
    Da:1863  Fr:1865  Ha:1863
    Mh:1864  Mu:1868  Va:1864
    Wm:1868
Ein glücklicher Familienvater
- C3
    Da:1858  Dr:1855  Fr:1860
    Ha:1857  Mu:1868
Des Herrn Magisters Perrücke
- C1 (1851-68)
    Ha:1851  Wm:1852
Jettchen am Fenster - C1
(1851-68)
    Fr:1856
Eine kleine Erzählung ohne
Namen - C1 (1851-68)
    Bn:1864  Da:1857  Dr:1856
    Fr:1855  Ha:1855  Mu:1869
    Va:1856  Wm:1855
Meines Onkels Schlafrock - F5
(1851-68)
    Da:1860
Nichte und Tante - C1 (1851-
68)
    Bn:1835  Da:1854  Dr:1838
    Fr:1851  Ha:1847
Eine Räubergeschichte - F1 -
Fr
    Wm:1860
Das Salz der Ehe - F1 (1851-
68)
    Bn:1848  Da:1855  Dr:1848
    Fr:1851  Wm:1856
Der schwarze Peter - F1
(1851-68)
    Da:1855  Dr:1851  Fr:1852
    Ha:1851  Mu:1868  Va:1877
    Wm:1852
Sperling und Sperber o. Der
Sündenbock - F1
    Da:1858  Fr:1857  Ha:1857
Die Stiefmama - C2 (1851-68)
    Bn:1836
Eine stille gemütliche Woh-
nung - C1 (1851-68)
    Fr:1865
Tantchen Unverzagt! - C3
(1851-68)
    Da:1857  Fr:1860  Ha:1855
Vor dem Balle - C1 (1851-68)
    Va:1856
Verwandlungen - C2 (1851-68)
    Bn:1838

**GOTTER, FRIEDRICH WILHELM**
Gotha 1746-1797 Gotha
Ref: Brüm 18, Goe 4/1, Ko Th,
ADB, NDB, OC

Ein alter Fuchs wird nicht
geprellt - F1
    Wm:1794
Der argwöhnische Ehemann - C5
- Eng (1778)
    Bn:1778  Dr:1779  Fr:1778
    Ha:1777  Mh:1779  Va:1781
    Wm:1793
Die Basen - C3 - It (1795)
    Wm:1795
Die Comödie aus dem Stegreif
- C1 - Fr
    Ha:1777
Der Ehescheue - C5 - Fr
(1777)
    Bn:1777  Dr:1779  Fr:1778
    Ha:1777  Mh:1779  Mu:1778
    Va:1783
Die Erbschleicher - C5 (1789)
    Bn:1789  Dr:1789  Fr:1795
    Ha:1789  Mh:1788  Va:1791
    Wm:1789
Die falschen Entdeckungen -
C3 - Fr (1774)
    Bn:1792  Da:1818  Dr:1778
    Fr:1793  Mh:1827  Mu:1776
    Va:1774
Der Faschingsstreich o. Die
Dame als Kapitän [Der weib-
liche Hauptmann] - C5 - Fr
(1778)
    Bn:1778  Ha:1776  Mh:1779
    Va:1774
Gabriele de Vergy - T3 - Fr
    Lg:1774  Wm:1772
Jeanette - C3 - Fr (1777)
    Bn:1778  Dr:1777  Ha:1776
    Mh:1779  Mu:1784  Va:1778
Juliane von Lindorak - D5 -
It - with F. Schröder (1779)
    Bn:1779  Dr:1782  Fr:1778
    Ha:1778  Lg:1780  Mh:1779
    Va:1780  Wm:1791
Der Kobold - C4 - Fr (1778)
    Bn:1784  Fr:1778  Ha:1778
    Lg:1788  Va:1778
Der Liebhaber ohne Namen - C5
- Fr
    Bn:1787  Dr:1783  Mh:1783
    Va:1783
Der Mann, der seine Frau
nicht kennt - C2 - Fr (1781)
    Bn:1782  Dr:1781  Fr:1782
    Ha:1785  Mh:1783

Mariane - T3 - Fr (1786)
    Bn:1776   Da:1815   Dr:1785
    Fr:1778   Ha:1776   Lg:1779
    Mh:1781   Mu:1782
Die Maskerade o. Die drei-
fache Heirat - C2 - Fr (1773)
    Dr:1778   Va:1776
Medea - D1 (1775)
    Bn:1777   Dr:1779   Fr:1794
    Ha:1776   Lg:1775   Mh:1778
    Mu:1779   Va:1778   Wm:1791
Merope - T5 - Fr (1774)
    Bn:1783   Da:1810   Fr:1777
    Lg:1775   Mh:1778   Va:1775
    Wm:1773
Die Mutter - C5 - Fr (1783)
    Va:1783
Nanine o. Das besiegte
Vorurteil - C3 - Fr
    Va:1778
Das öffentliche Geheimnis -
C5 - It (1781)
    Bn:1782   Dr:1781   Fr:1780
    Ha:1779   Mh:1780   Va:1781
    Wm:1781
Orest und Elektra - T5 - Fr
(1774)
    Bn:1784   Lg:1774   Mh:1779
    Va:1773   Wm:1772
Die sanfte Frau - C3 - It
    Dr:1779   Mh:1779
Der schwarze Mann - C2 - Fr
(1775)
    Bn:1783   Da:1813   Fr:1793
    Ha:1786   Lg:1810   Mh:1784
    Va:1784   Wm:1785
Trunkner Mund, wahrer Mund -
C1 - Fr (1779)
    Bn:1779
Die unversehene Wette - C1 -
Fr (1781)
    Bn:1787   Dr:1781   Fr:1793
    Ha:1784
Veit von Solingen - C4 - Fr
(1784)
    Dr:1786   Va:1784
Der Weise in der Tat - D5 -
Fr (1782)
    Bn:1787   Da:1791   Mh:1782
Zwei Onkels für einen - C1 -
Fr (1781)
    Bn:1786   Dr:1784   Fr:1782
    Ha:1782   Mh:1782

**GOTTSCHALL, KARL RUDOLF**
[Pseud.: Karl Rudolf]
Breslau 1823-1909 Leipzig
Ref: Brüm 19, Ko Th, OC

Amy Robsart - T5 (1877)
    Lg:1876   Va:1879   Wm:1847
Arabella Stuart - T5 (1877)
    Bn:1889   Lg:1877
Auf roter Erde - D5 (1780)
    Lg:1879
Die Diplomaten - C4 (1865-80)
    Bn:1856
Ferdinand von Schill - D5
(1850)
    Ha:1849   Lg:1870
Herzog Bernhard von Weimar -
T5 (1871)
    Bn:1873   Lg:1871
Hieronymous Snitger, der
Volkstribun von Hamburg -
(1848)
    Ha:1849
Katharina Howard - T5 (1866)
    Bn:1872   Da:1868   Fr:1874
    Lg:1869   Mh:1871   Mu:1868
    Va:1865   Wm:1868
Lambertine von Merincourt -
D5 (1850)
    Lg:1868
Lord Byron in Italian - D
(1847)
    Ha:1847
Die Marseillaise - D1 (1849)
    Ha:1849
Mazeppa - T4 (1865-90)
    Dr:1859   Lg:1872
Der Nabob - T5 (1866)
    Fr:1868   Lg:1866   Wm:1862
Pitt und Fox - C5 (1854)
    Bn:1874   Dr:1854   Fr:1854
    Ha:1854   Mh:1855   Mu:1855
    Va:1864   Wm:1860
Die Rose vom Kaukasus - D2
(1871)
    Fr:1852   Lg:1865   Mh:1874
Schulröschen - C5 (1886)
    Fr:1886   Lg:1884   Wm:1885
Der Spion von Rheinsberg - C5
(1886)
    Fr:1883   Lg:1882
Ein Vater auf Kündigung - C4
    Fr:1876   Lg:1875
Der Vermittler - C4 (1880)
    Lg:1878   Mu:1879   Wm:1879

**GOTTSCHED, LUISE ADELGUNDE
VICTORIA**, née Kulmus
Danzig 1713-1762 Leipzig
Ref: Brüm 18, Goe 3, Ko Th,
ADB, NDB, OC

Die Hausfranzösin - C5 (1744)
    Ha:1767

Das Testament - C5 (1745)
    Bn:1771
Die Widersprecherin - C1 - Fr
(1742)
    Dr:1778   Va:1770

**GOTTWALD**

Die Universalerben - C4
    Dr:1848

**GÖTZE, AUGUSTE** [Pseud.:
A. Weimar]
Weimar 1840-1908 Leipzig
Ref: Brüm 19, Ko Th

Magdalena - D4 (1879)
    Bn:1881   Lg:1881   Wm:1879
Viktoria Accoramboni - T5
(1878)
    Wm:1878

**GÖTZE, C.**
Ref: Goe 11

Die Flucht o. Der Reisewagen
des Emigranten - D5 - Fr
    Wm:1836
Marie o. Die drei Epochen -
D3 - Fr
    Wm:1838

**GRAMMERSTÖTTER, CARL EDUARD**
Vienna 1789-1833 Pressburg
Ref: Goe 11, Ko Th

Die Braut aus Arkadien - F4
    Mh:1831   Va:1834
Männerfreundschaft - C4 - Eng
    Bn:1834   Dr:1830   Va:1824
Der verkehrte Roman - C4
    Bn:1831   Va:1832
Die Zwillinge - C2
    Va:1827

**GRANDJEAN, MORITZ ANTON**
Vienna 1821-1885 Vienna
Ref: Brüm 19, Ko Th

Am Klavier - C1 - Fr
    Bn:1853   Da:1855   Dr:1853
    Fr:1853   Ha:1858   Va:1853
    Wm:1855
Der Blaubart - C1 - Fr (1866)
    Da:1853   Va:1852
Er kann nicht lesen o. Ein
anonymer Brief - F1 (1862)
    Da:1872   Fr:1868   Ha:1862
Die Haarlocke - F1 - Fr
    Va:1857

Das hohe C - C1 (1858)
    Dr:1856   Fr:1856   Va:1857
Ein Hut - C1 - Fr (1858)
    Dr:1855   Va:1855
Immer zu Hause - F1 - Fr
(1864)
    Bn:1870   Dr:1854   Fr:1873
Ludwig der Vierzehnte - C1
(1875)
    Fr:1875
Einen Namen will er sich
machen - C1 (1863)
    Fr:1852
Die neue Magd - F1 (1875)
    Va:1878
Das Pamphlet - C1 - Eng
(1853)
    Bn:1851   Fr:1851   Va:1851
Rote Haare - F1 (1853)
    Bn:1852   Da:1872   Fr:1851
    Ha:1852   Va:1852
Der Stiefvater - C1 - Fr
(1866)
    Dr:1854   Fr:1854   Va:1854
Der Topfgucker o. Mein Mann
mengt sich in alles - C1
    Da:1870

**GRANICHSTÄDTEN, EMIL**
Vienna 1847-1904 Berlin
Ref: Brüm 19, Ko Th

Frau [Witwe] Scarron - C1
(1878)
    Fr:1883   Lg:1878   Va:1878

**GRANS, AGNES CHARLOTTE ELISE**
Leipa 1828-?
Ref: Brüm 19, Ko Th

Die Tochter des Lotsen - D4
    Lg:1868   Wm:1865
Über den Ozean - D5
    Wm:1859

**GRANS, HEINRICH**
Braunschweig 1822-1893 Bres-
lau
Ref: Brüm 19, Ko Th

Adrienne Lecouvreur - D5 - Fr
(1851)
    Bn:1880

**GRASER, K.**

Hempel, Krempel und Stempel -
C1
    Dr:1853

**GRAVEN, CHARLOTTE von**
[Pseud. of Charlotte von
Gravenreuth]
1808-1877 Berlin
Ref: Brüm 19, Ko Th

Feenhände - C5 - Fr
    Bn:1871   Da:1859   Ha:1858

**GREIF, MARTIN** [Pseud. of
Friedrich Hermann Frey]
Speyer 1839-1911 Kufstein
Ref: Brüm 19, Ko Th, NDB, OC

Corfiz Ulfeldt - T5 (1873)
    Mh:1878   Va:1875
Heinrich der Löwe - D (1887)
    Mu:1888
Konradin, der letzte
Hohenstaufe - T (1889)
    Mu:1890
Marino Falieri - T5 (1879)
    Va:1878
Nero - T5 (1877)
    Va:1876
Die Pfalz am Rhein - D (1887)
    Mu:1888
Prinz Eugen - D5 (1880)
    Mu:1883   Va:1880

**GRIEBEN, FERDINANDE** [Pseud.:
W. Egbert]
Angermünde 1844-?
Ref: Brüm 19, Ko Th

Knalleffekte der Natur - C4
(1881)
    Fr:1881

**GRIEPENKERL, WOLFGANG ROBERT**
Hofwyl 1810-1868 Braunschweig
Ref: Brüm 19, Ko Th, ADB,
NDB, OC

Auf der hohen Rast - D4
(1859)
    Bn:1859
Ideal und Welt - D5 (1855)
    Bn:1854   Dr:1855   Wm:1854
Robespierre - T5 (1849)
    Fr:1850   Ha:1850

**GRILLPARZER, FRANZ**
Vienna 1791-1872 Vienna
Ref: Brüm 18, Goe 8, Ko Th,
ADB, NDB, OC

Die Ahnfrau - T5 (1817)
    Bn:1818   Da:1819   Dr:1817
    Fr:1817   Ha:1817   Lg:1818
    Mh:1818   Mu:1817   Va:1817
    Wm:1819
Ein Bruderzwist in Habsburg -
T5 (1873)
    Va:1872
Esther - D2 (1877)
    Bn:1875   Da:1873   Dr:1876
    Fr:1869   Ha:1878   Lg:1868
    Mh:1869   Va:1868
Das goldene Vließ: Der Gast-
freund, Die Argonauten, Medea
(1822)
    Bn:1826   Mu:1822   Va:1821
    Wm:1885
Die Jüdin von Toledo - T5
(1873)
    Bn:1888   Va:1873
König Ottokars Glück und Ende
- T5 (1825)
    Bn:1830   Ha:1830   Lg:1829
    Mh:1829   Mu:1874   Va:1825
Libussa - T5 (1872)
    Va:1874
Medea - T4 (1822)
    Bn:1826   Da:1827   Dr:1840
    Fr:1860   Ha:1823   Lg:1825
    Mh:1864   Mu:1830   Va:1821
Des Meeres und der Liebe
Wellen - T5 (1840)
    Bn:1874   Da:1855   Dr:1852
    Fr:1862   Ha:1870   Mu:1856
    Va:1831   Wm:1882
Sappho - T5 (1819)
    Bn:1818   Da:1818   Dr:1819
    Fr:1818   Ha:1818   Lg:1818
    Mh:1820   Mu:1818   Va:1818
    Wm:1818
Der Traum ein Leben - D4
(1840)
    Bn:1878   Da:1844   Dr:1835
    Fr:1835   Ha:1843   Lg:1877
    Mu:1835   Va:1834
Ein treuer Diener seines
Herrn - T5 (1830)
    Dr:1830   Ha:1830   Va:1828
Weh dem, der lügt - C5 (1840)
    Ha:1885   Mu:1885   Va:1838
    Wm:1839

**GRIMM. HERMANN**
Kassel 1828 - 1901 Berlin
Ref: Brüm 19, Ko Th, OC

Demetrius - D5 (1854)
    Bn:1854

GROCH, FRIEDRICH   see Albert, Karl

GROLLER, BALDUIN
Arad/Hungary 1848-1916 Vienna
Ref: Brüm 19, Ko 3

Gewagtes Spiel - C3
    Fr:1890

GROSS, FERDINAND
Vienna 1849-1900 Vienna
Ref: Brüm 19, Ko Th

Der erste Brief - C1 (1883)
    Fr:1882

GROSS, KARL  [Pseud.: Carlo Dolce]
Budapest 1838-1916 Baden
Ref: Ko 3

Ein Feuilleton - C1 (1863)
    Va:1874

GROSSE, JULIUS WALDEMAR
Erfurt 1828-1902 Torbole
Ref: Brüm 19, Ko Th, NDB, OC

Gudrun - D5 (1870-71)
    Wm:1872
Die Herzogin von Ferrara - T5
with H. Herold (1884)
    Wm:1888
Meister Dürers Erdenwallen -
D1 (1871)
    Mu:1871  Wm:1871
Tiberius - T5 (1876)
    Bn:1878  Mu:1878  Va:1875
    Wm:1875
Die Ynglinger - T (1870-71)
    Mu:1860

GROSSMANN, GUSTAV FRIEDRICH
WILHELM
Berlin 1744-1796 Hanover
Ref: Brüm 18, Goe 4/1, Ko Th,
ADB, NDB, OC

Die Feuersbrunst - D3 (1773)
    Dr:1790  Va:1774
Henriette o. Sie ist schon
verheiratet - C5 (1783)
    Bn:1777  Da:1777  Fr:1777
    Ha:1775  Mh:1778  Mu:1777
    Va:1777  Wm:1795

Nicht mehr als sechs Schüs-
seln - D5 (1780)
    Bn:1780  Dr:1780  Fr:1779
    Ha:1780  Lg:1788  Mh:1781
    Mu:1782  Va:1782  Wm:1801
Wilhelmine von Blondheim - D3
(1775)
    Fr:1780

GRUA, ERNST
Berlin 1848-1879 Berlin
Ref: Brüm 19, Ko Th

Die weiße und die rote Rose -
D4 (1879)
    Bn:1881

GRUBE, MAX
Dorpat 1854-1934 Meiningen
Ref: Brüm 19, Ko Th, NDB

Strandgut - D1 (1885)
    Lg:1885

GRUBER, LUDWIG   see Anzengruber, Ludwig

GRÜNDORF, CARL
Riegersdorf 1830-1906 Vienna
Ref: Brüm 19, Ko Th

Ein Guldenzettel - F2 (1862)
    Da:1863  Dr:1858
Noblesse oblige - D1 (1873)
    Va:1870
Ein Opfer der Consuln - F1
(1872)
    Fr:1870  Lg:1872  Va:1869

GRÜNSTEIN, JOSEPH RUDOLF
Vienna 1841-1926 Schwerin
Ref: Brüm 19, Ko Th

Maidenspeech - D1 (1876)
    Bn:1876  Fr:1877  Mu:1878

GRUTSCH, FRANZ XAVER

Agnes Sorel - D5
    Va:1848

GUBITZ, FRIEDRICH WILHELM
Leipzig 1786-1870 Berlin
Ref: Brüm 18, Goe 9, Ko Th,
ADB, NDB

Der Kaiser und die Müllerin -
C1 (1854)
    Bn:1850  Dr:1850  Fr:1850

Lieb' und Friede - D1 (1816)
Bn:1813
Lieb' und Versöhnen o. Die
Schlacht bei Leipzig - D1
(1816)
Bn:1816
Die selige Frau - D1 (1816)
Bn:1813
Sappho - D (1815)
Bn:1816
Ein Tag des Schicksals - T5
(1845)
Bn:1814
Die Talentprobe [Der Beruf
zur Kunst] - C1 (1813)
Bn:1813    Dr:1820    Fr:1817
Lg:1823    Mh:1821    Va:1824
Wm:1847

**GUMPPENBERG, HANNS von**
[Pseud.: Jodok]
Landshut 1866-1928 Munich
Ref: Brüm 19, Ko Th, ADB

Thorwald - T (1888)
Mu:1888

**GÜNTHER, ANTON** [Pseud. of
Elimar, Duke of Oldenburg]
Oldenburg 1844-1895 Erlaa
Ref: Brüm 19, Ko Th

Der arme Heinrich - C2 (1876-
79)
Da:1883    Lg:1886    Va:1883
Comtesse Dornröschen - D1
(1876-79)
Bn:1875    Va:1878
In Hemdsärmeln - F1 (1876-79)
Lg:1876    Va:1876
Ein passionierter Raucher -
C1 (1876-79)
Va:1875
Zu glücklich - C1 (1876-79)
Fr:1875

**GÜNTHER, LEOPOLD**
Berlin 1825-1902 Schwerin
Ref: Brüm 19, Ko Th

Der Herr von Lohengrin - C1
Fr:1876
Der Leibarzt - C4 (1885)
Bn:1881    Fr:1881    Lg:1880
Va:1884    Wm:1882
Mama muß heiraten [Ich ver-
heirate meine Mutter] - C1 -
with M. Günther (1874)
Da:1876    Fr:1875    Mu:1877
Va:1874

Die Nachrede - D4 (1889)
Lg:1887
Der neue Stiftsarzt - C4 -
with M. Günther (1883)
Bn:1883    Da:1885    Lg:1884
Die Tochter des Commerzien-
rats - C3 - with M. Günther
(1884)
Lg:1885

**GÜNTHER, MARIE**
Lübeck 1854-?
Ref: Brüm 19, Ko 3

Durch die Karten - C1 (1876)
Fr:1877
Mama muß heiraten [Ich ver-
heirate meine Mutter] - C1
with L. Günther (1874)
Da:1876    Fr:1875    Mu:1877
Va:1874
Der neue Stiftsarzt - C4
with L. Günther (1883)
Bn:1883    Da:1885    Lg:1884
Die Tochter des Commerzien-
rats - C3 - with L. Günther
(1884)
Lg:1885

**GUTTENBERG, ANDREAS JOSEF von**
Vienna 1770-1807 Croatia
Ref: Goe 5, Ko Th

Das Miniaturgemälde - C1 - Fr
Bn:1826
Der Onkel aus Indien - C
Fr:1796
Die Rückkehr ins Vaterland -
D5
Va:1801
Die Überlisteten - C1 - Fr
Va:1806
Die Versöhnung [Vergeben und
Vergessen] - C3 (1800)
Ha:1807
Die Verwechslung - C1 (1800)
Va:1800

**GUTTMANN**

Eine Rente - C3
Dr:1850

**GUTZKOW, KARL** [Pseud.: E. L.
Bulwer]
Berlin 1811-1878 Sachsen-
hausen
Ref: Brüm 19, Ko Th, ADB,
NDB, OC

Anonym - C5
  Dr:1846  Fr:1846  Mu:1846
Antonio Perez [Philipp und
Perez] - T5 (1863)
  Dr:1853  Mu:1853
Der dreizehnte November - D3
(1847)
  Bn:1845  Dr:1845  Ha:1848
  Mu:1845  Va:1845
Dschingiskhan - C1 (1876)
  Mu:1873  Va:1873
Ella Rose o. Die Rechte des
Herzens - D5 (1856)
  Bn:1856  Da:1856  Dr:1856
  Fr:1856  Mu:1856  Va:1856
Fremdes Glück - C1
  Dr:1853  Wm:1851
Der Gefangene von Metz - C5
  Bn:1871
Der Königslieutenant - C4
(1852)
  Bn:1869  Da:1857  Dr:1849
  Fr:1877  Ha:1856  Mh:1858
  Mu:1861  Va:1850  Wm:1862
Lenz und Söhne - C5 (1855)
  Dr:1855
Liesli - T3 (1850)
  Dr:1849  Ha:1850  Wm:1849
Lorbeer und Myrthe - D3
(1857)
  Bn:1856
Ottfried - D5 (1884)
  Bn:1849  Ha:1848  Mu:1848
  Va:1856  Wm:1854
Patkul - T5 (1842)
  Bn:1841  Da:1842  Ha:1841
  Mu:1841
Pugatscheff - D (1844)
  Ha:1844
Richard Savage o. Der Sohn
einer Mutter - T5 - Fr (1839)
  Bn:1840  Da:1842  Dr:1840
  Fr:1839  Ha:1839  Mu:1840
  Va:1842  Wm:1839
Die Schule der Reichen - D5
(1842)
  Ha:1841  Va:1841
Das Urbild des Tartuffe - C5
(1844)
  Bn:1845  Da:1845  Dr:1845
  Fr:1845  Ha:1845  Mh:1845
  Mu:1845  Va:1849  Wm:1845
Uriel Acosta - T5 (1848)
  Bn:1847  Da:1848  Da:1846
  Fr:1847  Ha:1847  Lg:1865
  Mh:1847  Mu:1848  Va:1849
  Wm:1848

Ein weißes Blatt - D5 (1844)
  Bn:1843  Dr:1842  Fr:1842
  Ha:1843  Lg:1864  Mu:1843
  Va:1843  Wm:1842
Werner o. Herz und Welt - D5
(1842)
  Bn:1841  Da:1844  Dr:1840
  Fr:1840  Ha:1840  Mu:1840
  Va:1840  Wm:1840
Die Wullenweber - D5 (1844)
  Dr:1847  Ha:1848
Zopf und Schwert - C5 (1844)
  Da:1844  Dr:1844  Fr:1844
  Ha:1844  Mh:1844  Mu:1844
  Va:1862  Wm:1848


**HAAKE, AUGUST**
Königsberg 1793-1864
Darmstadt
Ref: Ko Th, ADB

Der Bankrottirer - D2
  Dr:1847  Fr:1847

**HACKENTHAL, A.**

Eine Ehe von heut - D5
  Bn:1879

**HACKLÄNDER, FRIEDRICH WILHELM**
Burtscheid 1816-1877 Leoni am
Starnberger See
Ref: Brüm 19, Ko Th, ADB,
NDB, OC

Diplomatische Fäden - C3
  Lg:1876  Mu:1877  Va:1872
Der geheime Agent - C4 (1851)
  Bn:1851  Da:1854  Dr:1851
  Fr:1851  Ha:1851  Mh:1851
  Mu:1851  Va:1851  Wm:1851
Magnetische Kuren - C4 (1853)
  Bn:1853  Da:1852  Dr:1859
  Fr:1852  Ha:1854  Mu:1870
  Va:1852
Marionetten - C4 (1868)
  Bn:1867  Ha:1867  Mu:1869
Schuldig - F1 (1860)
  Bn:1854  Fr:1864  Va:1854
Der verlorene Sohn - C3
(1861)
  Va:1862
Zur Ruhe setzen - C4 (1857)
  Bn:1856  Va:1855

**HAFFNER, KARL**  [i.e. Karl
Schlachter]
Königsberg 1804-1876 Vienna
Ref: Brüm 19, Ko Th, ADB

Das Marmorherz (1845-46)
  Ha:1841
Ein Mann der Gesetze - D4
(1861)
  Fr:1850
Therese Krones - D4 (1862)
  Da:1876  Fr:1861  Va:1876
Der verkaufte Schlaf - Z
(1870)
  Ha:1843

**HAFNER, PHILIPP**
Vienna 1731 [1735?]-1764
Vienna
Ref: Brüm 18, Goe 4/1, Ko Th,
ADB, NDB, OC

Der Furchtsame - C3 (1812)
  Dr:1787  Va:1864

**HAGEMANN, FRIEDRICH GUSTAV**
Oranienbaum 1760-ca. 1830
Breslau
Ref: Brüm 18, Goe 5, Ko Th,
ADB

Der Doppelpapa - F3 (1810)
  Bn:1815  Da:1814  Dr:1818
  Fr:1817  Lg:1817  Mh:1818
Friedrich von Oldenburg o.
Der Strohmann - D3 (1794)
  Wm:1795
Der Fürst und sein Kammer-
diener - C1 (1792)
  Fr:1792  Ha:1792  Wm:1792
Großmut und Dankbarkeit - D4
(1810)
  Bn:1804
Iwan der alte dankbare Kosak
- D1 (1815)
  Bn:1816  Fr:1816  Ha:1816
Leichtsinn und gutes Herz -
C1 (1791)
  Bn:1793  Da:1810  Dr:1792
  Fr:1805  Ha:1790  Mh:1792
  Va:1792  Wm:1791
Ludwig der Springer - D5
(1793)
  Bn:1793  Da:1810  Fr:1793
  Ha:1793  Mh:1794  Mu:1816
  Wm:1792
Der Maitag - D4 (1794)
  Dr:1793  Fr:1794  Ha:1792
  Mh:1793  Va:1793

Die Martinsgänse - C1 (1798)
  Bn:1827  Da:1812  Dr:1798
  Fr:1804  Mh:1802  Wm:1800
Otto der Schütze - D5 (1791)
  Bn:1797  Da:1810  Fr:1793
  Mh:1793  Wm:1792
Vetter Paul o. Die Rache
eines Deutschen - D1 (1810)
  Bn:1816  Da:1815
Der Vogelbauer - D
  Fr:1799
Der Weihnachtsabend - D5
(1798)
  Dr:1799  Mu:1801

**HAGEMEISTER, JOHANN GOTTFRIED**
Greifswald 1761-1806 Breslau
Ref: Brüm 18, Goe 5, Ko Th,
ADB

Der Graf aus Deutschland - C5
(1791)
  Wm:1791
Das große Los - C1 (1791)
  Bn:1791  Da:1815  Dr:1791
  Fr:1799  Ha:1790  Mh:1794
  Va:1797  Wm:1791
Die Jesuiten - T5 (1787)
  Wm:1797
Johann von Procida o. Die
sicilische Vesper - T5 (1791)
  Bn:1792  Wm:1793
Waldemar, Herzog von Schles-
wig - D (1793)
  Ha:1785

**HAHN, RUDOLF**
Dresden 1815-1889 Berlin
Ref: Brüm 19, Ko Th

Der Alexandriner - D1
  Fr:1849
Ein alter Dienstbote - D1
(1866)
  Da:1865
Ein alter Pappenheimer - F3
  Ha:1857
Die dreiundsiebzig Kreuzer
des Herrn Stutzelberger - F1
  Fr:1865
Im Vorzimmer Sr. Excellenz -
D1 (1864)
  Bn:1869  Da:1862  Fr:1862
  Ha:1863  Lg:1867  Mu:1868
  Va:1862  Wm:1865
In Saus und Braus - F3
  Ha:1868
Ins Knopfloch - F1
  Lg:1866

Lokal-Nachrichten - C1
    Bn:1865  Fr:1866
Die Rückkehr des Landwehr-
manns - D1
    Fr:1849
Signor Pepita, mein Name ist
Meyer - F1 (1855)
    Ha:1856
Ein Weihnachtsabend - C1
    Dr:1857
Wie denken Sie darüber? - F1
(1855)
    Fr:1865  Ha:1845

**HALBE, JOHANN AUGUST**
Bautzen 1754-1823 Hamburg
Ref: Goe 5, Ko 3

Die Männerscheue - D5
    Bn:1799

**HALIRSCH, FRIEDRICH LUDWIG**
[Pseud.: K. E. Waller]
Vienna 1802-1832 Verona
Ref: Goe 11, Ko Th, ADB, NDB

Hans Sachs - D1 (1826)
    Ha:1828
Das Lustspiel - C4
    Va:1831
Ein Morgen auf Capri - D3
(1829)
    Va:1827

**HALLER, GUSTAV** [Pseud. of
Gustav Emil Barthel]
Ref: Brüm 19, Ko 3

Der Damenarzt - C4
    Va:1874

**HALM, FRIEDRICH** [Pseud. of
Eligius Franz Joseph von
Münch-Bellinghausen]
Cracow 1806-1871 Vienna
Ref: Brüm 19, Ko Th, ADB, OC

Der Adept - T5 (1828)
    Dr:1837  Ha:1839  Va:1836
Begum Somru - T5 (1872)
    Va:1867
Camoens - D1 (1838)
    Bn:1842  Da:1846  Dr:1843
    Fr:1840  Mu:1838  Va:1837
    Wm:1838
Donna Maria de Molina - D4 -
Sp
    Dr:1847  Va:1847

Der Fechter von Ravenna - T5
(1857)
    Bn:1854  Da:1855  Dr:1855
    Fr:1855  Ha:1854  Mu:1855
    Va:1854  Wm:1855
Griseldis - D5 (1837)
    Bn:1836  Dr:1836  Fr:1836
    Ha:1836  Mh:1837  Mu:1868
    Va:1835  Wm:1836
Imelda Lambertazzi - T5
(1842)
    Va:1838
Iphigenia in Delphi - D5
(1864)
    Va:1856
König und Bauer - D3 - Sp
(1842)
    Ha:1842  Va:1841
Ein mildes Urteil - T5 (1857)
    Mu:1840  Va:1840  Wm:1840
Die Pflegetochter - D1
    Va:1840
Sampiero - T5 (1857)
    Bn:1844  Va:1844
Der Sohn der Wildnis - D5
(1843)
    Bn:1842  Da:1842  Dr:1842
    Fr:1843  Ha:1842  Mh:1843
    Mu:1842  Va:1842  Wm:1842
Verbot und Befehl - D5 (1857)
    Ha:1848  Va:1848
Wildfeuer - D5 (1864)
    Da:1868  Fr:1864  Ha:1867
    Lg:1869  Va:1866  Wm:1867

**HAMMER, FRIEDRICH JULIUS**
Dresden 1810-1862 Pillnitz
Ref: Brüm 19, Ko Th, ADB

Auch eine Mutter - C1
    Dr:1859
Die Brüder - D5 (1856)
    Dr:1856

**HANNAMANN, OCTAVIAN AUGUST**
Vienna 1762-1808 Vienna
Ref: Goe 5, Ko 3

Die drei Körbchen - C3 (1802)
    Dr:1801  Va:1801
Die Hausehre - D5 (1804)
    Dr:1799  Fr:1800  Lg:1800
    Va:1799

**HANISCH, CARL**  see d'Elpons,
Friedrich Wilhelm von

**HANKER, GARLIEB**  see Epheu,
F. L.

**HARBOE, CHRISTINA JOHANNE**
von, née Falsen
Hadersleben ?-?
Ref: Goe 13

Der gewissenhafte Erbe - C5
   Va:1804

**HÄRING, GEORG WILHELM** see
Alexis, Willibald

**HARRYS, JOHANN GEORG**
Hanover 1780-1838 Hanover
Ref: Brüm 18, Goe 9, Ko 3

Adele - C2 (1836)
   Bn:1836   Ha:1836   Wm:1838
Der Bühnen-Dilettant - C1 -
Fr
   Bn:1836   Ha:1837
Drohungen o. Die Selbstmörder
C1 - Fr
   Bn:1835   Va:1844
Die Eisenbahn - C1 - Fr
(1834)
   Bn:1838
Das goldene Kreuz - C2 - Fr
(1835)
   Da:1838   Dr:1835   Fr:1835
   Ha:1835
König und Schauspieler - C1 -
Fr (1833)
   Fr:1835   Ha:1833
Löwenberg und Compagnie - C1
Fr (1836)
   Dr:1838   Fr:1836   Wm:1836
Sohn oder Braut - C1 (1835)
   Bn:1835   Dr:1835   Fr:1835
   Ha:1834
Student und Dame - C2 - Fr
(1838)
   Bn:1838   Ha:1839

**HARTER, ERNST** [Pseud. of
S. Mayer]

Der Verteidiger - D5
   Fr:1863

**HARTMANN, EDUARD von** see
Robert, Karl

**HARTMANN, MORITZ**
Duschnik/Bohemia 1821-1872
Vienna
Ref: Brüm 19, Ko 3, ADB, NDB,
OC

Gleich und gleich - D2
   Bn:1873   Fr:1864   Ha:1865
   Mu:1868   Va:1864   Wm:1871

**HASE**

Die glückliche Jagd - C2
   Bn:1783

**HASSAURECK, FRANZ JOSEF**
Vienna 1787-1836 Vienna
Ref: Goe 11, Ko 3

Der kurze Roman o. Die selt-
same Wette - C1 - Fr (1809)
   Bn:1809   Da:1812   Dr:1810
   Fr:1809   Va:1816
Der Vater und seine Kinder -
D3 - Fr (1807)
   Va:1806
Wiedervergeltung - C3 - Fr
(1811)
   Bn:1815   Va:1810

**HASSELSTEINER, FRANZ**
Vienna 1763-1837 Vienna
Ref: Goe 11, Ko 3

Die Cisterne - D4 - Fr
   Va:1811
Friedrich von Minski o. Das
Familiengericht - D3
   Va:1811
Johann von Calais - D3 - Fr
   Dr:1812   Va:1810
Die Jugend Heinrichs V. - C1
- Fr
   Va:1807

**HAUSSNER, FRIEDRICH WILHELM**

Der kleine Neger - C1
   Mh:1809

**HAYN, JULIANA**
Pest 1758-?
Ref: Goe 5, Ko Th

Der Dichterling o. Solche
Insekten gibts die Menge - C1
(1781)
   Va:1781

**HEBBEL, FRIEDRICH**
Wesselburen 1813-1863 Vienna
Ref: Brüm 19, Ko Th, ADB,
NDB, OC

Agnes Bernauer - T5 (1852)
   Mu:1852   Va:1868   Wm:1852

Demetrius - T5 (1864)
  Bn:1869
Genoveva - T5 (1843)
  Da:1864  Va:1854  Wm:1858
Gyges und sein Ring - T5
(1856)
  Va:1889
Herodes und Mariamne - T5
(1850)
  Bn:1874  Va:1849
Judith - T5 (1841)
  Bn:1840  Da:1869  Dr:1854
  Fr:1869  Ha:1840  Mh:1867
  Mu:1851  Va:1849  Wm:1864
Maria Magdalena - T3 (1844)
  Bn:1850  Fr:1883  Ha:1847
  Mu:1870  Va:1848
Michel Angelo - D2 (1855)
  Va:1861
Die Nibelungen (1862):
  Der gehörnte Siegfried - D1
  Bn:1862  Da:1869  Fr:1868
  Ha:1869  Lg:1867  Mh:1863
  Mu:1870  Va:1863  Wm:1861
  Siegfrieds Tod - T5
  Bn:1862  Da:1869  Fr:1868
  Ha:1869  Lg:1867  Mh:1863
  Mu:1870  Va:1863  Wm:1861
  Kriemhilds Rache - T5
  Bn:1862  Da:1869  Ha:1888
  Mh:1874  Mu:1872  Va:1871
  Wm:1861
Der Rubin - D2 (1851)
  Bn:1849

**HEERINGEN, GUSTAV ADOLF**  see
Wodomerius, Ernst

**HEIDEN, EUGENIE**  [Pseud. of
Eugenie Engelhardt]
Ries 1852-1927
Ref: Brüm 19, Ko 3

Der Herr Major auf Urlaub -
C4 - with F. Stahl (1889)
  Wm:1889
Jugendfreunde - C3
  Va:1884

**HEIDRICH, M.**

Passionen - F1
  Va:1878
Prinz Lieschen - C3
  Dr:1853

**HEIGEL, CAESAR MAXIMILIAN**
Munich 1783-1848/49
Ref: Brüm 18, Goe 11, Ko Th,
ADB

Alles à la Freischütz - F
  Mu:1825
Das war dein Glück o. Der
Liebhaber im Stroh - C1
(1821)
  Fr:1805  Mh:1805  Va:1804
Fiametta o. Die Zigeuner auf
Tegerna-Hora - D3
  Mu:1824
Hans von Dreisporn o. Die
Prüfung - C1
  Mu:1824
Das Husarenkind - D1
  Bn:1829  Fr:1832
Landolin o. Der Pfalzgrafen-
stein - D3
  Mu:1825
Ludwig von Ingolstadt - D1
  Fr:1805
Das Mädchen von Cattaro
  Mu:1824
Max Emanuel o. Die Klause in
Tyrol - D3 (1828)
  Mu:1824
Der Perückenstock - D1 (1821)
  Bn:1804  Da:1814  Dr:1804
  Fr:1805  Mh:1803  Va:1804
Der Schnabernack o. Kunst und
Liebesproben - F1
  Mh:1815  Mu:1822  Va:1816
Sonst und jetzt o. Die Neu-
jahrswünsche  - C1
  Mu:1824
Die Tollköpfe - C3
  Ha:1811
Das Weihnachtsgeschenk - F3
  Mu:1824
Die Zeitalter: So sind sie
gewesen/So waren sie/So sind
sie - C3 (1832)
  Bn:1810  Da:1811  Dr:1811
  Fr:1811  Ha:1810  Mh:1809
  Mu:1822  Va:1811  Wm:1813

**HEIGEL, KARL AUGUST**
Munich 1835-1905 Riva
Ref: Brüm 19, Ko Th

Freunde - D4 (1879)
  Lg:1881  Mu:1878
Hohenschwangau - D
  Mu:1886
Josefine Bonaparte - T (1882)
  Mu:1882
Des Kriegers Frau - T1 (1871)
  Bn:1870  Fr:1870  Mh:1871
  Mu:1870  Wm:1871
Marfa - D5 (1880)
  Bn:1862  Fr:1864  Mu:1870

Die schöne Zarin - T (1883)
    Mu:1884
Vor hundert Jahren - D (1880)
    Mu:1878

**HEINE, FERDINAND**
1798-1872 Dresden
Ref: Ko Th

Besser früher als später - C3
- Fr
    Dr:1850  Ha:1850
Der erste Waffengang - C2 -
Fr
    Da:1850  Dr:1843  Fr:1845
    Ha:1843
Hausmütterchen - D1 - Fr
    Bn:1847  Dr:1847  Va:1848
Herr Mannecke - F
    Ha:1845
Der Marronenverkäufer - C2 -
Fr
    Dr:1846
Der politische Koch - C1 - Fr
    Dr:1849
Ein Soldatenherz - D4 - Fr
    Dr:1845

**HEINE, HEINRICH**
Düsseldorf 1797-1856 Paris
Ref: Goe 8, Ko Th, ADB, NDB,
OC

William Ratcliff - T1 (1823)
    Fr:1888

**HEINEMANN, HEINRICH**
Bischofsburg 1842-1918
Tambach
Ref: Brüm 19, Ko Th

Auf glatter Bahn - C4 (1887)
    Bn:1887
Herr und Frau Hippokrates -
C4 (1886)
    Lg:1885
Der Schriftstellertag - C3
(1883)
    Da:1884  Fr:1883  Lg:1883

**HEINERSDORF, RICHARD**

Frau von Stein - C1
    Va:1859

**HEINRICH, KARL**  see Kette,
Hermann

**HEITER, AMALIE**  see Amalie
Marie Friederike, Princess
of Saxony

**HEITMANN, BARTHOLD**
Ochsenwerder 1808-1862
Hamburg
Ref: Brüm 19, Ko Th

Armin o. Die Schlacht im Teu-
toburger Walde (1846)
    Ha:1846

**HELBIG, FRIEDRICH**
Jena 1832-1896 Jena
Ref: Brüm 19, Ko Th

Gregor der Siebente - T5
(1878)
    Wm:1872
Die Komödie auf der Hoch-
schule - C4 (1878)
    Wm:1877

**HELD, LUDWIG**
Regensburg 1837-1900 Vienna
Ref: Ko Th

Hausse und Baisse - C3
    Va:1878
Die Näherin - F4 (1901)
    Fr:1882

**HELL, THEODOR**  [Pseud. of
Karl Gottlieb Theodor
Winkler]
Waldenburg 1775-1856 Dresden
Ref: Brüm 18, Goe 9, Ko 2, OC

Angelika - D5 (1811)
    Dr:1809  Lg:1807  Va:1836
Die beiden Galeerensklaven -
D3 - Fr (1824)
    Bn:1823  Da:1825  Dr:1823
    Ha:1824  Lg:1824  Mh:1833
    Wm:1824
Die beiden Sergeanten - D3 -
Fr (1825)
    Bn:1824  Da:1825  Dr:1824
    Ha:1824  Lg:1824  Mu:1833
    Va:1832  Wm:1824
Die Benefiz-Vorstellung - C5
Fr (1826)
    Bn:1825  Da:1827  Dr:1827
    Fr:1830  Ha:1826  Lg:1825
    Mh:1826  Mu:1829  Va:1827
Der Beruf zur Kunst - C1
(1805)
    Bn:1813  Da:1807  Dr:1820
    Fr:1814  Lg:1823  Va:1806

Ein Besuch im Narrenhause -
C1 - Fr (1820)
 Bn:1820  Dr:1819
Bianca von Toredo - D5 (1808)
 Bn:1806  Dr:1806  Fr:1807
 Ha:1806  Lg:1806  Mh:1808
 Mu:1808  Va:1806
Camilla - C2 - Fr (1835)
 Dr:1834
Caravaggio - D3 - Fr (1836)
 Dr:1835
Der Chevalier von St. Georges
- C3 - Fr
 Dr:1840  Fr:1841  Wm:1842
Christinens Liebe und Entsa-
gung o. Die Königin von sech-
zehn Jahren - D2 - Fr (1831)
 Bn:1828  Da:1829  Dr:1828
 Fr:1829  Ha:1828  Lg:1829
 Mh:1831  Mu:1830  Va:1832
 Wm:1834
Clementine - D1 - Fr (1823)
 Dr:1823  Lg:1823  Mu:1823
 Wm:1829
Der schwatzt ohne Ende - F1
 Bn:1821
Der Diplomat o. Wenn ichs
selbst nur wüßte - C2 - Fr
(1830)
 Da:1831  Dr:1828  Fr:1828
 Ha:1828  Lg:1828  Mh:1829
 Mu:1829  Va:1849  Wm:1828
Dominique o. Der Bund mit dem
Bösen - C3 - Fr
 Dr:1832  Wm:1832
Der Dorfarzt - D2 - Fr
 Wm:1841
Drei Tage aus dem Leben eines
Spielers - D3 - Fr (1830)
 Dr:1828  Ha:1830  Lg:1828
 Mh:1829  Mu:1829  Wm:1829
Der Ehrenhüter - C
 Bn:1832  Dr:1832
Die Elster - D3
 Dr:1816  Fr:1816  Lg:1816
Der Enkel - D1 - Fr (1831)
 Dr:1829
Erste Liebelei und erste
Liebe - C1 - Fr
 Dr:1826  Fr:1828  Lg:1826
 Mu:1826  Va:1826
Die Erzählungen der Königin
von Navarra - C5 - Fr
 Dr:1851
Die Familie [Das Haus]
Anglade - D3 - Fr (1818)
 Bn:1830  Dr:1818  Lg:1820
 Mh:1819  Va:1817
Fesseln - C3 - Fr (1843)
 Fr:1864  Lg:1842  Va:1842

Das Feuerlärm - C
 Fr:1811
Der Flatterhafte o. Er muß
heiraten - C3 (1809)
 Wm:1808
Flinte und Pinsel - C1 - Fr
 Bn:1825  Dr:1825
Die Flitterwochen - C2 - Fr
(1829)
 Dr:1827  Mh:1829  Mu:1826
 Va:1827
Geisterscenen - C4 (1805)
 Dr:1806
Der Gelehrte - C2 - Fr (1840)
 Wm:1833
Geliebt oder tot! - C1 - Fr
(1836)
 Dr:1836  Ha:1835
Die Gelübde - C2 (1805)
 Dr:1807  Va:1806
Der Geschäftige - C3
 Da:1815  Lg:1816  Va:1815
Die Gespenster - C5
 Mh:1807
Glück und Unglück - C1 - Fr
 Dr:1831  Fr:1831  Lg:1831
 Wm:1831
Der graue Mann - D3 - Fr
(1818)
 Dr:1818  Va:1818
Das Haus am Walle o. Der
Krieg in der Fronde - C3 - Fr
 Bn:1829  Dr:1829  Fr:1829
 Lg:1829  Mu:1829
Der Herr Gevatter - C1 - Fr
(1825)
 Bn:1822  Dr:1824  Wm:1829
Herr Habicht o. Der Hauswirt
unter Siegel - C1 (1809)
 Da:1812  Fr:1815
Der Hofmeister in tausend
Ängsten - C1 - Fr (1824)
 Bn:1847  Da:1824  Dr:1823
 Fr:1824  Ha:1844  Lg:1824
 Mh:1825  Mu:1824  Wm:1824
Jarvis - D4 - Fr (1842)
 Dr:1841  Fr:1844  Ha:1841
 Lg:1842
Jean Jacques Rousseaus
Schneider - F1 - Fr
 Da:1830
Karl XII. - C2 - Eng
 Dr:1830  Lg:1831
Der Kuß nach Sicht - C1 - Fr
(1826)
 Bn:1824  Dr:1825  Fr:1826
 Lg:1825
Lanrette - D1 - Fr (1837)
 Dr:1836

Licht und Schatten im Hause
von Sarning - D5 - Fr
   Bn:1812
Luise von Lignerolles - D5 -
Fr (1840)
   Dr:1838
Der lustige Rat - C2 - Fr
(1833)
   Bn:1835   Dr:1832   Ha:1832
   Lg:1832
Mahomed II. - T5
   Dr:1813
Malwine - D2 - Fr
   Dr:1833
Maria - D3 - Fr (1826)
   Dr:1825
Marie o. Die Zeiträume - D3 -
Fr
   Dr:1837   Va:1837
Die Memoiren des Teufels - C3
- Fr
   Dr:1843   Ha:1846   Va:1844
Michel Perrin o. Der Spion
wider Willen - C2 - Fr
   Da:1842   Dr:1834   Ha:1835
   Lg:1837   Mu:1834   Wm:1836
Der Mulatte - C3 - Fr (1841)
   Bn:1841   Dr:1840   Ha:1841
   Va:1841
Nur ein Stündchen war er
fort! - C1 - Fr (1805)
   Mh:1806   Va:1806
Das Opfer der Tochter - D
   Fr:1808
Oskar o. Wie schwer sind
Frauen zu betrügen! - C3 - Fr
(1844)
   Dr:1843   Va:1842   Wm:1844
Pferde und Wagen - C1 - Fr
   Dr:1826
Philipp - D1 - Fr
   Dr:1831
Die Pulververschwörung - C -
Fr (1843)
   Fr:1842
Der Räuber - C1 - Fr (1829)
   Bn:1824   Va:1824
Der Reisewagen eines Emi-
granten - D5 - Fr
   Da:1841   Dr:1836   Ha:1836
   Lg:1837
Der Schwätzer o. Nur er will
sprechen - C1 - Fr (1807)
   Bn:1808   Dr:1806   Mh:1806
   Va:1832
Sechzehn Jahre und schon so
alt - C1 - Fr
   Dr:1825
Sie ist wahnsinnig - D2 - Fr
   Dr:1835   Ha:1846

Der Staatsgefangene - C2
(1834)
   Bn:1831   Dr:1832   Ha:1833
   Mu:1833
Das Strudelköpfchen - C1 - Fr
(1808)
   Bn:1824   Da:1810   Dr:1805
   Ha:1830   Lg:1826   Mu:1816
   Va:1825
Ein Tag aus dem Jugendleben
Heinrich V. - C3 - Fr (1809)
   Dr:1813   Ha:1829
Die Tochter des Geizigen - D2
- Fr
   Dr:1835
Der Unschuldige muß viel
leiden - C3 - Fr (1823)
   Bn:1823   Da:1823   Dr:1823
   Fr:1823   Ha:1823   Lg:1823
   Mh:1825   Mu:1823   Va:1822
   Wm:1823
Die Unzertrennlichen - C1 -
Fr (1829)
   Bn:1825   Dr:1825   Lg:1826
Der Unbekannte im Gasthofe -
C1 - Fr
   Ha:1826
Der Vater der Debütantin [Das
erste Debüt] - C5 - Fr
   Dr:1838
Die Vernunftheirat - C2 - Fr
(1827)
   Bn:1827   Dr:1828   Ha:1848
   Mh:1828   Lg:1827
Wer nimmt ein Loos? - C1 - Fr
(1827)
   Bn:1821
Der Wunderring - C1
   Da:1821
Yelva o. Die Stumme [Die
Waise aus Rußland] - D2 - Fr
(1832)
   Bn:1849   Da:1850   Dr:1828
   Fr:1830   Ha:1829   Lg:1829
   Mu:1833   Va:1830
Zwei Jahre verheiratet o. Wer
ist daran schuld? - C1 - Fr
(1832)
   Da:1830   Dr:1830   Lg:1830
   Mu:1830   Va:1830

**HELMOLT, CHRISTIAN GEORG**
1728-1805

Der schöne Flüchtling - C5 -
Eng
   Va:1777
Der Ton der großen Welt - C2
- Eng
   Bn:1780

**HENLE, ELISE** [Pseud. of
Elise Levi, née Henle]
Munich 1832-1892 Frankfurt/M
Ref: Brüm 19, Ko Th

Durch die Intendanz - C5
(1878)
    Da:1878  Fr:1878  Ha:1881
    Lg:1878  Mh:1878  Mu:1878
    Va:1877
Der Erbonkel - C (1887)
    Fr:1889  Mu:1881
Die Wiener in Stuttgart - C5
(1879)
    Bn:1879

**HENRION, POLY** [Pseud. of
Leopold Kohl von Kohlenegg]
Vienna 1834-1875 Saalfeld
Ref: Brüm 19, Ko Th

Brididi - F1 - Fr (1872)
    Lg:1870
Für nervöse Frauen - C1
(1869)
    Fr:1867  Mu:1869  Va:1868
    Wm:1874
Geheime Mission - C
    Mu:1872
Hohe Gäste - F1 - with
G. Belly (1868)
    Fr:1867  Ha:1865
Im Tiergarten - D
    Fr:1886
König Mammon - D
    Fr:1870  Mu:1871  Wm:1870
Die Liebesdiplomaten - C1
(1863)
    Bn:1862  Fr:1862  Ha:1868
    Lg:1865  Mu:1869  Wm:1865
Macciavella - D2
    Bn:1872  Mu:1872
Strategie - C1
    Bn:1868
Ein unschuldiger Diplomat -
C1 - Fr (1865)
    Bn:1864

**HENSEL, SOPHIE FRIEDERIKE,**
née Sparmann
Dresden 1738-1789 Schleswig
Ref: Brüm 18, Goe 5, Ko 3,
ADB

Die Familie auf dem Lande -
D5 (1770)
    Ha:1770

**HENSEL, WILHELM**
Trebbin 1794-1861 Berlin
Ref: Goe 11

Ritter Hans o. Die Verwechslung - C1 (1818)
    Bn:1817

**HENSLER, KARL FRIEDRICH**
Vaihingen 1759-1825 Vienna
Ref: Brüm 18, Goe 5, Ko Th,
ADB, NDB, OC

Eugenius Skoko, Erbprinz von
Dalmatien - T5 (1798)
    Mh:1799

**HENZEN, KARL GEORG WILHELM**
[Pseud.: Fritz von Sakken]
Bremen 1850-1910 Leipzig
Ref: Brüm 19, Ko Th

Die Augen der Liebe - C3
    Lg:1880
Deutsche Studenten (1887)
    Lg:1887
Herr Studiosus Lessing - D1
(1880)
    Lg:1880
Im Reiche der Mütter - C1
(1890)
    Bn:1888  Fr:1886  Wm:1890
Luther - D5 (1883)
    Lg:1883  Wm:1883
Ossian - C1 (1877)
    Lg:1883

**HERKLOTS, KARL ALEXANDER**
Dulzen 1759-1830 Berlin
Ref: Brüm 18, Goe 11, Ko Th,
ADB

Herr Müßling [Müßiggang] o.
Wie die Zeit vergeht - C1 -
Fr
    Bn:1805  Dr:1805  Lg:1805
    Mu:1807  Va:1807
List und Liebe - C1
    Bn:1803
Der Prozeß - C2 (1794)
    Bn:1793  Wm:1792

**HERMANNSTHAL, FRANZ HERMANN
von**
Vienna 1799-1875 Vienna
Ref: Brüm 18, Ko Th, ADB

Die Blutrache - D1 (1831)
    Va:1824

Der letzte Ravenswood - T5
(1860)
   Va:1860
Ziani und seine Braut - T4
(1847)
   Bn:1847

**HEROLD, HEDWIG**
Dessau 1845-1900 Berlin
Ref: Brüm 19, Ko Th

Die Herzogin von Ferrara - T5
with J. Grosse (1884)
   Wm:1888

**HERRIG, HANS**
Braunschweig 1845-1892
Weimar
Ref: Brüm 19, Ko Th, ADB

Konradin - D4 (1881)
   Bn:1884  Wm:1887
Der Kurprinz - T (1876)
   Mu:1876
Nero - T5 (1883)
   Wm:1884

**HERRIGAU, WILIBERT** see Löhn-
Siegel, Maria Anna

**HERRMANN, BERNHARD ANTON**
Hamburg 1806-1876 Hamburg
Ref: Brüm 19, Ko Th, ADB

Alles durch die Frauen - C
   Ha:1845
Das Ehrenwort - D
   Ha:1843
Der Enkel - C1
   Fr:1864
Er weiß nicht, was er will -
C1 (1872)
   Dr:1856  Fr:1855  Ha:1857
   Lg:1864
Die ersten Koketterien - C1 -
Fr
   Ha:1849
Der Fleck - F
   Ha:1839
Der Freundschaftsdienst - C3
   Ha:1843
Die gelbe Rose - F
   Ha:1839
Johanna und Hannchen - C - Fr
   Fr:1846
Der Juwelier von St. James -
D
   Ha:1839

Kean - C5 - Fr
   Da:1840  Fr:1837  Ha:1836
   Mh:1839
Der König wider Willen - C2 -
Fr
   Dr:1838  Ha:1842  Va:1842
Lady Tartüffe - C5 - Fr
   Ha:1853
Louise Bernard - D5 - Fr
   Ha:1845
Der Maler - D3 - Fr
   Dr:1838  Fr:1839  Ha:1838
Mein Doppelgänger - F1 - Fr
   Fr:1856
Die Memoiren des Teufels - C3
- Fr
   Da:1843  Dr:1843  Fr:1842
   Ha:1842  Mh:1842  Wm:1842
Molière o. Das Leben eines
Schauspielers - C2 - Fr
   Fr:1842  Ha:1842  Wm:1842
Der Obrist von 16 Jahren - C
   Fr:1838  Ha:1837
Onkel und Neffe - C1
   Lg:1864
Das salische Gesetz - C2 - Fr
   Bn:1855
Der Schiffsjunge - C2 - Fr
   Wm:1846
Das Schreckens-Gewebe - F1
   Dr:1837  Ha:1837
Die Sclavin [Sclaven?] - D3 -
Fr
   Dr:1840  Ha:1840
Ein Silbergroschen - F1 - Fr
   Fr:1855
Die Tochter des Advokaten -
D2
   Va:1842
Unterricht für Ehefrauen - C2
   Va:1874
Der Vater der Debütantin - F4
- Fr
   Bn:1850  Da:1843  Dr:1856
   Fr:1838  Ha:1838  Wm:1845
Vater und Vormund - D3 - Fr
   Dr:1838  Fr:1839  Ha:1839
Voltaires Ferien - C2 - Fr
   Bn:1837  Da:1843  Dr:1843
   Fr:1839  Ha:1837  Wm:1837
Ein Weib aus dem Volke - D6 -
Fr
   Ha:1846
Das Weib des Soldaten - D1 -
Fr
   Ha:1851
Welche? - C1 - Fr (1863)
   Dr:1857

**HERRMANN, TH. G.**

Adrienne Lecouvreur - D5 - Fr
    Da:1852

**HERSCH, HERMANN**
Jüchen 1821-1870 Berlin
Ref: Brüm 19, Ko Th, ADB

Die Anna-Lise - C5 (1859)
    Bn:1859  Da:1859  Dr:1859
    Fr:1859  Ha:1858  Mu:1859
    Va:1858  Wm:1858
Sophonisbe - T5 (1859)
    Va:1857  Wm:1857

**HERWIG, H.**

Der Ingenieur - C4
    Fr:1881
Virginia - D5
    Fr:1877

**HERZENSKRON, HERMANN JOSEF**
Vienna 1792-1863 Vienna
Ref: Brüm 18, Goe 11, Ko Th,
ADB

Acht vernünftige Tage - C1
(1833)
    Bn:1833  Dr:1835  Va:1830
Der Bräutigam ohne Braut - C1
(1826)
    Bn:1831  Fr:1844  Ha:1849
    Va:1827
Der Gang ins Irrenhaus [Bed-
lams Nachbarschaft] - C1 - Fr
(1826)
    Dr:1833  Ha:1828  Va:1822
Das Häuschen in der Aue - C1
Fr (1826)
    Bn:1839  Va:1822
List und Strafe o. Die unver-
sehene Wette - C1 - Fr
    Va:1833
Die Perrücke - C1 (1839)
    Va:1839
Der schönste Tag des Lebens -
C1 - Fr (1828)
    Va:1826
Die Supplikanten in Verwir-
rung [Die Bittsteller in Ver-
legenheit] - C1 (1833)
    Bn:1833  Ha:1833  Va:1837
Die Witwe von 18 Jahren - C1
Fr (1833)
    Bn:1832  Va:1828
See Goedeke 11 for additional
listings.

**HERZL, THEODOR**
Budapest 1860-1904 Edlach
Ref: Brüm 19, Ko Th, NDB, OC

Der Flüchtling - C1 (1888)
    Va:1889
Wilddiebe - C4 - with
H. Wittmann (1891)
    Fr:1889  Va:1889

**HESSE, AUGUST WILHELM**
[Pseud.: J.C.H. Wages]
Strassburg 1805-1864 Berlin
Ref: Brüm 19, Ko Th

Ein Arzt - C1 - Fr (1869)
    Bn:1847  Ha:1845  Va:1851
    Wm:1850
s'Lorle o. Der Berliner im
Schwarzwald - F1 (1866)
    Fr:1851  Ha:1851
überall Irrtum - F1
    Ha:1857
Der Weihnachtsabend - Fr
    Fr:1855  Ha:1848

**HEUFELD, FRANZ**
Mainau 1731-1795 Vienna
Ref: Brüm 18, Goe 4/1, Ko Th,
ADB, NDB

Der Bauer aus dem Gebirge in
Wien - C3 - Fr (1767)
    Va:1767
Doktor Guldenschnitt - C5
(1781)
    Va:1782
Der Geburtstag - C3 (1767)
    Va:1779
Julie o. Wettstreit der
Pflicht und Liebe - C3 (1766)
    Ha:1767
Die Tochter des Bruder
Philipps - C1 (1771)
    Va:1769

**HEUN, CARL GOTTLIEB SAMUEL**
see Clauren, Heinrich

**HEYDEN, FRIEDRICH AUGUST von**
Nerfken 1789-1851 Breslau
Ref: Brüm 18, Goe 10, Ko Th,
ADB, NDB

Album und Wechsel - C5 (1842)
    Bn:1839
Das Feuer im Walde - D1
(1819)
    Dr:1821  Va:1820

Der Geschäftsführer - C5
(1842)
    Bn:1841
Haß, Ritterpflicht und Liebe
- D3 (1819)
    Va:1819
Die Modernen - C5 (1842)
    Bn:1840
Nadine - T5 (1842)
    Bn:1842
Renata - D5 (1816)
    Dr:1817    Ha:1818    Lg:1816
    Mu:1823

**HEYNE, CHRISTIAN LEBERECHT**
see Wall, Anton

**HEYSE, PAUL**
Berlin 1830-1914 Munich
Ref: Brüm 19, Ko Th, NDB, OC

Alkibiades - T3 (1880)
    Bn:1885    Wm:1882
Colburg - D5 (1868)
    Bn:1865    Da:1885    Lg:1882
    Mh:1877    Mu:1869    Wm:1870
Don Juans Ende - T5 (1883)
    Fr:1884    Lg:1885    Va:1885
Ehre um Ehre - D5 (1875)
    Bn:1869    Fr:1869    Mu:1874
    Va:1875    Wm:1869
Ehrenschulden - T1 (1884)
    Fr:1884    Mu:1886    Wm:1885
Elfride - T (1877)
    Mu:1883
Elisabeth Charlotte - D5
(1864)
    Bn:1860    Da:1860    Dr:1860
    Ha:1860    Mh:1860    Mu:1860
    Wm:1860
Die Franzosenbraut - D
    Mu:1871
Frau Lucrezia - T1 (1884)
    Fr:1885    Mu:1886    Wm:1885
Der Friede - D (1871)
    Mu:1871
Getrennte Welten - D (1886)
    Mu:1884
Die glücklichen Bettler - D3
- It (1867)
    Mu:1867    Wm:1870
Gott schütze mich vor meinen
Freunden - C (1888)
    Fr:1887
Graf Königsmark - T5 (1877)
    Fr:1883    Mu:1878
Die Grafen von der Esche - D5
    Da:1861    Va:1861

Hans Lange - D4 (1866)
    Bn:1864    Da:1865    Fr:1871
    Ha:1865    Lg:1865    Mh:1865
    Mu:1866    Va:1864    Wm:1865
Die Hochzeit auf dem Aventin
- T5 (1886)
    Fr:1885
Im Bunde der Dritte - D1
(1889)
    Fr:1883    Mu:1883    Va:1889
In sittlicher Entrüstung - C1
    Bn:1888
Ludwig der Bayer (1862)
    Mu:1862
Maria Moroni - T5 (1865)
    Bn:1866
Nur keinen Eifer - C1 (1889)
    Wm:1886
Prinzessin Sascha - D4 (1888)
    Wm:1888
Das Recht des Stärkeren - D3
(1883)
    Bn:1884    Wm:1888
Die Sabinerinnen - T5 (1859)
    Bn:1860    Mu:1858    Va:1859
    Wm:1858
Ein überflüssiger Mensch - D4
(1890)
    Wm:1889
Unter Brüdern - C1 (1884)
    Fr:1884    Mu:1885
Unter den Gründlingen - C
    Mu:1879
Der Venusdurchgang - C1
(1889)
    Fr:1885
Die Weisheit Salomos - D5
(1886)
    Mu:1890    Wm:1887
Weltuntergang - FP5 - (1889)
    Bn:1889    Wm:1889

**HIEMER, FRANZ KARL**
Rothenacker 1768-1822
Stuttgart
Ref: Brüm 18, Goe 7, Ko Th,
ADB, NDB

Der Totenschein - C3 - Fr
    Mh:1803

**HILL, ANNA**
Frankfurt/M 1860-1912
Frankfurt/M
Ref: Brüm 19, Ko Th

Compromittiert - F1 (1889)
    Fr:1890
Diana - F1 (1887)
    Fr:1888

**HILLER, F. C.**

Alte Sünden -C1 - Fr
    Dr:1851  Fr:1862
Der Regimentsprediger - Vv1
    Fr:1854

**HILLERN, WILHELMINE von**
Munich 1836-1916 Hohenaschau
Ref: Brüm 19, Ko Th, NDB

Die Augen der Liebe - C3
(1878)
    Bn:1876  Va:1878
Ein Autographensammler - D1
(1874)
    Bn:1870  Da:1877  Fr:1868
Die Geier-Wally - D5 (1880)
    Bn:1881  Da:1882  Fr:1882
    Lg:1882  Mu:1880  Wm:1880
Guten Abend - C1 (1873)
    Bn:1865

**HILTL, GEORG JOHANN**
Berlin 1826-1878 Berlin
Ref: Ko Th

Der Copist - D1 - Fr (1869)
    Bn:1858  Dr:1858  Fr:1860
    Ha:1859  Va:1858
Haß aus Liebe - D1 - Fr
    Bn:1858
Ein prächtiger alter Knabe -
C1 - Fr
    Bn:1853
Der Ritter der Damen - C1 -
Fr
    Bn:1857  Fr:1862  Ha:1857
    Wm:1857
Weiße Haare - C1 - Fr
    Fr:1865
Ein Zundhölzchen zwischen
zwei Frauen - F - Fr
    Fr:1866

**HINSBERG, JOSEF von**
Falkenstein 1764-1836 Munich
Ref: Brüm 18, Goe 6, Ko 3

Der Advokat o. Wer wird wohl
den Prozeß gewinnen? - C5
    Va:1788

**HIPPEL, THEODOR GOTTLIEB von**
Gerdauen 1741-1796 Königsberg
Ref: Brüm 18, Goe 4/1, Ko Th,
ADB, NDB, OC

Der Mann nach der Uhr - C1
(1760)
    Dr:1779  Ha:1767  Lg:1774
    Wm:1772

**HIRSCH, ARNOLD**
Horzitz 1815-1896 Vienna
Ref: Brüm 19, Ko Th

Blanca von Bourbon - T5
(1860)
    Dr:1860
Der Familiendiplomat - C3
(1859)
    Bn:1861  Da:1860  Dr:1860
    Fr:1860  Va:1860
Eine Gewissensfrage - D1 - Fr
    Va:1867
Postscriptum - C1 - Fr
    Va:1869
Eine Tour aus dem Contre-
Tanze - C1 - Fr (1862)
    Va:1862
Zu jung und zu alt - C1
(1864)
    Va:1866

**HIRSCH, FRANZ WILHELM**
Thorn 1844-1920 Berlin
Ref: Brüm 19, Ko 3

Der verlorene Sohn - D1
(1878)
    Lg:1879

**HOFFMANN, LEOPOLD ALOIS**
Niederwitting 1760 [1748?]-
1806 Wiener-Neustadt
Ref: Brüm 18, Goe 5, Ko Th,
NDB

Die Abenteuer des Herzens -
o. Suchen macht Finden - C5
(1786)
    Va:1785
Das Werther-Fieber - D5
    Va:1785

**HOFMANN, GEORG von**
Vienna 1769 [1771?] - 1845
Vienna
Ref: Goe 11, Ko 3

Das Jagdschloß - C3
    Bn:1828  Va:1819
Das Landleben - C3
    Va:1817
Ludwig und Louise o. Der 9.
Thermidor - D5
    Va:1815

**HOLBEIN, E.**

Mazarins Pathe - C2
  Dr:1859

**HOLBEIN, FRANZ IGNAZ von**
[Pseud.: Breitenstein]
Zistersdorf 1779-1855 Vienna
Ref: Brüm 18, Goe 6, Ko Th,
ADB, NDB

Das Alpenröslein, das Patent
und der Shawl - D3 (1822)
  Bn:1824  Da:1821  Dr:1820
  Fr:1821  Ha:1820  Lg:1824
  Mh:1821  Mu:1823  Va:1820
  Wm:1822
Der Brautschmuck - D5 (1811)
  Dr:1808  Va:1807.
Cagliostro - D1
  Bn:1833
Der Doppelgänger - C4
  Bn:1832  Da:1844  Dr:1833
  Fr:1834  Ha:1832  Lg:1834
  Mu:1832  Va:1832  Wm:1834
Einer von Beiden - C3 - Fr
  Va:1824
Fridolin - D2 (1806)
  Bn:1807  Da:1810  Dr:1806
  Fr:1808  Lg:1827  Mh:1807
  Mu:1806  Va:1806  Wm:1809
Der Fürst und der Minnesänger
- C4
  Va:1831
Genieren Sie sich nicht - C1
(1826)
  Bn:1826  Fr:1826  Va:1825
Der Jugendfreund - C3 - Fr
(1839)
  Bn:1840  Dr:1839
Der Krämer und die Herzogs-
braut - TC4
  Ha:1834
Leonidas - D5 (1812)
  Bn:1815  Fr:1815  Lg:1815
Liebe kann alles o. Die
bezähmte Widerspenstige - C4
- Eng (1822)
  Ha:1824  Lg:1822  Mh:1827
  Mu:1829
Die Männerschule - C3 - Fr
  Bn:1828  Dr:1831
Maria Petenbeck - D5 (1833)
  Bn:1833  Fr:1834  Ha:1833
Die Maskerade [Die Schlitten-
fahrt] o. Der Herr vom Hause
- C4
  Fr:1831  Lg:1831

Meister Martin der Küfner und
seine Gesellen - C5 (1825)
  Da:1829  Fr:1825  Mh:1825
  Va:1824  Wm:1829
Die Nachschrift - C1 (1826)
  Bn:1815  Lg:1815  Va:1815
Pantoffel und Degen - C4
  Da:1853  Fr:1861  Ha:1841
  Wm:1841
Die Proberollen - F1
  Bn:1815  Da:1816  Dr:1822
  Fr:1809  Lg:1815  Mh:1808
  Va:1807  Wm:1815
Der Regenschirm - C1
  Bn:1832  Ha:1833
Stadt und Land - C3 (1825)
  Bn:1825
Die Städterin und das Dorf-
mädchen - C2 - Fr
  Mu:1806
Der Stellvertreter - C2
  Bn:1847
Das Turnier zu Kronstein o.
Die drei Wahrzeichen - D5
(1820)
  Da:1818  Dr:1818  Fr:1818
  Ha:1820  Lg:1819  Mh:1820
  Mu:1826  Va:1818  Wm:1819
Der Tyrann von Syrakus o. Die
Bürgschaft - D5
  Fr:1810  Va:1806
Übereilung und Argwohn - D2
  Fr:1810  Va:1808
Die verhängnisvolle Wette o.
Gabriele von Belle-Isle - D5
Fr (1839)
  Bn:1843  Dr:1844  Fr:1841
  Ha:1840  Wm:1867
Der Verräter - C1 (1811)
  Bn:1811  Da:1814  Dr:1818
  Fr:1828  Ha:1820  Lg:1818
  Mh:1810  Va:1810  Wm:1814
Die Verräterin - C1 (1840)
  Da:1840  Wm:1836
Der Verstorbene - D3 (1811)
  Mh:1830  Va:1811
Der Vorsatz - C1 - (1819)
  Bn:1812  Da:1819  Dr:1809
  Lg:1819  Mu:1816  Va:1808
  Wm:1821
Die Waffenbrüder - D5 (1824)
  Fr:1824  Ha:1836  Va:1823
Das Wiedersehen - D1 (1812)
  Bn:1808  Da:1813  Fr:1810
  Lg:1815  Mu:1816  Va:1807
Der Wunderschrank - C4 (1823)
  Bn:1828  Da:1823  Dr:1822
  Fr:1822  Ha:1822  Lg:1822
  Mu:1822  Va:1822  Wm:1823

Der Zauberpark o. Der Liebe
Scherz und Ernst - C1
    Va:1836
Die Zufälle - C5 - Eng (1825)
    Va:1825

**HOLLPEIN, HEINRICH**
Vienna 1814-1888 Vienna
Ref: Ko Th

Er experimentiert - C1 (1861)
    Bn:1861  Fr:1862  Ha:1866
    Va:1861
In Ketten und Banden - C1
    Va:1866
Recrut und Dichter - C2
    Va:1863

**HOLSTEIN, FRANZ FRIEDRICH von**
Braunschweig 1826-1878 Leip-
zig
Ref: Ko Th, ADB

Der Heideschacht (1866)
    Mh:1873
Die Hochländer (1878)
    Mh:1876

**HOLTEI, KARL EDUARD von**
Breslau 1798-1880 Breslau
Ref: Brüm 18, Goe 9, Ko Th,
ADB, NDB, OC

Arm und reich - C
    Fr:1826
Der Berliner Droschken-
kutscher - C1 (1845)
    Dr:1836
Die Berliner in Wien - F1
(1825)
    Bn:1824  Lg:1825
Der Dichter im Versammlungs-
zimmer - C1
    Fr:1830
Dreiunddreißig Minuten in
Grüneberg - F1 (1839)
    Bn:1840  Da:1851  Dr:1836
    Fr:1853  Va:1842
Der dumme Peter - D2 (1836)
    Bn:1831  Da:1840  Ha:1836
    Lg:1833  Va:1835
Erich der Geizhals - D4
(1844)
    Bn:1842  Va:1841
Die Farben - C1 (1828)
    Bn:1824  Da:1822

Hans Jürge - D1 (1839)
    Bn:1833  Da:1858  Dr:1836
    Fr:1844  Ha:1833  Lg:1833
    Mu:1833  Va:1878
Jung oder alt? - C3 (1855)
    Bn:1855
Leonore - D3 (1829)
    Bn:1828  Da:1841  Dr:1833
    Fr:1829  Ha:1828  Lg:1870
    Mh:1829  Mu:1833  Va:1829
    Wm:1829
Lorbeerbaum und Bettelstab o.
Drei Winter eines Dichters -
D3 (1840)
    Bn:1833  Da:1851  Dr:1838
    Fr:1839  Ha:1833  Lg:1833
    Mu:1833  Wm:1853
Die Majoratsherren - D3
(1832)
    Bn:1830  Da:1831  Ha:1830
    Va:1835  Wm:1830
Margarete - F1 (1833)
    Bn:1832  Wm:1846
Robert der Teufel - D5 (1845)
    Bn:1831  Da:1831
Sechsunddreißig Jahre aus dem
Leben zweier Liebenden - F2
    Bn:1829  Mh:1830
Shakespeare in der Heimat o.
Die Freunde - D4 (1845)
    Bn:1840  Dr:1836  Fr:1839
    Ha:1840  Mu:1864  Va:1835
    Wm:1837
Sie schreibt an sich selbst -
C1 - Fr (1845)
    Bn:1841  Da:1860  Dr:1860
    Fr:1860  Ha:1857  Mu:1868
    Va:1842
Die Sterne - D4 (1845)
    Lg:1824
Der Theaterdiener - C1
    Dr:1836
Ein Trauerspiel in Berlin -
D3 (1838)
    Bn:1832  Ha:1833  Lg:1833
Die weiblichen Drillinge - C1
(1845)
    Da:1859  Dr:1836  Fr:1852
    Ha:1845  Va:1834
Die Wiener in Berlin - F1
(1824)
    Bn:1824  Da:1830  Dr:1825
    Fr:1825  Ha:1824  Lg:1824
    Mh:1825  Wm:1826
Die Wiener in Paris o. Der
12. Februar - D2 (1839)
    Bn:1855  Da:1857  Dr:1854
    Fr:1856  Ha:1849  Va:1835
    Wm:1850

Zum grünen Baum - D (1849)
    Ha:1849

**HOMBERG**

Ungesund - F1
    Va:1880

**HOMBURG, C.**

Eine Tasse Tee - C1 - Fr
    Bn:1862

**HOPFEN, HANS von**
Munich 1835-1904 Groß-
Lichterfelde
Ref: Brüm 19, Ko Th, NDB, OC

Aschenbrödel in Böhmen - D4
(1869)
    Lg:1869
Er hat so sollen sein - C
(1893)
    Fr:1889  Mu:1890
In der Mark - D5 (1870)
    Bn:1870  Da:1890  Fr:1885
    Lg:1886  Mh:1872  Mu:1885
    Wm:1872
Mutterglück - D3 - Fr
    Va:1865
Trudels Ball - C1
    Mu:1890  Wm:1889

**HOPP, FRIEDRICH**
Brünn 1789-1869 Vienna
Ref: Brüm 18, Ko Th

Doktor Fausts Zauberkäppchen
- F3 (1843)
    Da:1843  Dr:1843  Fr:1840
    Mh:1840  Wm:1865

**HORMAYR zu HORTENBURG, JOSEF**
Innsbruck 1781-1848 Munich
Ref: Goe 6, Ko Th, ADB, NDB,
OC

Friedrich von Österreich - D5
(1805)
    Va:1805
Leopold der Schöne - D5
(1806)
    Va:1806

**HORN, GEORG**
Bayreuth 1831-1897 Potsdam
Ref: Brüm 19, Ko Th

Das Brunnenmädchen - C4
    Da:1877  Fr:1863  Ha:1867

Experimente des Herzens - D4
    Fr:1859
Glückliche Flitterwochen - C1
(1860)
    Dr:1856  Fr:1855
Eine glühende Kohle - C1 -
with F. Wehl - (1861)
    Bn:1873  Dr:1857
Mademoiselle Bertin - C4
    Bn:1868
Unter dem Reichskammergericht
- C4
    Bn:1861  Fr:1862
Was die Welt regiert - C4
    Bn:1866  Mu:1868

**HORN, OTTO** see Bäuerle, Adolf

**HORN, UFFO DANIEL**
Trautenau 1817-1860 Trautenau
Ref: Brüm 19, Ko Th, ADB

Der Naturmensch - C4 - with
W. Gerle
    Ha:1839  Va:1840
Die Vormundschaft - C2 - with
W. Gerle (1836)
    Bn:1837  Dr:1839  Va:1837
    Wm:1837

**HORNBOSTEL, AUGST GOTTLIEB**
see Bohl, Otto Ernst

**HORNER, A. von**

Er ist nicht liebenswürdig -
C1
    Va:1874

**HORST, C. von** see Cramm
[-Burgdorf], C.F.Burghard

**HOSAUS, FRIEDRICH WILHELM**
Dessau 1827-1900 Dessau
Ref: Brüm 19, Ko Th

Johanna von Castilien - D5 -
Sp (1871)
    Wm:1870

**HOUWALD, ERNST von**
Straupitz 1778-1845 Lübben
Ref: Brüm 18, Goe 8, Ko Th,
ADB, NDB, OC

Die alten Spielkameraden - D2
(1823)
    Dr:1822  Ha:1822

Das Bild - T5 (1821)
    Bn:1821  Da:1821  Dr:1820
    Fr:1820  Ha:1820  Lg:1821
    Mh:1822  Mu:1820  Va:1821
    Wm:1820
Die Feinde - D3 (1825)
    Bn:1825  Dr:1824  Mh:1826
    Mu:1824  Va:1824  Wm:1825
Fluch und Segen - D2 (1821)
    Bn:1820  Da:1821  Dr:1820
    Fr:1821  Ha:1821  Lg:1821
    Mh:1823  Mu:1821  Wm:1821
Die Freistatt - T1 (1825)
    Da:1819  Lg:1822
Der Fürst und der Bürger - D3
(1823)
    Bn:1823  Da:1823  Dr:1823
    Ha:1824  Lg:1823  Mh:1830
    Wm:1824
Die Heimkehr - T1 (1821)
    Bn:1818  Da:1829  Dr:1818
    Fr:1819  Ha:1821  Lg:1819
    Mh:1821  Wm:1821
Der Leuchtturm - D2 (1821)
    Bn:1820  Dr:1820  Fr:1820
    Ha:1821  Lg:1821  Mh:1824
    Mu:1820  Va:1822  Wm:1821
Niemand kann seinem Schicksal
entgehen - F1 (1825)
    Da:1822
Die Seeräuber - T5 (1831)
    Va:1831
Der Schuldbrief - D1 (1833)
    Bn:1825  Da:1834

**HOYER, L.** see Ompteda, Baron
von

**HUBER, FRANZ XAVER**
Beneschau 1755-1809 Vienna
Ref: Brüm 18, Goe 5, Ko Th,
NDB

Julchen o. Liebe Mädchen,
spiegelt euch! - C5 (1793)
    Fr:1794  Va:1793
Die unvermutete Entdeckung o.
Nicht jeder Bräutigam ist so
glücklich - C5 (1795)
    Va:1795

**HUBER, LUDWIG FERDINAND**
Paris 1764-1804 Ulm
Ref: Brüm 18, Goe 5, Ko Th,
ADB, NDB, OC

Die Abenteuer einer Nacht -
C3 - Sp (1789)
    Bn:1789  Mh:1789

Der englische Kaper - C1
    Dr:1782  Ha:1787  Mh:1783
    Wm:1783
Ethelwolf o. Der König kein
König - D5 - Eng (1785)
    Dr:1785  Mh:1785
Das heimliche Gericht - T5
(1795)
    Mh:1790
Leichtsinn und kindliche
Liebe - C5 - Eng
    Mh:1795
Die magnetische Wunderkraft -
C2 - Fr (1790)
    Wm:1793
Der natürliche Sohn - D5 - Fr
    Bn:1804  Mh:1807
Offene Fehde - C3 - Fr (1788)
    Bn:1788  Da:1813  Dr:1787
    Ha:1787  Lg:1787  Mh:1787
    Wm:1789
Der verliebte Briefwechsel -
C5 - Fr (1797)
    Bn:1799  Dr:1799  Mh:1798
    Va:1798
Wer erst kommt, mahlt erst -
C3 - Fr
    Bn:1802

**HÜBNER, LORENZ**
Donauwörth 1751 [1752?]-1807
Munich
Ref: Brüm 18, Goe 5, Ko Th,
NDB

Kamma o. Die Heldin Bojariens
- D5 (1784)
    Bn:1785

**HUGO, KARL** [Pseud. of Karl
Hugo Bernstein]
Budapest 1808-1877 Milan
Ref: Brüm 19, Ko Th, ADB

Des Hauses Ehre - D3 (1859)
    Bn:1859  Da:1861

**HUNNIUS, ANTON CHRISTIAN**
Capellendorf 1764-?
Ref: Goe 4, Ko 3

Der Taubstumme - C3 (1791)
    Bn:1796  Fr:1799  Ha:1790
    Va:1792  Wm:1791

**HUSCHBERG, JOHANN FERDINAND**
Düsseldorf 1792-1852 Würzburg
Ref: Goe 11, ADB

Hannibal - T5 (1820)
  Va:1814

**HUTT, JOHANN**
Vienna 1774-1809 Vienna
Ref: Brüm 18, Goe 5, Ko Th

Der Buchstabe - C1 (1805-12)
  Ha:1823    Va:1807
Das war ich - C1 (1805-12)
  Bn:1807    Da:1810    Dr:1820
  Fr:1805    Ha:1864    Lg:1820
  Mh:1804    Mu:1868    Va:1803
  Wm:1812
Hab' ich nicht recht? - C3
(1805-12)
  Dr:1805    Fr:1805    Mh:1806
  Va:1804
Die Probe - C3 (1805-12)
  Ha:1824    Va:1808
Der rechte Weg - D1 (1805-12)
  Fr:1817    Va:1804
Die Wendungen - C2 (1805-12)
  Va:1808


**IFFLAND, AUGUST WILHELM**
Hanover 1759-1814 Berlin
Ref: Brüm 18, Goe 5, Ko Th,
ADB, NDB, OC

Achmed und Zenide - D5 (1798)
  Dr:1797    Mu:1815    Va:1796
Die Advokaten - D5 (1800)
  Bn:1795    Da:1811    Dr:1795
  Fr:1797    Ha:1815    Lg:1799
  Mh:1795    Mu:1796    Va:1795
  Wm:1796
Albert von Thurneisen - T5
(1788)
  Bn:1799    Dr:1782    Fr:1802
  Ha:1783    Lg:1782    Mh:1781
  Mu:1789    Va:1799    Wm:1799
Allzu scharf macht schartig -
D5 (1800)
  Bn:1793    Da:1818    Ha:1792
  Mh:1794    Mu:1793    Va:1793
  Wm:1794
Alte und neue Zeit - D5
(1799)
  Bn:1795    Da:1819    Fr:1792
  Ha:1792    Mh:1796    Mu:1794
  Va:1792    Wm:1794
Die Aussteuer - D5 (1799)
  Bn:1794    Da:1812    Dr:1794
  Fr:1795    Ha:1797    Mh:1795
  Mu:1798    Va:1794    Wm:1796

Das Bewußtsein - D5 (1788)
  Bn:1788    Dr:1787    Ha:1787
  Lg:1787    Mh:1786    Mu:1787
  Va:1802    Wm:1792
Die Brautwahl - D1 (1808)
  Bn:1826    Da:1825    Mh:1808
  Va:1808
Dienstpflicht - D5 (1800)
  Bn:1795    Da:1812    Dr:1794
  Fr:1796    Ha:1815    Lg:1803
  Mh:1795    Mu:1795    Va:1794
  Wm:1795
Die eheliche Probe - C1 - Eng
  Va:1801
Elise von Walberg - D5 (1799)
  Bn:1792    Da:1812    Dr:1813
  Fr:1791    Ha:1791    Lg:1806
  Mh:1791    Mu:1801    Va:1794
  Wm:1791
Das Erbteil des Vaters - D4
(1802)
  Bn:1800    Fr:1805    Lg:1801
  Wm:1802
Erinnerung - D5 (1799)
  Bn:1797    Da:1810    Dr:1797
  Fr:1798    Ha:1797    Lg:1798
  Mh:1798    Va:1797    Wm:1797
Die Familie Lonau - C5 (1802)
  Dr:1802    Fr:1803    Va:1801
Frauenstand - C5 (1799)
  Bn:1799    Da:1791    Ha:1790
  Mu:1792    Va:1790    Wm:1792
Friedrich von Österreich - D5
(1799)
  Dr:1791    Ha:1790
Der Fremde - C5 (1800)
  Bn:1798    Da:1811    Dr:1798
  Fr:1801    Ha:1801    Lg:1799
  Mh:1804    Va:1799    Wm:1799
Die Geflüchteten - D1 (1799)
  Mh:1795
Das Gewissen - D5 (1799)
  Bn:1797    Dr:1797    Mh:1797
  Wm:1797
Der gutherzige Polterer - C3
Sp (1812)
  Bn:1811    Lg:1818    Mh:1811
  Va:1812    Wm:1812
Die Hagestolzen - C5 (1799)
  Bn:1792    Da:1815    Dr:1791
  Fr:1792    Ha:1791    Lg:1799
  Mh:1791    Mu:1794    Va:1792
  Wm:1793
Die Hausfreunde - D5 (1808)
  Bn:1805    Dr:1805    Fr:1806
  Lg:1805    Mh:1805    Va:1805

Hausfrieden - C5 (1799)
    Bn:1796   Da:1814   Dr:1797
    Fr:1797   Ha:1796   Lg:1797
    Mh:1797   Mu:1816   Va:1797
    Wm:1797
Die Heimkehr - D5
    Bn:1806   Fr:1806   Mh:1806
    Va:1806
Heinrich des Fünften Jugend-
jahre - C3 - Fr (1808)
    Bn:1815   Da:1819   Fr:1809
    Mh:1809   Mu:1806
Der Herbsttag - D5 (1799)
    Bn:1791   Da:1812   Dr:1791
    Fr:1793   Ha:1790   Lg:1810
    Mh:1790   Mu:1793   Va:1791
    Wm:1791
Die Höhen - D5 (1801)
    Bn:1800   Da:1814   Va:1800
    Wm:1803
Hoffnung der Ruhe
    Ha:1788
Die Jäger - D5 (1786)
    Bn:1785   Da:1810   Dr:1785
    Fr:1792   Ha:1791   Lg:1785
    Mh:1785   Mu:1786   Va:1786
    Wm:1791
Die Kokarden - T5 (1800)
    Mu:1792
Der Komet - F1 (1799)
    Dr:1799   Fr:1808   Va:1798
    Wm:1798
Die Künstler - D5 (1801)
    Bn:1799   Dr:1800   Va:1800
Leichter Sinn - D5 (1799)
    Bn:1797   Da:1814   Dr:1797
    Ha:1797   Lg:1799   Mh:1798
    Va:1798   Wm:1797
Die Liebe auf dem Lande - C2
    Ha:1847   Va:1877
Der Magnetismus - C1 - (1788)
    Bn:1798   Da:1813   Dr:1787
    Fr:1787   Ha:1816   Lg:1787
    Mh:1787   Mu:1789   Va:1814
Der Mann von Wort - D5 (1800)
    Bn:1798   Dr:1798   Fr:1801
    Mh:1801   Va:1798   Wm:1801
Mittelweg ist Tugendprobe -
D5
    Mh:1788
Die Mündel - D5 (1786)
    Bn:1785   Da:1820   Dr:1785
    Fr:1792   Ha:1785   Lg:1785
    Mh:1784   Mu:1787   Va:1787
    Wm:1791
Der Oheim - C5 (1807)
    Dr:1806   Va:1806

Die Reise nach der Stadt - C5
(1800)
    Bn:1794   Da:1814   Dr:1793
    Fr:1794   Ha:1794   Mh:1794
    Va:1794   Wm:1794
Reue versöhnt - D5 (1798)
    Bn:1789   Dr:1789   Mu:1789
    Wm:1792
Die Ringe - D1
    Bn:1813
Scheinverdienst - D5 (1802)
    Bn:1794   Da:1818   Fr:1793
    Ha:1792   Mh:1794   Mu:1793
    Va:1793   Wm:1793
Die Seelenwanderung - C4
    Bn:1805
Selbstbeherrschung - D5
(1800)
    Bn:1798   Da:1819   Dr:1799
    Fr:1799   Lg:1799   Mh:1799
    Mu:1802   Va:1798   Wm:1800
Der Spieler - D5 (1800)
    Bn:1796   Da:1810   Dr:1795
    Fr:1796   Ha:1847   Lg:1796
    Mh:1796   Mu:1796   Va:1795
    Wm:1796
Das Vaterhaus - D5 (1802)
    Bn:1800   Da:1810   Fr:1800
    Ha:1801   Lg:1803   Mh:1800
    Mu:1801   Va:1800   Wm:1800
Verbrechen aus Ehrsucht - D5
(1786)
    Bn:1784   Da:1812   Dr:1784
    Fr:1797   Ha:1784   Lg:1784
    Mh:1784   Mu:1784   Va:1784
    Wm:1792
Das Vermächtnis - D5 (1799)
    Bn:1796   Da:1813   Dr:1795
    Fr:1795   Lg:1816   Mh:1797
    Mu:1796   Va:1795   Wm:1795
Der Veteran - D1 (1798)
    Bn:1798
Der Vormund - D5 (1800)
    Bn:1793   Da:1794   Fr:1795
    Ha:1794   Mh:1793   Mu:1796
    Va:1793   Wm:1794
Der Vorsatz
    Fr:1792
Vorurteile - D5
    Dr:1792   Fr:1792   Lg:1792
Wie man's treibt, so geht's -
C5
    Mh:1781
Wilhelm von Schenk - D5
    Mh:1781

**IMMERMANN, KARL LEBERECHT**
Magdeburg 1796-1840
Düsseldorf
Ref: Brüm 18, Goe 8, Ko Th,
ADB, NDB, OC

Alexis - T5 (1832)
   Mu:1885
Andreas Hofer o. Das Trauer-
spiel in Tirol - D5 (1828)
   Ha:1829   Mh:1845   Va:1863
   Wm:1853
Kaiser Friedrich der Zweite -
T5 (1828)
   Bn:1829   Ha:1829
Die Opfer des Schweigens
[Ghismonda] - D5 (1839)
   Bn:1838   Ha:1838   Wm:1838
Die schelmische Gräfin - C1
(1828)
   Bn:1827   Da:1828   Ha:1844
   Wm:1840
Das Tal von Ronceval - T
(1822)
   Fr:1823
Die Verkleidungen - C3 (1828)
   Bn:1829   Ha:1829


**JAFFE, RICHARD**
Posen 1861-1920 Berlin
Ref: Brüm 19, Ko Th

Das Bild des Signorelli - D4
(1900)
   Da:1890   Fr:1890   Mu:1890

**JEITTELES, ALOIS**
Brünn 1794-1858 Brünn
Ref: Goe 7, Ko Th, ADB, NDB,
OC

Auge und Ohr - C3 - Sp
   Va:1837
Die Hausgenossen - C3
   Fr:1845   Va:1843
Der Liebe Wahn und Wahrheit -
D3
   Va:1842

**JENTS, KARL**   see Stein, Karl

**JERRMANN, EDUARD**
Berlin 1798-1859 Berlin
Ref: Brüm 18, Ko Th, ADB

Ehrgeiz in der Küche
   Mh:1836

Der Schlaftrunk [Katharina
Howard] - T5 - Fr
   Dr:1834   Fr:1838   Ha:1834
   Wm:1836
Sybilla die Flamänderin - D5
Fr
   Bn:1854

**JERUSALEM, ERNST**
1845-?

Die Borgia - D5
   Lg:1876

**JESTER, ERNST FRIEDRICH**
Königsberg 1743-1822 Königs-
berg
Ref: Brüm 18, Goe 4/1, Ko Th,
ADB

Doktor Tonuccio - C5
   Bn:1798   Dr:1798   Mh:1798
   Va:1798
Das Duell o. Das junge Ehe-
paar - C1 (1769)
   Bn:1771   Dr:1778   Fr:1777
   Ha:1775   Mh:1779   Mu:1778
   Va:1769   Wm:1772
Freemann o. Wie wird das ab-
laufen? - D4
   Bn:1790   Dr:1791   Ha:1790
   Mh:1790   Va:1802
Die Trauer - C1 - Fr
   Dr:1777   Va:1769
Der Weise in der Tat o. Die
Hochzeit voller Unruhe - D5 -
Fr
   Va:1768

**JODOK** see Gumppenberg, Hanns
von

**JORDAN, WILHELM**
Insterburg 1819-1904 Frank-
furt/M
Ref: Brüm 19, Ko Th, NDB, OC

Durch's Ohr - C3 (1870)
   Bn:1878   Da:1884   Lg:1879
   Mh:1865   Mu:1878   Va:1882
   Wm:1876
Der falsche Fürst - D4
   Fr:1857
Graf und Grobschmied - D5
   Fr:1881
Die Liebesleugner - C3 (1855)
   Da:1855   Fr:1855   Mh:1855
   Wm:1855

Sein Zwillingsbruder - C5
(1883)
    Fr:1884  Mu:1879
Tausch enttäuscht - C5 (1884)
    Fr:1856
Die Witwe des Agis- T3 (1858)
    Bn:1859  Fr:1883  Mu:1858

**JÜNGER, JOHANN FRIEDRICH**
Leipzig 1759-1797 Vienna
Ref: Brüm 18, Goe 4/1, Ko Th,
ADB, NDB

Die Badekur - C2 (1785)
    Bn:1782  Dr:1782  Fr:1797
    Ha:1782  Lg:1782  Mh:1784
    Va:1784
Barbarossa - D5
    Dr:1795
Die beiden Figaro - C5 - Fr
(1804)
    Da:1826  Dr:1796  Fr:1833
    Mh:1822  Va:1799  Wm:1803
Die beiden Portraits o. Er
ist schwer zu befriedigen -
C1
    Da:1789  Mh:1785  Va:1784
Die Charlatans o. Der Kranke
in der Einbildung - C3 (1803)
    Dr:1796  Fr:1803  Va:1798
Dank und Undank - C3 - Fr
(1803)
    Dr:1789  Va:1788
Der doppelte Liebhaber - C3 -
Fr (1786)
    Bn:1787  Dr:1787  Va:1786
Das Ehepaar aus der Provinz -
C4 (1792)
    Dr:1791  Fr:1793  Mh:1793
    Va:1791  Wm:1792
Die Entführung - C3 (1792)
    Bn:1791  Dr:1787  Fr:1791
    Ha:1790  Lg:1812  Mh:1791
    Mu:1816  Va:1790  Wm:1792
Er mengt sich in alles - C5 -
Eng (1793)
    Bn:1791  Da:1811  Dr:1791
    Fr:1793  Lg:1791  Mh:1792
    Va:1791  Wm:1793
Die Flucht aus Liebe - C5
(1804)
    Dr:1796  Va:1801
Freundschaft und Argwohn - D5
(1785)
    Bn:1783  Dr:1782  Va:1793
Die Geschwister vom Lande -
C5 (1795)
    Bn:1792  Da:1814  Dr:1792
    Fr:1793  Mh:1793  Va:1791
    Wm:1794

Der Instinkt o. Wer ist der
Vater zum Kinde? - C1 - Fr
(1789)
    Bn:1786  Mh:1787  Va:1785
Das Kleid aus Lyon - C4
(1788)
    Dr:1787  Ha:1787  Mh:1788
    Va:1787
Der Krug geht so lange zum
Wasser, bis er bricht - C3
(1803)
    Dr:1794  Va:1798
Die Komödie aus dem Stegreif
- C1 - Fr (1795)
    Da:1813  Dr:1778  Fr:1817
    Ha:1816  Lg:1820  Mh:1780
    Va:1794
Maske für Maske - C3 - Fr
(1795)
    Bn:1792  Da:1814  Dr:1791
    Fr:1794  Lg:1812  Mh:1792
    Va:1792  Wm:1795
Der offene Briefwechsel - C5
(1785)
    Bn:1785  Fr:1792  Lg:1784
    Mh:1808  Va:1784  Wm:1786
Der Revers - C5 (1788)
    Bn:1788  Da:1810  Dr:1788
    Fr:1799  Ha:1790  Lg:1788
    Mh:1788  Va:1788  Wm:1792
Ein seltner Fall o. Die Mut-
ter, die Vertraute ihrer
Tochter - C3 - Fr (1803)
    Bn:1796  Dr:1798  Va:1798
Der Strich durch die Rechnung
- C4 (1785)
    Bn:1785  Da:1813  Dr:1783
    Fr:1792  Ha:1784  Lg:1783
    Mh:1785  Va:1784  Wm:1791
Stolz und Liebe - C5 (1804)
    Dr:1799  Va:1797
Der tolle Tag o. Die Hochzeit
des Figaro - C5 - Fr (1804)
    Va:1802
Der Ton unserer Zeiten - C1 -
Fr (1792)
    Dr:1794  Va:1804
Die unvermutete Wendung - C5
Eng (1793)
    Dr:1793  Mh:1790  Va:1789
Verstand und Leichtsinn - C5
(1786)
    Bn:1786  Dr:1786  Fr:1794
    Mh:1786  Va:1786  Wm:1791
Was sein soll, schickt sich
wohl - C3 (1803)
    Bn:1795  Dr:1794

Der Wechsel - C4 (1789)
   Bn:1795   Dr:1789   Fr:1792
   Ha:1790   Mh:1789   Mu:1790
   Va:1788   Wm:1791
Das Weiberkomplott - C5 - Fr
(1786)
   Dr:1785   Va:1785

**JUSTINUS, OSKAR** [Pseud. of
Oskar Justinus Cohn]
Breslau 1839-1893 Bad Nauheim
Ref: Brüm 19, Ko Th

Die Ehestifterin - C1
   Bn:1888
Gesellschaftliche Pflichten -
F4 - with H. Wilken (1881)
   Lg:1883
Griechisches Feuer - D4
(1887)
   Lg:1885   Va:1886
Der Herr Kommerzienrat [Kom-
merzienrat Königsberger] - D5
(1883)
   Fr:1883
Unser Zigeuner - C3 (1878)
   Da:1885   Fr:1880

**JUSTUS, M.**

Elisabeth Vernon - D4
   Wm:1882

**KADELBURG, GUSTAV**
Budapest 1851-1925 Berlin
Ref: Brüm 19, Ko Th, NDB

Die berühmte Frau - C3 - with
F. Schöntan (1899)
   Da:1888   Fr:1888   Mu:1888
   Wm:1888
Die Goldfische - C3 - with
F. Schöntan (1886)
   Da:1887   Fr:1887   Lg:1887
   Mu:1887   Va:1887   Wm:1887

**KAFFKA, JOHANN CHRISTOPH**
Regensburg 1754-1815 Riga
Ref: Brüm 18, Goe 5, Ko Th

Die Tempelherrn - T5 (1796)
   Wm:1791

**KAIBEL, KARL LUDWIG**
?-1864?
Ref: Goe 11, Ko Th

Benno von Flandern - D4
   Mh:1813
Die Dummköpfe - C1 - Fr
   Mh:1809
Die Jubelfeier - D1
   Mh:1816
Die Schildwache - D2 (1825)
   Da:1824   Mh:1809
Die verheirateten Junggesel-
len - C1
   Mh:1808

**KAISER, FRIEDRICH**
Biberach 1814-1874 Vienna
Ref: Brüm 19, Ko Th, ADB, NDB

Die Collecte - C
   Ha:1845
Die Dienstboten-Wirtschaft -
F4 (1852)
   Ha:1844
Doktor und Friseur o. Die
Sucht nach Abenteuern - F2
(1853)
   Fr:1850   Ha:1845
Ein edler Lump - F5 (1862)
   Fr:1886
Etwas Kleines - F3 (1861)
   Ha:1857
Die Frau Wirtin - D3 (1861)
   Da:1866   Ha:1856
Gute Nacht, Rosa! - D1 (1865)
   Va:1861
Jagdabenteuer - F2 (1864)
   Fr:1865
Junker und Knecht - F4 (1850)
   Fr:1851   Ha:1851
Mir fällt nichts ein - C2
   Fr:1852
Mönch und Soldat - D3 (1850)
   Fr:1850   Ha:1850   Lg:1867
Müller und Schiffmeister - F2
(1853)
   Ha:1844
Eine Posse als Medicin - F3
(1850)
   Fr:1852   Ha:1850
Des Schauspielers letzte
Rolle - C3 (1851)
   Fr:1849   Ha:1845
Sie ist verheiratet - F3
   Ha:1848
Stadt und Land - F4 (1872)
   Fr:1846   Ha:1844
Die Stumme von Ingouville -
D2
   Ha:1851
Verrechnet - F3 (1862)
   Fr:1852   Ha:1851

Der Zigeuner - F3 (1842)
    Fr:1852  Ha:1845

**KALCHBERG, JOHANN NEPOMUK von**
Schloß Pichl 1765-1827 Graz
Ref: Brüm 18, Goe 5, Ko Th,
ADB, NDB

Attila, König der Hunnen - T5
(1817)
    Dr:1813  Lg:1811
Wülfing von Stubenberg - D5
(1802)
    Va:1794

**KALISCH, DAVID**
Breslau 1820-1872 Berlin
Ref: Brüm 19, Ko Th, ADB,
NDB, OC

Die Aktienbudiker - F3 (1870-
71)
    Fr:1857  Ha:1856
Berlin bei Nacht - F3 (1850)
    Fr:1850  Ha:1849
Berlin [Das Volk], wie es
weint und lacht - FP3 - with
O.F.Berg
    Fr:1859  Wm:1859
Berlin wird Weltstadt - Vv1
(1870-71)
    Ha:1866
Börsenglück - F
    Fr:1852
Doctor Peschke - F1 (1870-71)
    Fr:1860  Ha:1857
Einer von unsre Leut - F3 -
with O.F.Berg (1859)
    Da:1861  Dr:1860  Fr:1860
    Ha:1860  Mu:1863  Wm:1866
Ein gebildeter Hausknecht -
F1 (1858)
    Da:1858  Dr:1858  Fr:1860
    Ha:1858  Mu:1861
Hunderttausend Taler - F3
(1848)
    Ha:1848
Die Mottenburger - F2  - with
A. Weihrauch
    Ha:1868
Münchhausen - F3
    Fr:1853  Ha:1853
Namenlos - F3 - with E. Pohl
(1863)
    Fr:1867  Ha:1864
Eine orientalische Frage - F1
(1863)
    Fr:1854

Otto Bellmann - F3 - Fr
(1857)
    Ha:1857
Peter Schlemihl - F1 (1850)
    Fr:1850
Sonntagsjäger o. Verplefft -
F1 - with G. Moser (1876)
    Fr:1863  Wm:1863
Vom Juristentage - F1 - with
A. Langer
    Fr:1863

**KALTENBRUNNER, KARL ADAM**
Enns 1804-1867 Vienna
Ref: Brüm 19, Ko 3, ADB, NDB

Ulrike - D5
    Va:1845

**KAMP, OTTO**
Coblenz 1850-1922 Bonn
Ref: Brüm 19, Ko Th

Der Volkszähler - C1 (1885)
    Fr:1885

**KARLWEIS, C.**  see Weiss, Karl

**KEIM, FRANZ**
Alt-Lambach 1840-1918 Brunn
am Gebirge
Ref: Brüm 19, Ko Th, NDB

Sulamith - T5 (1875)
    Va:1876

**KEMPELEN, LUDWIG von**

Das Bild des Bruders - D5
    Va:1835

**KERR, MAX**

Das Opferlamm - F3
    Lg:1885

**KETTE, HERMANN**  [Pseud.: Karl
Heinrich]
Einwinkel 1828-1908 Steglitz
Ref: Brüm 19, Ko Th

Carolina Brocchi - D5 (1876)
    Bn:1876
Friedrich des Großen Schwur-
gericht - D5 (1883)
    Wm:1883
König Saul - T5 (1860)
    Bn:1857

Nur keinen Studierten - F4
(1877)
    Lg:1883    Wm:1881

**KETTEL, JOHANN GEORG**
Brünn 1789-1862 Stuttgart
Ref: Goe 11, Ko Th, ADB

ABC - F2 - Eng
    Bn:1834    Da:1836    Dr:1836
    Fr:1834    Ha:1833    Wm:1834
Der betrogene Betrüger - C -
Fr
    Fr:1842
Drei Frauen und keine - F1 -
Fr (1838)
    Bn:1835    Dr:1839    Fr:1836
    Ha:1845    Wm:1838
Die falschen Vertraulich-
keiten - C3 - Fr
    Lg:1820
Der Findling - C2
    Bn:1833    Ha:1834
Ein Geheimnis - C3 - Fr
    Dr:1843    Fr:1843    Va:1844
Halifax - C4 - Fr
    Dr:1846
Der Kammerdiener des Emi-
granten - C2 - Fr
    Da:1855
Das lebende Bild - C3 - Fr
    Dr:1850
Richards Wanderleben - C4 -
Eng (1832)
    Bn:1831    Da:1837    Dr:1831
    Fr:1831    Ha:1831    Lg:1832
    Mh:1832    Mu:1831    Va:1832
    Wm:1832
Die Scheidung - C3 - Fr
    Bn:1850    Dr:1832    Ha:1833
    Lg:1832    Mu:1832
Vor Torschluß - F1 - Fr
(1858)
    Ha:1840    Lg:1844

**KETTENBURG, KUNO von der**
ca. 1775-1813 Schloß Schwerin
Ref: Brüm 18, Goe 6, Ko 3

Diego - T5 (1811)
    Bn:1812

**KIND, JOHANN FRIEDRICH**
Leipzig 1768-1843 Dresden
Ref: Brüm 18, Goe 9, Ko Th,
ADB, NDB

Der Abend am Waldbrunnen - D1
(1818)
    Bn:1818    Dr:1819    Lg:1818

Der Kirchhof von Savelthem -
D1
    Dr:1819
Die Morgenstunde [Das Morgen-
stündchen] - C1 (1806)
    Bn:1808    Dr:1807    Wm:1809
Das Nachlager in Granada - D2
(1817)
    Bn:1826    Da:1819    Dr:1818
    Fr:1818    Ha:1818    Mh:1820
    Va:1818    Wm:1824
Der Orangenbaum - C1 (1808)
    Bn:1815    Da:1814    Dr:1812
Petrus Appianus o. Achtung
der Wissenschaften - D2
(1818)
    Dr:1820    Va:1818
Die Truhe - D1 (1822)
    Da:1822    Dr:1821    Fr:1820
    Ha:1821
Van Dyks Landleben - D5
(1817)
    Bn:1830    Da:1828    Dr:1816
    Fr:1826    Ha:1818    Lg:1819
    Va:1817    Wm:1825

**KINKEL, JOHANN GOTTFRIED**
Oberkassel 1815-1882 Zurich
Ref: Brüm 19, Ko Th, ADB,
NDB, OC

Nimrod - T5 (1857)
    Lg:1878

**KISTNER, ANNA**   see Albert,
Anny

**KLÄGER, FRIEDRICH WILHELM**
Berlin 1817-1875 Braunschweig
Ref: Brüm 19, Ko Th, ADB

Abenteuer im Schloßgarten -
C1
    Da:1859
Ein Besuch Carl Seydelmanns -
D1
    Da:1860
Blumengift - C3 (1876)
    Da:1865
Ein Küchenroman - D1 (ca.
1872)
    Fr:1866
Ludwig Devrient - C1 (1869)
    Fr:1876
Der Präsident - C1 (1863)
    Da:1860    Dr:1861    Fr:1860
    Ha:1860    Mu:1872    Wm:1864

**KLÄHR, KARL**    [Pseud.: Karl
Fero]
Dresden 1773-1842 Meißen
Ref: Goe 6, Ko Th

Die Lotterielisten - C1
(1811)
    Bn:1819  Fr:1824  Wm:1813
Das Wachscabinet - C2 (1816)
    Dr:1817  Lg:1817

**KLAPP, MICHAEL**
Prague 1836-1888 Vienna
Ref: Brüm 19, Ko Th

Fräulein Kommerzienrat - C4
    Bn:1882  Fr:1882
Der Glückshafen - C4
    Fr:1881
Rosenkranz und Güldenstern -
C4 (1885)
    Bn:1884  Da:1879  Fr:1879
    Lg:1879  Mu:1879  Va:1878
Der selige Paul - C4 (1888)
    Va:1888

**KLAUSSMANN, ANTON OSKAR**
Breslau 1851-1916 Berlin
Ref: Ko 3

Alfreds Briefe - F4 - with
F. Brentano (1886)
    Fr:1886  Lg:1886  Wm:1886

**KLEIN, ANTON von**
Molsheim 1746-1810 Mannheim
Ref: Brüm 18, Goe 4/1. Ko Th,
ADB, NDB

Kaiser Rudolph - T (1787)
    Ha:1790  Mh:1810

**KLEIN, JULIUS LEOPOLD**
Miskolcz/Hungary 1810-1876
Berlin
Ref: Brüm 19, Ko Th, ADB,
NDB, OC

Heliodora - T5 (1867)
    Wm:1878
Die Herzogin - C5 (1848)
    Bn:1848  Mu:1871
Maria - T5 (1860)
    Bn:1859
Der Schützling - C3 (1850)
    Wm:1854
Zenobia - T5 (1844)
    Bn:1846  Fr:1885  Mu:1885

**KLEIST, HEINRICH von**
Frankfurt/O 1777-1811 Berlin
Ref: Goe 6, Ko Th, ADB, NDB,
OC

Die Hermannsschlacht - D5
(1821)
    Bn:1875  Dr:1861  Ha:1861
    Lg:1880  Mu:1871  Va:1875
    Wm:1888
Das Kätchen von Heilbronn o.
Die Feuerprobe - D5 (1810)
    Bn:1824  Da:1828  Dr:1819
    Fr:1816  Ha:1816  Lg:1820
    Mh:1813  Mu:1816  Va:1810
    Wm:1822
Penthesilea - T3 (1803)
    Bn:1876
Der Prinz von Homburg o. Die
Schlacht bei Fehrbellin - D5
(1821)
    Bn:1828  Da:1846  Dr:1821
    Fr:1821  Ha:1822  Lg:1827
    Mh:1826  Mu:1822  Va:1821
    Wm:1823
Die Waffenbrüder o. Die
Familie Schroffenstein - T5
(1803)
    Bn:1824  Da:1824  Fr:1824
    Ha:1836  Lg:1822  Mh:1826
    Va:1823
Der zerbrochene Krug - C3
(1811)
    Bn:1822  Da:1824  Dr:1828
    Fr:1832  Ha:1820  Mh:1827
    Mu:1846  Va:1850  Wm:1808

**KLEMM, CHRISTIAN GOTTLOB**
Schwarzenberg 1736-1811
Vienna
Ref: Brüm 18, Goe 5, Ko Th,
ADB

Der Schuldenmacher - C3
(1776)
    Va:1773
Die Schule der Liebhaber o.
Die Wahl eines Ehemanns - C3
- Eng (1767)
    Va:1776

**KLESHEIM, ANTON von**
Peterwardein 1809 [1812?
1816?]-1884 Baden/Vienna
Ref: Goe 5, Ko Th

Herr Spul o. Echtheit ohne
Schimmer - C5
    Va:1794

Die Kornwucherer - D5
   Dr:1798
Prüfung der Frauengeduld o.
Die Wiedervereblichung - D5
   Va:1793
Die Österreicher - C1
   Va:1796
Die Stiefmutter - D5
   Bn:1797  Dr:1797  Va:1795

**KLINGEMANN, AUGUST FRIEDRICH**
Braunschweig 1777-1831 Braun-
schweig
Ref: Brüm 18, Goe 6, Ko Th,
ADB, NDB, OC

Alfonso der Große - D5 (1820)
   Da:1813  Dr:1813  Fr:1812
   Lg:1812
Die Braut vom Kynast - D4
(1830)
   Bn:1828  Dr:1828
Die Brautnacht im Norden - T5
   Dr:1814
Columbus - D4 (1811)
   Bn:1809  Da:1814  Dr:1810
   Fr:1809  Ha:1822  Mh:1821
   Mu:1816
Deutsche Treue - D4 (1816)
   Bn:1812  Da:1814  Dr:1812
   Fr:1817  Ha:1814  Lg:1814
   Mh:1822  Wm:1823
Die Entdeckung von Amerika
[Die E. der neuen Welt] - D1
(1808)
   Da:1814  Dr:1809  Fr:1809
   Ha:1822  Mu:1816
Der ewige Jude [Ahasver] - T5
(1827)
   Bn:1825  Dr:1846  Mu:1827
Der Falkenstein - D1 (1824)
   Mh:1831  Wm:1826
Faust - T5 (1818)
   Bn:1816  Da:1822  Dr:1817
   Fr:1817  Lg:1816  Mh:1817
   Mu:1822
Die Maske - T5 (1797)
   Mu:1806  Wm:1797
Moses - D5 (1821)
   Bn:1831  Dr:1815  Fr:1820
   Ha:1816  Lg:1816  Mh:1820
Oedipus und Jokaste - T5
(1820)
   Bn:1812  Dr:1814  Wm:1813
Rodrigo und Chimene - T5 - Fr
(1817)
   Dr:1813  Mu:1813  Va:1813

Schill o. Das Deklamatorium
in Krähwinkel - C3 (1821)
   Bn:1810  Da:1811  Fr:1810
   Mh:1810
Das Vehmgericht - D5 (1820)
   Bn:1810  Da:1811  Dr:1814
   Fr:1810  Ha:1816  Mh:1810
   Mu:1810
Welf von Trudenstein o. Die
Grube zur Dorothea - D5
(1817)
   Fr:1813  Ha:1813  Mh:1813

**KLINGER, FRIEDRICH MAXIMILIAN**
Frankfurt/M 1752-1831 Dorpat
Ref: Brüm 18, Goe 4/1, Ko Th,
ADB, NDB, OC

Die falschen Spieler - C5
(1786)
   Va:1782
Der Günstling - T5 (1787)
   Mh:1787
Konradin von Schwaben - T5
(1786)
   Bn:1791  Fr:1793  Mh:1787
Stilpo und seine Kinder - T5
(1787)
   Ha:1783
Sturm und Drang - D5 (1786)
   Fr:1777  Lg:1777
Die Zwillinge - T5 (1776)
   Bn:1783  Dr:1781  Ha:1776
   Lg:1781  Va:1777

**KNEBEL, KARL LUDWIG**
Schloß Wallerstein 1744-1834
Jena
Ref: Brüm 18, Goe 4/1, ADB,
NDB, OC

Saul - T5 (1829)
   Wm:1811

**KNEISEL, RUDOLF**
Königsberg 1832-1899 Berlin
Ref: Brüm 19, Ko Th, ADB

Chemie für's Heiraten - F3
(1894)
   Da:1878
Desdemonas Taschentuch - F4
   Fr:1887  Lg:1887
Emmas Roman - C4 (1883)
   Fr:1879  Lg:1878
Die große Unbekannte - F4
   Lg:1886
Das Haus der Wahrheit - F4
   Va:1883

Die Kuckucks - C4 (1881)
  Lg:1882
Die Lieder des Musikanten -
FP4 (1866)
  Fr:1874   Wm:1861
Sein einziges Gedicht - F3
(1885)
  Lg:1878
Sie weiß etwas - F4 (1894)
  Fr:1886   Lg:1885
Die Tochter Belials - C5
(1872)
  Da:1872   Lg:1876
Wo ist die Frau? - C4
  Lg:1885
Eine Zeitungsente - F3
  Fr:1860

**KOBELL, FRANZ von**
Munich 1803-1882 Munich
Ref: Brüm 19, Ko 3, ADB, NDB,
OC

Die Brugger Marie - C
  Mu:1868

**KÖBERLE, GEORG**
Nonnenhorn 1819-1898 Dresden
Ref: Brüm 19, Ko Th, ADB

Heinrich IV. von Frankreich -
T5 (1851)
  Fr:1851   Wm:1852
Max Emanuels Brautfahrt - D
(1873)
  Mu:1870

**KOBERSTEIN, KARL FERDINAND**
Schulpforta 1836-1899 Berlin
Ref: Brüm 19, Ko Th, ADB

König Erich XIV. - T5 (1869)
  Bn:1871   Mu:1870
Was Gott zusammenfügt, das
soll der Mensch nicht schei-
den o. Um Nancy - C5 (1872)
  Bn:1873   Fr:1873   Lg:1872

**KOCH, KARL WILHELM**
Vienna 1785-1860 Vienna
Ref: Brüm 18, Ko Th

Er bezahlt alle - C1 - Fr
(1836)
  Dr:1834   Va:1834
Fester Wille o. Die Frau von
30 Jahren - C5 - Fr (1838-41)
  Va:1838

Das geraubte Kind - D2 - **Fr**
(1838-41)
  Va:1836
Haß und Liebe - C2 (1838-41)
  Va:1835
Die Jugendfreundin - C2 - Fr
(1838-41)
  Bn:1836   Dr:1838   Fr:1840
Die junge Pate - C1 - Fr
  Va:1832
Der Militair-Befehl - C2
(1838-41)
  Bn:1837   Ha:1838   Lg:1839
Nach Mitternacht - F1 - Fr
  Wm:1862
Ein nächtliches Abenteuer - C
  Ha:1845
Das Testament einer armen
Frau - D5 - Fr (1836)
  Fr:1835   Va:1833
Verläumdung - D4 - Fr
  Va:1841
Vierundzwanzig Stunden
Königin - C3
  Dr:1840
Die Vorleserin - D2 - Fr
(1836)
  Da:1865   Dr:1835   Fr:1836
  Ha:1836   Mu:1839   Va:1835
  Wm:1851

**KOHL von KOHLENEGG, LEOPOLD**
see Henrion, Poly

**KÖHLER, BRUNO**
Greiz 1855-1925 Berlin
Ref: Brüm 19, Ko Th

In dem Strudel - F4 (1886)
  Lg:1886

**KOLLER, BENEDIKT JOSEF**
Binddorf 1767-1817 Stuttgart
Ref: Brüm 18, Goe 5, Ko Th,
ADB

Der Hauskrieg - D5 - It
  Va:1807
Konrad, Herzog von Zähringen
- D5 (1814)
  Fr:1800
Künstlerrache - C1 - Fr
  Da:1817
Der Oculist - C5 (1800)
  Fr:1800

**KÖLLNER**

Die Erfüllung - T1
  Wm:1813

**KOMARECK, JOHANN NEPOMUK**
Prague 1757–after 1819
Ref: Goe 5, Ko Th

Ida o. Das Vehmgericht – D5
(1792)
   Wm:1793

**KÖNNERITZ, C. von**

Der Maler – C4
   Dr:1860

**KOPPEL-ELLFELD, FRANZ**
Eltville 1838–1920 Dresden
Ref: Brüm 19, Ko Th

Auf Kohlen – C5 (1873)
   Lg:1873
Marguerite – D (1887)
   Mu:1885

**KÖRNER, KARL THEODOR**
Dresden 1791–1813 Gadebusch
Ref: Brüm 18, Goe 7, Ko Th,
ADB, NDB, OC

Die Braut – C1 (1815)
   Bn:1814   Da:1814   Dr:1812
   Fr:1816   Ha:1816   Lg:1819
   Va:1812   Wm:1812
Die Gouvernante – F1 (1815)
   Bn:1818   Fr:1816   Wm:1819
Der grüne Domino o. Der un-
sichtbare Bräutigam – C1
(1815)
   Bn:1812   Da:1814   Dr:1813
   Fr:1816   Lg:1814   Mh:1815
   Mu:1822   Va:1812   Wm:1812
Hedwig, die Banditenbraut –
D3 (1815)
   Bn:1815   Da:1817   Dr:1815
   Fr:1813   Ha:1815   Lg:1815
   Mh:1816   Mu:1830   Va:1813
   Wm:1815
Der Nachtwächter – F1 (1812)
   Bn:1815   Da:1815   Dr:1821
   Fr:1816   Ha:1816   Lg:1818
   Mh:1815   Va:1812   Wm:1813
Rosamunde – T5 (1814)
   Bn:1815   Da:1815   Dr:1815
   Fr:1814   Lg:1815   Mu:1815
   Mu:1817   Wm:1816
Die Sühne o. Der 24. Mai – T1
   Wm:1812

Toni o. Die Franzosen auf
Domingo – D3 (1815)
   Bn:1812   Da:1816   Dr:1814
   Fr:1816   Ha:1816   Lg:1818
   Mh:1813   Mu:1816   Va:1812
   Wm:1812
Vater und Sohn o. Die un-
sichtbare Braut – C1
   Da:1815   Mh:1815   Wm:1812
Der Vetter aus Bremen – C1
(1815)
   Bn:1814   Dr:1815   Fr:1813
   Ha:1816   Lg:1821   Mh:1814
   Va:1812   Wm:1816
Zriny – T5 (1814)
   Bn:1814   Da:1815   Dr:1814
   Fr:1815   Ha:1816   Lg:1815
   Mh:1821   Mu:1817   Wm:1812
   Wm:1816

**KOROMPAY, JOSEPH**
Brünn ?–?
Ref: Goe 5, Ko Th

Anna Boleyn, Königin von Eng-
land – T5 (1794)
   Va:1792
Rudolph von Felseck o. Die
Schwarzthaler Mühle – D5
(1794)
   Va:1792

**KÖSTER, HANS**
Kritzow 1818–1900 Ludwigslust
Ref: Brüm 19, Ko Th

Der große Kurfürst – D5
(1851)
   Bn:1851
Hermann der Cherusker – D5
(1861)
   Bn:1862   Wm:1860
Ulrich von Hutten – T5 (1846)
   Wm:1865

**KOSTIA, KARL**   see Costa, Karl

**KÖSTING, KARL**
Wiesbaden 1842–1907 Dresden
Ref: Brüm 19, Ko Th

Im großen Jahr – D5 (1874)
   Lg:1874
Die neue Welt – D
   Fr:1872

**KOTZEBUE, AUGUST von**
Weimar 1761–1819 Mannheim
Brüm 19, Goe 5, Ko Th, ADB,
NDB, OC

Die Abendstunde - C1 (1809)
    Da:1815   Fr:1832   Va:1811
Adelheid von Italien - D6
Va:1823
Der alte Jüngling - F1 - Fr
    Wm:1821
Der alte Leibkutscher Peters
III. - C1 (1899)
    Da:1812
Die alten Liebschaften - C1
(1812)
    Bn:1812   Da:1811   Fr:1811
    Mh:1811   Va:1811   Wm:1811
Das arabische Pulver - F2
    Da:1812
Der arme Minnesänger - C1
(1811)
    Bn:1813   Da:1821
Der arme Poet - C1 (1813)
    Bn:1812   Da:1812   Dr:1812
    Fr:1812   Ha:1812   Lg:1817
    Mh:1812   Mu:1816   Va:1812
    Wm:1812
Armut und Edelsinn - C3
(1795)
    Bn:1794   Da:1810   Dr:1794
    Fr:1796   Ha:1793   Lg:1794
    Mh:1794   Mu:1795   Va:1794
    Wm:1795
Aufopferung - D3
    Bn:1796
Die barmherzigen Brüder - D1
(1803)
    Bn:1803   Da:1814   Dr:1815
Bayard - D5 (1801)
    Bn:1800   Da:1811   Dr:1800
    Fr:1802   Ha:1801   Lg:1820
    Mh:1800   Mu:1822   Wm:1801
    Wm:1800
Die beiden kleinen Auvergna-
ten D1 - Fr (1813)
    Da:1813   Dr:1813   Fr:1819
    Mh:1813   Wm:1813
Die beiden Klingsberge - C4
(1801)
    Bn:1799   Da:1811   Dr:1799
    Fr:1799   Ha:1816   Lg:1812
    Mh:1799   Va:1799   Wm:1799
Die Belagerung von Saragossa
o. Pachter Feldkümmels Hoch-
zeitstag - C4 (1811)
    Bn:1810   Da:1815   Dr:1811
    Mh:1812   Mu:1816
Belas Flucht - D2 (1813)
    Da:1813   Dr:1812   Fr:1812
    Mh:1812   Mu:1816
Die Bestohlenen - C1 (1817)
    Ha:1816   Mh:1817   Wm:1817

Der Besuch o. Die Sucht zu
glänzen - C4 (1802)
    Bn:1800   Da:1822   Dr:1801
    Fr:1800   Ha:1800   Mh:1801
    Va:1800   Wm:1800
Blind geladen - C1 (1811)
    Bn:1811   Da:1811   Dr:1810
    Fr:1811   Ha:1810   Lg:1830
    Mh:1811   Wm:1811
Blinde Liebe - C3 (1806)
    Bn:1805   Da:1812   Dr:1806
    Ha:1806   Va:1807   Wm:1807
Die Brandschatzung - C1
(1806)
    Bn:1805   Da:1810   Dr:1806
    Fr:1806   Ha:1805   Lg:1819
    Mh:1806   Mu:1816   Va:1827
    Wm:1808
Braut und Bräutigam in einer
Person - F2 (1814)
    Bn:1827   Da:1814   Dr:1814
    Fr:1814   Ha:1820   Mh:1815
    Va:1813
Der Brief aus Cadix - D3
(1813)
    Bn:1811   Da:1812   Dr:1811
    Fr:1811   Ha:1811   Lg:1816
    Mh:1812   Va:1811   Wm:1821
Bruder Moritz der Sonderling
- C3 (1791)
    Bn:1790   Dr:1790   Fr:1793
    Ha:1790   Lg:1791   Mh:1792
    Mu:1791   Wm:1791
Bruderzwist - D5 (1797)
    Bn:1832   Da:1811   Fr:1797
    Ha:1796   Mh:1797   Mu:1816
    Va:1796
Carolus Magnus - C3 (1806)
    Bn:1827   Dr:1820   Fr:1810
    Mu:1816
Colomanns Rache - D2
    Va:1815
Cora - D5
    Dr:1793
Die Corsen - D4 (1799)
    Bn:1798   Da:1810   Dr:1797
    Fr:1798   Ha:1797   Lg:1804
    Mh:1798   Va:1797   Wm:1798
Deodata - D4
    Dr:1820   Fr:1813
Der Deserteur - F1 (1808)
    Bn:1807   Da:1813   Lg:1796
    Va:1817   Wm:1808
Die deutsche Hausfrau - D3
(1813)
    Bn:1813   Da:1817   Fr:1812
    Ha:1820   Lg:1819   Mh:1812
    Va:1812   Wm:1812

Der deutsche Mann und die
vornehmen Leute - D4 (1818)
    Bn:1817  Fr:1818  Mh:1818
Die deutschen Kleinstädter -
C4 (1803)
    Bn:1802  Da:1810  Dr:1802
    Fr:1802  Ha:1802  Lg:1817
    Mh:1802  Mu:1803  Va:1802
    Wm:1803
Don Ranundo de Colibrados -
C4 (1803)
    Da:1810  Fr:1802  Lg:1802
    Mh:1812  Va:1815  Wm:1803
Das Dorf im Gebirge - D2
(1798)
    Bn:1814  Dr:1818  Ha:1811
    Lg:1823  Mh:1817  Va:1798
Drei Väter auf einmal - C1
    Da:1816  Fr:1816  Ha:1815
    Mh:1816
Die edle Lüge - D1 (1792)
    Bn:1794  Fr:1792  Ha:1791
    Wm:1791
Eduard in Schottland - D3
(1804)
    Bn:1803  Da:1811  Dr:1803
    Fr:1804  Ha:1820  Lg:1822
    Mh:1803  Mu:1816  Va:1804
Der Edukationsrat - C1
    Bn:1822  Da:1815  Dr:1821
    Fr:1816  Lg:1823  Mh:1816
    Va:1816  Wm:1816
Die eifersüchtige Frau - C2
- Eng (1820)
    Bn:1820  Da:1819  Dr:1820
    Fr:1820  Ha:1820  Lg:1822
    Mh:1822  Va:1819  Wm:1820
Die englischen Waren - F2
(1809)
    Bn:1815  Da:1815  Fr:1814
    Ha:1816  Wm:1810
Die Entdeckung im Posthause -
C1
    Wm:1817
Das Epigramm - C4 (1801)
    Bn:1798  Da:1811  Dr:1798
    Fr:1801  Lg:1817  Mh:1799
    Va:1798  Wm:1799
Die Erbschaft - C1 - It
(1808)
    Bn:1808  Da:1811  Dr:1807
    Fr:1808  Mh:1810  Mu:1808
    Va:1810  Wm:1810
Der Eremit auf Formentera -
D2 (1784)
    Dr:1790  Mu:1790  Va:1793
Falsche Scham - D4 (1798)
    Bn:1796  Fr:1813  Fr:1796
    Ha:1795  Mh:1796  Va:1796
    Wm:1796

Fedor und Pauline - C4
    Bn:1809
Die Feuerprobe - C1 (1811)
    Bn:1813  Da:1811  Fr:1811
    Mh:1811  Va:1815  Wm:1813
Die französischen Klein-
städter - C4 - Fr (1803)
    Bn:1802  Dr:1804  Fr:1808
    Va:1802  Wm:1802
Die Freimaurer - C1 - It
(1818)
    Bn:1817  Da:1817  Dr:1818
    Fr:1818  Lg:1819  Mh:1818
    Wm:1817
Der Gala-Tag in Krähwinkel -
C3
    Da:1812  Fr:1807  Lg:1821
    Mh:1807
Die gefährliche Nachbarschaft
[Schneider Fips] - C1 (1806)
    Bn:1813  Da:1810  Dr:1816
    Fr:1803  Ha:1816  Lg:1816
    Mh:1810  Va:1806  Wm:1806
Der Gefangene - C1 (1800)
    Bn:1832  Da:1815  Dr:1799
    Va:1798
Der gerade Weg der beste - C1
(1817)
    Bn:1816  Da:1817  Fr:1816
    Lg:1820  Mh:1817  Mu:1816
    Wm:1817
Das Gespenst - D4 (1808)
    Dr:1811
Das Geständnis [Die Beichte]
- C1 (1806)
    Bn:1806  Da:1810  Dr:1814
    Fr:1805  Ha:1805  Lg:1806
    Mh:1806  Mu:1816  Wm:1806
Das geteilte Herz - C1 (1813)
    Bn:1812  Da:1813  Dr:1813
    Fr:1812  Ha:1815  Lg:1818
    Mh:1814  Va:1812  Wm:1813
Gisela - D4 (1817)
    Bn:1817  Fr:1819  Mh:1821
    Wm:1818
Die Glücklichen - C1 (1811)
    Bn:1810  Da:1814  Va:1811
Graf Benjowsky o. Die Ver-
schwörung auf Kamtschatka -
D5 (1795)
    Bn:1798  Da:1818  Dr:1803
    Fr:1794  Ha:1794  Lg:1796
    Mh:1796  Va:1794  Wm:1792
Der Graf von Burgund - D4
(1798)
    Bn:1795  Da:1811  Dr:1796
    Fr:1796  Ha:1795  Lg:1805
    Mh:1796  Mu:1815  Va:1795
    Wm:1816

Die Großmama - C1 (1816)
    Bn:1816   Da:1816   Dr:1816
    Ha:1815   Lg:1816   Mh:1817
    Mu:1816   Va:1816   Wm:1816
Gustav Wasa - D5 (1801)
    Bn:1800   Da:1811   Dr:1800
    Fr:1800   Ha:1801   Mh:1801
    Mu:1800   Va:1800   Wm:1800
Der Hahnenschlag - D1 (1803)
    Bn:1803   Da:1810   Dr:1803
    Fr:1805   Mh:1805   Va:1803
    Wm:1807
Des Hasses und der Liebe
Rache - D5 (1816)
    Bn:1815   Da:1816   Dr:1815
    Fr:1815   Ha:1815   Mh:1816
    Mu:1816   Wm:1815
Der häusliche Zwist - C1 -
(1810)
    Bn:1810   Da:1810   Dr:1810
    Fr:1810   Ha:1820   Lg:1809
    Mh:1809   Mu:1816   Va:1809
    Wm:1812
Heinrich Reuß von Plauen o.
Die Belagerung von Marienburg
- D5 (1805)
    Bn:1805   Da:1814   Dr:1814
    Fr:1814   Mh:1825   Va:1810
Die hübsche kleine Putz-
macherin - C1 - Fr (1805)
    Da:1823   Dr:1805   Va:1804
Hugo Grotius - D4 (1803)
    Bn:1803   Fr:1804   Va:1803
    Wm:1804
Die Hussiten vor Naumburg im
Jahre 1432 - D5 (1803)
    Bn:1802   Da:1815   Dr:1803
    Fr:1803   Ha:1804   Lg:1802
    Mh:1803   Va:1803   Wm:1804
Die Indianer in England - C3
(1790)
    Bn:1789   Da:1811   Dr:1790
    Fr:1792   Ha:1789   Lg:1819
    Mh:1790   Mu:1790   Va:1790
    Wm:1791
Das Intermezzo o. Der Land-
junker zum ersten Mal in der
Residenz - C5 (1809)
    Bn:1808   Da:1810   Dr:1808
    Fr:1808   Ha:1816   Lg:1817
    Mh:1808   Mu:1816   Va:1808
    Wm:1809
Johanna von Montfaucon - D5
(1800)
    Bn:1799   Da:1810   Dr:1799
    Fr:1801   Ha:1816   Lg:1799
    Mh:1800   Mu:1823   Va:1799
    Wm:1804
Kaiser Claudius - D1 (1807)
    Da:1813   Fr:1806

Kapitän Belronde - C3 - Fr
(1817)
    Da:1818   Dr:1820   Fr:1818
    Lg:1820   Wm:1819
Das Kind der Liebe - D4
(1790)
    Bn:1790   Da:1813   Dr:1814
    Fr:1794   Ha:1790   Lg:1790
    Mh:1790   Mu:1792   Va:1791
    Wm:1791
Der kleine Deklamator - D1
(1809)
    Bn:1816   Da:1810   Mh:1813
    Va:1810
Die kleine Zigeunerin - D4
(1809)
    Bn:1809   Da:1810   Ha:1809
    Mh:1817   Wm:1816
Die kluge Frau im Wald o. Der
stumme Ritter - D5 (1801)
    Bn:1827   Da:1820   Dr:1799
    Fr:1801   Mu:1816   Va:1799
Die Komödiantin aus Liebe -
C1 (1811)
    Bn:1813   Da:1812   Mh:1811
Die Kreuzfahrer - D5 (1803)
    Bn:1802   Da:1810   Dr:1814
    Fr:1803   Ha:1815   Lg:1808
    Mh:1804   Mu:1816   Wm:1818
Das Landhaus an der Heer-
straße - C1 (1809)
    Bn:1809   Da:1810   Dr:1809
    Fr:1814   Ha:1808   Mh:1810
    Va:1810
Lasarilla - D5
    Dr:1809
Der Leineweber - D1 (1808)
    Bn:1816   Da:1811   Dr:1808
    Fr:1832   Va:1807
Das liebe Dörfchen - D1
(1807)
    Da:1813   Dr:1808   Fr:1807
    Ha:1816   Mh:1819
Der liefländische Tischler -
D3 - Fr
    Va:1809
Lohn der Wahrheit - D5 (1801)
    Bn:1799   Da:1810   Dr:1799
    Fr:1802   Mh:1799   Va:1798
    Wm:1799
Der Lügenfeind - D1 (1812)
    Da:1814   Fr:1811   Mh:1812
    Va:1811
Das Lustspiel am Fenster - F1
(1807)
    Da:1815   Fr:1814   Va:1817
Mädchenfreundschaft o. Der
türkische Gesandte - C1
(1805)
    Bn:1805   Wm:1824

Der Mann von vierzig Jahren -
C1 - Fr (1795)
    Bn:1794   Dr:1796   Fr:1803
    Va:1795   Wm:1795
Marie - D1 (1818)
    Dr:1819   Ha:1817   Mh:1819
    Va:1817
Die Masken - D1 (1813)
    Bn:1818   Da:1813   Dr:1812
    Fr:1812   Va:1812
Max Helfenstein - C2 (1811)
    Bn:1811   Da:1812   Dr:1811
    Fr:1811   Mh:1811   Mu:1816
    Wm:1811
Menschenhaß und Reue - D5
(1789)
    Bn:1789   Da:1813   Dr:1789
    Fr:1792   Ha:1789   Lg:1789
    Mh:1789   Mu:1790   Va:1789
    Wm:1791
Die Nachtmütze des Propheten
Elias - F1 (1814)
    Da:1813
Die Negersklaven - D (1795)
    Fr:1795
Die neue Frauenschule - C3 -
Fr (1811)
    Bn:1811   Da:1812   Dr:1812
    Fr:1811   Ha:1816   Mh:1811
    Va:1813   Wm:1811
Das neue Jahrhundert - F1
(1801)
    Bn:1799   Da:1812   Dr:1800
    Fr:1799   Va:1799
Octavia - T5 (1801)
    Bn:1800   Da:1810   Dr:1800
    Fr:1802   Mh:1803   Va:1800
    Wm:1801
Der Oheim vom Lande - D4
    Va:1817
Der Opfertod - D3 (1798)
    Da:1815   Fr:1800   Lg:1798
    Va:1797
Die Organe des Gehirns - C3
(1806)
    Bn:1805   Da:1811   Dr:1805
    Fr:1806   Mh:1807   Va:1805
    Wm:1807
Pachter Feldkümmel von Tip-
pelskirchen - F5 (1811)
    Bn:1810   Da:1811   Dr:1811
    Fr:1810   Lg:1816   Mh:1812
    Wm:1811
Pagenstreiche - F5 (1804)
    Bn:1803   Da:1811   Dr:1803
    Fr:1805   Ha:1816   Lg:1805
    Mh:1803   Mu:1801   Va:1809
    Wm:1804

Der Papagoy - D3 (1792)
    Bn:1791   Dr:1791   Fr:1793
    Mh:1791   Va:1804   Wm:1792
La Peyrouse - D2 (1798)
    Bn:1796   Fr:1800   Mh:1796
Das Posthaus in Treuenbriet-
zen - C1 (1808)
    Da:1810   Dr:1821
Der Prozeß um des Esels
Schatten in Krähwinkel - F1
(1810)
    Bn:1809   Fr:1809   Mh:1831
    Va:1810   Wm:1810
Die Quäker - D1 (1812)
    Bn:1812   Da:1812   Ha:1815
    Ha:1812   Mu:1830   Va:1811
Das rächende Gewissen - D4
(1799)
    Dr:1800   Mh:1801   Va:1798
Der Rehbock o. Die schuld-
losen Schuldbewußten - C3
(1816)
    Bn:1814   Da:1815   Fr:1815
    Ha:1814   Lg:1818   Mh:1815
    Mu:1815   Va:1815   Wm:1815
Die respektable Gesellschaft
- F1 (1813)
    Bn:1812   Da:1813   Fr:1812
    Ha:1820   Mh:1812   Va:1812
Rollas Tod o. Die Spanier in
Peru - T5 (1796)
    Bn:1794   Da:1812   Dr:1796
    Fr:1794   Mh:1794   Va:1795
    Wm:1796
Die Rosen des Herrn von
Malesherbes - D1 - Fr (1813)
    Bn:1812   Da:1813   Dr:1813
    Fr:1813   Ha:1812   Lg:1816
    Mh:1812   Mu:1816   Va:1812
    Wm:1812
Der Rotmantel - C4 (1817)
    Bn:1816   Da:1816   Mh:1817
    Va:1816
Rübezahl - D1 (1804)
    Da:1814
Die Rückkehr der Freiwilligen
o. Das patriotische Gelübde -
C1 (1815)
    Bn:1814   Mu:1815
Rudolph von Habsburg und
König Ottokar von Böhmen - D6
(1816)
    Bn:1813   Da:1815   Dr:1815
    Fr:1815   Ha:1815   Lg:1815
    Mh:1819   Mu:1816   Wm:1815
Der Russe in Deutschland - C4
(1806)
    Bn:1828   Da:1814   Dr:1813
    Fr:1810   Mh:1807

Der Samtrock - C1 (1807)
    Da:1816  Dr:1816  Fr:1806
    Lg:1816  Mh:1810
Der Schauspieler wider Willen
- C1 - Fr (1803)
    Bn:1811  Da:1812  Dr:1810
    Fr:1811  Lg:1817  Mh:1805
    Va:1827  Wm:1812
Der schelmische Freier - C1
(1815)
    Bn:1830  Da:1814  Dr:1831
    Mh:1831
Die schlaue Witwe - F1 (1803)
    Da:1812  Fr:1807  Mh:1805
Das Schreibpult - D5 (1800)
    Bn:1798  Da:1812  Dr:1798
    Fr:1798  Ha:1816  Lg:1820
    Mh:1798  Va:1798  Wm:1799
Der Schutzgeist - D6
    Bn:1814  Da:1815  Dr:1814
    Fr:1815  Ha:1815  Lg:1814
    Mh:1816  Mu:1815  Wm:1817
Die Seelenwanderung o. Der
Schauspieler wider Willen auf
eine andere Manier - F1
(1816)
    Bn:1816  Fr:1824  Fr:1830
    Ha:1816  Mh:1817
Das Schmuckkästchen o. Der
Weg zum Herzen - D4 (1806)
    Fr:1805  Va:1805
Die Seeschlacht und die Meer-
katze - F1 (1809)
    Bn:1809  Da:1813  Fr:1815
Die Selbstmörder - D1 (1819)
    Dr:1819
Die seltene Krankheit - F2
(1814)
    Bn:1827  Da:1814  Mh:1820
Das seltsame Testament - C1
    Va:1796
Der Shawl - C1 (1815)
    Bn:1814  Da:1814  Dr:1816
    Fr:1814  Da:1820  Lg:1816
    Mh:1815  Mu:1816  Va:1814
    Wm:1815
Die silberne Hochzeit - D5
(1799)
    Bn:1797  Dr:1801  Fr:1798
    Ha:1797  Mh:1798  Va:1798
    Wm:1798
Der Sklavenhandel - D5
    Dr:1795
Die Sonnenjungfrau - D5
(1791)
    Bn:1790  Da:1811  Fr:1792
    Ha:1790  Lg:1791  Mh:1790
    Va:1791  Wm:1793

Sorgen ohne Not und Not ohne
Sorgen - C5 (1810)
    Bn:1809  Da:1811  Dr:1810
    Fr:1809  Ha:1816  Mh:1810
    Va:1810  Wm:1820
Die Sparbüchse o. Der arme
Kandidat - C1
    Bn:1804  Da:1811  Dr:1804
    Mh:1805
Der Spiegel - C1 (1818)
    Da:1817  Va:1817
Das Strandrecht - D1 (1807)
    Bn:1807  Da:1812  Dr:1806
    Fr:1807  Ha:1820  Lg:1806
    Mh:1810  Va:1815
Die Stricknadeln - D4 (1805)
    Bn:1804  Da:1810  Dr:1804
    Ha:1816  Lg:1822  Mh:1805
    Mu:1823  Wm:1805
Die Stumme - C1 (1808)
    Bn:1808  Da:1813  Fr:1809
    Va:1808
Sully und Quinault
    Va:1813
Das Tal von Almeria - D1
(1812)
    Da:1812  Mh:1813
Das Taschenbuch - D3 (1818)
    Bn:1817  Da:1818  Dr:1818
    Fr:1818  Ha:1820  Lg:1817
    Mh:1818  Va:1817  Wm:1817
Der Taubstumme o. Der Abbé
de l'Epée - D4 - Fr
    Bn:1801  Da:1810  Dr:1801
    Fr:1800  Ha:1816  Lg:1800
    Mh:1800  Va:1800  Wm:1820
Die Tochter Pharaonis - C1
(1804)
    Bn:1817  Da:1811  Fr:1807
    Mh:1813  Va:1804  Wm:1818
Der tote Neffe - C1 - Fr
(1804)
    Dr:1804  Fr:1805  Mh:1803
    Va:1803  Wm:1808
Der Trunkenbold - F2
    Da:1820
U.A.w.g. o. Die Einladungs-
karte - F1 (1818)
    Bn:1817  Da:1817  Dr:1818
    Fr:1821  Ha:1817  Lg:1817
    Mh:1818  Va:1817  Wm:1817
Ubaldo - T5 (1808)
    Bn:1809  Da:1811  Dr:1813
    Fr:1810  Lg:1808  Mh:1810
    Va:1809  Wm:1810
Üble Laune - D4 (1799)
    Bn:1797  Da:1811  Dr:1797
    Fr:1799  Ha:1797  Mh:1798
    Va:1797  Wm:1798

Die Uhr und die Mandeltorte -
C1 (1804)
    Va:1816
Die Unglückliche[n] - C1
(1798)
    Bn:1797   Da:1811   Dr:1796
    Fr:1798   Mh:1798   Va:1798
    Wm:1807
Die Uniform des Feld-
marschalls Wellington - C1
    Bn:1815   Da:1816   Mh:1816
    Wm:1817
Unser Fritz - D1 (1803)
    Bn:1828   Dr:1803   Fr:1802
    Mh:1805   Va:1802
Der Unvermählte - D4 (1808)
    Bn:1808   Da:1819   Dr:1806
    Fr:1807   Lg:1819   Mh:1809
    Va:1808   Wm:1809
Der Vater von ungefähr - C1 -
Fr
    Bn:1803   Dr:1800   Fr:1805
    Ha:1820   Mh:1803   Va:1803
    Wm:1808
Der verbannte Amor o. Die
argwöhnischen Eheleute - C4
(1810)
    Bn:1809   Da:1810   Dr:1809
    Fr:1809   Ha:1816   Lg:1816
    Mh:1810   Va:1809   Wm:1832
Die Verkleidungen - F2 (1819)
    Bn:1819   Da:1819   Mu:1830
Der Verläumder - D5 (1796)
    Bn:1795   Da:1815   Dr:1806
    Fr:1795   Ha:1795   Mh:1802
    Mu:1797   Va:1805   Wm:1796
Verlegenheit und List - C3 -
Fr (1820)
    Bn:1819   Da:1819   Dr:1820
    Fr:1820   Lg:1820   Mh:1822
    Va:1826   Wm:1822
Das verlorene Kind - D1
(1806)
    Da:1811   Dr:1806   Fr:1807
    Va:1806
Der Verschwiegene wider Wil-
len o. Die Fahrt von Berlin
nach Potsdam - C1 (1816)
    Bn:1817   Da:1816   Dr:1816
    Fr:1816   Ha:1815   Lg:1816
    Va:1815   Wm:1846
Die Versöhnung - D5 (1798)
    Bn:1796   Dr:1796   Wm:1796
Die Verwandtschaften - C5
(1798)
    Bn:1797   Da:1811   Dr:1797
    Fr:1798   Ha:1797   Lg:1819
    Mh:1797   Mu:1816   Va:1797
    Wm:1798

Der Vielwisser - C5 (1817)
    Bn:1816   Da:1816   Dr:1816
    Fr:1816   Ha:1815   Lg:1816
    Mh:1819   Wm:1819
Der weibliche Jakobiner-Klub
- C1 (1791)
    Wm:1791
Wer weiß wozu das gut ist -
F1 (1815)
    Fr:1832   Mh:1819
Der Westindier - C5 - Eng
(1816)
    Bn:1827   Mh:1823   Mu:1823
Der Wildfang - C3 (1798)
    Bn:1795   Da:1811   Dr:1798
    Fr:1800   Mh:1795   Mu:1816
    Va:1818   Wm:1798
Der Wirrwarr - F5 (1803)
    Bn:1801   Da:1811   Dr:1801
    Fr:1802   Ha:1820   Lg:1819
    Mu:1816   Va:1818   Wm:1802
Die Witwe und das Reitpferd -
C1 (1796)
    Da:1810   Dr:1797   Wm:1796
Die Wüste - D1 (1818)
    Bn:1817   Da:1817   Wm:1818
Die Zerstreuten - F1 (1810)
    Bn:1809   Da:1811   Dr:1809
    Fr:1809   Ha:1816   Lg:1816
    Mh:1810   Va:1809   Wm:1809
Das zugemauerte Fenster - C1
(1811)
    Bn:1810   Da:1811   Dr:1810
    Ha:1816   Lg:1817   Mh:1811
    Mu:1816   Wm:1814
Der Zitherschläger und der
Gaurichter - C3 (1817)
    Dr:1818   Fr:1816   Mh:1817
Zwei Nichten für eine - C2
(1814)
    Bn:1827   Da:1813   Dr:1814
    Fr:1813   Ha:1816   Mh:1814
    Va:1813   Wm:1815

**KOTZEBUE, WILHELM**   see
Augustsohn, Wilhelm

**KRAATZ, KURT**
Wiesbaden 1856-1925 Wiesbaden
Ref: Ko Th

Antoinette - D4 - with
H. Norweg
    Da:1888   Fr:1888

**KRAUS, KONRAD**
Mainz 1833-1886 Mainz
Ref: Brüm 19, Ko Th

Eine Notlüge - F3 (1880)
    Da:1882

**KRATTER, FRANZ**
Oberndorf 1758-1830 Lemberg
Ref: Brüm 18, Goe 5, Ko Th,
ADB

Athenais - D5
    Va:1818
Eginhard und Emma - D5 (1801)
    Va:1801
Die Familie Klinger - D5
(1802)
    Dr:1797
Der Friede am Pruth - D5
(1799)
    Dr:1798
Die Kriegskameraden - C5
(1791)
    Mh:1793  Va:1791
Das Mädchen von Marienburg -
D5 (1795)
    Bn:1793    Da:1811    Dr:1794
    Fr:1794    Ha:1793    Lg:1795
    Mh:1793    Mu:1793    Va:1793
    Wm:1794
Die Pflegesöhne - T5
    Bn:1813    Dr:1816    Lg:1814
    Va:1812
Sebastian der Unechte, König
von Portugal - D5
    Da:1825  Va:1814
Die Sklavin in Surinam - D5
(1804)
    Da:1814    Dr:1814    Mh:1805
    Wm:1801
Die Verschwörung wider Peter
den Großen. Menzikoff und
Natalie - T5 (1794)
    Fr:1794    Mh:1791    Va:1794
    Wm:1793
Der Vicekanzler - D5 (1789)
    Mh:1789  Va:1789

**KRAUS, P.**

Der eifersüchtige Dichter
    Mh:1878
Die Liebesprobe
    Mh:1864

**KRAUSENECK, JOHANN CHRISTOPH**
Zell 1738-1799 Bayreuth
Ref: Brüm 18, Goe 4/1, Ko Th

Die Goldmacher - C2 (1772)
    Fr:1780

Die Werbung für England - C1
(1776)
    Ha:1776

**KREMPLSETZER, GEORG**
Vilsbiburg 1827-1871
Vilsbiburg
Ref: Ko Th, ADB

Der Vetter auf Besuch (1863)
    Mu:1876

**KRETSCHMANN, KARL FRIEDRICH**
Zittau 1738-1809 Zittau
Ref: Brüm 18, Goe 4/1, Ko Th,
ADB, OC

Der alte böse General - C3
(1787)
    Bn:1787    Dr:1787    Lg:1787
    Mh:1787
Die Familie Eichenkron o.
Rang und Liebe - C5 (1786)
    Mh:1787  Va:1786
Seidne Schuhe - C2
    Dr:1780

**KRICKEBERG, SOPHIE FRIEDERIKE**
Hanover 1770-1842 Berlin
Ref: Goe 11, Ko Th, ADB

Die Ehrenrettung - D2 - Fr
(1836)
    Bn:1827    Da:1831    Ha:1827
    Va:1827
Herr l'Espérance o. Die Kunst
Stellen zu erlangen - Vv1 -
Fr (1817)
    Bn:1817
Der Kammerdiener - C1 - Fr
    Bn:1814    Da:1830    Dr:1832
    Fr:1824    Lg:1824    Mh:1829
    Mu:1831    Va:1829

**KRÜGER, ALBERT PETER JOHANN**
Altona 1810-1881 [1883?]
Hamburg
Ref: Brüm 19, Ko Th

Ein alter Seemann - F4
    Ha:1854
Die Bummler von Hamburg - F4
(1860-62)
    Ha:1858
König Wein - F5
    Fr:1852  Ha:1852
Das Mädchen vom Dorf - D3
(1861)
    Bn:1854    Fr:1854    Ha:1853

Rübezahl - Z3
Ha:1851
Ein schöner Traum - C1 (1860-
66)
Va:1883
Wurm und Würmer - F3
Ha:1857

**KRÖGER, JOHANN CHRISTIAN**
Berlin 1722-1750 Hamburg
Ref: Brüm 18, Goe 4/1, Ko Th,
ADB

Herzog Michel - C1 (1751)
Bn:1776  Ha:1767  Lg:1750
Mh:1781
Die Kandidaten - C5 (1748)
Ha:1767

**KRUSE, GEORG** [Pseud.:
G. Krusemann]
Neu-Strelitz 1830-1908 Berlin
Ref: Brüm 19, Ko Th

Die Brautschau - C4 (1879)
Lg:1880

**KRUSE, HEINRICH**
Stralsund 1815-1902 Stralsund
Ref: Brüm 19, Ko Th

Die Gräfin - T5 (1870)
Bn:1871  Lg:1869  Va:1871
Marino Faliero - T5 (1877)
Bn:1876
Wullenweber - T5 (1870)
Bn:1872

**KRUSE, LAURIDS**
Copenhagen 1778-1840 Paris
Ref: Brüm 18, Goe 9, Ko Th

Ezzelino, Tyrann von Padua -
T5 (1821)
Ha:1820  Va:1816
Die Witwe - T5 (1821)
Ha:1821

**KRUSEMANN, G.**   see Kruse,
Georg

**KUFFNER, CHRISTOPH**
Vienna 1780-1846 Vienna
Ref: Brüm 18, Goe 9, Ko Th,
ADB, NDB

Cervantes in Algier - D5
(1820)
Da:1819  Va:1819

Guido von Ostenthal [Ulrich,
Herzog von Württemberg] - D5
(1840)
Va:1834
Die Maltheser - D3 (1840)
Va:1838
Tarpeja - T5 (1825)
Va:1813

**KUGLER, FRANZ THEODOR**
Stettin 1808-1858 Berlin
Ref: Brüm 19, Ko Th, ADB, NDB

Der Doge von Venedig - T5
(1849)
Bn:1850
Lindane - Z
Ha:1835

**KÜHN, JULIUS EDUARD**
Leipzig 1831-after 1871 Leip-
zig
Ref: Brüm 19, Ko 3

Cola di Rienzi - D5 (1872)
Lg:1872

**KÜHNE, FERDINAND GUSTAV**
Magdeburg 1806-1888 Dresden
Ref: Brüm 19, Ko Th, ADB,
NDB, OC

Demetrius - T5 (1859)
Bn:1858
Kaiser Friedrich in Prag -
(1857)
Mh:1844
Kuß und Gelübde - D5 (1859)
Dr:1861

**KURANDA, IGNAZ**
Prague 1811-1884 Vienna
Ref: Ko 3, ADB, NDB

Die letzte weiße Rose - T5
(1834)
Bn:1844  Fr:1840  Va:1844
Wm:1841

**KURLÄNDER, FRANZ AUGUST von**
Vienna 1777-1836 Vienna
Ref: Brüm 18, Goe 11, Ko Th,
ADB

Das Abenteuer im Gasthofe -
C2 - Fr (1815)
Dr:1818  Va:1814
Der achtzigste Geburtstag -
D1 - Fr (1837)
Da:1837  Va:1836

Die Altistin - C2 - Fr (1835)
    Da:1838   Fr:1835   Va:1834
Der aufrichtigste Freund - C1
- Fr (1830)
    Dr:1830   Ha:1839   Va:1831
Die Charade - C2 (1818)
    Bn:1818   Dr:1819   Va:1819
Das ändert die Sache - C1 -
Fr (1826)
    Da:1826   Lg:1826
Der Ehemann als Bittsteller -
C3 - Fr (1831)
    Mu:1830   Va:1830
Die Ehescheidung - C2 - Fr
(1832)
    Ha:1832   Va:1832
Eins für zehn - C1 - Fr
(1823)
    Ha:1824   Va:1825   Wm:1823
Ewig - C2 - Fr (1834)
    Bn:1834   Da:1837   Dr:1855
    Fr:1833   Ha:1833   Va:1833
Die Familie Rosenstein - D3 -
Fr (1820)
    Dr:1820   Va:1819
Flattersinn und Liebe - C4 -
Fr (1826)
    Bn:1825   Dr:1826   Ha:1826
    Va:1825
Freuden und Leiden eines
Kranken - C1 (1830)
    Ha:1831   Mu:1832   Va:1829
Die Freunde als Nebenbuhler -
C2 (1834)
    Bn:1834   Va:1832
Das Geheimnis - D1 - Fr
(1831)
    Da:1831   Va:1830
Die Geldheirat - C4 - Fr
(1829)
    Va:1828   Wm:1829
Das goldene Kreuz - D2 - Fr
(1837)
    Bn:1835   Va:1835
Der Großonkel - C2 - Fr
(1819)
    Fr:1819   Va:1817
Die Heirat aus Vernunft - D3
- Fr (1828)
    Da:1828   Lg:1845   Mu:1830
    Va:1827   Wm:1827
Der Hochzeitstag - C2 - Fr
(1829)
    Dr:1830   Mh:1829   Mu:1830
    Va:1830
Eine Hütte und sein Herz - C3
- Fr (1836)
    Bn:1836   Ha:1836   Va:1836
Jenny - D4 - Fr (1813)
    Bn:1812   Da:1817   Va:1811

Julius von Krack [Der junge
Krack] o. Alles wahr [Ein
Lügner, der die Wahrheit
spricht] - F1 - Fr (1824)
    Da:1824   Va:1823
Der junge Husaren-Obrist - C1
Fr (1822)
    Mh:1822   Va:1821
Kindliche Liebe - D1 (1824)
    Bn:1823
Die Liebeserklärung - C2 - Fr
(1822)
    Bn:1821   Va:1821
Der Lügner und sein Sohn - C1
Fr (1811)
    Da:1815   Fr:1817   Lg:1816
    Mh:1811   Va:1811
Neues Mittel, Töchter zu ver-
heiraten - C1 - Fr (1828)
    Bn:1827   Da:1828   Mu:1829
Das Portrait der Erbin - C3 -
Fr (1811)
    Bn:1811   Da:1811   Mu:1815
    Va:1809
Die Reise nach Dieppe - C2
(1822)
    Mu:1822   Va:1822
Schüchtern und dreist - C1 -
Fr (1827)
    Da:1830   Lg:1827   Mu:1826
    Va:1827   Wm:1827
Die Schutzfrau - C1 - Fr
(1833)
    Ha:1833   Va:1832
Der sechzigjährige Jüngling -
C2 - Fr (1820)
    Fr:1819   Va:1819
Die seltsame Entführung - C1
(1820)
    Bn:1820   Dr:1820   Va:1819
Shakespeare als Liebhaber -
C1 - Fr (1818)
    Bn:1817   Da:1817   Dr:1817
    Va:1817
Die Tochter des Geizigen - D3
- Fr (1836)
    Da:1838   Va:1835
Der Tote in Verlegenheit - C3
- Fr (1826)
    Bn:1826   Da:1827   Va:1826
    Wm:1826
Der verwundete Liebhaber - C1
- Fr (1812)
    Bn:1825   Lg:1817   Mh:1821
    Va:1812
Warum? - C1 - Fr (1834)
    Dr:1834   Mu:1834   Va:1834
Welche von beiden? - C1
(1819)
    Va:1818   Wm:1819

Zwei Tage auf dem Lande - C1
(1813)
   Mh:1816
Der Zweikampf - D1 - Fr
(1828)
   Da:1842  Dr:1828  Mu:1829
See Goedeke 11 for additional
listings.

**KURNICK, MAX**
Santomyschl 1819-1881 Breslau
Ref: Brüm 19, Ko Th

Ein Mann - C3 (1852)
   Bn:1853

**KÜRNBERGER, FERDINAND**
Vienna 1821-1879 Munich
Ref: Brüm 19, Ko Th, ADB,
NDB, OC

Firdusi - T (1902)
   Mu:1871

**KÜSTNER, CARL THEODOR**
Leipzig 1784-1864 Berlin
Ref: Goe 11, Ko Th, ADB, NDB

Die beiden Brüder - T4 (1833)
   Lg:1824
Die Ehemänner als Junggesel-
len - C1 - Fr (1815)
   Bn:1825  Da:1815  Lg:1828
Feder und Schwert - C1 -
(1815)
   Bn:1815 .Mh:1815
Die Vermählte - D3 (1815)
   Dr:1814  Lg:1813

**LAFONTAINE, AUGUST HEINRICH**
Braunschweig 1758-1831 Halle
Ref: Brüm 18, Goe 5, Ko 3,
ADB, NDB, OC

Die Prüfung der Treue o. Die
Irrungen - C3 (1805)
   Bn:1806
Die Tochter der Natur - D3
(1805)
   Bn:1828  Va:1798

**LAMBRECHT, MATTHIAS GEORG**
[Pseud.: Friedrich Laub]
Hamburg 1748-1826 Munich
Ref: Brüm 18, Goe 5, Ko Th

Betrug aus Liebe - C4
   Va:1786
Der Empfindliche - C1
   Dr:1806
Der falsche Stanislaus [Die
lästige Würde] - C3 - Fr
(1811)
   Mh:1811
Der gutherzige Alte - C1 - Fr
   Lg:1818  Va:1800
Liebe und Freundschaft - C4
(1801)
   Dr:1805
List gegen Bosheit - C3
(1799)
   Dr:1792
Der Lohn der Dankbarkeit - D1
   Dr:1809
Das sechzehnjährige Mädchen
o. Unschuld und Liebe - D3
Fr (1787)
   Dr:1787  Mh:1788
Die stolze Spröde - C1 - Fr
   Dr:1805
Und er soll dein Herr sein o.
Die Überraschung nach der
Hochzeit - C5 - Eng (1786)
   Mh:1784

**LA MOTTE, KARL AUGUST DE**
ca. 1768-1841
Ref: Goe 6, Ko 3

Die Ausgewanderten in Wien -
D3
   Bn:1805  Mh:1803
Der beste Wucher - D5 (1806)
   Dr:1804  Mh:1805
Ida Münster - T5 (1806)
   Dr:1807  Fr:1805  Lg:1808
   Mh:1803

**LAMPE, KARL**   see Werther,
Karl Ludwig

**LAMPERT, ALBERT**
1758-1831

Männertreue - C1
   Va:1816

**LANDESMANN, HEINRICH**   see
Lorm, Hyronimus

**LANDSBERG**

Karl der Kühne - C1
   Va:1875

**LANGE**

Der Mentor - C3
  Bn:1882  Fr:1857

**LANGENSCHWARZ, LEOPOLD**
[Pseud.: Karl Zwengsahn]
Rödelheim 1801-after 1867
Ref: Brüm 19, Goe 10, Ko Th

Dschingiskhan - T5
  Bn:1849
Glück und Talent - D5
  Da:1850
Peter im Frack - C4
  Bn:1849  Da:1849  Dr:1849
  Va:1849
Tiphonia - T5
  Bn:1848  Dr:1848  Va:1848

**LANGER, ANTON**
Vienna 1824-1879 Vienna
Ref: Brüm 19, Ko Th, ADB, NDB

Eine Vereinsschwester - F1
(1876)
  Fr:1883
Eine verfolgte Unschuld - F1
with E. Pohl (1873)
  Fr:1863
Vom Juristentage - F1 - with
D. Kalisch (1862)
  Da:1863  Fr:1863
Vom Land und von der See - C1
  Ha:1868
Ein Wort an den Minister - D1
  Da:1867  Fr:1868

**LARCESO, MAX**  see Cosmar,
Alexander

**LA ROCHE, SOPHIE von**
Kaufbeuren 1730-1807 Offen-
bach
Ref: Brüm 18, Goe 4, Ko 2,
ADB, OC

Die Erbschaft - C3
  Fr:1780

**L'ARRONGE, ADOLF**  [i.e. A.
Aronsohn]
Hamburg 1838-1908 Kreuzlingen
Ref: Brüm 19, Ko Th, NDB, OC

Doktor Klaus - C5 (1878)
  Da:1879  Fr:1879  Lg:1878
  Mu:1879  Va:1883  Wm:1878

Hasemanns Töchter - FP4
(1877)
  Da:1878  Fr:1878  Lg:1878
  Mh:1878  Mu:1878  Va:1883
  Wm:1880
Haus Lonei - C4 (1880)
  Da:1881  Fr:1880  Lg:1881
  Va:1880
Der Kompagnon - C4 (1880)
  Da:1881  Fr:1881  Lg:1881
  Mu:1881  Va:1881
Mein Leopold - FP3 (1873)
  Dr:1875  Fr:1874  Mh:1875
  Mu:1874  Va:1883  Wm:1886
Papa hat's erlaubt - F1 -
with G. Moser (1872)
  Da:1876  Fr:1872  Wm:1882
Der Registrator auf Reisen -
F3 - with G. Moser (1872)
  Da:1876  Fr:1875  Mu:1873
  Wm:1874
Die Sorglosen - C3 (1882)
  Fr:1883  Lg:1883  Va:1882
  Wm:1882
Der Weg zum Herzen - C4
(1884)
  Lg:1886
Wohltätige Frauen - C4 (1879)
  Da:1880  Fr:1880  Lg:1879
  Mu:1879  Va:1879  Wm:1879

**LAUB, FRIEDRICH**  see Lambrecht, Matthias Georg

**LAUBE, HEINRICH**  [Pseud.:
H. Campo]
Sprottau 1806-1884 Vienna
Ref: Brüm 19, Ko Th, ADB,
NDB, OC

Adrienne Lecouvreur - D5 - Fr
  Va:1851
Ein alter Franzose - C1 - Fr
  Va:1860
Die Bernsteinhexe - D5 (1846)
  Bn:1844  Ha:1844
Birnbaum und Sohn - D4 - Fr
  Va:1854
Böse Zungen - D5 (1868)
  Da:1872  Fr:1870  Ha:1868
  Lg:1868  Mh:1868  Mu:1868
  Va:1873  Wm:1868
Capitän Bitterlin - C1 - Fr
  Va:1861
Cato von Eisen - C3 - Sp
(1875)
  Bn:1858  Dr:1859  Fr:1858
  Ha:1858  Lg:1877  Mh:1858
  Va:1858

Demetrius - T5 (1872)
    Da:1869   Fr:1869   Lg:1869
    Mh:1869   Wm:1870
Die Furcht vor der Freude -
D1 - Fr (1878)
    Va:1854
Das Fräulein von Sieglière -
D4 - Fr (1875)
    Va:1852
Gottsched und Gellert - D5
(1847)
    Bn:1846   Dr:1845   Fr:1846
    Ha:1846   Lg:1869   Mh:1845
    Mu:1848   Va:1862   Wm:1847
Graf Essex - T5 (1856)
    Bn:1856   Da:1856   Dr:1857
    Fr:1856   Mh:1856   Mu:1857
    Va:1856   Wm:1856
Der Hauptmann von der Schaar-
wache - C2 - Fr (1878)
    Bn:1851   Ha:1858   Va:1851
Die Karlsschüler - D5 (1847)
    Bn:1847   Da:1847   Dr:1846
    Fr:1847   Ha:1847   Mh:1846
    Mu:1846   Va:1848   Wm:1847
Der kleine Richelieu - C2 -
Fr
    Bn:1876
Der letzte Brief - C3 - Fr
(1875)
    Va:1860
Mein Stern - C1 - Fr
    Va:1854
Mitten in der Nacht - F1 - Fr
(1874)
    Va:1878
Monaldeschi o. Die Abenteurer
- T5 (1845)
    Bn:1842   Dr:1842   Fr:1844
    Ha:1844   Mu:1844   Va:1843
    Wm:1843
Montrose, der schwarze Mark-
graf - T (1859)
    Da:1860   Mu:1860   Va:1859
Die Mördergrube - F1 - Fr
    Va:1852
Nicolo Zaganini, der große
Virtuos - Vv1
    Bn:1830   Da:1830   Ha:1830
Prinz Friedrich - D5 (1854)
    Fr:1848   Ha:1850   Mh:1848
    Va:1879   Wm:1854
Rokoko o. Die alten Herren -
D5 (1846)
    Bn:1845   Dr:1842   Fr:1858
    Ha:1846   Mu:1870   Va:1851
    Wm:1853
Schauspieler - C4
    Va:1883

Der Statthalter von Bengalen
- D4 (1868)
    Fr:1868   Ha:1867   Lg:1867
    Mh:1867   Mu:1867   Va:1867
    Wm:1867
Struensee - T5 (1847)
    Bn:1848   Da:1845   Ha:1845
    Mh:1844   Mu:1845   Va:1849
    Wm:1854

**LAUBE, SAMUEL GOTTLIEB**
Thorn 1781-1835 Berlin
Ref: Goe 6, Ko 3

Ariodante - T5 (1805)
    Dr:1809

**LAUDES JOSEF GOTTWILL**
Vienna 1741-1780 Vienna
Ref: Brüm 18, Goe 4, Ko Th

Es ist nicht alles Gold, was
glänzt - C (1773)
    Ha:1773
Der Franzos in Wien - C2 - Fr
(1776)
    Va:1776
Nacht und ungefähr - C1 - It
(1771)
    Va:1780
Die verliebten Zänker - C3
It (1764)
    Dr:1779   Fr:1780   Va:1764

**LAUFS, KARL**
Mainz 1858-1900 Kassel
Ref: Brüm 19, Ko Th

Pension Schöller - F (1898)
    Fr:1890
Ein toller Einfall - F (1891)
    Fr:1888

**LEBRUN, CARL AUGUST**
Halberstadt 1792-1842 Hamburg
Ref: Brüm 18, Goe 11, Ko Th,
ADB

Album der Weiberlist - C
    Ha:1840   Mu:1839
Aller Welt Freund - C1 - Fr
(1826)
    Bn:1825   Da:1826   Ha:1826
Aller Welt Vetter - C1 - Fr
(1826)
    Da:1826   Fr:1826
Alles gefoppt o. Der erste
April - C1 (1818)
    Dr:1817   Fr:1818

Der alte Jüngling - F1 (1820)
      Da:1821   Fr:1834   Lg:1831
      Wm:1821
Der Backenstreich [Drei Bak-
kensteiche] - C2
      Ha:1842
Die beiden Philibert - C3
(1820)
      Da:1818   Fr:1817   Ha:1819
      Mh:1830   Va:1817   Wm:1819
Bestrafter Ehrgeiz o. Marquis
und Schuhmacher - D2 - Fr
      Ha:1839
Brief und Antwort - C1 - Fr
(1833-34)
      Bn:1820   Dr:1834   Fr:1821
      Ha:1820   Lg:1821   Wm:1822
Casanova im Fort St. André -
C3 (1837)
      Bn:1838   Ha:1837   Lg:1837
Die diebische Elster o. Der
Schein trügt - D3 - Fr (1816)
      Ha:1818   Mu:1817
Der Empfindliche - C1 (1826)
      Bn:1833   Dr:1844
Er ist sein eigner Gegner -
C3 - Fr (1822)
      Bn:1821
Erbschaft und Heirat - C2
      Ha:1840
Ein Fehltritt - D2 - Fr
(1833-34)
      Bn:1836
Die Fledermäuse o. Klug soll
leben! - F1 (1825)
      Bn:1833   Da:1825   Fr:1825
Eine Freundschaft ist der
andern wert - C3 - Fr (1825)
      Bn:1827   Dr:1834   Fr:1823
      Ha:1823   Va:1823
Eine geheime Leidenschaft -
D3 - Fr
      Ha:1840   Mu:1840
Hans Luft - D3 - Fr (1830)
      Dr:1833   Fr:1832   Ha:1834
      Mh:1830
Der Holländer - C3 (1839)
      Ha:1839
Humoristische Studien [Der
tote Neffe] - F2 - Fr (1825)
      Bn:1819   Da:1825   Dr:1829
      Fr:1825   Lg:1825   Mh:1825
      Wm:1825
Ich irre mich nie o. Der Räu-
berhauptmann - F1 - Fr (1820)
      Bn:1821   Da:1821   Dr:1823
      Fr:1823   Ha:1820   Lg:1824
      Mh:1826   Wm:1821

Die Intrige aus dem Stegreif
- F2 (1823)
      Bn:1829   Ha:1822
Die kinderlose Ehe - F1
(1833-34)
      Bn:1833   Ha:1832
Die Kunst, wohlfeil zu leben
- C3 - Eng (1835)
      Bn:1827   Lg:1834
Der Lachenbüsser - C2 - Fr
      Dr:1839   Ha:1841
Lehrer, Schüler und Korrektor
- C1 - Fr (1822)
      Bn:1835   Dr:1821   Ha:1822
      Lg:1823
Lehr-, Wehr- und Nährstand -
C1 (1837)
      Ha:1837
Der Liebe und des Zufalls
Spiel - C2 - Fr (1834)
      Bn:1840   Fr:1840
Der Mann mit der eisernen
Maske - D5 - Fr (1838)
      Bn:1832   Da:1838   Dr:1833
      Fr:1832   Ha:1831   Lg:1832
      Mu:1832   Wm:1853
Memoiren eines Husaren-
Offiziers - C1 - Fr (1827)
      Lg:1829
Mittel und Wege - F3 - Eng
(1822)
      Bn:1823   Da:1821   Fr:1822
Nummer 777 - C1 - Fr (1822)
      Bn:1822   Da:1821   Dr:1822
      Fr:1821   Ha:1821   Lg:1822
      Mh:1822   Va:1825   Wm:1822
Pommersche Intriguen o. Das
Stelldichein - C3 (1822)
      Bn:1820   Da:1820   Dr:1820
      Ha:1820   Lg:1824
Postwagenabenteuer - F3 - Fr
(1827)
      Bn:1827   Mh:1827
Die Puritanerin - D2 - Fr
(1838)
      Dr:1834   Va:1834
Die Schauspieler - C5 - Fr
(1822)
      Fr:1821   Ha:1821
Shakespeare - D1 (1818)
      Ha:1819
Spiele [Launen] des Zufalls -
C3 (1827)
      Bn:1826   Da:1827   Dr:1829
      Fr:1840   Lg:1830   Va:1826
Sympathie - C2 (1825)
      Dr:1823   Va:1823

Der Sylvesterabend o. Die
Nachtwächter - F2 (1820)
    Da:1837  Fr:1831  Ha:1818
    Lg:1820  Va:1821  Wm:1821
Der tote Gast - C4 (1838)
    Da:1841  Ha:1838
Der Unschlüssige - C1 - Fr
(1820)
    Ha:1820
Van Bruck, Rentier - C2 - Fr
    Bn:1842  Dr:1842  Ha:1842
    Lg:1842
Vater Dominique o. Sauer ist
süß - D1 - Fr (1833)
    Bn:1832  Dr:1832  Fr:1833
    Ha:1832
Die Verstorbenen - F1 (1826)
    Bn:1825  Da:1825  Dr:1825
    Fr:1826  Mh:1825  Mu:1833
    Va:1826  Wm:1832
Verwechslungen - C2 - Fr
(1826)
    Bn:1826  Mh:1828  Wm:1827
Vielliebchen o. Das Tagebuch
- C1 (1826)
    Bn:1825  Fr:1825  Ha:1824
    Lg:1838  Mu:1838
Der Weiberfeind - F2 (1824)
    Fr:1823
Der Wetterableiter - F2 - Fr
(1837)
    Bn:1837  Dr:1837  Ha:1837
Wohl zu bekommen - C1 - Fr
    Ha:1840
Zeitungstrompeten - C2 - Fr
(1827)
    Bn:1828
Zwei Namenstage für einen -
F3 (1839)
    Ha:1839

**LECHNER, FRIEDRICH** see
Mosenthal, Salomon Hermann

**LEDERER, J. JOACHIM** [Pseud.:
Felix Wagner]
Prague 1808-1876 Dresden
Ref: Brüm 19, Ko Th, ADB

Geistige Liebe o. Gleich und
gleich gesellt sich gern - C2
    Bn:1848  Da:1849  Dr:1849
    Fr:1848  Ha:1849  Mu:1869
    Va:1847  Wm:1842
Häusliche Wirren - C3 - with
W. Gerle (1839)
    Bn:1852  Dr:1851  Fr:1852
    Ha:1852  Mu:1883  Wm:1850

Die kranken Doctoren - C3 -
with W. Gerle
    Va:1842
Die rettende Tat o. Die weiblichen Studenten - C3
    Dr:1858  Fr:1858  Ha:1858
    Va:1854

**LEHNARD**

Der verwünschte Brief - F3 -
Fr
    Ha:1844

**LEISEWITZ, JOHANN ANTON**
Hanover 1752-1806 Braun-
schweig
Ref: Brüm 18, Goe 4/1, Ko Th,
ADB, NDB, OC

Julius von Tarent - T5 (1776)
    Bn:1776  Dr:1789  Fr:1780
    Ha:1777  Mh:1784  Mu:1785
    Va:1785  Wm:1796

**LEITERSHOFEN von**  see Wolff,
Pius Alexander

**LEMBERT, JOSEF WENZEL** [i.e.
Wenzel Tremler]
Prague 1779-1851 Mödling
Ref: Brüm 18, Goe 9, Ko 3

Die beiden Louisen - C4 - Fr
    Va:1838
Das Blümlein Wunderhold - D4
    Va:1830
Die Brautwahl - C3 - Fr
(1821)
    Bn:1817  Ha:1829  Mh:1821
    Va:1823
Der Dichter und der Schau-
spieler o. Das Lustspiel im
Lustspiel - C3 - Fr (1813)
    Bn:1814  Da:1812  Dr:1812
    Mh:1812  Va:1812  Wm:1814
Der Ehemann auf Schleichwegen
- C3 - Fr (1825)
    Da:1825  Mh:1825
Der Ehemann in der Klemme -
C1 (1816)
    Mh:1830
Ehrgeiz in der Küche - F1 -
Fr (1827)
    Bn:1825  Da:1827  Fr:1831
    Lg:1831  Va:1826  Wm:1830
Er sucht sich selbst - C1 -
Fr
    Fr:1849  Wm:1851

Die Feinde - D4
    Dr:1814
Der Frack und die Livrée - C1
Fr
    Da:1835   Dr:1835   Wm:1824
Frauenjahre zählt man nicht -
C3 - It
    Va:1825
Freund und Krone - D4 (1836)
    Va:1832
O Freundschaft - C4 - Fr
    Va:1849
Die Geheimnisse - C1 - Fr
    Bn:1820   Ha:1822   Mh:1821
    Va:1819
Der gute Rat - C1 - Fr
    Va:1840
Die homöopathische Kur - C3 -
Fr (1845)
    Va:1838
Kenilworth [Emmy Robsart] -
D5 (1845)
    Bn:1822   Fr:1824   Mu:1823
    Va:1825   Wm:1829
König Richard in Palästina -
D4
    Va:1827
König Stanislaus o. List und
Liebe - C3 - Fr (1812)
    Bn:1811   Da:1811   Dr:1810
    Va:1825
Lebt er oder ist er tot? - C1
Fr
    Fr:1849
Der Mann meiner Frau - C3 -
Fr (1834)
    Da:1833   Fr:1833   Lg:1834
    Mu:1832   Va:1831
Männer denken, Frauen lenken
- C3
    Va:1822
Männerspiegel - C1 (1816)
    Fr:1813   Mu:1816   Va:1813
Maria Stuarts erste Gefangen-
schaft - D4 (1827)
    Bn:1825   Fr:1823   Va:1835
    Wm:1828
Der Mentor - C1 - Fr (1836)
    Da:1838   Fr:1861   Va:1834
Nach Mitternacht - C1 - FR
    Va:1840
Der Nachtwächter - D5 - Fr
    Bn:1832
Das öffentliche Geheimnis -
C4 - Sp (1824)
    Bn:1821   Da:1821   Dr:1821
    Fr:1824   Ha:1821   Lg:1821
    Mh:1823   Mu:1850   Va:1820
    Wm:1824

Onkel Adam und Nichte Eva -
C2 (1823)
    Bn:1825   Da:1823   Mh:1825
    Mu:1822   Va:1822
Der Papa und sein Söhnchen -
F3 - Fr (1812)
    Bn:1825   Da:1812   Dr:1811
    Fr:1811   Va:1813
Rache für Rache - C5 - Fr
    Va:1832
Ränke und Schwänke - C3 - Fr
(1813)
    Bn:1812   Da:1813   Dr:1812
Die Reise zur Hochzeit - D3 -
Fr (1822)
    Bn:1822   Da:1822   Dr:1822
    Fr:1821   Ha:1821   Lg:1831
    Mh:1821   Va:1820   Wm:1822
Der Schwiegersohn eines Mil-
lionairs - D5 - Fr
    Ha:1845
Der Trauring - D3 (1813)
    Da:1812   Wm:1814
Unbewußte Liebe - C2 - Fr
    Va:1840   Wm:1839
Die Untröstlichen - C3 - Fr
(1834)
    Fr:1831   Va:1830
Vergebliche Mühe - C3 (1817)
    Bn:1815   Dr:1815   Ha:1816
    Mu:1820   Va:1816
Die Verwandten des Groß-
Veziers - F1 - Fr (1816)
    Va:1815
Wahn und Wahnsinn - D2 - Fr
(1836)
    Mh:1836   Va:1835

**LENZ, JAKOB MICHAEL REINHOLD**
Seßwegen/Livonia 1751-1792
Moscow
Ref: Brüm 18, Goe 4/1, Ko Th,
ADB, NDB, OC

Der Hofmeister o. Die Vor-
teile der Privaterziehung -
C5 (1774)
    Bn:1778   Ha:1778   Mh:1780

**LENZ, JOHANN REINHOLD** called
Kühne, also Lenz-Kühne
Pernau/Livonia 1778-1854 Riga
Ref: Brüm 18, Goe 4/1, Ko Th,
ADB

Der Buckelige - D5 - Eng
    Ha:1836

Die Flucht nach Kenilworth -
T5 (1826)
    Da:1827   Dr:1823   Ha:1822
    Lg:1823   Mh:1824   Va:1822
Frauenwert - D
    Ha:1840
Paoli o. Korsika und Genua -
D3 - Fr
    Ha:1823
Ruy Blas - D5 - Fr
    Ha:1839
Die Tochter des Gefangenen -
D6 - Fr
    Ha:1847

**LEONHARD, ERNST**  see Elsner,
Oskar

**LEPEL, BERNHARD von**
Meppen 1818-1885 Prenzlau
Ref: Brüm 19, Ko Th, ADB, NDB

König Herodes - T5 (1860)
    Bn:1857

**LEROY**

Er bezaubert - D3
    Lg:1878

**LESSING, GOTTHOLD EPHRAIM**
Kamenz 1729-1781 Braunschweig
Ref: Brüm 18, Goe 4/1, Ko Th,
ADB, NDB, OC

Die alte Jungfer - C3 (1749)
    Fr:1783   Lg:1770
Emilia Galotti - T5 (1772)
    Bn:1772   Da:1810   Dr:1774
    Fr:1777   Ha:1772   Lg:1772
    Mh:1778   Mu:1779   Va:1772
    Wm:1772
Der Freigeist - C5 (1755)
    Bn:1767   Dr:1777   Fr:1768
    Ha:1767   Lg:1770   Mh:1779
    Mu:1780   Wm:1772
Die Juden - C1 (1754)
    Bn:1775   Dr:1780   Fr:1775
    Ha:1770   Lg:1771   Mu:1779
Der junge Gelehrte - C3
(1754)
    Fr:1783   Lg:1771
Minna von Barnhelm - C5
(1767)
    Bn:1768   Da:1811   Dr:1771
    Fr:1767   Ha:1767   Lg:1767
    Mh:1777   Mu:1774   Va:1767
    Wm:1768

Miß Sara Sampson - T5 (1755)
    Bn:1767   Dr:1771   Fr:1780
    Ha:1767   Lg:1767   Mh:1779
    Mu:1772   Va:1771   Wm:1771
Der Misogyn - C3 (1755)
    Ha:1768   Va:1769
Nathan der Weise - D5 (1779)
    Bn:1783   Da:1812   Dr:1818
    Fr:1806   Ha:1803   Lg:1818
    Mh:1805   Mu:1814   Va:1819
    Wm:1801
Philotas - T1 (1752)
    Bn:1774   Ha:1780   Va:1782
Der Schatz - C1 (1755)
    Ha:1767   Lg:1770   Va:1771
    Wm:1792
Der Schlaftrunk - C3 (1784)
    Da:1785   Lg:1785   Mh:1786

**LESSING, KARL GOTTHELF**
Kamenz 1740-1812 Breslau
Ref: Brüm 18, Goe 4/1, Ko Th,
ADB, NDB, OC

Die Bankrottier - C5 (1780)
    Va:1778
Die Kindermörderin - T5
(1777)
    Bn:1777
Die reiche Frau - C5 (1780)
    Bn:1776   Ha:1775   Mu:1776

**LEUTNER, EMANUEL**  see
Raupach, Ernst

**LEVEZOW, KONRAD**
Stettin 1770-1835 Berlin
Ref: Brüm 18, Goe 6, Ko Th,
ADB, NDB

Der Fischer von Colberg - D2
(1814)
    Bn:1814
Innocentia - T5 (1823)
    Bn:1823
Iphigenia in Aulis - T5
(1805)
    Bn:1804   Dr:1813   Lg:1813
Ratibor und Wanda - D5 (1819)
    Bn:1819

**LEVI, ELISE**  see Henle, Elise

**LEWALD, JOHANN KARL AUGUST**
Königsberg 1792-1871 Munich
Ref: Brüm 18, Goe 11, Ko Th,
ADB, NDB

Der Diamentenraub zu Paris -
D4
    Mu:1823  Va:1824
Es ist die rechte Zeit - C2
(1829)
    Bn:1828  Mu:1822
Das Fräulein von Scuderi - D4
    Mu:1823
Fürst Blaubart - D4
    Mu:1823

**LICHTENSTEIN, KARL AUGUST von**
Lahm 1767-1845 Berlin
Ref: Goe 11, Ko Th, ADB

Erste Liebe o. Erinnerungen
aus der Kindheit - C1 - Fr
(1826)
    Bn:1826  Ha:1826
Die Kostgänger - C1 - Fr
(1824)
    Bn:1824
Der Nachbar - C1 - Fr (1827)
    Bn:1827
Nichtchen und Großonkel - C1
- Fr (1824)
    Bn:1824
Die Stiefmutter - C1 - Fr
(1841)
    Bn:1841
Der Vormund - D1 - Fr (1827)
    Bn:1827

**LIEBHABER, AMALIE LOUISE**
[Pseud.: Amalie Louise]
Wolfenbüttel 1781-1845 Berlin
Ref: Goe 10, Ko Th

Der Apfel von Balsora - D3
    Bn:1831

**LILIENCRON, DETLEV von**
Kiel 1844-1909 Alt Rahlstedt
Ref: Brüm 19, Ko Th, NDB, OC

Arbeit adelt - D2 (1887)
    Lg:1887
Knut der Herr - D5 (18850
    Lg:1886

**LINDAU, PAUL**
Magdeburg 1839-1919 Berlin
Ref: Brüm 19, Ko Th, NDB, OC

Die beiden Leonoren - C4
(1904)
    Fr:1889  Mu:1888  Va:1889
    Wm:1890
Diana - D5 (1873-81)
    Bn:1873  Va:1873

Ein Erfolg - C4 (1875)
    Bn:1874  Da:1888  Fr:1879
    Lg:1874  Mu:1875  Va:1874
    Wm:1874
Frau Susanne - D5 - with
H. Lubliner (1885)
    Fr:1885  Mu:1885  Va:1885
Galeotto - D3 - Sp (1887)
    Fr:1887  Lg:1887  Mu:1887
    Va:1888  Wm:1887
Gräfin Lea - D5 (1880)
    Bn:1880  Fr:1880  Lg:1880
    Mu:1880  Wm:1879
In diplomatischer Sendung -
C1 (1873-81)
    Bn:1873  Fr:1876  Mu:1872
    Va:1872  Wm:1872
Johannistrieb - D4 (1878)
    Bn:1878  Da:1878  Fr:1878
    Lg:1878  Mu:1878  Va:1878
    Wm:1878
Jungbrunnen - C4
    Fr:1882  Lg:1882  Mu:1881
Maria und Magdalena - D4
(1873-81)
    Bn:1872  Da:1873  Fr:1873
    Lg:1873  Mh:1873  Mu:1873
    Va:1872  Wm:1872
Mariannens Mutter - D4 (1885)
    Fr:1890  Wm:1883
Marion - D4 (1873-81)
    Lg:1870
Die Schatten - D (1889)
    Fr:1889  Mu:1889
Schnell gefreit - D4 - Eng
    Da:1877  Fr:1876  Mu:1882
Die Sonne - D (1890)
    Mu:1891
Tante Therese - D4 (1876)
    Bn:1875  Lg:1877  Mh:1876
    Mu:1876  Va:1875  Wm:1875
Verschämte Arbeit - D3 (1873-
81)
    Bn:1880  Mu:1881  Va:1881
    Wm:1880
Der Zankapfel - F1 (1876)
    Bn:1875  Mu:1880  Wm:1877

**LINDEN, GUSTAV**  see Stein,
Karl

**LINDERER, ROBERT**
Erfurt 1824-1886 Berlin
Ref: Ko Th

Welche Lust Soldat zu sein! -
C1 (ca 1859-64)
    Dr:1861

**LINDNER, ALBERT**
Sulza 1831-1888 Dalldorf
Ref: Brüm 19, Ko Th, ADB, NDB

Die Bluthochzeit o. Die Bar-
tholomäusnacht - T4 (1871)
   Bn:1874   Da:1887   Dr:1877
   Fr:1877   Lg:1872   Va:1873
   Wm:1886
Brutus und Collatinus - T5
(1867)
   Bn:1867   Lg:1867   Mh:1865
   Mu:1888   Va:1867
Der Hund des Aubry - D3
(1869)
   Lg:1869
Stauf und Welf - D5 (1867)
   Wm:1867

**LINDNER, FRIEDRICH GEORG**
Mitau 1772-1845 Stuttgart
Ref: Goe 8

Das Abenteuer auf Extrapost -
C2
   Va:1803

**LINDOLF, ALFRED**  see
Stieglitz, Nikolaus

**LINGG, HERMANN**
Lindau 1820-1905 Munich
Ref: Brüm 19, Ko Th, NDB, OC

Die Bregenzer Klause - D
(1887)
   Mu:1887
Catalina - T (1864)
   Mu:1866
Clytia - D (1883)
   Mu:1883
Doge Candiano - D (1873)
   Mu:1876

**LIPPERT, FRIEDRICH KARL**
Neuburg 1758-1803 Vienna
Ref: Goe 11, Ko Th

Flattersinn und Liebe - D5
   Va:1801
Keiner ist, was er scheint -
C3 - Fr
   Va:1798
Das Komplott o. Die Männer-
feindin - C4
   Dr:1802   Va:1800
Papirius praetextatus o. Die
römischen Weiber waren auch
Weiber - C2
   Va:1803

Das Rezept - D1
   Va:1800
Die seltsame Audienz - C2
(1812)
   Da:1829   Va:1800

**LOGAU, GOTTHOLD**

Ein deutsches Herz - T5
   Bn:1848   Dr:1848   Fr:1849

**LOHMEYER, JULIUS**
Neiße 1834-1903 Berlin
Ref: Brüm 19, Ko Th

Der Stammhalter - F1 (1882)
   Bn:1882   Mu:1883

**LÖHN-SIEGEL, MARIA ANNA**
[Pseud.: Wilibert von Her-
rigau]
Naundorf 1830-1902 Dresden
Ref: Brüm 19, Ko 3

Gefahr über Gefahr - C4 - It
(1861)
   Dr:1858
Treumann von Sachsen - D5
   Lg:1873

**LORM, HYRONIMUS**  [Pseud. of
Heinrich Landesmann]
Nikolsburg 1821 - 1902 Brünn
Ref: Brüm 19, Ko 3, OC

Die Alten und die Jungen - D1
   Bn:1862   Va:1862
Das Forsthaus - D3
   Va:1864
Der Herzensschlüssel - C1
   Bn:1852   Dr:1852   Va:1851

**LOTZ, HANS GEORG**
Hamburg 1784-1844 Hamburg
Ref: Brüm 18, Goe 9, Ko Th,
ADB

Die Freier
   Ha:1817
Der junge Offizier - C2 - Eng
   Va:1838
Nach Sonnenuntergang - C2 -
Fr (1835)
   Bn:1833   Da:1835   Dr:1834
   Fr:1834   Ha:1833   Lg:1834
   Mu:1834   Va:1834   Wm:1834
Der Schleichhändler - D3 - Fr
   Fr:1823
Der Wechsel - C1 (1824)
   Ha:1825   Lg:1824

**LÖWEN, JOHANN FRIEDRICH**
Klausthal 1727-1771 Rostock
Ref: Brüm 18, Goe 4/1, Ko Th,
ADB

Ich habe es beschlossen - C3
- Fr (1765-66)
   Ha:1767
Die neue Agnese - C1 - Fr
   Ha:1767   Lg:1775   Va:1769
Das Rätsel - C1 (1765-66)
   Ha:1767

**LÖWENTHAL, MAX von**
Vienna 1799-1872 Traunkirchen
Ref: Goe 11, Ko Th

Anna Lovell - D4
   Bn:1843
Die beiden Schauspieler - C3
   Va:1839

**LUBARSCH, RUDOLF**   see
Schubar, L.

**LUBLINER, HUGO**   [Pseud.: Hugo
Bürger]
Breslau 1846-1911 Berlin
Ref: Brüm 19, Ko Th, OC

Die Adoptirten - C4 (1876)
   Lg:1879
Auf der Brautfahrt - C4
(1881-82)
   Bn:1880   Fr:1880   Lg:1880
   Mu:1880   Va:1881   Wm:1880
Aus der Großstadt - D4 (1883)
   Bn:1883   Da:1881   Lg:1883
   Va:1883
Die von Kleewitz - C4
   Lg:1884
Die Frau ohne Geist - C4
(1881-82)
   Bn:1879   Da:1880   Fr:1879
   Lg:1879   Mu:1879   Va:1880
Frau Susanne - D5 - with
P. Lindau (1885)
   Fr:1885   Mu:1885   Va:1885
Der Frauenadvokat - D3 (1876)
   Bn:1875   Fr:1876   Mu:1884
   Va:1874
Gabriele - D4 (1881-82)
   Bn:1878   Fr:1879   Lg:1879
   Mu:1878
Gold und Eisen - D4 (1881-82)
   Bn:1881   Fr:1881   Lg:1882
Gräfin Lambach - D4 (1886)
   Lg:1886   Va:1887
Der Jourfix - C4 (1892)
   Fr:1882   Lg:1882   Va:1882

Die Mitbürger - C4 (1884)
   Bn:1884
Der Name - D4
   Bn:1889
Sheridans Modelle - C4 (1876)
   Bn:1875   Va:1875

**LUBOJATZKY, FRANZ**
Dresden 1807-1887 Dresden
Ref: Brüm 19, Ko 3

Der Vierzehnte - C3
   Dr:1850
Die Volksadvokaten - C2
   Dr:1848

**LUDWIG, CARL**

Photographirt
   Mh:1879

**LUDWIG, OTTO**
Eisfeld 1813-1865 Dresden
Ref: Brüm 19, Ko Th, ADB, OC

Der Erbförster - T5 (1853)
   Bn:1876   Dr:1850   Fr:1883
   Ha:1861   Mh:1864   Mu:1850
   Va:1850
Die Makkabäer - T5 (1854)
   Bn:1853   Dr:1853   Fr:1870
   Lg:1869   Mh:1862   Mu:1855
   Va:1852

**MAIEN, CARL**   see Wolfsohn,
Wilhelm

**MAIER, JAKOB**
Mannheim 1739-1784 Mannheim
Ref: Goe 5, Ko Th, OC

Essserig-Esserogum o. Die
mißlungene Spekulation - C1
   Mh:1784
Fust [Faust] von Stromberg -
D6 (1782)
   Bn:1799   Da:1813   Fr:1792
   Mh:1782   Mu:1802   Va:1805
Der Sturm von Boxberg - D3
(1778)
   Mh:1781

**MAJLATH, JOHANN NEPOMUK von**
Pest 1786-1855 Starnberger
See
Ref: Brüm 18, Goe 12, Ko 3,
ADB

Der junge Ehemann - C3 - Fr
    Mu:1832   Va:1828
Das Ladenmädchen - C4 - Fr
    Va:1837
Die Zwillingsschwestern - T4
    Va:1832

**MALTEN, D. C.**

Er muß taub sein - F1 - Fr
    Da:1868

**MALTITZ, GOTTHILF AUGUST von**
Königsberg 1794-1837 Dresden
Ref: Brüm 18, Goe 11, Ko Th,
OC

Der alte Student - D2 (1828)
    Bn:1828   Dr:1835   Fr:1830
    Ha:1828   Lg:1832   Mh:1833
    Wm:1868
Fürst, Minister, Bürger o.
Das Pasquill - D4 (1829)
    Bn:1848   Fr:1849   Lg:1848
Hans Kohlhas - T5 (1827)
    Bn:1827   Da:1841   Dr:1835
    Fr:1830   Ha:1828
Die Leibrente - C1 (1838)
    Bn:1836   Dr:1835   Fr:1838
    Ha:1838   Lg:1837
Ritter Roststaub - (1835)
    Bn:1826   Da:1828   Ha:1826
Schwur und Rache - T4 (1826)
    Bn:1825   Wm:1826

**MALZ**

Herr Hampelmann im Eilwagen -
C
    Ha:1835

**MAMROTH, FEDOR**
Breslau 1851-1907 Frankfurt/M
Ref: Ko Th

Der neue Paganini - C1 - with
O. Weiß
    Va:1883
Die Reise nach Sumatra - F4 -
with O. Weiß
    Va:1883

**MAND, J. E.**  see Goldschmidt,
Karl

**MANSFELDT, JULIUS**
Braunschweig 1797-?
Ref: Ko 3

Carl der Zweite - D5
    Bn:1834

**MANSEN, GUSTAV**  see Putlitz,
Gustav Heinrich Gans

**MARBACH, HANS**
Leipzig 1841-1905 Leipzig
Ref: Brüm 19, Ko Th

Lorenzino von Medici - T5
(1875)
    Lg:1876
Marius in Minturnä - D1
(1875)
    Bn:1875
Timoleon - T5 (1869)
    Lg:1871

**MARIUS, CARL**  see Weber, Carl
von

**MARR, MARTIN HEINRICH**
Hamburg 1797-1871 Hamburg
Ref: Brüm 18, Ko Th, ADB

Bajazzo und seine Familie -
D5 - Fr (1850)
    Da:1851   Fr:1851   Ha:1851
Ein Börsenspekulant - D3 - Fr
    Wm:1855
Das Leben eines Ehrgeizigen -
D (1835)
    Ha:1835

**MARR, WILHELM**

Alter und junger Adel - C3
    Va:1875
Beim Gewitter - C1
    Va:1877
Eine Geschichte aus Kentucky
- C2
    Lg:1874   Va:1875
Noblesse oblige - C3
    Lg:1874

**MARSANO, WILHELM**
Prague 1797-1871 Görz
Ref: Brüm 18, Goe 11, Ko Th,
ADB

Die Brautschau - F5
    Da:1829   Va:1833
Die Helden - F1 (1830)
    Bn:1829   Da:1830   Dr:1831
    Fr:1831   Ha:1851   Lg:1831
    Mh:1832   Mu:1829   Va:1829
    Wm:1837

Der Rosamundens Turm o. Rit-
terliche Treue - D5
  Bn:1832  Lg:1834  Va:1829

**MARTERSTEIG, MAX**
Weimar 1853-1926 Cologne
Ref: Brüm 19, Ko Th

Im Pavillon - F1 (1878)
  Wm:1877

**MARTIN, KARL CHRISTIAN**

Die Frau als Witwe und Jung-
fer - C1 - Fr
  Va:1782
Liebe wirkt schnell - C1
  Va:1782

**MAUTNER, EDUARD**
Pest 1824-1889 Baden
Ref: Brüm 19, Ko Th, ADB

Christiane - D4 - Fr
  Va:1872
Der Courier - C1
  Va:1853
Eglantine - D4 (1863)
  Da:1866  Fr:1874  Ha:1863
  Mu:1863  Va:1863
Enterbt - D4
  Va:1881
Feodora - D4 - Fr
  Va:1883
Der Hofball - C1
  Va:1870
In dem Augarten - D1 (1880)
  Va:1880
Kriegslist - C1 (1878)
  Lg:1880  Va:1877
Die Lerche - C1 - Fr
  Va:1882
Eine Mutter vor Gericht - D1
(1872)
  Fr:1871
Das Preislustspiel - C3
(1852)
  Bn:1851  Da:1853  Fr:1851
  Mu:1851  Va:1851
Die Sanduhr - D1 (1871)
  Va:1869
Die Strike der Schmiede - D1
  Fr:1870  Lg:1870
Während der Börse - C1 (1856)
  Dr:1859  Fr:1869

**MAY, ANDREAS**
Bamberg 1817-1899 Munich
Ref: Brüm 19, Ko Th, ADB

Die Amnestie - D5 (1867)
  Lg:1866
Cinq-mars - T5 (1867)
  Dr:1849  Mu:1848
Der Courier in die Pfalz - C
(1867)
  Mu:1869
Die Heimkehr - D (1881)
  Mu:1881
Der König der Steppe - D
(1849)
  Mu:1849
Das Stammschloß - D5 (1881)
  Fr:1868  Mu:1868

**MAYER, S.**  see Harter, Ernst

**MEDDLHAMMER, ALBIN JOHANN
BAPTIST von**  see Albini

**MEISL, KARL**
Laibach 1773-1853 Vienna
Ref: Brüm 18, Goe 11, Ko Th,
ADB, OC

Carolo Carolini, der Bandi-
tenhauptmann - D5 (1801)
  Mu:1816  Va:1801
Die Damenhüte im Theater - F1
(1820)
  Mu:1831  Va:1818
Er ist mein Mann - D1 (1824)
  Bn:1823  Mh:1825  Va:1816
Der falsche Paganini [Vir-
tuose] - F2
  Mh:1830  Va:1828
Der Neffe als Braut des
Oheims - F
  Mh:1824  Va:1823
Der Pantoffelbruder - F3
  Mh:1829  Va:1829
See Goedeke 11 for additional
listings.

**MEISSNER, ALFRED**
Teplitz 1822-1885 Bregenz
Ref: Brüm 19, Ko Th, ADB, OC

Die Fruchthändlerin - D6 - Fr
  Fr:1852
Der Prätendent von York - T5
(1857)
  Va:1855  Wm:1855
Reginald Armstrong - T5
(1853)
  Bn:1852  Va:1852

MEISSNER, AUGUST GOTTLIEB
Bautzen 1753-1807 Fulda
Ref: Brüm 18, Goe 4/1, Ko Th,
ADB, OC

Die gegenseitige Probe - C1 -
Fr (1777)
   Dr:1780  Va:1779
Johann von Schwaben - T5
(1780)
   Bn:1787  Dr:1783  Ha:1784
Der Schachspieler - C1 (1782)
   Dr:1782
Der stürmische [aufbrausende]
Liebhaber - C3 - Fr (1778)
   Dr:1778  Ha:1779
Der Verschwender - C5 - Fr
   Dr:1779

MEJO, WILHELM
1821/31-1888 Berlin
Ref: Ko Th

Ein feiner Diplomat - C1 - Fr
   Da:1883  Lg:1886
Lustspiel aus dem Leben - C4
   Va:1881

MELS, AUGUST [Pseud. of
Martin Cohn]
Berlin 1829-1894 Summerdale,
Illinois
Ref: Brüm 19, Ko Th, ADB

Die beste Reise - C2
   Va:1876
Heines junge Leiden - D3
(1871)
   Fr:1876  Lg:1874  Mu:1880
   Va:1873
Der Staatsanwalt - D4 (1875)
   Lg:1879

MENNER, JOSEPH STEPHAN von
Brünn 1774-1823 Vienna
Ref: Goe 11, Ko Th

Maria von Burgund [Maria,
Tochter Karls des Kühnen] -
D4 (1807)
   Fr:1808  Va:1807

MEYER, FRIEDRICH [Pseud.:
Friedrich Meyer von Waldeck]
Arolsen 1824-1899 Heidelberg
Ref: Brüm 19, Ko Th

Der Pate des Kardinals - D1
(1855)
   Bn:1872

MEYER, FRIEDRICH LUDWIG
WILHELM
Harburg 1759-1840 Bramstädt
Ref: Brüm 18, Goe 4/1, Ko Th,
ADB

Der Autor - C2 - Eng (1783)
   Va:1783
Imogen - D5 - Eng (1782)
   Va:1782
Kronau und Albertine - D5 -
Fr - with F. Schröder (1783)
   Dr:1785  Va:1783
Der seltne Freier o. Alter
schützt vor Torheit nicht -
C3 - Fr (1781)
   Bn:1782  Dr:1782  Mh:1782
   Va:1781
Taps o. Wie gewonnen, so zer-
ronnen - F2 - Fr (1793)
   Va:1793
Treue und Undank - C1 (1782)
   Bn:1782  Dr:1782  Va:1782
Die Übereilung - C1 - Eng
(1790)
   Bn:1789  Da:1815  Dr:1790
   Fr:1795  Ha:1788  Mh:1788
   Wm:1793
Die Versuchung - C1 - Fr
   Wm:1802

MEYERN-HOHENBERG, GUSTAV von
Kalvörde 1826-1878 Konstanz
Ref: Brüm 19, Ko Th, ADB

Die Cavaliere - D5 - Fr
(1874)
   Bn:1869  Mh:1868  Mu:1868
Heinrich von Schwerin - D5
(1859)
   Bn:1858  Dr:1858  Fr:1863
   Wm:1858
Prinz Eugen - D4
   Da:1861

MEYR, MELCHIOR
Ehringen 1810-1871 Munich
Ref: Brüm 19, Ko Th, ADB, OC

Agnes Bernauerin [Herzog Al-
brecht o. Vater und Sohn] -
T5 (1862)
   Bn:1852  Da:1866  Fr:1852
   Mu:1854  Va:1864
Karl der Kühne - T (1862)
   Mu:1858
Liebe um Liebe und Treue um
Treue
   Mu:1855

**MICHELL, GUSTAV**
Stolberg 1842-?
Ref: Ko Th

Therese - D3 (1878)
   Wm:1878

**MIKOLASCH, J. E.**

Die verhängnisvolle Reise -
C3
   Va:1845

**MIKSCH, J. R.**

Der Ehestifter - C2
   Bn:1837  Dr:1832  Lg:1832
   Va:1837  Wm:1831
Die Mitgift - C1 - It
   Dr:1832

**MILLENET, JOHANN HEINRICH**
[Pseud.: M. Tenelli]
Berlin 1785-1859 Gotha
Ref: Goe 11, Ko Th, ADB

Die Damen unter sich - C1 -
Fr (1837)
   Bn:1830  Dr:1831  Ha:1830
   Mu:1834  Va:1834  Wm:1830
Er muß nach Magdeburg - C2
(1850)
   Fr:1850
Er und sie - F1 - Fr
   Lg:1846
Die Kinder Eduards von Eng-
land - T3 - Fr
   Wm:1838
Mademoiselle - C2 - Fr
   Bn:1839  Ha:1839
Die Mönche - C3 - Fr
   Bn:1837  Fr:1850  Fr:1848
   Ha:1839
Papchen - C3
   Bn:1838  Ha:1839
Der Prinz von Ungefähr - C2 -
Fr (1819)
   Bn:1818  Da:1819
Die Scheidung - C3 - Fr
   Wm:1832
Der Übel größtes ist die
Schuld - D2
   Wm:1831
Der Verstorbene - F1
   Bn:1840
Zwei Jahre nachher o. Wer
trägt die Schuld? - C1 - Fr
   Wm:1830

**MINDING, JULIUS**
Breslau 1808-1850 New York
Ref: Brüm 19, Ko 3

Papst Sixtus V. - T5 (1870)
   Bn:1874  Lg:1872

**MISCH, ROBERT**
Schloß Zurczyn 1860-1929 Ber-
lin
Ref: Brüm 19, Ko Th

Die Liebesleugnerin - D
(1886)
   Fr:1887

**MITZENIUS, ADOLPH**
Darmstadt 1831-1889 Gießen
Ref: Brüm 19, Ko 3

Harun al Raschid, der König
der Nacht - D5 (1867)
   Da:1866

**MÖLLER, HEINRICH FERDINAND**
Olbersdorf 1745-1798 Fehrbel-
lin
Ref: Goe 4/1, Ko Th, ADB

Der Graf von Waltron o. Die
Subordination - D5 (1776)
   Bn:1777  Dr:1778  Fr:1777
   Ha:1777  Mh:1782  Mu:1786
   Va:1776
Sophie o. Der gerechte Fürst
D3 (1777)
   Bn:1778
Wikkinson und Wandrop - D5
(1779)
   Dr:1781

**MORLÄNDER, MORITZ** [i.e.
Engländer]
Eisenstadt 1819-1898 Budapest
Ref: Ko 3

Theatralischer Unsinn - F4
(ca. 1876)
   Fr:1862  Ha:1855

**MOSEN, JULIUS**
Marieney 1803-1867 Oldenburg
Ref: Brüm 19, Goe 13, Ko Th,
ADB, OC

Die Bräute von Florenz - T5
(1842)
   Dr:1841

Herzog Bernhard von Weimar -
T5 (1855)
   Bn:1866  Dr:1842  Mh:1847
Johann von Österreich - T5
(1863)
   Dr:1846
Otto III. - T5 (1842)
   Dr:1839
Der Sohn des Fürsten - T5
(1855)
   Da:1845  Fr:1847  Ha:1845
   Mu:1847

**MOSENTHAL, SALOMON HERMANN**
[Pseud.: Friedrich Lechner]
Kassel 1821-1877 Vienna
Ref: Brüm 19, Ko Th, ADB, OC

Cäcilia von Albano - D5
(1851)
   Bn:1850  Va:1849
Conrad Vorlauf - T5 (1878)
   Va:1872
Deborah - FP4 (1850)
   Bn:1849  Da:1850  Dr:1849
   Fr:1849  Ha:1849  Mh:1850
   Mu:1849  Va:1864  Wm:1849
Die deutschen Komödianten -
D5 (1863)
   Bn:1864  Fr:1863  Ha:1862
   Mh:1862  Va:1862  Wm:1863
Der Dorflehrer - D1 (1852)
   Da:1855  Va:1852
Düweke - D5 (1860)
   Fr:1860  Va:1859
Gabriele von Precy - D4
(1852)
   Va:1853
Der Goldschmied von Ulm - FP3
   Bn:1856  Dr:1856
Isabella Orsini - D5 (1870)
   Bn:1870  Da:1872  Fr:1876
   Lg:1870  Mu:1869  Va:1869
Madeleine Morel - D5 (1878)
   Va:1871
Maryna - D5 (1871)
   Va:1870
Parisina - T - (1878)
   Va:1875
Pietra - T5 (1865)
   Bn:1864  Mh:1864  Va:1865
Der Schulze von Altenbüren -
D4 (1868)
   Fr:1868  Ha:1868  Lg:1868
   Mh:1868  Mu:1868  Va:1867
Die Sirene - C4 (1870)
   Bn:1874  Lg:1875  Mu:1874
   Va:1874  Wm:1874
Die Sklaven - D (1847)
   Ha:1849

Der Sonnwendhof - FP5 (1857)
   Bn:1854  Da:1854  Dr:1854
   Fr:1854  Ha:1854  Mh:1855
   Mu:1867  Va:1854  Wm:1854

**MOSER, GUSTAV von**
Spandau 1825-1903 Görlitz
Ref: Brüm 19, Ko Th, OC

Alfred - F4
   Fr:1886  Lg:1886
Ein amerikanisches Duell - C1
(1874)
   Bn:1872
Aus Liebe zur Kunst - F1
(1873)
   Da:1863  Fr:1862  Ha:1862
   Wm:1864
Der Bibliothekar - F4 (1878)
   Bn:1880  Da:1880  Fr:1880
   Lg:1880  Mu:1880  Va:1880
   Wm:1880
Der Bojar o. Wie denken Sie
über Rumänien? - F1 (1872)
   Fr:1871
Der Bureaukrat - C4
   Fr:1887  Lg:1885  Wm:1888
Der Elefant - C4 (1873-94)
   Bn:1873  Fr:1873  Lg:1873
   Mu:1873  Wm:1873
Er soll dein Herr sein - C1
(1867)
   Fr:1873  Va:1859  Wm:1864
Fanny o. Ebbe und Flut - C1
   Va:1861
Eine Frau, die in Paris war -
C1 (1866)
   Fr:1863  Va:1861
Glück bei Frauen - C4 (1885)
   Bn:1883  Lg:1882
Die Gouvernante - C1 (1872)
   Bn:1872  Fr:1871  Wm:1872
Der Hausarzt - C1 (1873-94)
   Bn:1881  Mu:1879  Va:1879
Hektor - F1 (1877)
   Da:1878  Fr:1877  Va:1877
   Wm:1877
Herrn Kaudels Gardinen-
predigten - C1 (1874)
   Bn:1869  Da:1870  Fr:1870
   Mu:1870  Wm:1870
Der Hypochonder - C4 (1878)
   Da:1877  Fr:1877  Lg:1877
   Mu:1877  Va:1877  Wm:1877
Hypothekennot - C1 (1872)
   Bn:1871  Mu:1871
Ich werde mir den Major ein-
laden - C1 - Fr (1862)
   Da:1861  Dr:1861  Fr:1867
   Ha:1861  Va:1876  Wm:1867

Kalte Seelen - C4 (1881)
    Va:1882
Eine kranke Frau - F3 - with
W. Drost (1883)
    Fr:1863  Wm:1875
Krieg und Frieden - C5 - with
F. Schöntan (1880)
    Da:1880  Fr:1880  Lg:1880
    Mu:1880  Va:1880  Wm:1880
Die Leibrente - F5 (1901)
    Fr:1885  Lg:1885
Die Leiden junger Frauen - C1
(1867)
    Bn:1860  Fr:1866
Mädchenschwüre - C3 (1877)
    Bn:1878  Va:1878
Mit Vergnügen - F4 - with
O. Girndt
    Da:1886  Fr:1886  Lg:1884
    Va:1883
Ein moderner Barbar - C1
(1861)
    Da:1870  Fr:1871  Lg:1867
    Va:1859
Moritz Schnörche o. Die
Bürgermeisterwahl - F1 - with
R. Benedix (1862)
    Da:1874  Dr:1861  Fr:1863
Die Novizen - D3
    Bn:1862
Onkel Grog - C3 (1878)
    Lg:1878
Papa hat's erlaubt - F1 -
with A. L'Arronge (1872)
    Da:1876  Fr:1872  Wm:1882
Reflexe - C1 (1877)
    Bn:1877  Va:1878
Der Registrator auf Reisen -
F3 - with A. L'Arronge (1879)
    Da:1876  Fr:1875  Mu:1873
    Wm:1874
Reif von Reiflingen - F5
(1882)
    Da:1882  Fr:1882  Lg:1882
    Mu:1882  Va:1882
Der Salontiroler - C4 (1873-
94)
    Da:1885  Fr:1884  Lg:1885
Der Schimmel - C1 (1877)
    Da:1880  Fr:1877  Va:1877
Der Sklave - C4 - Rus
    Lg:1877  Va:1881  Wm:1877
Der Soldatenfreund - F5 -
with O. Girndt
    Lg:1887
Sonntagsjäger o. Verplefft -
F1 - with D. Kalisch (1876)
    Fr:1863  Wm:1863

Splitter und Balken - C1
(1872)
    Fr:1873  Va:1872  Wm:1886
Die Sternschnuppe - F4 - with
O. Girndt
    Fr:1887  Lg:1886
Das Stiftungsfest - F3 (1873)
    Bn:1871  Da:1872  Fr:1872
    Lg:1872  Mu:1872  Va:1872
    Wm:1872
Ein Stoff von Gerson - C1
(1876)
    Fr:1873
Die Sünderin - C1 (1888)
    Lg:1872
Ultimo - C5 (1874)
    Da:1874  Fr:1874  Lg:1874
    Mh:1874  Mu:1874  Va:1874
    Wm:1874
Unsere Frauen - C5 - with
F. Schöntan (1881)
    Da:1881  Fr:1881  Lg:1881
    Mu:1881  Va:1873  Wm:1881
Der Veilchenfresser - C3
(1874)
    Da:1876  Fr:1876  Lg:1875
    Mh:1875  Mu:1874  Va:1876
    Wm:1875
Vernachlässigt die Frauen
nicht - C1 (1867)
    Lg:1868
Die Versucherin - C1 (1876)
    Da:1875  Fr:1875  Va:1875
    Wm:1874
Wenn man Whist spielt - C1
(1866)
    Fr:1863
Wenn Männer ausgehen wollen -
C1
    Fr:1863
Wie denken Sie über Rußland?
o. Der erste Dienst - C1
(1861)
    Da:1859  Fr:1859  Va:1859
    Wm:1860
Der Zugvogel - F4 - with
F. Schöntan (1880)
    Va:1882

**MOSING, GUIDO KONRAD**
[Pseud.: Guido Conrad]
Vienna 1824-1907 Vienna
Ref: Brüm 19, Ko Th

Atho, der Priesterkönig - T5
(1877)
    Va:1876
Das Fräulein von Lanvy - D5
(1871)
    Va:1871

**MOYS de SONS, KARL**
Munich 1827-1894 Gardone
Ref: Brüm 19, Ko Th

Ein deutscher Standesherr -
D4 (1879)
    Bn:1880  Mu:1879  Va:1880
Die Spinne - C (1884)
    Mu:1881

**MÜHLBACH, LUISE** [Pseud. of
Klara Mundt, née Müller]
Neubrandenburg 1814-1873 Berlin
Ref: Brüm 19, Ko 3, ADB, OC

Lady Ellen - C3
    Bn:1845  Ha:1844
Ein Vormittag in Sanssouci -
C2
    Da:1860

**MÜLLER, ARTHUR**
Neumarkt 1830-1873 Munich
Ref: Brüm 19, Ko Th, ADB

Geächtet o. Otto der Große
und sein Haus (1867)
    Mu:1869
Gute Nacht, Hänschen! - C1
(1865)
    Ha:1868
Die Kaiserglocke von Speyer -
D
    Mu:1871
Der schwarze Wilhelm - D1
(1860)
    Fr:1861
Die Verschwörung der Frauen
o. Die Preußen in Breslau -
C4 (1875)
    Da:1859  Fr:1858  Ha:1858
    Mu:1872
Ein vest Burg ist unser Gott
- FP4 (1861)
    Wm:1861
Das Wichtel o. Ein guter
Hausgeist - D5 (1866)
    Da:1862

**MÜLLER, HUGO**
Posen 1830-1881 Niederwalluf
Ref: Brüm 19, Ko Th

Adelaide - D1 (1869)
    Bn:1869  Da:1869  Fr:1868
    Ha:1868  Lg:1868  Mh:1869
    Va:1883  Wm:1869
Die Arbeiter - D - Fr (1870)
    Mu:1870

Bartelmanns Leiden - D5 - It
    Da:1872
Der Diplomat der alten Schule
- C3 (1867)
    Bn:1869  Lg:1867  Mu:1881
    Va:1872
Duft - C1 (1872)
    Da:1870  Fr:1872
Fürst Emil - D5 (1868)
    Lg:1868
Gewonnene Herzen - FP3 (1875)
    Wm:1871
Im Wartesaal erster Klasse -
C1 (1865)
    Bn:1866  Da:1865  Fr:1864
    Ha:1866  Lg:1865  Va:1874
    Wm:1864
Onkel Moses - D1 (1872)
    Da:1881  Fr:1869  Lg:1869
Welcher? - C (1871)
    Fr:1872  Mu:1871
Zwei Brüder - D5
    Bn:1868

**MÜLLER, JOHANN HEINRICH**
Halberstadt 1738-1815 Vienna
Ref: Brüm 19, Goe 5, Ko Th

Der Ausgang o. Die Genesung -
C3
    Va:1778
Der Heuchler - D5 - Fr (1788)
    Va:1788
Die Neugierige - C4 - Fr
(1783)
    Va:1783
Nina o. Wahnwitz aus Liebe -
C1 - Fr (1788)
    Va:1788
Der Optimist o. Der Mann, dem
alles behagt - D5 - Fr
    Va:1788
Präsentirt das Gewehr! - C2
(1775)
    Bn:1776  Da:1779  Ha:1777
    Mh:1780  Va:1775
Die unähnlichen Brüder o.
Unglück prüft das Herz - C5
(1771)
    Mu:1772  Va:1771
Was ist's? - C1 (1786)
    Va:1786
Wind für Wind! - F3 (1786)
    Va:1786

**MÜLLER, KAROLINE**
1806-?

Das Geheimnis - C3 - Fr
    Va:1839

Der Reise-Commis - C2 - Fr
    Va:1839
Die Schwestern - D2 - FR
    Va:1839

**MÜLLER, OTTO**
Schotten am Vogelsberg 1816-
1894 Frankfurt/M
Ref: Brüm 19, Ko Th, ADB

Charlotte Ackermann - D5
(1854)
    Da:1854   Fr:1854   Ha:1854
    Va:1855

**MÜLLER, WOLFGANG** [Pseud.:
Wolfgang Müller von Königs-
winter]
Königswinter 1816-1873 Bad
Neuenahr
Ref: Brüm 19, Ko Th, ADB, OC

Ein Autographensammler - D1
    Bn:1870   Fr:1868
Die Frau Kommerzienrätin - C3
(1872)
    Da:1868
In der Kur - F1 (1872)
    Fr:1864
Sie hat ihr Herz entdeckt -
C1 (1865)
    Bn:1870   Da:1864   Fr:1864
    Ha:1867   Lg:1865   Mu:1867
    Va:1867   Wm:1866
Über den Parteien - C5 (1872)
    Va:1869

**MÖLLNER, ADOLF**
Langendorf 1774-1829 Weißen-
fels
Ref: Brüm 18, Goe 8, Ko Th,
ADB, OC

Die Albaneserin - T5 (1820)
    Bn:1820   Ha:1820   Lg:1820
    Mu:1822   Va:1820   Wm:1820
Der Blitz [Blitzstrahl] - C1
(1820)
    Bn:1814   Da:1818   Dr:1817
    Fr:1814   Mh:1818   Va:1815
    Wm:1814
Der Gebesserte o. Ein Aben-
teuer in Spaa - C1
    Fr:1820
Die großen Kinder - C2 (1820)
    Bn:1813   Da:1818   Dr:1816
    Fr:1814   Ha:1816   Lg:1815
    Mh:1815   Va:1813   Wm:1813

Die Onkelei o. Das französi-
sche Lustspiel - C1 - Fr
(1820)
    Bn:1818   Da:1819   Dr:1817
    Fr:1818   Lg:1819   Mh:1825
    Va:1817   Wm:1819
Die Rückkunft aus Surinam -
C3 (1815)
    Bn:1812   Fr:1815   Va:1813
Die Schuld - T4 (1816)
    Bn:1814   Da:1818   Dr:1814
    Fr:1814   Ha:1815   Lg:1815
    Mh:1814   Mu:1816   Va:1813
    Wm:1814
Die Vertrauten - C2 - Fr
(1815)
    Bn:1812   Da:1814   Dr:1814
    Fr:1814   Ha:1816   Lg:1817
    Mh:1814   Mu:1816   Va:1812
    Wm:1812
Der Wahn o. Der 29. Februar -
D1 (1812)
    Bn:1816   Lg:1812   Va:1815
Yngard, König der Normannen -
T4 (1817)
    Bn:1817   Da:1820   Dr:1817
    Mh:1822   Mu:1820   Va:1816
    Wm:1827
Die Zweiflerin - D1 - Fr
(1817)
    Bn:1812   Da:1817   Dr:1820
    Lg:1818   Va:1816

**MÜNCH-BELLINGHAUSEN, ELIGIUS
FRANZ JOSEPH von** see Halm,
Friedrich

**MUNDT, KLARA** see Mühlbach,
Luise

**MURAD EFFENDI** [i.e. Franz v.
Werner]
Vienna 1836-1881 The Hague
Ref: Brüm 19, Ko Th, ADB

Bogadil - C1 (1874)
    Bn:1875   Mu:1875
Marino Faliero - T5 (1871)
    Lg:1875
Mirabeau - T5 (1875)
    Va:1875
Selim der Dritte - T5 (1872)
    Va:1872

**NAUMANN**

Der edle Egoist - D3
Dr:1795

**NAUNDORFF, A. JULIUS**  see
Dornau, Julius

**NEPOS, FRANZ**  see Pocci,
Franz von

**NESSELRODE, F. G. von**
Ref: Goe 5

Der adelige Tagelöhner - D3
(1774)
Dr:1779
Die doppelte Kindesliebe - D3
(1780)
Dr:1787
Wer hätte das gedacht? - C3
(1779)
Dr:1781

**NESTROY, JOHANN NEPOMUK**
Vienna 1801-1862 Graz
Ref: Brüm 19, Ko Th, ADB, OC

Der Affe und der Bräutigam -
F3 (1890-91)
Da:1843  Dr:1838  Ha:1849
Va:1836
Die beiden Nachtwandler o.
Der verwünschte Zopf - Z2
(1890-91)
Da:1844  Dr:1837  Fr:1837
Ha:1845  Mu:1872  Va:1836
Der böse Geist Lumpazivaga-
bundus o. Das liederliche
Kleeblatt - F3 (1835)
Bn:1834  Da:1836  Dr:1834
Fr:1834  Ha:1834  Lg:1834
Mu:1834  Va:1833  Wm:1835
Eulenspiegel o. Schabernack
über Schabernack - F4 (1841)
Da:1842  Dr:1850  Fr:1836
Mu:1845  Va:1835
Der Färber und sein Zwil-
lingsbruder - F3 (1890-91)
Ha:1844  Va:1840
Frühere Verhältnisse - F1
(1890-91)
Fr:1885  Va:1862
Glück, Mißbrauch und Rückkehr
o. Das Geheimnis des grauen
Hauses - C (1845)
Ha:1841  Va:1838
Das Haus der Temperamente -
F2 (1890-91)
Da:1855  Va:1837

Hinüber-herüber - F1 (1890-
91)
Ha:1845  Va:1844
Einen Jux will er sich machen
- F4 (1844)
Da:1845  Dr:1842  Fr:1843
Ha:1842  Mu:1862  Va:1842
Wm:1857
Kampl - F3 (1890-91)
Ha:1852  Va:1852
Liebesgeschichten und Hei-
ratssachen - F3 (1890-91)
Ha:1844  Va:1843
Das Mädel aus der Vorstadt -
F (1845)
Ha:1847  Mu:1845  Va:1841
Mein Freund - F3 (1890-91)
Fr:1851  Va:1851
Nur Ruhe - F1 (1890-91)
Fr:1851  Va:1843
Der Schützling - F4 (1890-91)
Fr:1847  Ha:1847  Va:1847
Der Talisman - F3 (1843)
Da:1865  Dr:1841  Fr:1841
Ha:1841  Mu:1845  Va:1840
Wm:1859
Tannhäuser - F3 (1924-30)
Fr:1857  Ha:1858  Va:1857
Tritsch-Tratsch - F1 (1890-
91)
Fr:1847  Va:1833
Umsonst - F1 (1890-91)
Fr:1865  Va:1857
Unverhofft - C3 - Fr (1848)
Dr:1845  Fr:1853  Ha:1845
Mu:1845  Va:1845
Die verhängnisvolle
Faschingsnacht - F3 (1841)
Ha:1845  Mu:1839  Va:1839
Der Zerrissene - F3 (1845)
Da:1848  Dr:1844  Fr:1847
Ha:1844  Va:1844  Wm:1847
Zu ebener Erde und erster
Stock - F3 (1838)
Da:1839  Dr:1836  Fr:1836
Mu:1836  Va:1835  Wm:1863

**NEUBRINGER, FERDINAND LUDWIG**
Düsseldorf 1836-1895
Frankfurt/M
Ref: Brüm 19, Ko Th

Das Gastmahl des Pontius - T
(1887)
Fr:1887
Laroche - T5 (1882)
Fr:1882
Die Marquise von Pommeray - T
(1875)
Fr:1876

**NEUERT, HANS** [i.e. Reitinger]
Munich 1838-1912 Zurich
Ref: Brüm 19, Ko Th

Der Geigenmacher von Mitten-
wald - FP3 - with L. Gang-
hofer (1884)
    Fr:1885 Mu:1884 Wm:1886
Der Herrgottschnitzer von Am-
mergau - FP5 - with L. Gang-
hofer (1880)
    Dr:1884 Fr:1884 Mu:1880
Wm:1885
Im Austragstübchen - FP4
(1885)
    Fr:1884 Mu:1882 Wm:1885
Der Prozeßhandel - FP4 - with
L. Ganghofer (1881)
    Fr:1884 Mu:1881 Wm:1885
Der Schlagring - FP (1882)
    Fr:1885 Mu:1879

**NEUSTADT, BERNHARD FERDINAND**
Berlin 1796-? Breslau
Ref: Brüm 18, Ko Th

Ben David der Knabenräuber -
D5 (1832)
    Fr:1831 Ha:1837 Lg:1832

**NEUSTÄTTER, FERDINAND**

Pflichten - D1
    Da:1870 Mu:1872

**NIBAUR, A. von**

In der Theaterloge - C1
    Bn:1860 Dr:1861 Va:1861

**NIEMEYER, ANTON CHRISTIAN**
Halle 1783-?
Ref: Brüm 18, Goe 7, Ko Th

Der Cid - T5 - Fr (1808)
    Bn:1806 Wm:1806
Die Hintergangenen - C1 - Fr
(1808)
    Bn:1811
Die Testamentsklauseln - C1
    Bn:1822

**NIENDORF, MARC ANTON**
Niemegk 1826-1878 Nieder-
lößnitz
Ref: Brüm 19, ADB

Wahl und Qual - D1
    Fr:1871

**NISSEL, FRANZ**
Vienna 1831-1893 Gleichenberg
Ref: Brüm 19, Ko Th, ADB, OC

Agnes von Meran - T5 (1877)
    Va:1879 Wm:1879
Heinrich der Löwe - D5 (1858)
    Dr:1859 Va:1858
Perseus von Makedonien - T5
(1862)
    Va:1862
Ein Wohltäter - D3 (1854)
    Mh:1858 Va:1856
Die Zauberin am Stein - P4
(1864)
    Ha:1863 Va:1862

**NISSEN**
Hamburg

Der eigne Richter - D
    Ha:1786

**NOAK**

Der Nachtwandler wider Willen
- F1
    Va:1877

**NOLTE, VINCENT**
Livorno 1770-1856 Paris
Ref: Goe 11, ADB

Die Zigeunerin - D5 - Fr
(1830)
    Mh:1831

**NORDECK zu NORDECK, KARL
THEODOR**
1793-1853
Ref: Goe 10, Ko 2

Tancred und Clorinde - T5
(1821)
    Ha:1819

**NORWEG, HANS**

Antoinette - D4 - with
K. Kraatz
    Da:1888 Fr:1888

**OCHSENHEIMER, FERDINAND**
Mainz 1765-1822 Vienna
Ref: Brüm 18, Goe 5, Ko Th,
ADB

Der Brautschatz - C1 (1807)
    Va:1814
Er soll sich schlagen - C1
(1792)
    Da:1813   Dr:1797   Fr:1808
Das Manuskript - D1 (1791)
    Dr:1795   Mh:1791

**OEHLENSCHLÄGER, ADAM GOTTLOB**
Westerbroe 1779-1850 Copen-
hagen
Ref: Brüm 18, Goe 6, Ko Th,
OC

Axel und Walburg - T5 (1810)
    Bn:1817   Da:1820   Dr:1817
    Lg:1815   Mh:1824   Va:1814
Correggio - T5 (1816)
    Bn:1828   Da:1817   Dr:1828
    Fr:1818   Ha:1817   Lg:1819
    Mh:1818   Mu:1818   Va:1815
    Wm:1819
Dina - T5 (1850)
    Dr:1845   Va:1846
Die Drillingsbrüder von
Damascus - D5 (1839)
    Bn:1832
Hakon Jarl - T5 (1809)
    Dr:1816   Lg:1816
Die Ludlamshöhle - D5 (1818)
    Da:1819   Mu:1823   Wm:1818
Robinson in England - C5
(1821)
    Wm:1822

**OLFERS, MARIA von**  [Pseud.:
Maria Werner]
Berlin 1826-1924 Berlin
Ref: Brüm 19

Frauenkampf [Der Damenkrieg]
C3 - Fr
    Bn:1876   Da:1852   Fr:1851
    Wm:1851
Der Freiwillige - C3 - Fr
    Fr:1854   Wm:1855
Die Geldfrage - C5
    Fr:1857
Onkel Tom - D4
    Fr:1853

**ORTLEB, F. WOLDEMAR**  see
Clement, Lothar

**OSENHEIM**

Der Freund aus der Provinz -
C2 - Fr
    Va:1836

**OSTSEE, JOHANNES von der**  see
Falk, Johann Daniel

**OSWALD, TH.**

Gasthaus-Abenteuer - F3
    Bn:1848   Da:1851   Fr:1848

**OTTO, REINHARD**

Ein Morgen Peters des
Großen - D
    Fr:1880

**PABST, JULIUS**
Wilhelmsruhe 1817-1881
Dresden
Ref: Brüm 19, Ko Th

Die Tonkunst und vier
deutsche Meister - D1 (1859)
    Dr:1859

**PACHLER, FAUSTUS**  [Pseud.:
C. Paul]
Graz 1819-1892 Graz
Ref: Brüm 19, Ko Th

Loge Nr. 2 - C1 (1876)
    Va:1877

**PALFFY, FERDINAND von**
Vienna 1774-1840 Vienna
Ref: Ko Th

Die besondere Familien-
Eigenschaft - C3
    Va:1806

**PANNASCH, ANTON**
Brussels 1789-1855 Vienna
Ref: Brüm 18, Goe 11, Ko 2,
ADB

Alboin - T5 (1835)
    Va:1833
Die Christnacht - D1 (1837)
    Va:1836
Clemence Isaure - T5 (1835)
    Mu:1826   Va:1835

Czerny Georg - D5 (1847)
　　Va:1849
Der Erbgraf - D1
　　Va:1847
Der Findling - T1 (1826)
　　Va:1817
Die Grafen von Montalto - T5
(1826)
　　Va:1824
Johnsons Tod - D2 - Eng
　　Va:1839
Maximilian in Flandern - D5
(1835)
　　Va:1837
Die Wette - C4 (1840)
　　Bn:1840　Va:1840

**PANSE, KARL**
Naumburg 1798-1871 Weimar
Ref: Brüm 19, Goe 11, Ko 2

Die Fischerin von Island - T5
　　Dr:1829　Lg:1830
Der König und sein Kind - T
　　Wm:1845

**PAPE, GEORG**

Die Reisenden - C1
　　Va:1788

**PASSY, JOSEPH**
Vienna 1786-1820 Vienna
Ref: Brüm 18, Goe 6, Ko 2

Die Verschreibung - C1
　　Bn:1810　Va:1810

**PAUERSBACH, JOSEF von**
Ref: Brüm 18, Goe 5

Der Herr Gevatter o. Etwas
für Land und Eheleute - C1 -
Fr (1778)
　　Va:1778
Die indianische Witwe o. Der
Scheiterhaufen - C1 - Fr
(1772)
　　Lg:1782　Va:1772
Der redliche Bauer und der
großmütige Jude - C3 - Eng
(1774)
　　Va:1774
Der Tote, ein Freier - C2 -
Fr (1778)
　　Va:1778

**PAUL, C.** see Pachler, Faustus

**PAUL, C. A.**

Das bin ich - C1 (1869)
　　Da:1871　Fr:1870

**PAWLOFF, CAROLINE von**
Jaroslaw 1812-?

Eine übereilte Ehe - C2
　　Bn:1860　Dr:1859

**PELZEL, JOSEF BERNHARD**
Reichenau 1745-1804
Ref: Brüm 18, Goe 5, Ko 2,
ADB

Die Hausplage - C5 (1770)
　　Va:1770
Hedwigis von Westenwang o.
Die Belagerung von Wien - T5
(1780)
　　Va:1780
Das Liebhaber-Duell - C2 -
Eng
　　Va:1789
Viel gewagt und Nichts gewon-
nen - F2 - Eng
　　Va:1789
Yariko - T1 (1770)
　　Va:1771

**PERFALL, KARL** [Pseud.:
Theodor von der Ammer]
Landsberg 1851-1924 Cologne
Ref: Brüm 19, Ko 2, OC

Die Brüder - D
　　Mu:1889

**PERINET, JOACHIM**
Vienna 1765-1816 Vienna
Ref: Brüm 18, Goe 5, Ko 2,
ADB, OC

Das Freikorps - C3 (1788)
　　Va:1788
Der Geisterseher
　　Lg:1794

**PERRON, PAUL** [Pseud. of
Oskar Riecke]
Hamburg 1848-1909 Hamburg
Ref: Brüm 19, Ko 2

Warum haben Sie das nicht
gleich gesagt? - F1 (1876)
　　Bn:1880

PESCHKAU, EMIL    [Pseud.:
Emil Bauer]
Ref: Brüm 19, Ko 2

Gefährliche Leute - F1
    Fr:1883
Ein Reiseabenteuer - F1
(1883)
    Da:1884

PETERMANN, KARL MAXIMILIAN
Bayreuth 1722-1794 Bayreuth
Ref: Goe 4

Der Gleichgültige - C5 (1773)
    Bn:1775  Dr:1780

PEUCER, FRIEDRICH
Buttstädt 1779-1849 Weimar
Ref: Brüm 18, Goe 11

Die Familie Riquebour - C1 -
Fr (1835)
    Bn:1835  Wm:1831
Hernani o. Castilianische
Ehre - D5 - Fr (1834)
    Wm:1830
Der Wanderer und die Päch-
terin - D1 (1821)
    Wm:1815

PHILIPPI, FELIX
Berlin 1851-1921 Berlin
Ref: Brüm 18, Ko 2, OC

Der Advokat - D5 (1886)
    Wm:1887
Daniela - D4 (1888)
    Bn:1886  Fr:1886  Mu:1886
    Wm:1886
Irrlicht - D (1886)
    Mu:1885
Meeresleuchten - C1 (1887)
    Fr:1887

PICHLER, KAROLINE, née
Greiker
Vienna 1769-1843 Vienna
Ref: Brüm 18, Goe 5, Ko 2,
ADB, OC

Germanicus - T5 - Fr (1822)
    Va:1812
Heinrich von Hohenstaufen -
T5 (1822)
    Bn:1814  Ha:1816  Mh:1821
    Mu:1815  Va:1813  Wm:1815
Wiedersehen - D2 (1822)
    Va:1814

PIDERIT, THEODOR
Detmold 1826-1912 Detmold
Ref: Brüm 19, Ko 2

Gründlich kuriert - C3
    Fr:1877

PILLWITZ, FERDINAND

Rataplan, der kleine Tambour
- Vv1 - Fr
    Da:1835  Dr:1833  Fr:1833
    Ha:1844  Mh:1832  Mu:1834
    Wm:1833

PIRAZZI, EMIL
Offenbach 1832-1898 Offenbach
Ref: Ko 2, ADB

Auf der Hochzeitsreise - C1
(1890)
    Da:1882  Fr:1878
Die Erbin von Maurach - D5
(1875)
    Da:1876  Fr:1876
Rienzi, der Tribun - T5
(1873)
    Da:1878  Fr:1884  Wm:1874

PLATEN, AUGUST, GRAF von
Ansbach 1796-1835 Syrakus
Ref: Brüm 18, Goe 8, Ko 2,
ADB, OC

Treue um Treue - D4 (1828)
    Wm:1854
Der Turm mit sieben Pforten -
C1 (1828)
    Wm:1854

PLESSNER, E. L.

Eine halbe Stunde Aufenthalt
- F1 (1858)
    Da:1866

PLÖTZ, JOHANN von
Munich 1786-1856 Munich
Ref: Brüm 18, Goe 11, Ko 2

Das Abenteuer einer Neujahrsnacht - C3 (1835)
    Bn:1832  Mu:1831
Dumm und gelehrt - F1 (1844)
    Da:1847  Lg:1858
Die Hintertreppe o. Die Gunst
der Kleinen - Fr (1821)
    Bn:1820  Dr:1820  Fr:1830
    Lg:1830  Mu:1821

Poesie und Prosa - C1 (1817)
Va:1819
Der Ruf o. Die Journalisten -
C1 - Fr (1840)
Bn:1843  Da:1845
Stolz der Geburt und Stolz
des Glücks o. Der Kaufmann
von Hamburg - C5 (1835)
Mu:1826
Das Testament eines Schau-
spielers o. Die beiden Debü-
tanten - F1
Wm:1841
Der verwunschene Prinz - F3
(1844)
Bn:1844  Da:1845  Dr:1844
Fr:1844  Ha:1844  Lg:1844
Mu:1843  Va:1850  Wm:1845

**PLÜMICKE, KARL MARTIN**
Wollin 1749-1833 Dessau
Ref: Brüm 18, Goe 5, Ko 2,
ADB

Der Besuch nach dem Tod - D3
Bn:1783
Henriette o. Der Husarenraub
- D5 (1780)
Bn:1779  Dr:1780  Ha:1780
Lg:1780  Mh:1781  Va:1804
Lanassa - T5 - Fr (1782)
Bn:1781  Dr:1785  Fr:1784
Ha:1782  Lg:1785  Mh:1782
Mu:1784  Va:1783  Wm:1784
Miß Jenny Wharton - C3 (1775)
Bn:1776
Der Volontair - C1 (1775)
Bn:1778

**POCCI, FRANZ von** [Pseud.:
Franz Nepos]
Munich 1809-1876 Munich
Ref: Brüm 19, Ko 2, ADB, OC

Gevatter Tod - FP (1855)
Mu:1858

**POHL, EMIL**
Königsberg 1828-1901 Ems
Ref: Brüm 19, Ko 2

Die alte Schachtel - F3
Ha:1866
Arm und reich - F2
Ha:1862
Auf eigenen Füßen - F - with
H. Wilken (1883)
Fr:1878
Bruder Liederlich - F1 (1882)
Fr:1865  Ha:1863

Die drei Langhänse - C3
Da:1880
Er will sich auszeichnen - F1
Ha:1868
Der Goldonkel - F3 (1862)
Da:1868  Fr:1862  Ha:1862
Wm:1862
Herr Meidinger und sein Con-
trabaß - F1 (1865)
Fr:1863
Jeremias Grille - F1 (1863)
Fr:1874
Der Jongleur - F3 (1882)
Ha:1860
Eine leichte Person - F3
(1882)
Ha:1864
Namenlos - F3 - with
D. Kalisch (1864)
Fr:1867  Ha:1864
Pech-Schulze - F1
Fr:1867
Sachsen in Preußen - F1
(1858)
Fr:1861  Ha:1855
Die Schulreiterin - C1 (1885)
Da:1886  Fr:1885  Lg:1885
Mu:1885  Va:1888  Wm:1886
Seine Dritte - F1 (1860)
Fr:1866
Sie stottert - F1
Lg:1886
Die Sterne wollen es - C3
(1881)
Da:1862  Mu:1870
Unruhige Zeiten o. Lietzes
Memoiren - F3 (1862)
Ha:1862  Wm:1863
Eine verfolgte Unschuld - F1
with A. Langer (1873)
Fr:1863  Ha:1862
Vom landwirtschaftlichen
Balle - C1 (1886)
Fr:1886  Lg:1886
Zahnschmerzen - F1 (1874)
Lg:1870
Zeitgemäß - F3
Ha:1866

**PÖHNL, HANS**
Vienna 1849-?
Ref: Brüm 19

Der arme Heinrich - D (1887)
Mu:1886
Gismunda - D (1887)
Mu:1887

POLL, J.

Der tote Fisch - F4
    Va:1878

PRECHTLER, OTTO
Grieskirchen 1813-1881
Innsbruck
Ref: Brüm 19, Ko 2, ADB

Adrienne - D5 (1847)
    Dr:1849  Va:1847
Cäcilie - T5
    Va:1855
Er muß beweisen - C1
    Bn:1853
Er sucht seine Braut - C2
    Da:1850  Dr:1853  Fr:1850
    Va:1850
Falconiere - T5 (1846)
    Va:1846
Isfendiar - D4 (1843)
    Va:1843
Johanna von Neapel - T5
(1850)
    Va:1850
Die Kinder des Königs - D5
    Va:1864
Die Kronenwächter - D5 (1844)
    Va:1844
Michel Colomb - D5 (1854)
    Va:1854
Paolo Rocca - D1 (1852)
    Dr:1852  Fr:1853  Va:1852
Die Rose von Sorrent - D5
(1849)
    Va:1849
Die Waffen der Liebe - D2
(1842)
    Va:1842

PREUSS, A.
Ref: Goe 11

Der galante Abbé - C2 - Fr
    Fr:1856
Der junge Ehemann - C3 - Fr
(1830)
    Bn:1829  Dr:1838  Fr:1841
    Lg:1833

PRIEM, JOHANN PAUL
Nuremberg 1815-1890 Nuremberg
Ref: Brüm 19, Ko 2

Die Dänen in Holstein - D
    Fr:1848

PRIX, ADALBERT  [Pseud. of
Margarete Bernbrunn]
Munich 1788-1861 Ischl
Ref: Goe 11, Ko Th

Das Abenteuer in Venedig - D4
Fr
    Va:1838
Die drei gefahrvollen Nächte
- D6 - Fr
    Va:1840
Die Gabe, für sich einzuneh-
men - Vv3 - Fr
    Va:1843
Herr und Diener o. Das
geheimnisvolle Haus - D5 - Fr
    Va:1839
Das Irrenhaus in Dijon - D3 -
Fr
    Bn:1838  Fr:1832  Mh:1832
    Mu:1831  Va:1831
Der Reisewagen des Flücht-
lings - D4
    Va:1837
Das Spielhaus zu Langen-
schwalbach - D4
    Va:1836
Das Testament einer armen
Frau - D5 - Fr
    Bn:1833  Ha:1833

PRÖLSS, JOHANNES
Dresden 1853-1911 Eßlingen
Ref: Brüm 19, Ko 2

Renaissance - C (1889)
    Fr:1890
Unsere Zeitung - C4 (1888)
    Da:1888  Fr:1888  Mu:1889

PRÖLSS, ROBERT  [Pseud.: Carl
Robert]
Dresden 1821-1906 Dresden
Ref: Brüm 19, Ko 2

Katharina Howard - T5 (1865)
    Va:1877
Das Recht der Liebe - C
(1847)
    Fr:1882

PRÜLLER

Die schöne Klosterbäuerin -
D4
    Ha:1852

PRUTZ, ROBERT EDUARD
Stettin 1816-1872 Stettin
Ref: Brüm 18, Ko 2, ADB, OC

Karl von Bourbon - D5 (1845)
    Da:1844  Ha:1842  Wm:1842
Moritz von Sachsen - T5
(1845)
    Bn:1844  Da:1844  Fr:1844
    Ha:1844  Mu:1844  Va:1845

PUTLITZ, GUSTAV HEINRICH GANS
[Pseud.: Gustav Mansen]
Retzin 1821-1890 Retzin
Ref: Brüm 19, Ko 2, ADB, OC

Die alte Schachtel - C1
(1888)
    Bn:1868  Da:1869  Fr:1869
    Ha:1868  Lg:1868  Mu:1869
    Va:1868  Wm:1869
Badekuren - C1 (1853)
    Bn:1848  Da:1852  Dr:1849
    Fr:1848  Ha:1848  Lg:1869
    Mu:1868  Wm:1848
Die blaue Schleife - C5
(1850-55)
    Bn:1847  Ha:1847
Die böse Stiefmutter - D1
(1869-72)
    Bn:1871  Da:1876  Fr:1876
    Mu:1871  Va:1872  Wm:1871
Der Brockenstrauß - C1 (1864)
    Bn:1850  Fr:1850  Wm:1850
Die Compagnons - C5
    Mu:1876  Wm:1876
Doktor Raimond - C4
    Bn:1873  Lg:1873  Mh:1873
    Wm:1873
Don Juan d'Austria - T5
(1863)
    Bn:1860  1861  Mh:1861
    Va:1861
Familienzwist und -Frieden -
C1 (1853)
    Bn:1848  Dr:1849  Fr:1849
    Ha:1848  Va:1849  Wm:1849
Eine Frau, die zu sich selbst
kommt - C2 (1852)
    Bn:1850  Wm:1850
Friede - C1
    Bn:1871  Wm:1871
Gut gibt Mut - C3 (1869-72)
    Bn:1869  Fr:1870  Lg:1870
    Mu:1870  Wm:1870
Ein Hausmittel - C1 (1853)
    Bn:1848  Dr:1848  Va:1848
Die Herrin von Lichtenwarth -
C3
    Fr:1870

Das Herz vergessen - C1
(1853)
    Bn:1850  Dr:1850  Fr:1852
    Wm:1849
Die Idealisten - D5
    Bn:1881  Lg:1881  Mu:1882
    Wm:1881
Liebe im Arrest - C1 (1850-
55)
    Da:1857  Dr:1854  Fr:1860
    Va:1854  Wm:1866
Die Lützower Jäger - D1
    Ha:1863
Rolf Berndt - D5 (1879)
    Bn:1879  Da:1880  Fr:1879
    Lg:1879  Mh:1879  Mu:1879
    Va:1880  Wm:1879
Der Salzdirektor - C3 - with
W. Alexis (1851)
    Bn:1849  Da:1849  Fr:1851
    Ha:1862  Wm:1854
Das Schwert des Damokles - F1
(1878)
    Bn:1886  Da:1870  Fr:1863
    Ha:1862  Mu:1886  Wm:1866
Seine Frau - C1 (1850-55)
    Bn:1850  Da:1850  Dr:1850
Spielt nicht mit dem Feuer -
C3 (1887)
    Bn:1866  Da:1867  Fr:1867
    Ha:1868  Lg:1867  Mh:1867
    Mu:1867  Va:1872  Wm:1867
Ein Ständchen - C1 (1893)
    Bn:1869  Fr:1869  Lg:1869
    Wm:1874
Ein Tag Wahrheit - C
    Mu:1874
Das Testament des großen Kur-
fürsten - D5 (1859)
    Bn:1858  Da:1859  Dr:1859
    Fr:1858  Ha:1858  Mh:1858
    Mu:1858  Va:1858  Wm:1859
Über's Meer - C1 (1864)
    Da:1857  Dr:1856  Ha:1856
    Va:1857
Um die Krone - D5 (1869-72)
    Bn:1865  Da:1865  Fr:1866
    Ha:1865  Mh:1865  Va:1865
Unerträglich - C1 (1869-72)
    Bn:1867  Da:1874  Fr:1878
    Mu:1886  Wm:1874
Vatersorgen - C3
    Da:1849  Ha:1849
Vom Herzen - D3
    Dr:1856
Waldemar - D5 (1863)
    Bn:1863  Lg:1885  Mu:1886
Wilhelm von Oranien in White-
hall - D5 (1864)
    Bn:1862  Va:1862  Wm:1862

Die Zeichen der Liebe - C1
(1869-72)
    Bn:1865   Fr:1871   Ha:1865
Zwei Tassen - C1 (1869-72)
    Bn:1871   Mu:1873

**PUTLITZ, KARL von**
Marienburg 1775-1822 Münster
Ref: Brüm 18, Goe 6, Ko 2

Marpha - T5
    Va:1809

**RÄDER, GUSTAV**
Breslau 1810-1868 Teplitz
Ref: Brüm 19, Ko 2, ADB

Der artesische Brunnen - F4
(1859-67)
    Dr:1845   Fr:1846   Ha:1844
Fuchs und Luchs - C1 (1859-
67)
    Dr:1850   Fr:1851
Jupiters Reiseabenteuer - F4
- Fr
    Ha:1847
Nur Wahrheit - F3 (1859-67)
    Ha:1854
Ein Prophet - F4 (1859-67)
    Ha:1854
Robert und Bertram o. Die
lustigen Vagabunden - F4
(1859-67)
    Da:1857   Dr:1856   Fr:1858
    Ha:1856   Mh:1856   Mu:1866
    Wm:1859
Der Weltumsegler wider Willen
- D4 (1859-67)
    Fr:1845   Ha:1837   Wm:1845

**RAIMUND, FERDINAND**
Vienna 1790-1836 Pottenstein
Ref: Brüm 18, Goe 11, Ko 2,
ADB, OC

Der Alpenkönig und der Men-
schenfeind - Z3 (1837)
    Bn:1830   Da:1837   Dr:1830
    Fr:1841   Ha:1829   Lg:1832
    Mh:1835   Mu:1831   Va:1828
    Wm:1831

Der Bauer als Millionär o.
Das Mädchen aus der Feenwelt
- Z3 (1837)
    Bn:1830   Da:1837   Dr:1831
    Fr:1831   Ha:1830   Lg:1829
    Mh:1832   Mu:1831   Va:1826
    Wm:1832
Der Diamant des Geisterkönigs
- Z2 (1837)
    Bn:1831   Da:1845   Dr:1839
    Fr:1839   Ha:1831   Lg:1832
    Mu:1827   Va:1824   Wm:1843
Die gefesselte Phantasie o.
Der Harfenist - Z2 (1837)
    Bn:1832   Ha:1832   Mu:1831
    Va:1828
Moisasurs Zauberfluch - Z2
(1837)
    Bn:1837   Mu:1831   Va:1827
Die unheilbringende Krone -
Z2 (1837)
    Mu:1869   Va:1829
Der Verschwender - Z3 (1837)
    Bn:1837   Da:1841   Dr:1837
    Fr:1838   Ha:1836   Lg:1836
    Mh:1838   Mu:1835   Va:1834
    Wm:1837

**RAMBACH, FRIEDRICH EBERHARD**
Quedlinburg 1767-1826 Reval
Ref: Brüm 18, Goe 5, Ko 2,
ADB, OC

Die Brüder - D1 (1798)
    Da:1813
Der große Kurfürst von Rathe-
now - D4 (1795)
    Bn:1795
Margot o. Das Mißverständnis
- C1 (1798)
    Dr:1803   Va:1798
Otto mit dem Pfeile - T5
(1797)
    Bn:1797   Wm:1797
Der Scheintote - C1 - Fr
(1802)
    Va:1803
Der Verstossene - D5 (1800)
    Dr:1798

**RANK, JOSEPH**
Friedensthal 1816-1896 Vienna
Ref: Brüm 19, Ko 2, ADB, OC

Heidenglück - Z1
    Wm:1859
Der Herzog von Athen - D5
    Wm:1855
König Manfreds Kinder - D1
    Wm:1858

**RASPE, RUDOLF ERICH**
Hanover 1737-1794
Muckross/Ireland
Ref: Goe 4, ADB, OC

Soliman der Zweite - C - Fr
(1765)
    Lg:1800

**RATSCHKY, JOSEF FRANZ von**
Vienna 1757-1810 Vienna
Ref: Brüm 18, Goe 4, Ko 2,
ADB

Bekir und Gulroni - D1 - Fr
(1780)
    Va:1780
Der verlogne Bediente - C2 -
Eng (1781)
    Va:1781

**RAUPACH, ERNST BENJAMIN**
[Pseud.: Emanuel Leutner]
Straupitz 1784-1852 Berlin
Ref: Brüm 18, Goe 8, Ko 2,
ADB, OC

Adelheid von Burgund - T5
(1851)
    Bn:1838
Agnes von Hohenstaufen - D2
    Bn:1827
Ahnenstolz in der Küche - C4
    Bn:1825  Dr:1825
Alanghu - D3 (1827)
    Bn:1825
Die alte und die junge Gräfin
- C3
    Ha:1838  Wm:1837
Die beiden Nachtwächter - F5
    Bn:1826
Die Bekehrten - C5 (1827)
    Bn:1826  Da:1827  Fr:1826
    Mh:1828  Mu:1829
Die Bettler - D1 (1832)
    Bn:1829  Da:1830  Dr:1830
    Fr:1831  Ha:1830  Lg:1830
    Mh:1832  Mu:1832  Va:1829
Boris Gudonow - T5
    Bn:1840
Der Cardinal und der Jesuit -
TC4
    Bn:1835  Wm:1834
Corona von Saluzzo - D4
(1840)
    Bn:1834  Dr:1838  Fr:1841
    Ha:1839  Va:1834
Das Creditiv - C3
    Bn:1828

Cromwell Protektor - D5
(1841-44)
    Bn:1833  Dr:1834  Wm:1833
Cromwells Ende - T5 (1841-44)
    Bn:1833  Da:1851  Dr:1834
    Fr:1841  Ha:1844  Mh:1836
    Mu:1847  Va:1839  Wm:1834
Der Degen - C2 (1831)
    Bn:1829  Da:1838  Dr:1841
    Lg:1832  Wm:1830
Denk' an Cäsar - C3 (1832)
    Bn:1833  Ha:1839
Der Dolch - T5
    Va:1853
Das doppelte Rendezvous - C3
    Bn:1832
Ein Drama ohne Titel - D5 -
Fr (1843)
    Da:1841  Fr:1852
Drei Wünsche - Z3
    Wm:1835
Elisabeth Farnese - C4 (1850)
    Bn:1840
Engel und Dämon - C3 - Fr
    Dr:1841
Die Erdennacht - T5 (1820)
    Bn:1821  Lg:1820  Wm:1821
Die feindlichen Brüder o. Der
Doktor und der Apotheker - F4
(1834)
    Bn:1829  Da:1830  Dr:1829
    Fr:1830  Ha:1846  Lg:1829
    Mu:1830  Va:1841
Die Frauen von Elbing - D4
    Bn:1831  Wm:1833
Die Freunde - T5 (1825)
    Wm:1824
Der Fürst über alle - C5
    Bn:1827  Da:1829  Fr:1827
    Va:1829
Die Fürsten Chawansky - T5
(1818)
    Bn:1820  Da:1828  Dr:1820
    Fr:1831  Ha:1823  Lg:1823
    Mh:1822  Mu:1821  Va:1819
Die Gefesselten - D5 (1821)
    Wm:1821
Die Geheimnisse - D4
    Bn:1838
Genoveva - T5 (1834)
    Bn:1828  Fr:1832  Ha:1835
    Va:1830  Wm:1829
Der geraubte Kuß - C1 (1827)
    Bn:1825  Da:1827  Dr:1829
    Fr:1826  Lg:1825
Die Geschwister - D5 (1846)
    Bn:1837  Da:1839  Dr:1839
    Fr:1838  Ha:1838  Lg:1830
    Mh:1839  Mu:1839  Wm:1838
    Wm:1838

Die gewagte Kur - F3 (1845)
    Bn:1839
Gute Miene zum bösen Spiel -
F1
    Bn:1832   Wm:1835
Hahn und Hector - C4 (1840)
    Bn:1832   Ha:1839
Das Harfenmädchen - D3 (1842)
    Bn:1831   Fr:1832   Ha:1832
    Va:1832
Heinrich VI., 1. Teil - D5
(1837)
    Bn:1837
Heinrich VI., 2. Teil - T5
(1837)
    Bn:1830   Dr:1834   Fr:1830
    Ha:1831   Mu:1833
Ideal und Leben - D5 (1847)
    Dr:1841
Jacobine von Holland - D5
(1852)
    Bn:1832
Das Jubiläum - D1
    Bn:1839
Kaiser Friedrich I., 1. Teil
[Friedrich in Mailand] - T5
(1837)
    Bn:1835
Kaiser Friedrich I., 2. Teil
[Friedrich und Alexander] -
T5 (1837)
    Bn:1835
Kaiser Friedrich I., 3. Teil
[Friedrich und Heinrich der
Löwe] - T5 (1837)
    Bn:1835
Kaiser Friedrich I., 4. Teil
[Friedrichs Abschied] - T5
(1837)
    Bn:1836
Kaiser Friedrich II., 2. Teil
[Friedrich und sein Sohn] -
T5 (1837)
    Bn:1832   Da:1840   Dr:1834
    Fr:1837   Ha:1832   Wm:1833
Kaiser Friedrich II., 4. Teil
[Friedrichs Tod] - T5 (1837)
    Bn:1833   Wm:1833
König Enzio - T5 (1837)
    Bn:1831   Da:1842   Dr:1831
    Fr:1838   Ha:1831   Lg:1832
    Mh:1838   Mu:1832   Va:1832
    Wm:1832
König Friedrich - T5 (1837)
    Bn:1831
König Konradin - T5 (1837)
    Bn:1834   Dr:1835   Fr:1839
    Ha:1835   Mu:1834   Va:1835
    Wm:1835

König Manfred - T5 (1837)
    Bn:1834   Dr:1836   Wm:1835
König Philipp - T5 (1837)
    Bn:1830
Kritik und Antikritik - C4
(1827)
    Bn:1825   Fr:1826   Mh:1830
Laßt die Toten ruhen! - C3
(1826)
    Bn:1825   Da:1826   Dr:1826
    Fr:1826   Ha:1827   Lg:1825
    Mh:1828   Wm:1824
Die Lebensmüden - C5 (1849)
    Bn:1839   Da:1863   Dr:1839
    Fr:1864   Ha:1839   Lg:1839
    Va:1841   Wm:1840
Die Leibeigenen o. Isidor und
Olga - T5 (1826)
    Bn:1825   Da:1826   Dr:1825
    Fr:1825   Lg:1825   Mh:1826
    Mu:1826   Wm:1827
Lorenzo und Cäcilia - T4
(1818)
    Mh:1828   Wm:1819
Löwenklau - C4
    Da:1827
Das Märchen im Traum - D3
(1836)
    Bn:1832   Dr:1833
Maria, Königin von Schottland
- T5 (1858)
    Bn:1838
MDCCXL o. Die Eroberung von
Grüneberg - C5
    Bn:1840
Das Melodrama - F2
    Bn:1831
Mulier taceat in ecclesia o.
Die kluge Königin - TC3
(1836)
    Bn:1833   Da:1844   Ha:1834
Der Müller und sein Kind - D5
(1835)
    Bn:1830   Da:1843   Fr:1831
    Ha:1830   Lg:1835   Mh:1832
    Mu:1835   Wm:1830   Wm:1843
Der Narr seiner Freiheit - C2
(1837)
    Bn:1836
Der Nasenstüber - C3 (1835)
    Bn:1830   Da:1831   Dr:1833
    Fr:1831   Ha:1830   Lg:1832
Der Nibelungenhort - T5
(1834)
    Bn:1828   Dr:1833   Ha:1835
    Mu:1833   Va:1828

Der Platzregen als Ehepro-
kurator - F2 (1830)
    Bn:1829   Da:1831   Dr:1834
    Fr:1860   Ha:1830   Lg:1830
    Mh:1830   Mu:1833   Wm:1830
Der Prinz und die Bäuerin -
T5 (1840)
    Bn:1836
Rafaele - T5 (1828)
    Bn:1826   Fr:1827   Mh:1829
    Wm:1833
Das Ritterwort - D4
    Bn:1828   Fr:1829   Ha:1835
    Va:1829   Wm:1829
Robert der Teufel - D5 (1834)
    Fr:1832   Va:1833
Die Royalisten - D4 (1841)
    Bn:1829   Da:1829   Dr:1831
    Fr:1829   Ha:1846   Lg:1831
    Mu:1830   Va:1853   Wm:1832
Saat und Frucht - D5
    Bn:1850
Schuld und Buße - T5
    Va:1830
Die Schule des Lebens - D5
(1841)
    Bn:1835   Da:1843   Dr:1837
    Fr:1839   Ha:1836   Mh:1839
    Wm:1837
Die Schleichhändler - F4
(1830)
    Bn:1828   Da:1829   Dr:1829
    Fr:1828   Ha:1828   Mh:1829
    Mu:1830   Va:1830   Wm:1829
Scherz und Herz - C
    Fr:1843
Das Sonett - C3 (1833)
    Bn:1829   Dr:1832   Fr:1842
    Ha:1830   Lg:1830
Ein Sonntag aus Schelles
Jugendleben - F3
    Bn:1828
Der Stiefvater - C3 (1833)
    Bn:1829   Dr:1830   Fr:1832
    Ha:1830   Lg:1830
Tassos Tod - T5 (1835)
    Bn:1833   Dr:1834   Fr:1837
    Ha:1840   Mu:1834   Va:1834
    Wm:1834
Themisto - T5 (1840)
    Bn:1835
Die Tochter der Luft - T5 -
Sp (1829)
    Bn:1827   Ha:1830   Lg:1827
    Va:1826   Wm:1827
Vater und Tochter - D5
    Bn:1828   Va:1828

Der versiegelte Bürgermeister
- F2 (1829)
    Bn:1828   Da:1829   Dr:1829
    Fr:1828   Mh:1828   Wm:1828
Die Versucherin [Ohne Glauben
keine Liebe] - C3 (1844)
    Bn:1829   Va:1831
Vor hundert Jahren - D4
(1848)
    Bn:1838   Da:1842   Dr:1840
    Fr:1838   Ha:1838   Va:1850
    Wm:1840
Vormund und Mündel - D5 - Eng
(1835)
    Bn:1828   Ha:1835   Lg:1828
    Va:1827   Wm:1828
Der Wechsler - C3 (1832)
    Fr:1827   Ha:1827   Lg:1833
    Wm:1827
Der weibliche Bruder - C3
    Va:1832
Der Zeitgeist - F4 (1835)
    Bn:1830   Da:1838   Dr:1831
    Fr:1831   Ha:1830   Lg:1831
    Va:1851   Wm:1830

**RAUPACH, PAULINE**, née Werner
[Pseud.: A. P.]

Der Bruderkuß - C1
    Bn:1839
Ehemann und Junggeselle - C4
    Bn:1843
Eine einfache Geschichte - D2
    Bn:1863
Die Frau im Hause - C3
    Bn:1842   Da:1860   Dr:1852
    Fr:1856   Ha:1847   Wm:1846
Die Grundsätze - C5
    Bn:1852
Die Kadetten - C3
    Bn:1841
Marie - D4
    Bn:1840   Dr:1841
Noch ist es Zeit - D3
    Bn:1839   Da:1843   Dr:1839
    Fr:1839   Wm:1841
Sie kann nicht schweigen - C2
    Bn:1839
Ein Wort des Fürsten - D5
    Bn:1841

**RAUTENSTRAUCH, JOHANN**
Erlangen 1746-1801 Vienna
Ref: Brüm 18, Goe 4, Ko 2,
ADB

Der Jurist und der Bauer - C2
(1773)
   Bn:1776  Da:1810  Dr:1778
   Fr:1779  Ha:1786  Mh:1779
   Wm:1773  Wm:1797
Die unversehene Wette o. Wer
viel weiß, weiß noch nicht
alles - C2 - Fr (1771)
   Va:1771

**REBMANN, ANDREAS GEORG**
Kitzingen 1768-1824 Wiesbaden
Ref: Brüm 18, Goe 5, Ko 2,
ADB

Der Universalfreund - C5
(1796)
   Dr:1795

**REDWITZ, OSKAR von**
Lichtenau 1823-1892 Gilgen-
berg
Ref: Brüm 19, Ko 2, ADB, OC

Der Doge von Venedig - (1863)
   Mu:1861
Die Gräfin von Provence - C
   Mu:1880
Philippine Welser - D5 (1859)
   Bn:1859  D859  R859
   Fr:1859  Ha:1858  Mh:1858
   Mu:1858  Va:1877  Wm:1861
Psychologische Studien - C
(1872)
   Mu:1873
Schloß Monbonheur - D5
   Va:1882
Der Zunftmeister von Nürnberg
- D5 (1860)
   Bn:1860  Da:1860  Dr:1861
   Fr:1860  Mh:1860  Mu:1860

**REIBISCH**

Heinrich der Löwe - T5
   Dr:1844

**REICHARD, HEINRICH AUGUST**
Gotha 1751-1828 Gotha
Ref: Brüm 18, Goe 4/1, Ko 2,
ADB

Die Freier o. Worauf verfällt
ein Frauenzimmer nicht - C1
   Bn:1778
Das Muttersöhnchen - C3 - It
   Dr:1779
Nacht und ungefähr - C1 - It
(1779)
   Mh:1779

Der Schwätzer - C1 - Fr
   Fr:1780  Lg:1791
Sind die Verliebten nicht
Kinder? - C3 - It (1778)
   Fr:1778
Der Teufel steckt in ihm [Er
hat den Teufel im Leibe] o.
Die seltsame Probe - C2 - Eng
   Bn:1784  Dr:1781  Mh:1780
   Va:1774
Die Ungetreuen - C1 - Fr
(1779)
   Mh:1779  Va:1777

**REIL, JOHANN FRIEDRICH**
Ehrenbreitstein 1773-1843
Penzing
Ref: Brüm 18, Goe 11, Ko 2

Der erste Mai o. Der reiche
Poet - C
   Va:1816
Der Pulverturm - D
   Va:1824
Tranquillus - D - Fr
   Va:1822
Der verstellte Postmeister -
C1
   Mh:1806

**REIMAR, REINALD** see Glaser,
Adolf

**REIN, LUDWIG** see Würkert,
Ludwig Friedrich

**REINBECK, GEORG von**
Berlin 1766-1849 Stuttgart
Ref: Brüm 18, Goe 6, Ko 2,
ADB

Der Dichter - C1 (1821)
   Va:1813
Die Doppelwette o. Er muß
sich malen lassen - C5 (1818)
   Bn:1811  Fr:1807
Gordon und Montrose - T5
(1821)
   Dr:1817
Graf Rasowsky o. Nicht alles
ist falsch, was glänzt - D4
(1805)
   Bn:1801
Herr von Hopfenheim - F4
(1805)
   Wm:1802
Der Quartier-Zettel - C3
(1818)
   Bn:1816  Da:1822

Die Virginier - C3 (1817)
    Va:1813
Der Westindier - C5 - Eng
(1822)
    Da:1813   Mh:1812   Va:1813

**REINHARD, KARL**
Gotha 1760-1799 Breslau
Ref: Brüm 18, Goe 5, Ko 2

Der Pasquillant - D2 (1792)
    Ha:1792

**REINHARDT, LUDWIG**
Königsberg 1842-1875 Weimar
Ref: Brüm 19

Edward - T5 (1873)
    Wm:1873

**REINHOLD, KARL WILHELM**
Hamburg 1777-1841 Hamburg
Ref: Goe 6, Ko 2, ADB

Die Postkutsche zu Bocksdorf
- C5 - Fr (1808)
    Dr:1808
Die Eheleute vor der Hochzeit
o. Sie sind zu Hause - C1 -
Fr (1809)
    Dr:1811

**REITLER, MARZELLIN ADALBERT**
see  Arter, Emil

**RIEGGER, JOHANN NEPOMUK von**
Ref: Goe 5

Pamela als Mutter - C3 - It
    Va:1764

**REINICKE**

Feuer in der Mädchenschule -
C1 - Fr
    Wm:1865

**REITZENSTEIN, MARIANNE
SOPHIE**, née Weikard
1770-1823 Nemmersdorf
Ref: Goe 5

Die Kriegslist - C1 (1794)
    Va:1792
Reue mildert Verbrechen - D5
    Va:1792

**RELLSTAB, LUDWIG**  [Pseud.:
Freimund Zuschauer]
1799 Berlin-1860 Berlin
Ref: Brüm 18, Goe 11, Ko 2,
ADB, OC

Die drei Tanzmeister - F1
(1836)
    Bn:1834
Eugen Aram - T5 (1839)
    Bn:1839   Dr:1839   Fr:1840
    Ha:1839
Franz von Sickingen - T5
(1844)
    Bn:1843
Die Venetianer - D5
    Bn:1837

**REUTER, FRITZ**
Stavenhagen 1810-1874
Eisenach
Ref: Brüm 19, Ko 2, ADB, OC

Die drei Langhänse - C (1858)
    Ha:1878
Hanne Nüte und de lütte Pudel
- C4 (1859)
    Va:1883
Jochen Päsel, wat bist Du
vorn Esel - F1
    Fr:1883   Va:1883
Onkel Bräsig - D5
    Va:1883
Ut der Franzosentid - D3
(1860)
    Fr:1883   Va:1883

**RHEINISCH, ALBIN**
Malborghet 1845-1892 Berlin
Ref: Brüm 19

Die Freunde der Frau - C3
(1883)
    Bn:1883

**RIECKE, OSKAR**  see Perron,
Paul

**RIEGEN, JULIUS**  [Pseud. of
Julius Nigrivon St. Albino]
1849-1895 Weidlingen

Mariensommer - C1
    Va:1874

**RIESCH, FRANZ JOSEPH von**
Dresden 1793-1833 Berlin
Ref: Brüm 18, Goe 11, Ko 2

Die Bleiklammern von Venedig
- D3
    Mu:1821
Germanikus - T5 - Fr (1818)
    Bn:1817  Dr:1818  Wm:1821
Graf Heinrich und Heinrich
Graf - C
    Va:1820

**RIESE, FRIEDRICH WILHELM** see
Friedrich, Wilhelm

**RING, MAX**
Zauditz 1817-1901 Berlin
Ref: Brüm 19, Ko 2

Alle spekulieren - C5 - with
R. Bürkner
    Bn:1851  Wm:1851
Ein deutsches Königshaus - D5
    Fr:1870
Die Genfer - T (1850)
    Ha:1850
In Charlottenburg - D4
    Bn:1874
Marguerite - D5 - Fr
    Ha:1864
Scarrons Liebe - C1 (1860)
    Bn:1851
Unsere Freunde - C5
    Bn:1859  Ha:1859  Va:1860
Der verlorene Sohn - C1
    Bn:1875

**RITTER, ERNST** [Pseud. of
Emilie Binzer] .
Berlin 1801-1891 Munich
Ref: Brüm 19, Ko 2

Die Gauklerin - D5
    Va:1846
Die Neuberin - D3
    Bn:1853  Va:1846
Ruth - D5
    Lg:1874  Va:1858

**ROBERT, CARL** see Prölß,
Robert

**ROBERT, LUDWIG**
Berlin 1778-1832 Baden Baden
Ref: Brüm 18, Goe 8, Ko 2,
ADB, OC

Blind und lahm - C1 (1824)
    Bn:1819  Da:1824  Fr:1819
    Ha:1824  Va:1820
Carl II. o. Das Labyrinth von
Woodstock - C3 - Fr
    Bn:1828  Va:1828

Es wird zur Hochzeit gebeten
- C1 (1825)
    Bn:1823
Die Macht der Verhältnisse -
T5 (1819)
    Bn:1815  Da:1825  Fr:1819
    Ha:1816  Lg:1819  Mh:1815
    Wm:1826
Neue Proberollen - D1 (1828)
    Bn:1826  Lg:1826
Ein Schicksalstag in Spanien
- C3 (1839)
    Bn:1828
Die Tochter Jephthas - T5
(1820)
    Fr:1812  Ha:1830  Mh:1812
Der tote Gast - C2
    Bn:1828  Mu:1830
Die Überbildeten - C1 - Fr
(1826)
    Dr:1831  Fr:1817

**ROBERT, KARL** [Pseud. of
Eduard von Hartmann]
Berlin 1842-1906 Groß-
Lichterfelde
Ref: Brüm 19, Ko Th, OC

Das Recht der Liebe - C5
    Fr:1882

**ROCHLITZ, JOHANN FRIEDRICH**
Leipzig 1770-1842 Leipzig
Ref: Brüm 18, Goe 5, Ko 2,
ADB, OC

Antigone - T3
    Wm:1809
Es ist die Rechte nicht - C2
(1803)
    Dr:1802  Fr:1804  Va:1803
    Wm:1800
Die Freunde - D1
    Lg:1822
Jedem das Seine - C1 (1803)
    Wm:1801
Revanche - C2 (1803)
    Dr:1804  Mh:1806  Wm:1804
So geht's - C1
    Dr:1806  Wm:1805

**ROGER, ANTON** see Ascher,
Anton

**RÖHSE, F.**
Ref: Goe 11

Gisela - D4
    Bn:1817

ROLLER, MAX [Pseud. of
Friedrich Gottlieb Julius
Burchard]
Rostock 1767-1807 Rostock
Ref: Goe 5, Ko 3

Der väterliche Fluch o. Die
Dichterfamilie - C5 (1793)
   Bn:1794  Dr:1795  Mh:1796

ROLTSCH, RICHARD
Weimar 1854-?
Ref: Brüm 19, Ko 2

Das vierblätterige Kleeblatt
- C4 (1879)
   Wm:1885

ROMANUS, KARL FRANZ
Leipzig 1731-1787 Dresden
Ref: Goe 4, Ko 2

Die Brüder o. Die Schule der
Väter - C5 (1761)
   Bn:1771  Fr:1780  Ha:1767
   Lg:1775
Crispin [Frontin] als Diener,
Vater und Schwiegervater - C3
(1761)
   Ha:1767  Mu:1778
Frontin, ein Vater im Notfall
- C3
   Bn:1771
Das Mündel - C1 - Fr
   Va:1769
Die unerwartete Veränderung -
C5
   Bn:1771
Die Verläumder - C5 - Fr
(1778)
   Dr:1781

ROQUETTE, OTTO
Krotoschin 1824-1896 Darm-
stadt
Ref: Brüm 19, Ko 2, ADB, OC

Der deutsche Festkalender -
C5 (1865)
   Bn:1865
Der Feind im Hause - T5
(1867-77)
   Bn:1875  Da:1881
Das Haus Eberhard - C4
   Bn:1862  Da:1885
Lanzelot - D5
   Da:1888  Mu:1890
Die Probepredigt - C2
   Dr:1850

Der Rosengarten - D5
   Da:1875
Sebastian - T5
   Da:1883
Waldeinsamkeit - C1 (1851)
   Dr:1851

RÖMER, DR.  see Deinhard-
stein, Johann Ludwig

RÖMER, GEORG CHRISTIAN
Kriegsfeld 1766-1829
Karlsruhe
Ref: Goe 7, Ko 2

Die beiden Neffen - C3 - Fr
   Wm:1814
Der Bürgermeister von Saardam
o. Die beiden Peter - C3 - Fr
(1822)
   Bn:1822  Dr:1822  Fr:1822
   Ha:1820  Lg:1821  Mh:1819
   Wm:1821
Der Empfindliche - C1 - Fr
   Mh:1810
Das Testament des Onkels - D3
(1808)
   Bn:1807  Dr:1808  Va:1808

ROSE, FELIX  see Christern,
Johann wilhelm

ROSEN, JULIUS [Pseud.:
Nikolaus Duffek]
Prague 1833-1892 Görz
Ref: Brüm 19, Ko 2, ADB

Citronen - C4 (1870-88)
   Bn:1875  Da:1876  Fr:1876
   Lg:1876  Mu:1875  Va:1876
Deficit - C4 (1870-88)
   Lg:1884
Die Dilettanten - C4 (1870-
88)
   Va:1878
Das Ei des Kolumbus - C2
   Va:1879
Ein Engel - C3 (1870-88)
   Bn:1870  Da:1871  Fr:1871
   Mu:1870  Va:1874
Entweder-oder - C3
   Va:1865
Feinde - C3 (1870-88)
   Va:1877
Fromme Wünsche - C (1870-88)
   Fr:1881  Mu:1871
Garibaldi - F1 (1870-88)
   Da:1870  Fr:1868  Ha:1868
Gespenster - F3
   Lg:1884

Größenwahn - F4
  Lg:1877   Mu:1878
Der große Wurf - C4
  Lg:1878
Halbe Dichter - F3 (1870-88)
  Lg:1884
Hohe Politik - C1 (1870-88)
  Bn:1865   Da:1866   Lg:1865
Il baccio - F1 (1870-88)
  Fr:1865   Lg:1865   Va:1879
Im Schlafe - C1 (1870-88)
  Lg:1872   Va:1879
Ins volle Leben - C4
  Va:1875
Ja, so sind wir - F4
  Va:1878
Kanonenfutter - C3 (1870-88)
  Bn:1868   Da:1869   Fr:1869
  Lg:1868   Va:1878
Die Kompromittierten - C3
(1870-88)
  Bn:1864   Fr:1866   Lg:1865
  Wm:1864
Ein Knopf - C1 (1870-88)
  Fr:1869   Lg:1874
O diese Mädchen - F4
  Va:1884
Mamas Augen - C1 (1870-88)
  Bn:1887   Fr:1888
Der Mann in der Flasche - C4
  Va:1881
O diese Männer - F4 (1870-88)
  Da:1877   Fr:1877   Lg:1877
  Ha:1877   Mu:1876   Va:1876
  Wm:1876
Maschinen - F4
  Va:1881
Des Nächsten Hausfrau - C3
(1870-88)
  Bn:1863   Da:1872   Fr:1881
  Mu:1870   Va:1873
Nächstenliebe - C
  Fr:1890
Nervus rerum - F4
  Va:1879
Nullen - C4 (1870-88)
  Bn:1866
Ein schlechter Mensch - C3
(1870-88)
  Da:1865   Fr:1868   Lg:1865
Die schönste Tat - D1
  Va:1882
Ein Schutzgeist - C3 (1870-
88)
  Fr:1890   Va:1875
Schwere Zeiten - C4 (1870-88)
  Bn:1874   Da:1875   Fr:1874
  Va:1874
Starke Mittel - F4
  Va:1879

Unter dem Mikroskop - C3
  Va:1873
Der wunde Fleck - F4
  Lg:1885

**ROSINO**

Die Frau von dreißig Jahren -
C4
  Wm:1839

**RÖSSLER, A. von**

Conrad Slör - C5
  Da:1865

**ROSSMANN, W.**

Lady Macbeth - C1
  Bn:1877

**ROST, ALEXANDER**
Weimar 1816-1875 Weimar
Ref: Brüm 19, Ko 2, ADB

Berthold Schwarz o. Die
deutschen Erfinder - D5
(1867-68)
  Wm:1864
Kaiser Rudolf in Worms - D5
(1867-68)
  Wm:1841
Landgraf Friedrich mit der
gebissenen Wange - D5 (1867-
68)
  Dr:1848   Fr:1848   Ha:1848
  Wm:1848
Ludwig der Eiserne o. Das
Wundermädchen aus der Ruhl -
FP5 (1867-68)
  Wm:1860
Das Regiment Madlo - T5
(1867-68)
  Wm:1857
Der ungläubige Thomas - D5
(1875)
  Wm:1872

**ROTT, MORITZ** [i.e. Rosen-
berg]
Prague 1797-1867 Berlin

Vergeltung - D3
  Lg:1831   Va:1829

**RUBLACK, AUGUST**
Lieberose 1787-1854 Marbach
Ref: Goe 6, Ko 2

Clarissa - T4
    Dr:1816   Lg:1816
Liebe um Liebe - D1 (1818)
    Dr:1818

**RÖDIGER**

Tellmar und seine Familie -
D3
    Dr:1804

**RUDOLF, B.**   see Bunge, Rudolf

**RUDOLPH, KARL**   see Gottschall, Karl Rudolph

**RÜFFER, FRIEDRICH**
Berlin 1851-1899
Ref: Brüm 19, Ko 2

Der Wildfang - C1
    Lg:1878


**SAAR, FERDINAND von**
Vienna 1833-1906 Döbling
Ref: Brüm 19, Ko 2, OC

Die beiden de Witt - T5
(1875)
    Va:1879   Va:1878

**SAKKEN, FRITZ von**   see Henzen, Karl Georg Wilhelm

**SALLMANN, F. B.**

Sophie van der Daalen - D5
    Bn:1800

**SANGALLI, ELISABETH**
Heinrichswalde 1828-1901
Weimar

Die Macht der Vorurteile - D5
    Fr:1848   Ha:1847

**ST. ALBINO, JULIUS NIGRIVON**
see Riegen, Julius

**SANNENS [SANNENZ von SENSEN-
STEIN], FRIEDRICH KARL**
Neuhaus 1761-1849 Vienna
Ref: Brüm 18, Goe 5, Ko 2

Die Büsten o. Der Sylvester-
abend - C1
    Va:1820

Der Deutsche und der Musel-
mann - D3
    Va:1792
Der Ehemann - C4
    Va:1796
Der hagestolze Liebhaber - C3
    Dr:1799
Heirat durch Konvention - C3
    Va:1801
Karl der Kühne - D5
    Dr:1801
Der Kriegsgefangene - D5
    Va:1807
Das Rendezvous - C3
    Va:1815
Die Schachpartie - C4
    Va:1796
Der Sohn aus Indien - o.
Diesmal hat die Liebe wieder
Komödie gespielt - C5
    Va:1790
Die Theatersucht - C3
    Va:1815
Der zerrissene Brief - D3
    Va:1804

**SAPHIR, MORITZ GOTTLIEB**
Lovas-Berény 1795-1858 Baden
Ref: Brüm 18, Goe 9, Ko 2,
ADB, OC

Das Sololustspiel - C3 (1871)
    Bn:1843   Dr:1843

**SAUL, DANIEL**
Balhorn 1854-1903 Jugenheim
Ref: Brüm 19, Ko 2

Die Stoiker - C1 (1889)
    Fr:1889

**SAVITS, JOSZA**
Török-Becse/Hungary 1847-1915
Munich
Ref: Ko 2

Nach dem Kriege - D1 - Fr
    Wm:1872
Das Spiel des Zufalls und der
Liebe - C3 - Fr
    Wm:1881

**SCHACK, ADOLF FRIEDRICH von**
[Pseud.: Felix Adolphi]
Schwerin 1815-1894 Rome
Ref: Brüm 19, Ko 2, ADB, OC

Die Pisaner - T (1871)
    Mu:1875

Timandra - T5 (1879)
  Mu:1884  Wm:1888

**SCHADOW**

Der Referendar - C3
  Dr:1782

**SCHAFER, W.**

Ein Kritiker in Verlegenheit
- C1
  Fr:1859
Nur keine Konkurrenz - C4
  Fr:1861

**SCHALL, CHRISTIAN HEINRICH**
Ref: Goe 7

Die erste Liebe - C5
  Wm:1798
Die Ränke - C5 - Eng
  Va:1797  Wm:1797
Der seltne Freund - D5 - Sp
  Va:1799
Das Vorurteil - C5 - Eng
(1798)
  Wm:1797

**SCHALL, KARL**
Breslau 1780-1833 Breslau
Ref: Brüm 18, Goe 9, Ko 2,
ADB

Eigene Wahl - C2 (1826)
  Bn:1825  Da:1825  Fr:1825
  Ha:1825  Lg:1825  Va:1825
  Wm:1826
Das Kinderspiel o. Die ver-
nünftigen Leute - C1 (1825)
  Da:1825
Der Knopf am Flausrock - C2
(1832)
  Bn:1832  Ha:1833
Der Kuß und die Ohrfeige [Das
Sonett] - C1 (1817)
  Bn:1811  Da:1817  Dr:1830
  Fr:1812  Ha:1821  Mh:1818
  Va:1820  Wm:1811
Mehr Glück als Verstand - C1
(1817)
  Bn:1812  Fr:1815  Wm:1816
Schwert und Spindel o. Ehret
die Frauen - C3 (1832)
  Bn:1833
Theatersucht [Das Liebhaber-
theater] - C3 (1817)
  Bn:1815  Da:1817  Dr:1815
  Fr:1816  Ha:1817  Lg:1815
  Va:1815

Trau, schau, wem? [Die Not-
lügen] - C1 (1817)
  Bn:1812  Da:1817  Dr:1818
  Fr:1815  Ha:1817  Lg:1818
  Mh:1817  Va:1814  Wm:1816
Die unterbrochene Whistpartie
o. Der Strohmann - C2 (1817)
  Bn:1814  Da:1817  Dr:1815
  Fr:1816  Ha:1816  Lg:1815
  Mh:1816  Va:1815  Wm:1817

**SCHARFF von SCHARFFENSTEIN,
HERMANN**

Johanna I., Königin von
Neapel - T5 - Fr
  Dr:1852  Fr:1849

**SCHAUFERT, HIPPOLYT AUGUST**
Winterweilen 1835-1872 Speyer
Ref: Brüm 19, Ko 2, ADB

Der Erbfolgekrieg - C4 (1872)
  Fr:1872  Mu:1873  Va:1873
Schach dem König - C5 (1869)
  Da:1869  Fr:1869  Lg:1869
  Mu:1869  Va:1868  Wm:1869
1683 - D5
  Va:1869

**SCHEMENAUER**

Das Gartenhaus - C4
  Dr:1807

**SCHENCK, GUSTAV**  see Stab,
R. L.

**SCHENK, EDUARD von**
Düsseldorf 1788-1841 Munich
Ref: Brüm 18, Goe 8, Ko 2,
ADB, OC

Albrecht Dürer in Venedig -
D1 (1829)
  Bn:1828  Da:1829  Dr:1829
  Fr:1835  Ha:1832  Mu:1828
  Va:1828  Wm:1829
Belisar - T5 (1829)
  Bn:1828  Da:1840  Dr:1827
  Fr:1827  Ha:1828  Lg:1827
  Mh:1827  Mu:1826  Va:1827
  Wm:1829
Die Griechen in Nürnberg - C3
(1835)
  Mu:1835
Henriette von England - T5
(1833)
  Mu:1826

Die Krone von Cypern - D5
(1835)
    Da:1840   Dr:1842   Ha:1834
    Lg:1834   Mu:1832   Va:1833

**SCHICKH, JOSEF KILIAN**
Vienna 1799-1851 Vienna
Ref: Goe 11, Ko 2

Die Entführung vom Maskenball
- F3
    Ha:1844   Va:1835
Die Hammerschmiedin von
Steiermark - F1
    Ha:1846   Va:1842
Der Kobold - F3
    Ha:1839   Mu:1839   Va:1838
See Goedeke 11 for additional
listings.

**SCHIEBELER, DANIEL**
Hamburg 1741-1771 Hamburg
Ref: Brüm 18, Goe 4, Ko 2,
ADB, OC

Die Schule der Jünglinge - C1
(1767)
    Ha:1768

**SCHIFF, DAVID HERMANN**
Hamburg 1801-1867 Hamburg
Ref: Goe 10, Ko 2, ADB

Agnes Bernauerin - T5 (1831)
    Bn:1831

**SCHIKANEDER, EMANUEL**
Straubing 1751-1812 Vienna
Ref: Brüm 18, Goe 5, ADB, OC

Die bürgerlichen Brüder - D5
    Fr:1812   Va:1797
Der redliche Landmann - D5
(1792)
    Dr:1794
See Goedeke 11 for additional
listings.

**SCHILDBACH, JOHANN GOTTLIEB**
Ref: Goe 5, Ko 2

Glück durch Unglück - C1
(1808)
    Dr:1828
Pauline - D3 (1805)
    Dr:1806
Die Rekrutierung - D1 (1793)
    Dr:1792

**SCHILLER, FRIEDRICH**
Marbach 1759-1805 Weimar
Ref: Brüm 18, Goe 5, Ko 2,
ADB, OC

Die Braut von Messina - T4
(1803)
    Bn:1803   Da:1811   Dr:1806
    Fr:1805   Ha:1803   Lg:1805
    Mh:1805   Mu:1808   Va:1810
    Wm:1803
Demetrius - T5 (1805)
    Fr:1864   Ha:1862   Mu:1834
    Va:1859
Don Carlos - T5 (1787)
    Bn:1788   Da:1831   Dr:1789
    Fr:1798   Ha:1787   Lg:1787
    Mh:1788   Mu:1789   Va:1809
    Wm:1791
Die Jungfrau von Orleans - T5
(1801)
    Bn:1801   Da:1817   Dr:1802
    Fr:1806   Ha:1801   Lg:1801
    Mh:1802   Mu:1812   Va:1802
    Wm:1803
Kabale und Liebe - T5 (1784)
    Bn:1787   Da:1812   Dr:1785
    Fr:1784   Ha:1785   Lg:1789
    Mh:1784   Mu:1788   Va:1808
    Wm:1796
Maria Stuart - T5 (1801)
    Bn:1801   Da:1811   Dr:1804
    Fr:1802   Ha:1801   Lg:1801
    Mh:1804   Mu:1803   Wm:1814
    Wm:1800
Die Piccolomini - D5 (1800)
    Bn:1799   Da:1817   Dr:1819
    Fr:1801   Ha:1805   Lg:1825
    Mh:1807   Mu:1804   Va:1814
    Wm:1799
Die Räuber - T5 (1781)
    Bn:1783   Da:1831   Dr:1782
    Fr:1801   Ha:1782   Lg:1782
    Mh:1782   Mu:1784   Wm:1792
Turandot, Prinzessin von
China - TC5 - It (1802)
    Bn:1802   Da:1855   Dr:1802
    Fr:1807   Ha:1802   Lg:1823
    Mh:1843   Va:1851   Wm:1802
Die Verschwörung des Fiesko
zu Genua - T5 (1784)
    Bn:1784   Da:1811   Dr:1786
    Fr:1783   Ha:1785   Lg:1821
    Mh:1784   Mu:1789   Va:1787
    Wm:1806
Wallensteins Lager - D1
(1800)
    Bn:1803   Da:1817   Dr:1803
    Fr:1814   Ha:1805   Lg:1825
    Mh:1807   Mu:1804   Wm:1798

Wallensteins Tod - T5 (1800)
      Bn:1799   Da:1814   Dr:1803
      Fr:1801   Ha:1805   Lg:1800
      Mh:1808   Mu:1804   Va:1814
      Wm:1799
Wilhelm Tell - D5 (1804)
      Bn:1804   Da:1813   Dr:1805
      Fr:1805   Ha:1804   Lg:1805
      Mh:1808   Mu:1806   Va:1827
      Wm:1804

**SCHILLING, FRIEDRICH GUSTAV**
Dresden 1766-1839 Dresden
Ref: Goe 5, Ko 2, ADB

Die Flitterwoche - C1
      Bn:1818   Dr:1818

**SCHINK, JOHANN FRIEDRICH**
Magdeburg 1755-1835 Sagan
Ref: Brüm 18, Goe 4/1, Ko 2,
ADB

Die Beschämten o. Die Weib-
lichkeit in ihrer Stärke und
Schwäche - C5 - Eng
      Va:1789
Dahlbeck, der verlorene Sohn
[Der wiedergefundene Sohn] -
C3
      Dr:1794   Va:1794
Gassner II. o. Die bezähmte
Widerbellerin - C4 - Eng
      Bn:1787   Fr:1792   Ha:1781
      Lg:1792
Gianetta Montaldi - T5 (1777)
      Bn:1787   Ha:1775   Va:1781
Wie man's macht, so geht's! -
D5 - Fr
      Va:1780

**SCHIRMER, ADOLF**
Hamburg 1821-1886 Vienna
Ref: Brüm 19, Ko 2, ADB

Ein guter Tag Ludwigs des
Elften - D4
      Fr:1851   Lg:1850
Ein verhängnisvolles Bild -
F3
      Va:1879

**SCHLECHTA, FRANZ XAVER von**
Vienna 1796-1875 Vienna
Ref: Brüm 18, Ko 2

Cimburga von Masovien - D4
(1826)
      Va:1825

**SCHLEGEL, AUGUST WILHELM von**
Hanover 1767-1845 Bonn
Ref: Brüm 18, Goe 6, Ko 2,
ADB, OC

Ion - D5 - Lat (1803)
      Wm:1802
Die Wunder des Kreuzes o. Die
Reue des Sünders - T3 - Sp
      Mh:1824   Mu:1822

**SCHLEGEL, FRIEDRICH von**
Hanover 1772-1829 Dresden
Ref: Brüm 18, Goe 6, Ko 2,
ADB, OC

Alarcos - T2 (1802)
      Wm:1802

**SCHLEGEL, JOHANN ELIAS**
Meißen 1719-1749 Soroe
Ref: Brüm 18, Goe 4/1, Ko 2,
OC

Canut der Gütige - T5 (1746)
      Bn:1786   Ha:1767   Va:1769
Hermann - T5 (1743)
      Bn:1772
Die stumme Schönheit - C2
(1747)
      Bn:1771   Ha:1767
Triumph der guten Frauen - C5
(1746)
      Dr:1779   Ha:1767   Lg:1774
      Mh:1779   Mu:1778   Va:1769
      Wm:1772
Die Trojanerinnen - T5 (1747)
      Va:1782

**SCHLEICH, MARTIN** [Pseud.:
Martin Bertram]
Munich 1827-1881 Munich
Ref: Brüm 19, Ko 2, ADB

Ansässig o. Der Zunftzwang -
FP (1862)
      Ha:1865   Mu:1861
Die Bauernkomödie - C
      Mu:1878
Bürger und Junker - D4 (1862)
      Fr:1872   Mu:1855
Drei Kandidaten - C5 (1862)
      Dr:1860   Fr:1860   Mu:1858
      Va:1858
Der Ehrgeizige - C
      Mu:1877
Die Haushälterin - C1 (1862)
      Fr:1866
Kraft und Stoff - C (1874)
      Mu:1879

Die letzte Hexe - C3 (1862)
    Fr:1856   Mu:1856
Veit Stoß und sein Sohn - D
(1862)
    Mu:1883

**SCHLEMM, THEODOR**

Roxelane - T5
    Bn:1866

**SCHLENKERT, FRIEDRICH
CHRISTIAN**
Dresden 1757-1826 Tharand
Ref: Brüm 18, Goe 5, Ko 2,
ADB, OC

Bürgertreue - D5
    Va:1798

**SCHLESINGER, SIGMUND**
Waag-Neustadtl 1832-1918
Vienna
Ref: Brüm 19, Ko 2

Am Freitag - C1 (1865)
    Fr:1862   Mu:1870   Va:1861
Derby - C
    Fr:1889
Das Ende vom Anfang - C1
(1890)
    Va:1890
Ein ernster Heiratsantrag -
C1
    Va:1855
Ein Gastspiel - C1
    Va:1886
Glühlämpchen - C1
    Va:1886
Gustel von Blasewitz - D1
(1863)
    Bn:1861   Da:1872   Dr:1861
    Fr:1862   Va:1860   Wm:1863
Der Hausspion - C2 (1864)
    Bn:1862   Ha:1863   Va:1864
Der Kopf auf dem Bilde - C1
    Va:1879
Lange Flitterwochen - C1
    Va:1862
Ein liberaler Kandidat - C
(1872)
    Mu:1872
Liselotte - D1 (1872)
    Bn:1869   Mu:1869   Va:1869
Mein Sohn - C1 (1863)
    Va:1860
Mit der Feder - C1 (1863)
    Bn:1860   Da:1860   Dr:1860
    Fr:1860   Ha:1860   Mu:1868
    Va:1860   Wm:1861

Nicht schön - C1 (1863)
    Bn:1861   Va:1860
Ein Opfer der Patienten - C1
    Va:1863
Ein Opfer der Wissenschaft -
C1
    Va:1862
Rauchwolken - D1
    Va:1875
Die Rose vom Schlachtfeld -
C1
    Va:1886
Die Schraube des Glücks - C1
    Ha:1864   Va:1864
Die Schwestern von Rudolstadt
- D1 (1874)
    Lg:1874   Va:1874
Das Trauerspiel des Kindes -
D2 (1876)
    Bn:1876   Va:1875
Vogelfrei - F1
    Va:1879
Die Verschwörung der Hofdamen
- C2
    Va:1880
Wenn man nicht tanzt - C1
(1863)
    Fr:1861   Va:1861
Wer das Größere nicht ehrt,
ist das Kleinere nicht wert -
C1 (1890)
    Va:1890
Zahlen beweisen - C1
    Va:1882

**SCHLETTER, SALOMON FRIEDRICH**
1739-1801
Ref: Goe 5, Ko 2

Betrug für Betrug o. Wer hat
nun die Wette gewonnen - C3
(1780)
    Va:1781   Dr:1782   Va:1780
Der Eilfertige [Die Eil-
fertigen] - C2 (1783)
    Dr:1789   Va:1783
Der glückliche Geburtstag -
C3 (1777)
    Bn:1778   Dr:1784   Fr:1777
    Mu:1778
Karl von Freystein - D - It
    Dr:1782
Lohn und Strafe - D1 (1785)
    Dr:1792   Fr:1792   Mh:1804
    Va:1816
Die philosophische Dame o.
Gift und Gegengift - C5 - It
(1784)
    Dr:1790   Va:1784

Die Rechnung ohne den Wirt -
C1 (1780)
   Dr:1783   Va:1781
Die Vormünder - C5 - It
(1781)
   Bn:1786   Dr:1788
Wahrheit ist gut Ding - C5 -
It (1781)
   Dr:1782   Mh:1789   Va:1781

**SCHLICHT, FRIEDRICH GUSTAV**
Eisleben 1758-?
Ref: Goe 5

Otto der Schütz - D4 (1782)
   Dr:1783

**SCHLÖNBACH, KARL ARNOLD**
Wissen an der Sieg 1817-1866
Coburg
Ref: Brüm 19, Ko 2, ADB

Anton und Cordelia - D5
(1856)
   Dr:1856
Extreme berühren sich - C3
   Wm:1863
Gustav III. - D5 (1852)
   Ha:1848
Nicht jede Liebe ist Liebe -
C4
   Dr:1851

**SCHLOSSER, JOHANN LUDWIG**
Hamburg 1738-1815 Bergedorf
Ref: Brüm 18, Goe 4/1, Ko 2

Freund und Feind o. Der Zwei-
kampf - C5 (1767)
   Dr:1784   Ha:1767   Va:1770
   Wm:1772
Der Glücksritter o. Die Liebe
steht ihren Günstlingen bei -
C5 - Fr
   Va:1783

**SCHMELKA, HEINRICH**
Schwedt 1777-1837 Pankow
Ref: Goe 11, Ko 2, ADB

Wenn nur der Rechte kommt -
C1 (1822)
   Da:1822

**SCHMID, CHRISTIAN HEINRICH**
Eisleben 1746-1800 Gießen
Ref: Goe 5, Ko 2, ADB

Die Gunst der Fürsten o.
Elisabeth und Essex - T5 -
Eng (1773)
   Va:1773
Das Landmädchen o. Die
listige Einfalt - C5 - Eng
(1776)
   Va:1776

**SCHMID, HERMANN THEODOR von**
Weizenkirchen 1815-1880
Munich
Ref: Brüm 19, Ko 2, ADB, OC

Bretislav - T (1853)
   Mu:1843
Camoens - T (1853)
   Mu:1843
Columbus - T (1875)
   Mu:1857
Eine deutsche Stadt - T5
(1853)
   Da:1870   Mu:1849
Don Quijote - D
   Mu:1861
Fürst und Stadt - FP
   Mu:1858
Herzog Christoph der Kämpfer
- D (1853)
   Mu:1847
Ludwig im Bart - T
   Mu:1865
Poesie und Prosa - C
   Mu:1869
Rose und Distel - D1 (1876)
   Bn:1876   Mu:1876
Tassilo - T
   Mu:1859
Der Tatzelwurm - FP (1873)
   Mu:1866
Der Theuerdank - C (1853)
   Mu:1863
Die Z'widerwurz'n - FP (1878)
   Fr:1890   Mu:1878

**SCHMID, JOHANN FRIEDRICH**
Langensalza 1729-1791 Meusel
Ref: Goe 4/1

Wer ist in der Liebe unbes-
tändig? - C2 (1778)
   Va:1777
Zu gut ist nicht gut - C5 -
Eng (1778)
   Bn:1777   Dr:1779   Ha:1777
   Mh:1789   Va:1777

**SCHMIDT, A.**

Die Liebe auf der Alm - D3
    Dr:1834

**SCHMIDT, ELISE**
Berlin 1824-?
Ref: Brüm 19, Ko 2

Der Genius und die Gesellschaft - D5 (1849)
    Bn:1850  Dr:1850
Macchiavelli - T5 (1853)
    Bn:1853

**SCHMIDT, FRIEDRICH LUDWIG**
Hanover 1772-1841 Hamburg
Ref: Brüm 18, Goe 5, Ko 2,
ADB

Berg und Tal o. Die Ver-
wechslung - C5 (1819)
    Bn:1819  Fr:1820  Ha:1820
Cervantes Portrait - C3 - Fr
(1804)
    Bn:1803  Da:1819  Dr:1803
    Ha:1806  Wm:1803
Gleiche Schuld, gleiche
Strafe - C3 - Fr (1824)
    Dr:1834  Va:1833
Johann Vasmer, Bürgermeister
von Bremen - T5 (1812)
    Bn:1811  Dr:1811  Fr:1811
    Va:1810
Der leichtsinnige Lügner - C3
(1813)
    Bn:1813  Da:1815  Dr:1810
    Fr:1814  Lg:1831  Mh:1815
    Va:1812  Wm:1817
Lorenz Stark o. Die deutsche
Familie - D5 (1804)
    Bn:1802  Da:1812  Dr:1803
    Fr:1803  Ha:1816  Lg:1804
    Mh:1802  Va:1803  Wm:1805
Der Mann im Feuer o. Der
Bräutigam auf der Probe - C3
    Bn:1827  Dr:1819
    Bn:1808  Da:1814  Dr:1834
Die Neugierigen - C3 - It
(1808)
    Bn:1827  Da:1811  Dr:1808
    Fr:1806  Mh:1816  Va:1805
    Wm:1834
Nur er will sprechen - C1 -
Fr (1808)
Die rätselhafte Kranke - C2 -
It
    Dr:1832

Der rechte Arzt - C4 (1807-
11)
    Bn:1809  Dr:1809  Va:1808
Die Teilung der Erde - C3
(1824)
    Da:1823  Ha:1823  Lg:1823
Die ungleichen Brüder - C3
(1816)
    Bn:1828  Da:1817  Dr:1811
    Fr:1834  Va:1811  Wm:1817
Weiberpolitik - C4 (1801)
    Mh:1808
Die Weihnachtsfeier - D3
    Bn:1833  Va:1806

**SCHMIEDER, HEINRICH GOTTLIEB**
Dresden 1763-1828 St. Peters-
burg
Ref: Brüm 18, Goe 5, Ko 2,
ADB

Die große Toilette - C5
    Mh:1788
Der gutherzige Sohn - C1 - Fr
(1791)
    Mh:1790

**SCHNEEGANS, LUDWIG**
Strasbourg 1842-1922 Vienna
Ref: Brüm 19, Ko 2

Jan Bockhold - T (1877)
    Mu:1877
Maria, Königin von Schottland
- T (1868)
    Mu:1870
Samuel, hilf! - C (1881)
    Mu:1882

**SCHNEIDER, LOUIS** [Pseud.:
L. W. Both]
Berlin 1805-1878 Potsdam
Ref: Brüm 19, Ko 2, ADB

Der Bandit - D2 - Eng
    Dr:1834
Er amüsiert sich doch! - F1 -
Fr
    Bn:1829
Der erste Eindruck - C1 - Fr
    Bn:1829  Dr:1833
Der Erwartete - C1 - Fr
    Bn:1829
Eine Frau, die sich aus dem
Fenster stürzt - C1 - Fr
    Dr:1847
Fritz, Ziethen und Schwerin -
D1
    Fr:1844

Gebrüder Forster - D5 - Eng
  Lg:1833
Hans und Grete - C1
  Fr:1850   Ha:1851
Der Heiratsantrag auf Hel-
goland - C2 (1844)
  Bn:1840   Da:1842   Dr:1842
  Fr:1841   Ha:1840   Mu:1868
  Va:1842   Wm:1845
Ihr Bild - C1 - Fr (1846)
  Fr:1849   Va:1857
Jeder fege vor seiner Tür -
C1 - Fr (1842)
  Dr:1844
Die junge Pate - C1 - Fr
  Bn:1830   Da:1836   Dr:1831
  Ha:1847   Lg:1831   Mu:1832
  Mu:1832
Karl XII. auf Rügen - C4 -
Eng
  Ha:1845   Mh:1831   Mu:1867
  Wm:1831
Der Kurmärker und die Picarde
- C1 (1859)
  Dr:1847   Fr:1848   Ha:1845
  Mu:1870   Wm:1848
Die Memoiren des Teufels - C3
(1843)
  Va:1864
Michel Perrin o. Die Spion
wider Willen - C2 - Fr
  Bn:1838   Ha:1844   Mh:1836
  Va:1849
Monaldeschi - T3 - Fr
  Mh:1831
Der Oberst von 18 Jahren - C1
Fr (1839)
  Bn:1862
Der Onkel als Nebenbuhler -
C1 - Fr
  Da:1835
Die Quitzows - D5
  Bn:1846
Die Schnellpost - C1
  Bn:1832
Die schöne Müllerin - C1 - Fr
(1843)
  Bn:1843   Da:1844   Dr:1848
  Fr:1848   Ha:1845   Bn:1850
  Wm:1844
So geht's - C1 - Fr
  Lg:1833
Vergeltung - C1 - Fr
  Bn:1829
Versuche - C
  Fr:1848   Ha:1852

SCHNELLER, JULIUS
Strasbourg 1777-1833 Freiburg
Ref: Goe 7, Ko 2, ADB

Gefangenschaft aus Liebe - C5
Fr
  Va:1804
Vitellia - T5 (1801)
  Va:1804

SCHNETGER, ALEXANDER

Mahomed und Irene - D5
  Dr:1859

SCHÖDLER, F.

Der verwünschte Brief - C2
  Da:1843   Dr:1840

SCHOLZ, BERNHARD
Wiesbaden 1831-1871 Wiesbaden
Ref: Brüm 19, Ko 2, ADB

Gustav Wasa o. Maske für
Maske - D4 (1870)
  Da:1868   Fr:1872   Ha:1868
  Mh:1872   Mu:1869   Va:1868
Hans Waldmann - T5 (1869)
  Fr:1857
Eine moderne Million - D5
(1870)
  Bn:1871   Lg:1871

SCHÖNFELD, KARL
Budapest 1854-?
Ref: Brüm 19, Ko 2

Künstlernamen - C - with
F. Schöntan (1892)
  Fr:1890
Eine Lüge - D (1889)
  Fr:1889
Mit fremden Federn - C4
(1888)
  Da:1888   Fr:1888
Ein Psycholog - C (1890)
  Fr:1889

SCHÖNTAN, FRANZ von
Vienna 1849-1913 Vienna
Ref: Brüm 19, Ko 2, OC

Die berühmte Frau - C3 - with
G. Kadelburg (1899)
  Da:1888   Fr:1888   Mu:1888
  Wm:1888
Cornelius Voß - C4 (1902)
  Da:1888   Fr:1888   Va:1888
Frau Direktor Striese - F4
  Lg:1886
Die goldene Spinne - F4
(1886)
  Lg:1885

Die Goldfische - C4 - with
G. Kadelburg (1886)
    Da:1887  Fr:1887  Lg:1887
    Mu:1887  Va:1887  Wm:1887
Kleine Hände - C3 - Fr (1883)
    Va:1883
Krieg im Frieden - C5 - with
G. Moser (1880)
    Da:1880  Fr:1880  Lg:1880
    Mu:1880  Va:1880  Wm:1880
Das letzte Wort - C4 (1902)
    Da:1889  Wm:1890
Das Mädchen aus der Fremde -
C4 (1880)
    Lg:1879  Va:1880
Der Raub der Sabinerinnen -
F4 - with P. Schöntan (1885)
    Da:1884  Fr:1884  Lg:1884
    Mu:1885  Wm:1884
Roderich Heller - C4 (1884)
    Bn:1884  Da:1884  Fr:1884
    Lg:1884  Mu:1884  Va:1883
Der Schwabenstreich - C4
(1883)
    Da:1883  Fr:1882  Lg:1882
    Va:1882  Wm:1887
Sodom und Gomorrha - F4
(1880)
    Da:1879  Fr:1880
Die Spatzen - F3
    Fr:1882  Lg:1882
Unsre Frauen - C5 - with
G. Moser (1881)
    Da:1881  Fr:1881  Lg:1881
    Mu:1881  Va:1873  Wm:1881
Villa Blancmignon - C3 - Fr
(1885)
    Lg:1885
Der Zugvogel - F4 - with
G. Moser (1880)
    Va:1882

**SCHÖNTAN, PAUL von**
Vienna 1853-1905 Berlin
Ref: Brüm 19, Ko 2, OC

Der Raub der Sabinerinnen -
F4 - with F. Schöntan (1885)
    Da:1884  Fr:1884  Lg:1884
    Mu:1885  Wm:1884

**SCHRADER, A.**
Ref: Goe 11

Rataplan der kleine Tambour -
C1 - Fr
    Bn:1824
Wie gewonnen, so zerronnen -
C1 - Fr
    Bn:1824

**SCHRAMBL, FRANZ ANTON**
Vienna 1751-1803 Vienna
Ref: Brüm 18, Goe 5, Ko 2

Edwin und Emma - D5 (1779)
    Bn:1780  Va:1779

**SCHREIBER, A.**

Ein großer Redner - C4
    Fr:1862  Ha:1862
Der Jesuit und sein Zögling -
C4
    Ha:1862
Lieschen Wildermuth - C4
    Ha:1864  Lg:1867

**SCHREIBER, ALOYS WILHELM**
Bühl 1761-1841 Baden-Baden
Ref: Brüm 18, Goe 5, Ko 2,
ADB, OC

Die Erbschaft - C1 (1789)
    Mh:1792
Hermann und Marbod o. Der
erste deutsche Bund - D1
    Bn:1815  Fr:1814

**SCHREYER, OTTO**
Frankfurt/M 1831-1914 Hamburg
Ref: Brüm 19, Ko 2

Nicht zu Hause - C1 (1876)
    Fr:1878
Das Triumvirat - D1 (1870)
    Fr:1878  Va:1874

**SCHRÖDER, FRIEDRICH LUDWIG**
Schwerin 1744-1816 Rellingen
Ref: Brüm 18, Goe 4/1, Ko 2,
ADB, OC

Adelheid von Salisbury - T3
Fr (1804)
    Bn:1811  Fr:1811  Mu:1786
    Va:1783
Die Adelsucht o. Ehrgeiz und
Liebe - C2 - Fr (1791)
    Dr:1792  Ha:1786  Mh:1787
    Mu:1791  Va:1790
Der Advokatenspiegel - C5
    Fr:1813  Va:1812
Der alte Junggeselle - C3 -
Fr
    Va:1818
Der Arglistige
    Ha:1771
Ataliba, der Vater seines
Volkes - D5
    Bn:1794

Der Autor - C2 - Eng
  Va:1783
Beverly o. Der englische
Spieler - D5 - Eng (1791)
  Dr:1780   Ha:1786   Lg:1783
  Va:1780   Wm:1794
Das Blatt hat sich gewendet -
C5 - Eng (1831)
  Bn:1786   Da:1811   Dr:1786
  Fr:1806   Ha:1785   Mh:1789
  Va:1785
Brüder Belfield - C5 - Eng
  Dr:1779
Der Diener zweier Herren - C2
It (1794)
  Bn:1794   Da:1815   Dr:1778
  Ha:1772   Lg:1820   Mh:1813
  Va:1820   Wm:1790
Doktor Brummer - C3 - Fr
  Va:1783
Die dürftige Familie - D3 -
Fr
  Va:1781
Der eifersüchtige Ungetreue -
C3 - Fr (1831)
  Ha:1787   Va:1782
Die Eifersüchtigen o. Keiner
hat Recht - C4 - Eng (1790)
  Bn:1789   Da:1822   Dr:1789
  Fr:1793   Ha:1786   Mu:1790
  Va:1791   Wm:1791
Der Essigmann mit seinem
Schubkarren - D5 - Fr
  Da:1810   Dr:1781   Fr:1804
  Ha:1775   Lg:1799   Mh:1787
  Wm:1798
Eugenie - C1 - Fr
  Ha:1785
Der Fähndrich o. Der falsche
Verdacht - D3 (1786)
  Bn:1783   Da:1812   Dr:1782
  Fr:1780   Ha:1782   Lg:1782
  Mh:1782   Mu:1785   Va:1782
  Wm:1791
Die Freimaurer - C3
  Va:1784
Die Gefahren der Verführung -
D4 - Fr (1831)
  Bn:1783   Ha:1778   Va:1781
Glück bessert Torheit - C5 -
Eng (1802)
  Dr:1782   Ha:1783   Mh:1782
  Va:1782   Wm:1795
Die glücklichen Bettler - C3
It
  Bn:1779   Dr:1780
Große Toilette - C5
  Dr:1788   Ha:1788   Lg:1788
Gustav Wasa - T5 - Eng
  Va:1782

Die gute Mutter o. Erst sieh,
dann spring! - C1
  Ha:1785
Die gute Tochter - C5
  Va:1780
Die heimliche Heirat - C5 -
Fr (1831)
  Dr:1778   Ha:1786   Va:1781
Die Heirat aus Irrtum - C1 -
Fr (1804)
  Bn:1790   Dr:1787   Ha:1786
  Va:1784
Die Heirat durch ein Wochen-
blatt - F1 - Fr (1803)
  Bn:1787   Da:1811   Dr:1786
  Fr:1794   Ha:1786   Mh:1788
  Va:1784   Wm:1795
Incle und Yariko - D3 - Eng
(1794)
  Bn:1794   Wm:1795
Irrtum auf allen Ecken - C5 -
Eng (1810)
  Da:1811   Dr:1789   Mh:1809
  Va:1784   Wm:1801
Jeder fege vor seiner Tür -
D1 - Fr (1810)
  Bn:1808   Da:1812   Dr:1793
  Fr:1793   Va:1783
Juliane von Lindorack - D5 -
It - with F. Gotter (1831)
  Bn:1779   Dr:1782   Fr:1778
  Ha:1778   Lg:1780   Mh:1779
  Va:1780   Wm:1791
Jugend hat selten Tugend - D4
Fr
  Mh:1780
Die Komödie - C1
  Va:1783
Kronau und Albertine - D5 -
Fr - with F.L W. Meyer (1783)
  Dr:1785   Va:1783
Die Lästerschule - C5 - Eng
  Lg:1790   Mh:1781   Va:1782
  Wm:1819
Der Murrkopf - C3
  Dr:1783
Die Physiognomie - C5
  Va:1782
Das Portrait der Mutter o.
Die Privatkomödie - C4 (1790)
  Bn:1790   Da:1812   Dr:1790
  Fr:1793   Ha:1786   Lg:1793
  Mh:1790   Mu:1790   Va:1789
  Wm:1795
Der Richter - D2 - Fr
  Va:1782
Der Ring I - C5 (1786)
  Bn:1786   Da:1812   Fr:1798
  Ha:1785   Mh:1786   Mu:1785
  Va:1783   Wm:1795

Der Ring II o. Die unglück-
liche Ehe durch Delikatesse -
C4 - Eng (1792)
    Bn:1791  Da:1813  Dr:1790
    Ha:1788  Lg:1803  Mh:1791
    Mu:1790  Va:1789  Wm:1795
Der Schneider und sein Sohn -
C5 - Eng
    Bn:1811  Da:1817  Dr:1816
    Fr:1821  Ha:1811  Lg:1816
    Mh:1819  Va:1820
Der Schulgelehrte - C2 - Eng
    Dr:1783  Va:1782
Stille Wasser sind tief - C4
Eng (1805)
    Bn:1795  Da:1810  Dr:1786
    Fr:1799  Ha:1785  Lg:1799
    Mh:1788  Va:1784  Wm:1791
Die Stimme der Natur - D4
    Dr:1827  Ha:1827
Tankred - T5 - Fr
    Dr:1789  Va:1783
Der taube Liebhaber - C2 -
Eng (1804)
    Bn:1783  Dr:1782  Ha:1780
    Va:1782
Das Testament - C4 - Eng
(1786)
    Bn:1786  Dr:1782  Ha:1782
    Mh:1782  Mu:1786
Um sechs Uhr ist die Ver-
lobung - C5 - Eng (1805)
    Bn:1786  Dr:1786  Ha:1786
    Mh:1786  Va:1785
Die unglückliche Heirat - T3
Eng (1804)
    Bn:1787  Ha:1786  Va:1784
Die unmögliche Sache - C4 -
Fr (1831)
    Da:1783  Mh:1785  Wm:1783
Die Vatergrille - C3 - Eng
    Va:1782
Die väterliche Rache o. Liebe
für Liebe - C4 - Eng (1784)
    Bn:1787  Dr:1783  Fr:1805
    Ha:1784  Mh:1783  Va:1783
Die verdächtige Freundschaft
- C4
    Dr:1784  Ha:1786  Va:1783
Der vernünftige Narr o.
Keiner versteht den andern -
C1 - Fr (1804)
    Fr:1808  Ha:1785  Mh:1799
    Va:1784
Die Versuchung - C1 - Fr
    Dr:1783  Va:1782

Der Vetter in Lissabon - D3
(1786)
    Bn:1786  Da:1813  Dr:1786
    Fr:1810  Ha:1786  Lg:1786
    Mh:1785  Mu:1785  Va:1784
    Wm:1793
Victorine o. Wohltätigkeit
trägt Zinsen - C4 - Eng
(1786)
    Bn:1787  Dr:1786  Fr:1792
    Ha:1786  Mh:1785  Mu:1786
    Va:1784  Wm:1796
Die [vier] Vormünder - C3 -
Eng
    Bn:1792  Da:1814  Dr:1792
    Ha:1784  Mh:1784  Va:1806
Die Wankelmütige o. Der weib-
liche Betrüger - C3 - Eng
(1831)
    Dr:1782  Ha:1782  Mh:1784
    Va:1782
Weder einer noch der andere -
F1
    Fr:1793  Va:1783
Wenn sie böse sein könnten,
so wären sie es - C3 - Fr
    Va:1784
Wer ist sie? - C3 - Eng
(1790)
    Ha:1786  Va:1795
Die Zwillingsbrüder - C5 - Fr
    Dr:1782  Ha:1775  Mh:1793
    Mu:1792  Va:1782  Wm:1792

SCHUBAR, L. [Pseud. of
Rudolf Lubarsch]
Ref: Brüm 19

Der Günstling o. Keine
Jesuiten mehr - C4 (1847)
    Bn:1846  Fr:1846  Ha:1845
Joseph Haydn - C4
    Bn:1847

SCHUBERT, FRIEDRICH KARL
Munich 1832-1892 Munich
Ref: Brüm 19, Ko 2

Florian Geyer - T
    Mu:1883
Vom Regen in die Traufe - C3
- Sp (1873)
    Fr:1875
Wlasta - T (1875)
    Mu:1877

SCHÜCKING, LUISE von   see
Gall, Luise von

**SCHULTES, KARL**
Ansbach 1822-1904 Hanover
Ref: Brüm 19, Ko 2

Eine Partie Schach - D2
(1882)
    Mu:1881    Va:1884

**SCHULTZ, KARL GUSTAV THEODOR**
[Pseud.: Paul Sirano]
Danzig 1835-1900 Königsberg
Ref: Brüm 19, Ko 2

Schuld aus Schuld - D (1878)
    Mu:1878

**SCHUMMEL, JOHANN GOTTLIEB**
Seidendorf 1748-1813 Breslau
Ref: Goe 4/1, Ko 2, ADB, OC

Die Eroberung von Magdeburg -
D (1776)
    Ha:1774

**SCHUSELKA [-BRÜNING], IDA**
Königsberg 1817-1903

Eine kleine Gefälligkeit - F
- Fr
    Fr:1887
Die Plappermühle - C1
    Bn:1857
Der Reichtum der Arbeit - D2
- Fr
    Ha:1853
Sie will sich trennen - C1
    Dr:1851    Ha:1852
Vater und Sohn - D5 - Fr
    Va:1860

**SCHUSTER, PAUL ROBERT**
[Pseud.: Paul Venator]
Markneukirchen 1841-1877
Leipzig
Ref: Brüm 19, Ko 2

Perpetua - T4 (1876)
    Lg:1876

**SCHÜTZ, FRIEDRICH**
Prague 1845-1908 Vienna
Ref: Brüm 19, Ko 2

Alte Mädchen - C1 (1887)
    Fr:1886    Va:1887
Täuschung auf Täuschung - D5
(1869)
    Fr:1870    Va:1872

**SCHÜTZE, JOHANN STEPHAN**
Olvenstedt 1771-1839 Weimar
Ref: Brüm 18, Goe 9, Ko 2,
ADB

Die Journalisten - C1 (1806)
    Dr:1808    Wm:1807
Der König von gestern - C1
(1818)
    Bn:1824    Dr:1828    Fr:1833
    Ha:1818    Lg:1833    Wm:1831
Was doch die Vorstellung tut!
- C1 (1831)
    Bn:1831

**SCHWARZ, GEORG**
Ref: Goe 5

Luise - D4
    Dr:1794

**SCHWARZSCHILD, HEINRICH**
Frankfurt/M 1803-1878
Frankfurt/M
Ref: Brüm 19, Ko 2, ADB

Herzog Richelieu o. Der Hof
des Regenten - D
    Fr:1842

**SCHWEITZER, JEAN BAPTISTA von**
Frankfurt/M 1833-1875 Brien-
zer See
Ref: Brüm 19, Ko 2, ADB

Cousin Emil - C1 (1876)
    Fr:1875
Die Darwinianer - C3 (1875)
    Da:1875    Fr:1875    Lg:1875
Drei Staatsverbrecher - D5
(1876)
    Fr:1875    Lg:1873
Epidemisch - F4 (1876)
    Da:1874    Fr:1874    Lg:1873
    Va:1875
Großstädtisch - F4 (1876)
    Da:1875    Fr:1875    Lg:1876
Theodelinde - F1 (1876)
    Fr:1873
Das Vorrecht des Genies - C4
    Lg:1874

**SEIBOLD, ANTON**

Das Liebesgeständnis - C5
    Mh:1794

**SEIDEL, F. W.**

Künstlerliebe o. Die moderne
Galathe - C1
   Bn:1831

**SEIDEL, HEINRICH**
Leipzig ?-?
Ref: Goe 7

Abdallah, König von Persien -
T5 (1827)
   Bn:1830
Eginhard und Emma - D5 (1837)
   Mu:1832

**SEIDEL, KARL AUGUST GOTTLIEB**
Löbau 1754-1822 Dessau
Ref: Brüm 18, Goe 5, Ko 2

Der Fehler in Formalibus - C3
(1779)
   Va:1790
Die Macht der kindlichen
Liebe - D5 (1789)
   Dr:1790
Die Strafsache - D2
   Dr:1790

**SEIDL, JOHANN GABRIEL**
Vienna 1804-1875 Vienna
Ref: Brüm 18, Goe 9, Ko 2, OC

Das erste Veilchen - D1
(1833)
   Va:1831
Lucretia - T5 - Fr
   Va:1844

**SEIPP, CHRISTOPH LUDWIG**
Worms 1747-1793 Vienna
Ref: Goe 5, Ko 2

Für seine Gebieterin sterben
- T5 (1785)
   Dr:1787

**SELLEN, GUSTAV** see Alvensleben, Karl Ludwig

**SENF, FRANZ TRAUGOTT**
Ref: Goe 5

Wohltun macht glücklich - D5
(1790)
   Dr:1790

**SERENA, A.** see Amalie Marie
Friederike, Princess of
Saxony

**SERLITZ, GUSTAV**

Ein Opfer - C1
   Va:1877

**SESSA, KARL BOROMÄUS**
[Pseud.: Samson Eidex]
Breslau 1786-1813 Breslau
Ref: Brüm 18, Goe 11, Ko 2

Die Luftschiffer - F1 (1824)
   Bn:1826
Die Sonntagsperrücke - C1
(1825)
   Da:1825  Fr:1825  Wm:1825
Unser Verkehr - F1 (1814)
   Bn:1815  Fr:1817  Lg:1817
   Mh:1820  Wm:1822

**SIEGERT, GEORG** [Pseud.:
Ludwig Biron]
Weißenohe 1836-1921 Munich
Ref: Brüm 19, Ko 2

Klytämnestra - T5 (1871)
   Bn:1883  Fr:1881  Lg:1882
   Mu:1885

**SIEGFRIED, JOHANN SAMUEL**
Königstein 1775-1840
Ref: Goe 5, Ko 2

Nadir Amida, König von Persien - T5 (1807)
   Dr:1809  Mh:1808

**SIEGMUND, FRIEDRICH** see
Albrecht, Friedrich Johann

**SIEVERS, GEORG LUDWIG PETER**
Braunschweig 1766-after 1830
Ref: Brüm 18, Goe 6, Ko 2

Die komische Ehe - C1 - Fr
(1802)
   Mh:1801  Wm:1803

**SIGL, OTTO**
Ascholtshausen 1839-1902
Munich
Ref: Brüm 19, Ko 2

Im Altertumskabinet - C1
(1875)
   Bn:1875

SIRANO, PAUL   see Schultz,
Karl Gustav Theodor

SMIDT, HEINRICH
Altona 1798-1867 Berlin
Ref: Brüm 18, Goe 10, Ko 2,
ADB, OC

Bruder Kain - D4 (1852)
    Bn:1842   Dr:1842   Fr:1842
    Ha:1841   Va:1843   Wm:1842
Es ist schlimmer als es war -
C3 - Sp (1832)
    Bn:1832
Die Frau Schwiegermutter - D4
(1850)
    Bn:1845
Die Herausforderung - C1
(1837)
    Bn:1833
Juan Maiquez - D2 (1843)
    Bn:1842
Kaufmann und Seefahrer - D4
(1844)
    Ha:1842
Der Lumpensammler von Paris -
D5 - Fr (1847)
    Bn:1847   Ha:1847
Mein Herr Onkel - C3 (1848)
    Bn:1844   Da:1848
Der Sarazene - T5 - Fr (1833)
    Lg:1834
Unterm Regenbogen - C1 (1856)
    Va:1857

SODEN, FRIEDRICH JULIUS
HEINRICH von
Ansbach 1754-1831 Nuremberg
Ref: Brüm 18, Goe 5, Ko 2,
ADB, OC

Aurore o. Das Kind der Hölle
- (1795)
    Fr:1792
Der Blinde - D5 (1798)
    Mh:1800
Die deutsche Hausmutter - D5
(1797)
    Va:1799
Ernst Graf von Gleichen - D5
(1791)
    Fr:1792   Lg:1792   Mh:1792
Franzesko Pizarro o. Der
Schwur im Sonnentempel - D5
(1814)
    Fr:1815
Inez de Castro - T5 (1791)
    Bn:1786   Dr:1789   Mh:1820
    Mu:1793   Wm:1793

Die lange Nase - C1
    Da:1818   Mu:1831
Die Negerin o. Lilliput,
2. Teil - C5 (1790)
    Mh:1789
Rosalie von Felsheim o. Lil-
liput, 1. Teil - C5 (1790)
    Bn:1787   Mh:1786
Versöhnung und Ruhe o. Men-
schenhaß und Reue, 2. Teil -
D5 (1801)
    Va:1801
Virginia - T5 (1814)
    Dr:1807   Lg:1807

SOMMER, G.

Antonie - D3
    Dr:1808
Der Habsüchtige - C3
    Dr:1810

SONDERSHAUSEN, KARL
Weimar 1792-1882 Weimar
Ref: Brüm 18, Goe 11, Ko 2,
ADB

Der neue Orpheus - C1 (1823)
    Wm:1820

SONNLEITHNER, JOSEF
Vienna 1766-1835 Vienna
Ref: Goe 11, Ko 2, ADB, OC

Baron Blitz o. Er macht keine
Umstände - C3 - Fr
    Va:1814
Der Botaniker - C2 - Fr
(1806)
    Bn:1811   Da:1814   Dr:1808
    Lg:1816   Mh:1813   Va:1806
    Wm:1809
Claudine - D3 - Fr (1806)
    Va:1806
Diesmal meint er's so - C3 -
Fr (1805)
    Va:1805
Dir wie mir - C1 (1812)
    Bn:1809   Da:1820   Va:1812
    Wm:1813
Die Gartenmauer - C1 - Fr
(1805)
    Da:1814   Fr:1808   Va:1805
Die kurze Ehe - C1 - Fr
(1805)
    Bn:1816   Va:1804   Wm:1809
Liebe und Geheimnis o. Wel-
cher ist mein Vater? - C1 -
Fr (1807)
    Mh:1813   Va:1807   Wm:1808

Die Scheinehre - C1
  Dr:1810
Die Überraschung - C1 (1815)
  Va:1814
Die Wette - C1 - Fr (1805)
  Da:1806  Va:1805  Wm:1806

**SONTAG, KARL**
Berlin 1828-1900 Dresden
Ref: Brüm 19, Ko 2

Frauen-Emanzipation - F1
(1871)
  Da:1885  Fr:1888  Lg:1874

**SPECKNER, JOSEPH VALENTIN von**
Munich ?-1784 Munich
Ref: Goe 5, Ko 2

William Buttler, Baronet von
Yorkshire - T5 (1772)
  Mu:1772

**SPIELHAGEN, FRIEDRICH**
Magdeburg 1829-1911 Berlin
Ref: Brüm 19, Ko 2, OC

Hans und Grete - D5 (1876)
  Bn:1870  Lg:1870  Va:1870
In eiserner Zeit - T5 (1891)
  Fr:1890
Liebe um Liebe - D4 (1875)
  Bn:1875  Lg:1877  Mu:1877
  Va:1875
Der lustige Rat - C4 (1875)
  Va:1877
Die Philosophin - D4 (1887)
  Mu:1887  Wm:1887

**SPIESS, CHRISTIAN HEINRICH**
Freiberg 1755-1799 Schloß
Bezdiekau/Bohemia
Ref: Brüm 18, Goe 5, Ko 2,
ADB, OC

Die drei Töchter - C3 (1782)
  Bn:1783  Dr:1783  Fr:1793
  Ha:1783  Mh:1786  Va:1782
  Wm:1791
Das Ehrenwort - C4 (1790)
  Bn:1790  Dr:1791  Fr:1792
  Va:1794
Die Folgen einer einzigen
Lüge - D4 (1792)
  Dr:1792  Fr:1792  Lg:1792
  Va:1815
Friedrich, Graf von Toggen-
burg - D4 (1794)
  Bn:1794

General von Schlenzheim - D5
(1785)
  Bn:1782  Fr:1807  Ha:1783
  Mh:1783  Mu:1816  Va:1803
  Wm:1794
Klara von Hoheneichen - D4
(1790)
  Bn:1791  Da:1812  Dr:1791
  Fr:1791  Ha:1791  Lg:1797
  Mh:1791  Mu:1816  Va:1796
  Wm:1791
Liebe und Mut macht alles gut
- C3 (1793)
  Dr:1793  Fr:1793
Maria Stuart - T5 (1784)
  Bn:1787  Fr:1795  Lg:1788
  Mh:1791  Va:1784
Stadt und Land - C3 (1791)
  Dr:1791

**SPRICKMANN, ANTON MATTHIAS**
Münster 1749-1833 Munich
Ref: Brüm 18, Goe 14, Ko 2,
ADB, OC

Das Mißverständnis - D1
  Va:1778
Der Schmuck - C5 (1779)
  Bn:1780  Dr:1780  Ha:1779
  Lg:1780  Mh:1782  Va:1779
  Wm:1800

**STAB, R. L.**  [Pseud. of
Gustav Schenck]
Berlin 1830-1905 Werder
Ref: Brüm 19, Ko 2

Sekt, Abend- und Morgenszene
- D1 (1879)
  Bn:1877

**STADE, J. F. A.**  see
Albrecht, Johann Friedrich
Ernst

**STÄGEMANN**

Die Namensvetter - F3
  Bn:1877

**STAHL, FRANCIS**
Tilsit 1844-1902 Berlin
Ref: Brüm 19, Ko 2

Der Herr Major auf Urlaub -
C4 - with E. Heiden (1889)
  Wm:1889
Tilli - C4 (1888)
  Bn:1885  Fr:1888  Lg:1886
  Mu:1886  Wm:1886

**STARKE, GEORG**
Hanover 1815-1858 Hamburg
Ref: Ko 2

Ränke und Schwänke - F3
(1853)
   Fr:1854
Der Universalerbe - C2 (1853)
   Fr:1853

**STARKE, KARL**
Linz 1743-?
Ref: Goe 5, Ko 2

Soliman der Zweite o. Die
drei Sultaninnen - C3 - Fr
   Va:1770

**STAWINSKY, KARL**
Berlin 1794-1866 Berlin
Ref: Brüm 18, Goe 11, Ko 2,
ADB

Der dreißigste Geburtstag -
C1 - Fr (1837)
   Bn:1830
Das Familienleben Heinrichs
IV. - C1 - Fr (1832)
   Bn:1829  Dr:1829  Mu:1832
   Wm:1829
Das hohe C - C1
   Lg:1857
Der Mann meiner Frau - C3 -
Fr (1841)
   Bn:1830  Ha:1831  Lg:1831
   Wm:1831
Die Quäker und die Tänzerin -
C1 - Fr (1833)
   Dr:1833  Ha:1832  Lg:1832
   Mh:1832
Der Spion - D4 - Fr
   Bn:1829  Ha:1830  Lg:1830
   Mu:1829

**STEGMAYER, MATTHÄUS**
Vienna 1771-1820 Vienna
Ref: Brüm 18, Goe 11, Ko 2,
ADB

Albrecht, Landgraf von
Thüringen - D4
   Dr:1815  Mu:1816  Va:1806
Alfonso [Pedro] der Gerechte
- D4 - Eng
   Dr:1812  Bn:1807
Die Eroberung von Jerusalem -
D (1805)
   Fr:1808  Va:1805

Schein und Wirklichkeit - C4
   Dr:1812  Lg:1816  Va:1805
See Goedeke 11 for additional
listings.

**STEIGENTESCH, AUGUST ERNST
von**
Hildesheim 1774-1826 Vienna
Ref: Brüm 18, Goe 5, Ko 2,
ADB

Der Briefwechsel - C3 (1808)
   Bn:1812  Dr:1809  Mh:1809
   Va:1807
Die Entdeckung - C2 (1798)
   Bn:1799  Da:1811  Dr:1800
   Fr:1799  Lg:1816  Mh:1803
   Mu:1816  Va:1806  Wm:1809
Die Entfernung - C2 (1808)
   Va:1806
Die Freier - C4 (1798)
   Fr:1796  Mh:1806
Die Kleinigkeiten - C1 (1813)
   Da:1811  Dr:1808  Fr:1809
   Lg:1822  Mh:1809  Bn:1807
   Wm:1809
Das Landleben - C3
   Dr:1819  Fr:1807
Man kann sich irren - C1
(1813)
   Bn:1827  Da:1813  Dr:1828
   Fr:1834  Lg:1830  Va:1814
Die Mißverständnisse - C1
(1808)
   Bn:1817  Da:1812  Dr:1811
   Fr:1809  Ha:1824  Lg:1823
   Mh:1828  Va:1807  Wm:1809
Die Prüfung - C1 (1808)
   Dr:1811  Va:1809
Der Schiffbruch o. Die Erben
C1 - Fr (1798)
   Bn:1799  Da:1811  Dr:1799
   Mh:1799  Mu:1829  Va:1799
   Wm:1809
Die Versöhnung - C (1795)
   Fr:1794
Verstand und Herz - C1 (1808)
   Bn:1809  Da:1814  Fr:1810
   Ha:1827  Wm:1807
Die Verwandten - C3 (1813)
   Da:1814  Fr:1814  Wm:1814
Die Verwöhnten - C3
   Va:1808
Wer sucht, findet, auch was
er nicht sucht - C1 (1813)
   Da:1814  Mh:1811  Wm:1810
Die Zeichen der Ehe - C3
(1808)
   Da:1814  Dr:1829  Lg:1826
   Mh:1814  Va:1810  Wm:1810

**STEIN, FRIEDRICH ADOLF** see
Elz, Alexander

**STEIN, KARL** [Pseud.: Karl
Jents, Gustav Linden]
Neubrandenburg 1773-1855 Berlin
Ref: Brüm 18, Goe 6, Ko 2,
ADB

Die Bundesgenossen [Die Verbündeten] - C4 (1810)
  Dr:1809  Fr:1809
Garrick - D1 (1818)
  Bn:1817
Der goldene Löwe o. Des
Schicksals Tücke - D4 (1818)
  Bn:1817
Der neue Proteus - C4 (1808)
  Da:1813  Dr:1808  Ha:1808
  Lg:1808  Mh:1809  Va:1808
Der rechte Mann - C3 (1811)
  Da:1811  Dr:1810
Shakespeares Bestimmung - D1
(1818)
  Bn:1819  Va:1819
Ein Tag in der Hauptstadt -
C3 (1807)
  Da:1814  Fr:1808
Die Zurückkunft des Fürsten -
C1 (1805)
  Wm:1805

**STEIN, OSWALD**  see Wörle,
Karl Heinrich Theodor

**STEINAU, AUGUST**
Ref: Goe 11

Die Eilpost - C2
  Lg:1833
Der Prinz und der Kammerpächter - C3
  Bn:1825  Dr:1824  Lg:1825
Die Wasserfahrt nach Gohlis
o. Das erste Fischerstecken
in Leipzig
  Lg:1827

**STEIN-KOCHBERG, FELIX von**

Lucy - T5
  Wm:1871
Der vierte Oktober - C1
  Wm:1883

**STEINSBERG**

Die Proberollen - F1
  Wm:1811

Unverhofft kommt oft - C5
  Dr:1810  Lg:1810

**STEPHANIE, CHRISTIAN GOTTLOB**
[Stephanie der Ältere]
Breslau 1733-1798 Vienna
Ref: Brüm 18, Goe 4/1, Ko 2,
ADB, OC

Die eifersüchtige Ehefrau -
C5 - Eng
  Va:1769
Der Galeerensklave - o.
Belohnung der kindlichen
Liebe - C5 - Fr
  Va:1769
Die Grille o. Eifersucht
neuer Art - C5 - Fr
  Va:1789
Der gutherzige Murrkopf - C4
- It (1773)
  Va:1772
Der Kaufmann aus London - T5
- Eng
  Va:1778
Die Liebe in Corsica o. Welch
ein Ausgang! - D5 (1770)
  Va:1770
Der neue Weiberfeind und die
schöne Jüdin - C1 (1774)
  Va:1773
Die neueste Frauenschule o.
Was fesselt uns Männer? - C5
- Eng (1770)
  Dr:1777  Ha:1771  Va:1770

**STEPHANIE, GOTTLIEB**
[Stephanie der Jüngere]
Breslau 1741-1800 Vienna
Ref: Brüm 18, Goe 4/1, Ko 2,
ADB, OC

Die abgedankten Offiziere -
C5 (1771)
  Bn:1771  Dr:1778  Lg:1775
  Mh:1780  Va:1770
Der allzugefällige Ehemann -
C3 - Eng (1778)
  Va:1775
Die Art eine Bedienung zu erhalten - C5 (1780)
  Mh:1784
Die Bekanntschaften im Bade -
C5 (1780)
  Bn:1777  Va:1775
Die bestrafte Neugierde - C5
(1776)
  Dr:1778  Lg:1775  Va:1773
  Wm:1773

Christoph Ehrlich - C1 - Fr
Va:1785
Der Deserteur aus Kindesliebe
- C3 (1776)
Bn:1796  Dr:1783  Ha:1774
Lg:1775  Mh:1779  Va:1773
Der Eigensinnige - C5
Bn:1774
Gräfin Freyenhof o. Vater und
Tochter in Gefahr - C5 - Fr
(1771)
Va:1771
Hannibal von Donnersberg o.
Der geizige Soldat - C5
Va:1784
Der Hofmeister o. Das Mutter-
söhnchen - C3 - It
Va:1780
Die Kriegsgefangenen o. Große
Begebenheiten aus kleinen Ur-
sachen - D5 (1774)
Bn:1774  Dr:1777  Lg:1775
Mh:1784  Va:1771
Die Liebe für den König - D5
(1776)
Bn:1774
Das Liebesgeständnis - C5
Va:1793
Das Loch in der Türe - C4
(1781)
Bn:1781  Da:1819  Dr:1781
Ha:1781  Mh:1781  Va:1781
Macbeth o. Das neue steinerne
Gastmahl - T5 (1774)
Va:1772
Monsieur Fips o. Alter
schützt vor Torheit nicht -
C1 - Fr
Dr:1783  Va:1782
Die Nacht zu Abenteuern - C3
Fr
Dr:1788  Va:1788
Die neugierige Wirtin - C5
Mh:1782
Nichts - C1
Va:1779
Der Oberamtmann und die
Soldaten - D5 - Sp (1787)
Bn:1781  Dr:1783  Va:1780
Der Ostindienfahrer o. Die
Liebe heilt nichts - C3
(1787)
Dr:1781  Ha:1782  Va:1781
Die reiche Freierin - C5
Va:1784
Der Schauspieldirektor - D1
Va:1786
Die Schule der Damen - C5
Dr:1789  Lg:1790

Sie lebt in der Einbildung
[Das Mädchen in der Irre] -
C3 (1780)
Va:1775
So muß man Füchse fangen - C5
(1787)
Va:1784
Der Spleen o. Der Eine hat zu
viel, der Andere hat zu wenig
C3 (1778)
Bn:1774  Dr:1778  Mh:1781
Va:1774
Der Tadler nach der Mode - C5
(1776)
Bn:1819  Fr:1777  Lg:1775
Mh:1781  Wm:1774
Die Überraschung - C1
Va:1778
Der unglückliche Bräutigam -
C3 (1772)
Va:1772
Der Unterschied bei Dienst-
bewerbungen - C5 (1777)
Dr:1783  Va:1777
Das vermeinte Kammermädchen -
C3 - Fr
Va:1783
Die Werber - C5 - Eng (1771)
Dr:1777  Ha:1771  Lg:1778
Mh:1781  Mu:1772  Va:1769
Die Wildschützen - C3 (1777)
Bn:1777  Va:1777
Die Wirtschafterin o. Der
Tambour bezahlt alles - C3
(1771)
Mh:1779  Mu:1771  Va:1770
Die Wohlgeborene o. Heiraten
macht alles gut - C5 (1771)
Bn:1771  Dr:1778  Va:1770
Die Wölfe in der Herde - C5
(1778)
Dr:1775  Va:1775

**STEPPES, ADOLPH**
Hirschhorn 1796-after 1858
Ref: Brüm 18, Ko 2

Amaranth und Ghismonda - D6
(1858)
Da:1853
Homöopathie - C1 - Fr
Da:1840
Rita o. Die geheimnisvolle
Maske - Fr (1842)
Da:1844

**STERN, OSKAR**  see Bittong,
Franz

**STETTENHEIM, JULIUS**
Hamburg 1831-1916 Berlin
Ref: Brüm 19, Ko 2

Gottes Segen bei Cohn - F3
    Ha:1861

**STEUB, LUDWIG**
Aichach 1812-1888 Munich
Ref: Brüm 19, Ko 2, ADB

Das Seefräulein - C (1873)
    Mu:1868

**STIEGLITZ, NIKOLAUS** [Pseud.:
Alfred Lindolf]
Hanover 1830-1894 Vienna
Ref: Brüm 19, Ko 2

Moses Mendelssohn - D1 (1874)
    Wm:1874

**STOBITZER, HEINRICH**
Waldsassen 1856-1929
Ref: Brüm 19, Ko 2

Funken unter der Asche - C
(1886)
    Mu:1885
Ihre Ideale - C (1883)
    Mu:1884

**STOLL, JOSEPH LUDWIG**
Vienna 1778-1815 Vienna
Ref: Brüm 18, Goe 6, Ko 2,
ADB

Amors Bild - F1 (1808)
    Va:1808   Wm:1807
Scherz und Ernst - C1 - Fr
(1804)
    Da:1810   Dr:1804   Fr:1809
    Mh:1809   Va:1819   Wm:1803
Streit und Liebe - C2 (1810)
    Wm:1806

**STRAUSS, FR.**

Schuld um Schuld
    Mh:1875

**STRECKFUSS, ADOLF FRIEDRICH**
Gera 1778-1844 Berlin
Ref: Brüm 18, Goe 7, Ko 2,
ADB

Der Vergleich - C2
    Dr:1807

**STURZ, HELFRICH PETER**
Darmstadt 1736-1779 Bremen
Ref: Brüm 18, Goe 4/1, Ko 2,
ADB, OC

Julie und Belmont - T5 (1767)
    Bn:1774   Dr:1779   Ha:1767
    Mh:1774   Wm:1779

**SUDERMANN, HERMANN**
Matziken 1857-1928 Berlin
Ref: Brüm 19, Ko 2, OC

Die Ehre - D4 (1890)
    Bn:1889   Fr:1890   Mu:1890

**SVENSON, IWAN**   see Eulenberg-
Hertefeld, Philipp von

**SWIEDACK, KARL**   see Elmar,
Karl

**SYLVA, CARMEN** [Pseud. of
Elisabeth, Queen of Rumania]
Neuwied 1843-1916 Bucarest
Ref: Brüm 19, Ko 2

Dämmerung - D1
    Wm:1889

**SYLVESTER**

Der Bastard - T
    Ha:1838

**TEMPEL, J.**

Am ersten Sonntag - C1
    Fr:1874   Lg:1875   Mu:1876

**TEMPELTEY, KARL ERNST EDUARD**
[Pseud.: Karl Ernst]
Berlin 1832-1919 Coburg
Ref: Brüm 19, Ko 2

Cromwell - D5 (1883)
    Lg:1883
Daheim - D5 (1861)
    Bn:1861   Wm:1873
Hie Welf, hie Waiblingen - D5
(1859)
    Lg:1883   Mu:1886   Wm:1885
Klytämnestra - T5 (1857)
    Bn:1856   Dr:1856   Fr:1856
    Ha:1856   Mh:1856   Mu:1857
    Va:1856   Wm:1856

TENELLI, M. see Millenet,
Johann Friedrich

TEUTSCHER, MARIE ANTONIE
Vienna 1752-1784 Vienna
Ref: Goe 4/1, Ko 2

Fanny o. Die glückliche
Wiedervereinigung - D5 (1774)
  Bn:1774

THALE, ADALBERT vom [Pseud.
of Karl von Decker]
Berlin 1784-1844 Mainz
Ref: Brüm 18, Goe 11, Ko Th,
ADB

Die Gastrollen - F2
  Bn:1828
Guten Morgen, Vielliebchen -
C1 (1839)
  Bn:1833  Da:1839  Dr:1836
  Fr:1838  Lg:1838
Der Hagelschlag - C1
  Bn:1821  Da:1828
Das Konzert zu München - D1
(1821-27)
  Da:1830
Liebe im Krieg und Krieg um
Liebe - C1
  Bn:1834
Margot Stofflet - D4 (1828)
  Bn:1827  Mh:1828
Der Theaterdichter - C3 - Eng
  Bn:1820
Das Vorlegeschloß - F2 - Eng
  Bn:1820  Ha:1822

THILO, FRIEDRICH GOTTLIEB
Roda 1749-1825 Frohburg
Ref: Brüm 18, Goe 5, Ko 2,
ADB

Die ungleichen Freunde - C2
(1780)
  Bn:1777  Dr:1778

THUMB-NEUBURG, KARL von
Stuttgart 1785-1831 Stuttgart
Ref: Brüm 18, Goe 11, Ko 2,
ADB

Das Dachstübchen - C1 - Fr
(1825)
  Bn:1824
Ehestandsrepressalien - C1
(1820)
  Bn:1817

Die Familie Aglade o. Der
Schmuck - D3 (1818)
  Bn:1820  Da:1820  Fr:1816
  Mu:1817
Das Geschenk des Fürsten - C3
Fr (1824)
  Bn:1822
Der wahrhafte Lügner - C1 -
Fr
  Bn:1823  Dr:1825  Fr:1823
  Lg:1824  Mu:1830
Die Wette - C1 - Fr
  Mh:1809

TIECK, LUDWIG
Berlin 1773-1853 Berlin
Ref: Brüm 18, Goe 6, Ko 2,
ADB, OC

Ritter Blaubart - D5 (1797)
  Bn:1845
Der gestiefelte Kater - D3
(1797)
  Bn:1844
Rotkäppchen - D1 (1800)
  Da:1873

TIETZ, FRIEDRICH
Königsberg 1803-1879 Berlin
Ref: Goe 11, Ko 2, ADB

Eine Braut auf Lieferung - C4
- It (1872)
  Dr:1857  Ha:1857  Lg:1874
Drei Arrestanten - C4 - Fr
(1869)
  Dr:1857
Englischer Spleen o. Der
Geliebte in der Einbildung -
F1 (1829)
  Bn:1827
Die theatralische Landpartie
o. Kabale und Liebe - F1
(1828)
  Bn:1828
Ein Verschwörer - D4 - Fr
(1868)
  Bn:1860

TILLING, WOLF

Timon von London - D4
  Va:1876

TIMLICH, KARL
Asch 1744-1825 Vienna
Ref: Goe 5, Ko 2

Adelheid von Ungarn o. Der
Wettstreit weiblicher Freundschaft - T5 - Fr (1784)
    Va:1783

**TÖPFER, KARL**
Berlin 1792-1871 Hamburg
Ref: Brüm 18, Goe 11, Ko 2,
ADB, OC

Der Aufruhr im Serail - Z
    Ha:1841
Der beste Ton - C4 (1830)
    Bn:1828   Da:1828   Dr:1828
    Fr:1829   Ha:1829   Lg:1829
    Mh:1829   Mu:1828   Va:1829
    Wm:1828
Das Bild der Mutter - D4
    Dr:1822   Ha:1854   Va:1855
Die blonden Locken - D1
(1822)
    Bn:1826   Va:1819
Böttcher, der Goldmacher - C4
(1851)
    Bn:1847   Ha:1847
Bube und Dame o. Schwache
Seiten - C3 (1835)
    Bn:1834   Dr:1834   Ha:1834
    Lg:1834   Wm:1834
Bürgertum und Adel - D4
    Ha:1846   Va:1848
Canovas Jugendliebe - C4
    Bn:1847   Ha:1845   Va:1844
Cyprian und Barbara - C1
(1822)
    Da:1829   Fr:1823   Ha:1822
    Lg:1821
Die Einfalt vom Lande - C4 -
Eng (1839)
    Bn:1835   Da:1845   Dr:1835
    Fr:1837   Ha:1835   Mh:1836
    Mu:1835   Va:1844   Wm:1835
Der Empfehlungsbrief - C4
(1833)
    Bn:1823   Dr:1823   Fr:1823
    Ha:1823   Lg:1823   Mh:1830
    Mu:1824   Va:1823   Wm:1823
Freien nach Vorschrift o.
Wenn Sie befehlen - C4 (1835)
    Bn:1831   Da:1842   Dr:1831
    Fr:1832   Ha:1831   Lg:1832
    Va:1831   Wm:1832
Der galante Abbé - C3
    Ha:1842
Gebrüder Foster o. Das Glück
mit seinen Launen - D5 - Eng
(1841)
    Bn:1832   Da:1838   Dr:1832
    Fr:1833   Ha:1832   Mh:1833
    Mu:1833   Va:1832   Wm:1833

Hermann und Dorothea - D4
(1835)
    Bn:1823   Da:1826   Dr:1824
    Fr:1824   Ha:1850   Lg:1824
    Mh:1827   Va:1820   Wm:1823
Des Herzogs [Königs] Befehl -
C4 (1834)
    Bn:1829   Da:1840   Dr:1821
    Fr:1822   Ha:1822   Lg:1821
    Mh:1832   Mu:1822   Va:1821
    Wm:1852
Karl XII. auf der Heimkehr -
C5 - Fr (1839)
    Bn:1830   Da:1831   Dr:1847
    Fr:1830   Ha:1830   Va:1830
Der Krieg mit dem Onkel - F4
(1835)
    Da:1830   Ha:1827
Laßt mich lesen - C1 (1839)
    Bn:1835   Dr:1855   Ha:1842
Nehmt ein Exempel daran! - C1
(1830)
    Bn:1828   Da:1828   Dr:1828
    Fr:1828   Ha:1830   Lg:1828
    Mh:1829   Mu:1830   Va:1828
    Wm:1829
Ein Pagenstückchen - F1
(1841)
    Ha:1845   Lg:1866   Va:1843
Der Pariser Taugenichts - C4
Fr (1839)
    Bn:1850   Da:1838   Dr:1836
    Fr:1837   Ha:1836   Mh:1837
    Va:1837   Wm:1837
Der reiche Mann o. Die Was-
serkur - C4 (1843)
    Bn:1839   Da:1842   Dr:1839
    Fr:1839   Ha:1840   Lg:1829
    Va:1839
Rosenmüller und Finke o. Ab-
gemacht - C5 (1851)
    Bn:1849   Da:1850   Dr:1850
    Fr:1850   Ha:1849   Mu:1850
    Mu:1868   Va:1850   Wm:1850
Schein und Sein - C5 (1830)
    Bn:1824   Da:1830   Dr:1825
    Fr:1825   Lg:1825   Mh:1830
    Mu:1824   Va:1824
Schloß Caradec - C4 (1840)
    Ha:1837
Strauß und Lanner - C1 - Fr
(1843)
    Bn:1843   Ha:1842   Wm:1843
Ein Stündchen in Pyrmont - C1
Fr (1841)
    Bn:1822   Fr:1824   Lg:1822
    Wm:1823

Ein Stündchen Incognito - D2
(1833)
    Bn:1829  Dr:1831  Fr:1824
    Ha:1830  Mu:1833  Va:1830
Ein Tag vor Weihnachten - D2
(1831)
    Bn:1829  Da:1829  Dr:1829
    Fr:1831  Ha:1830  Lg:1829
    Mu:1829  Va:1829  Wm:1829
Der Tagsbefehl - D2 (1843)
    Da:1820  Dr:1820  Fr:1820
    Lg:1820  Mh:1821  Va:1819
    Wm:1831
Tanzeszauber - C1
    Va:1842
Volk und Soldat - D5
    Ha:1848
Die Weiber im Harnisch - F3
(1843)
    Dr:1848  Ha:1841
Die weiße Pekesche - C1
(1851)
    Bn:1834  Da:1836  Dr:1834
    Fr:1837  Ha:1834  Va:1835
Die Zurücksetzung - C4 (1841)
    Bn:1837  Da:1844  Dr:1838
    Fr:1838  Ha:1837  Mh:1840
    Mu:1838  Va:1838  Wm:1842
Zwei Tableaux für Eines - C4
    Bn:1824  Fr:1820  Va:1820

**TÖRRING-CRONSFELD, JOSEF
AUGUST von**
Munich 1753-1826 Munich
Ref: Brüm 18, Goe 5, Ko 2,
ADB, OC

Agnes Bernauerin - T5 (1780)
    Bn:1781  Da:1812  Dr:1780
    Fr:1799  Ha:1781  Lg:1789
    Mh:1781  Mu:1799  Va:1781
Kaspar der Thorringer - T5
(1785)
    Bn:1788  Dr:1788  Fr:1799
    Ha:1789  Mu:1815

**TÖRRING-SEEFELD, ANTON
KLEMENS von**
Munich 1725-1812 Munich
Ref: Brüm 18, Goe 5, Ko 2,
ADB

Die Belagerung der Stadt
d'Aubigny - D5 (1778)
    Mu:1778

**TRAUEN**

Die Lady in Trauer - D5
    Da:1863  Fr:1863

Die Maikönigin - D5
    Ha:1864

**TRAUTMANN, FRANZ**
Munich 1813-1887 Munich
Ref: Brüm 19, Ko 2, ADB

Meine Ruh' will ich o.
Blemers Leiden - C (1864)
    Mu:1869

**TRAUTMANN, P. F.**

Auf Freiersfüßen - F3 (1855)
    Fr:1856
Don Juan in Wiesbaden - C1
    Dr:1856
Ein Don Juan wider Willen -
C3 - Fr (1852)
    Da:1855
Onkel Quäker - F1 (1851)
    Dr:1851
Die Zwillinge - D4
    Da:1859  Fr:1852  Ha:1853

**TREITSCHKE, GEORG FRIEDRICH**
Leipzig 1776-1842 Vienna
Ref: Brüm 18, Ko 2, ADB

Die Belagerung von Calais -
D5 - Fr
    Va:1836
Fernando und Marie - D5
    Va:1808
Gustav in Darlekarlien o. Die
Minengräber in Schweden - D5
- Fr
    Va:1805
Mariana - D5 - Eng (1838)
    Dr:1838  Ha:1845  Va:1834
Die Schweden in Eger - D5
    Va:1839
Des Stranders Tochter - D5 -
Eng (1840)
    Dr:1839  Ha:1838  Va:1837

**TRELLER, FRANZ EDMUND**
Kassel 1843-1908 Kassel
Ref: Brüm 19, Ko 2

Albrecht - D1
    Lg:1870
Doktor Sanftleben - F3
    Lg:1881

**TRESKOW, A. von**

Die Dame von Lyon o. Lieb'
und Stolz - C5
    Da:1838

**TREUMANN, KARL**
Hamburg 1823 - 1877 Baden
Ref: Ko 2, ADB

Liebestyrannei - C1 - Fr
    Lg:1868
Urlaub nach dem Zapfenstreich
- C1 - Fr
    Ha:1868

**TRIESCH, FRIEDRICH GUSTAV**
Vienna 1845-1907 Vienna
Ref: Brüm 19, Ko 2

Ein Anwalt - C4 (1881)
    Va:1881
Der Hexenmeister - C4 (1891)
    Fr:1885  Mu:1885  Va:1885
Neue Verträge - C4 (1880)
    Fr:1880  Lg:1881  Mu:1880
    Va:1880
Die Nixe - C3 (1891)
    Va:1887
Die reine Liebe - C1 (1877)
    Va:1878
Träume sind Schäume - C1
(1876)
    Va:1874

**TROMLITZ, A. von** [Pseud. of
Karl August von Witzleben]
Gut Tromlitz 1773-1839 Dres-
den
Ref: Brüm 18, Goe 10, Ko 2,
ADB

Die Douglas o. Familienzwist
- D5 (1826)
    Bn:1825  Fr:1825
Die Entführung - C3
    Bn:1823
Der Friedhof von St. Sebaldus
- D5
    Bn:1833

**TSCHISCHWITZ, BENNO JOHANN**
Schweidnitz 1828-1890
Schwiednitz
Ref: Brüm 19, Ko 2

Agnes von Meran - T5 (1874)
    Lg:1875

**UECHTRITZ, FRIEDRICH**
Görlitz 1800-1875 Görlitz
Ref: Brüm 19, Goe 11, Ko 2,
ADB, OC

Alexander und Darius - T5
(1827)
    Bn:1826  Va:1826
Das Ehrenschwert - T5
    Bn:1827
Rosamunde - T5 (1833)
    Dr:1832

**UHLAND, JOHANN LUDWIG**
Tübingen 1787-1862 Tübingen
Ref: Brüm 18, Goe 8, Ko 2,
ADB, OC

Herzog Ernst von Schwaben -
D5 (1818)
    Bn:1853  Da:1823  Fr:1847
    Ha:1818  Mh:1846  Va:1827
    Wm:1841
Ludwig der Bayer - D5 (1819)
    Lg:1885  Mh:1846  Mu:1826

**UNGER, FRIEDERIKE HELENE**
Berlin 1741-1813 Berlin
Ref: Brüm 18, Goe 4/1, Ko 2,
ADB, OC

Der Mondkaiser - F3 (1790)
    Wm:1791

**UNGER, H.**

Zwei Weihnachtsabende
    Mh:1871

**UNGERN-STERNBERG, ALEXANDER**
Estonia 1806-1868 Dannenwalde
Ref: Ko 2, ADB

Die Brieftasche - C1
    Wm:1841

**UNZER, JOHANN CHRISTOPH**
Wernigerode 1747-1809
Göttingen
Ref: Brüm 18, Goe 4/1, Ko 2,
ADB

Diego und Leonore - T5 (1775)
    Bn:1796  Ha:1778
Die Drossel - D1 - Fr (1782)
    Dr:1782  Mh:1784  Wm:1788

Die neue Emma - C3 (1782)
    Bn:1786   Fr:1792   Ha:1779
    Mh:1784   Va:1788


VASELLI, MARIE von, née von
Ernest
Breslau 1858-1923
Ref: Brüm 19, Ko 3

Mit dem Strome - C4 (1879)
    Mu:1880   Va:1879

VELDE, KARL FRANZ van der
Breslau 1779-1824 Breslau
Ref: Brüm 18, Goe 10, Ko 2,
ADB

Das wilde Heer - C1 (1822)
    Da:1822   Ha:1822

VENATOR, PAUL   see Schuster,
Paul Robert

VESPERTINUS   see Bürkner,
Robert Emanuel Heinrich

VIETOR, FERDINAND

Zwei Lustspiele - C1
    Da:1883

VILLINGER, HERMINE   [Pseud.:
Hermine Willfried]
Freiburg/Br 1849-1917
Karlsruhe
Ref: Brüm 19, Ko 2

Verloren und gewonnen - C1
(1883)
    Wm:1883

VINCKE, GISBERT von
Dortmund 1813-1892
Freiburg/Br
Ref: Brüm 19, Ko 2, ADB

Die erste Prüfung - C1 (1880)
    Wm:1873
Die Feuerprobe - C (1869)
    Mu:1872

VISCHER, OTTO
Stralsund 1852-1905 Todtmoos
Ref: Ko 2

Gaudeamus - C4 (1889)
    Bn:1889

O dieser Papa - C4 (1886)
    Lg:1886

VOGEL, WILHELM
Mannheim 1772-1843 Vienna
Ref: Brüm 18, Goe 11, Ko 2,
ADB

Adelma - D5 - Eng (1829)
    Dr:1828   Fr:1826   Lg:1831
    Mh:1830   Va:1826
Die Ähnlichkeit - C3 - Fr
(1806)
    Bn:1799   Da:1814   Dr:1799
    Fr:1814   Va:1800   Wm:1811
Der alte Prognostiker - F1
    Bn:1832
Der Amerikaner - C5 - It
(1808)
    Bn:1798   Da:1810   Dr:1798
    Fr:1804   Ha:1816   Mh:1800
    Mu:1815   Va:1799   Wm:1799
Bettina o. Grausamkeit und
Mutterliebe - D4
    Va:1820
Blanca von Wolfenbüttel o.
Der Blinde - D - Fr
    Mu:1821
Der Bräutigam in der Irre -
C3
    Bn:1801   Dr:1801
Christine von Schweden - D3
(1841)
    Da:1839   Fr:1836   Ha:1836
Das Duell-Mandat o. Ein Tag
vor der Schlacht bei Roßbach
- D5 (1843)
    Da:1843   Fr:1832
Don Aurelio - C4 - Sp
    Bn:1840   Dr:1841
Der ehrsüchtige Künstler o.
Die Annahmne an Kindesstatt -
D4 - Fr
    Va:1820
Er hat alle zum Besten - C5 -
Eng
    Mu:1830   Va:1829   Wm:1832
Der Erbvertrag [Das Majorat]
- D5 (1828)
    Bn:1826   Da:1831   Dr:1827
    Fr:1826   Lg:1826   Mh:1828
    Mu:1829   Va:1825   Wm:1827
Der Erste führt die Braut
heim - C3 - Fr
    Mh:1802   Va:1802
Der Essighändler - D2
    Bn:1827   Ha:1826   Va:1821

Gattin und Witwe zugleich -
D5
    Fr:1806   Lg:1800   Mh:1799
    Wm:1799
Die Gegenlist [List und
Gegenlist] - C3 - Fr
    Bn:1803   Dr:1803   Fr:1806
    Ha:1805   Va:1803
General Moreau o. Die drei
Gärtner - D1 (1818)
    Mh:1817   Va:1819
Gerechte Strafe - C3
    Mh:1816   Va:1814
Gleiches mit Gleichem - C5 -
It
    Bn:1798   Da:1821   Dr:1813
    Fr:1798   Ha:1797   Lg:1807
    Mh:1797   Va:1799   Wm:1798
Der gutherzige Alte - C1 - Fr
    Bn:1825   Va:1800
Der Gutmacher o. Alte Liebe
rostet wohl! - C3 - Fr
    Dr:1832   Fr:1833   Ha:1839
Ein Handbillet Friedrichs des
Großen o. Incognitos-
Verlegenheiten - C3 (1843)
    Bn:1843   Dr:1842   Fr:1844
    Wm:1844
Das Haus des Corregidors o.
Bunt über Eck - F3 - Fr
    Bn:1827   Va:1819
Die heimlich Vermählten - C1
- Fr (1818)
    Bn:1816   Dr:1823
Heinrich IV. vor Paris o. Die
Folgen eines Zweikampfs - D5
(1821)
    Lg:1832   Mh:1824   Va:1821
    Wm:1823
Der Hut - C1 (1809)
    Mh:1799   Va:1800
Der Invalide - D1 (1809)
    Mh:1801   Mu:1809   Va:1801
Die Journalisten - C4 - Fr
    Va:1820
Julius der kleine Findling -
D3
    Va:1802
Der König und der Stuben-
heizer - D1 (1809)
    Bn:1819   Da:1812   Fr:1807
    Lg:1817   Mh:1826   Va:1815
Der letzte Pagenstreich - C1
    Va:1819
Liebe hilft zum Rechte - C4 -
Sp
    Bn:1826   Lg:1828
Der Liebe Zauberkünste - C3
    Bn:1827   Dr:1819   Ha:1818
    Va:1819

Die Liebe zu Abenteuern o.
Abenteuer aus Liebe - C4 -
Eng
    Bn:1823   Va:1822
Der Nachschlüssel - D3 - Fr
    Bn:1839   Dr:1824   Mh:1828
    Va:1837
Pflicht und Liebe o. Wieder-
vergeltung - D5 - Fr
    Bn:1802   Da:1812   Dr:1802
    Fr:1801   Ha:1801   Mh:1801
    Va:1802   Wm:1802
Pinto o. Die Verschwörung in
Portugal - D4
    Bn:1802   Ha:1802   Lg:1808
    Wm:1807
Die Postwagenreise - C - FR
    Ha:1803
Reue und Ersatz [Der Ersatz]
- D4 (1808)
    Bn:1805   Da:1810   Fr:1803
    Ha:1802   Lg:1803   Mh:1808
    Mu:1829   Va:1802   Wm:1806
Die Schauspieler - C5 - Fr
    Da:1822   Va:1820
Schlecht spekuliert! - F2
    Bn:1832
Der Schlechtmacher o. Alte
Liebe rostet nicht! - C2 - Fr
    Da:1838   Dr:1832   Fr:1833
    Ha:1839
Der Schleichhändler - D3 - Fr
    Ha:1824
Der Schmeichler - C3 - Fr
    Va:1820
Das seltene Rezept - D1
(1809)
    Da:1814   Mu:1815
Der tote Gast - F4
    Va:1823
Die Tugend in Gefahr - D5 -
Fr
    Va:1800
Vater und Sohn - D5
    Dr:1814   Ha:1816
Verführung ist Tugendprobe -
D5 - Fr
    Ha:1800
Vier Schildwachen auf einem
Posten - C1 (1809)
    Bn:1817   Da:1810   Dr:1835
    Fr:1806   Ha:1809   Va:1815
Die Verschleierte [Die Dame
im Schleier; Der Schleier] -
C5 - It
    Bn:1798   Dr:1799   Fr:1805
    Mh:1798   Va:1799   Wm:1798
Witzigungen - C3 - Eng (1843)
    Bn:1839   Dr:1843   Ha:1836
    Lg:1842   Va:1853   Wm:1849

**VOIGT, FRIEDRICH TRAUGOTT**
Kamenz 1770-1814 Artern
Ref: Brüm 18, Goe 5, Ko 2,
ADB

Radegunde von Thüringen - T5
(1792)
Dr:1813

**VOLGER, EDUARD**
Landsberg 1847-1914 Leipzig
Ref: Brüm 19, Ko 2

Die junge Frau - C4 (1882)
Lg:1880

**VOLLMAR, ANTON**
Ottobeuren 1843-?
Ref: Brüm 19

Stauf - T5 (1881)
Fr:1881

**VOSS, JULIUS von**
Brandenburg 1768-1832 Berlin
Ref: Brüm 18, Goe 11, Ko 2,
ADB, OC

Die beiden Gutsherren - C5
(1820)
Bn:1819  Dr:1820  Fr:1820
Die blühende Jungfer - C3
(1816)
Bn:1815  Da:1828  Fr:1833
Ha:1815  Mh:1828  Va:1823
Wm:1819
Die Blume vom Ganges - C4
(1812)
Bn:1812
Chamaranthe - C1 (1810)
Bn:1810
Die Damenhüte im Theater - F1
(1819)
Bn:1818
Die Einnahme von Breda - D5
Ha:1816
Die Erbschaft aus Surinam -
C5 (1823)
Ha:1823
Des Fahnenjunkers Treue o.
Besser spät als gar nicht -
D3 (1825)
Bn:1825
Die Frankfurter Messe - F2
(1816)
Bn:1826  Lg:1822
Der geheime Registrator o.
Die versalzenen Klöße - C2
(1825)
Bn:1825

Die Grabrosen - T3 (1823)
Bn:1822
Die Griechheit - C5 (1807)
Bn:1807
Künstlers Erdenwallen - C5
(1810)
Bn:1810  Da:1814  Dr:1816
Fr:1812  Ha:1816  Lg:1816
Mh:1813  Mu:1831  Va:1842
Wm:1812
Die Pfarrei - C4 (1812)
Da:1812  Mh:1813
Quintin Messis - D2 (1825)
Bn:1822
Das Sprüchlein - C3 (1823)
Bn:1826  Da:1829
Ton des Tages - C3 - Fr
(1806)
Bn:1806
Das unterbrochene Konzert -
C5
Bn:1815
Die verblühte Jungfer - C2
(1816)
Bn:1815  Da:1828  Fr:1833
Ha:1815  Mh:1828  Wm:1819
Die zwölf schlafenden Jung-
frauen - D4 (1805)
Bn:1805  Mu:1823

**VOSS, RICHARD**
Pyritz 1851-1918 Berchtes-
gaden
Ref: Brüm 19, Ko 2, OC

Alexandra - D4 (1886)
Dr:1887  Fr:1886  Lg:1886
Mu:1887
Brigitta - T4 (1887)
Bn:1889  Fr:1886  Wm:1886
Eva - D (1889)
Fr:1889  Mu:1890
Der Mohr des Zaren - D5
(1883)
Bn:1884  Mu:1883
Pater Modestus - D5 (1883)
Fr:1882
Die Patrizierin - T5 (1881)
Fr:1881
Treu dem Herrn - D4 (1886)
Bn:1886
Unehrlich Volk - T5 (1884)
Mu:1884  Wm:1884
Wehe den Besiegten - D3
(1888)
Wm:1889
Zwischen zwei Herzen - D
(1895)
Fr:1889

**VULPIUS, CHRISTIAN AUGUST**
Weimar 1762-1827 Weimar
Ref: Brüm 18, Goe 5, Ko 2,
ADB, OC

Ehestandsproben - C4 (1791)
   Fr:1792
Karl XII. bei Bender [Sitah
Mani] - D5 (1800)
   Da:1816  Dr:1798  Mh:1819
   Va:1797
Leidenschaft und Liebe - T5
(1790)
   Dr:1790  Lg:1790
Der Liebe Sohn - D2 (1789)
   Mh:1789
Die Liebesproben - C (1790)
   Fr:1792
List und Unschuld - C1
   Mh:1794
Luftschlösser - C4 (1792)
   Wm:1791
Rikko - C2 (1793)
   Wm:1792
Rinaldo Rinaldini der Räuber-
hauptmann - D (1800)
   Fr:1805

**WACHT, GUSTAV** [Pseud. of
Friedrich Algardi]
Godesberg 1841-?
Ref: Brüm 19, Ko Th

Dolkuroff - D1 (1879)
   Da:1879  Lg:1882  Mh:1879
   Mu:1881
Sommerfrische
   Mh:1870

**WAGEMANN, BENEDIKT von**
Altdorf 1763-after 1835
Ehingen
Ref: Brüm 19, Goe 7, Ko 2

Der gutherzige Sonderling o.
Tadelsucht und Gleichmut - D5
   Va:1805

**WAGENER, FRIEDRICH**
Hamburg 1794-1833 Magdeburg
Ref: Brüm 18, Goe 13, Ko 2

Alter schützt vor Torheit
nicht - C2 (1833)
   Wm:1827

**WAGENSEIL, CHRISTIAN JAKOB**
Kaufbeuren 1756-1839 Augsburg
Ref: Brüm 18, Goe 4/1, Ko 2,
ADB

Die Freimaurer - C3
   Va:1784
Mustapha und Zeangir - T5 -
Fr (1823)
   Va:1782

**WAGES, J. C. H.** see Hesse,
August Wilhelm

**WAGNER, FELIX** see Lederer,
J. Joachim

**WAGNER, GOTTLIEB HEINRICH**
Leipzig 1774-1835 Leipzig
Ref: Brüm 18, Goe 6, Ko 2

Liebesnetze - C2 (1816)
   Wm:1807

**WAGNER, HEINRICH LEOPOLD**
Strasbourg 1747-1779
Frankfurt/M
Ref: Brüm 18, Goe 4/1, Ko 2,
ADB, OC

Evchen Humbrecht o. Ihr
Mütter, merkt's euch - T
(1779)
   Fr:1778
Der Familienstolz - D5
   Mh:1779
Die Reue nach der Tat - T6
(1775)
   Ha:1775

**WALDAU, J. K.**

Die Sklaven - D1
   Mh:1803

**WALDAU, L.**

Nur kein Talent - C1
   Fr:1890

**WALDHERR, WILLIBALD**

Eine Frau - D4
   Da:1853  Dr:1853  Fr:1853
   Ha:1853  Va:1853

**WALDSTEIN, MAX**
Dörzbach 1836-1919 Vienna
Ref: Brüm 19, Ko 2

In Franzensbad - F1
    Va:1879
Veilchenduft - C1
    Va:1877

**WALL, ANTON** [Pseud. of
Christian Leberecht Heyne]
Leuben 1751-1821 Hirschberg
Ref: Brüm 18, Goe 4/1, Ko Th,
OC

Der Arrestant - C3 (1780)
    Bn:1781   Dr:1781   Va:1781
Die beiden Billets - C1 - Fr
(1783)
    Bn:1784   Da:1815   Dr:1785
    Fr:1792   Ha:1786   Lg:1812
    Mh:1783   Va:1788   Wm:1791
Die Expedition o. Die Hoch-
zeit nach dem Tode - C3
(1781)
    Bn:1782   Dr:1781   Mh:1783
    Va:1782
Die gute Ehe - C1 - Fr (1784)
    Bn:1784   Dr:1787   Fr:1803
    Mh:1791
Der Herr im Hause - C3 (1785)
    Ha:1786
Der Stammbaum - C1 (1791)
    Bn:1788   Dr:1789   Fr:1797
    Mh:1791   Va:1798   Wm:1791
Das Verständnis - D1 - Fr
    Va:1800

**WALL, B.**

Aus der komischen Oper - C1 -
Fr
    Fr:1862   Va:1861   Wm:1869
Merinos Schafe - C1
    Lg:1865
Vier Uhr morgens - C1
    Lg:1864

**WALLER, K. E.**  see Halirsch,
Friedrich Ludwig

**WALLSEE, HEINRICH EGON**
Lomnitz 1849-?
Ref: Brüm 19, Ko 2

Die Verlorenen - D5
    Va:1881

**WALTER**

Das Jawort - C5
    Va:1810

**WALTHER, F.**  see Wimpfen,
Baron

**WALZEL, CAMILLO**  see Zell, F.

**WANGENHEIM, FRANZ THEODOR**
Hanover 1805-1849 Hanover
Ref: Ko 2

Die Juristen - D5 (1847)
    Fr:1845   Ha:1844

**WARBURG, W. von**

Mitgefangen, mitgehangen - 1
    Bn:1866

**WARTENBURG, KARL FRIEDRICH**
Leipzig 1826-1889 Gera
Ref: Brüm 19, Ko 2, ADB

Der Ring des Agamemnon - C1
    Wm:1877
Die Schauspieler des Kaisers
- D3 (1878)
    Bn:1878   Da:1882   Fr:1878
    Lg:1879   Mu:1885   Va:1879

**WARTENEGG, WILHELM von**
Vienna 1839-1914 Vienna
Ref: Brüm 19, Ko 2

Andreas Paumkirchen - T5
(1878)
    Va:1878
Maria Stuart in Schottland -
T5 (1870)
    Va:1871
Rosamunde - T5 (1873)
    Fr:1875   Mu:1877

**WARTTEL, HEINRICH**

Der Kuß - C1
    Da:1861

**WEBER, CARL von**  [Pseud.:
Carl Marius]

Der Araber - C1
    Lg:1886
Die von Hutten - T5
    Lg:1886

**WEBER, VINCENZ**
Trautenau 1809-1859 Märisch-
Trübau
Ref: Brüm 19, Ko 2, ADB

Spartacus - T5 (1846)
    Va:1845
Die Wahabitin - T4 (1847)
    Va:1849

**WEGENER, KARL FRIEDRICH**
Pommerania 1734-1787 [1782]
Berlin
Ref: Goe 4/1, Ko 2, ADB

Erich und Florentine o. Die
geprüfte Zärtlichkeit - C3
(1775)
    Bn:1775

**WEHL, FEODOR** [i.e. zu Wehlen]
Kunzendorf 1821-1890 Hamburg
Ref: Brüm 19, Ko 2, ADB

Alter schützt vor Torheit
nicht - C1 (1864-69)
    Bn:1844   Ha:1845
Ein Bräutigam, der seine
Braut verheiratet - C1 (1864-
69)
    Da:1855   Dr:1856   Ha:1857
    Wm:1853
Caprice aus Liebe, Liebe aus
Caprice - C1
    Bn:1849   Da:1849   Dr:1849
    Wm:1849
Eine Frau, welche die Zeitung
liest - C1 (1864-69)
    Dr:1850   Fr:1851
Eine glühende Kohle - C1 -
with G. Horn (1864-69)
    Bn:1873   Dr:1857
Gräfin Colonna o. Die
schwarze Maske - D5
    Ha:1847
Hölderlins Liebe - D1 (1852)
    Dr:1850
Der Kosmos des Herrn von Hum-
boldt - C1 (1864-69)
    Fr:1864   Lg:1867
Man soll den Teufel nicht an
die Wand malen - F1 (1864-69)
    Bn:1849   Fr:1849
Romeo auf dem Bureau - F1
(1864-69)
    Dr:1858   Fr:1874   Ha:1857
    Wm:1860
Die Tante aus Schwaben - C1
(1864-69)
    Bn:1869   Dr:1850   Fr:1860
    Wm:1872

**WEIDMANN, FRANZ KARL**
Vienna 1787-1867 Vienna
Ref: Brüm 18, Goe 11, Ko 2,
ADB

Die Belagerung von Solothurn
- D2 (1821)
    Dr:1820   Va:1819
Clementine von Aubigny - D4
(1816)
    Mh:1817   Va:1816
Die Geächteten - D4 (1826)
    Va:1823
Die Scharfenecker - D5 (1821)
    Bn:1833   Va:1822

**WEIDMANN, JOSEF**
Vienna 1742-1810 Vienna
Ref: Goe 5, Ko 2, ADB

Die drei Zwillingsschwestern
- C5 (1785)
    Va:1785
Der Landphilosoph o. Die
natürliche Weisheit - C3
    Va:1787
Der Neider o. So rächt man
sich an seinen Feinden - C5
(1786)
    Va:1786
Die Rückfälle o. Die Stärke
der Gewohnheit - C5 (1788)
    Va:1788
Der Sonderling o. Besser
schielend als blind - C5
    Dr:1786   Va:1785
Weibliche Eroberungssucht -
C5 (1788)
    Va:1787

**WEIDMANN, PAUL**
Vienna 1744-1810 Vienna
Ref: Goe 5, Ko 2, ADB, OC

Dido - T5 (1771)
    Va:1776
Der Fabrikant o. Das war ein
fürstlicher Zeitvertreib - C3
    Va:1789
Der Fuchs in der Falle - o.
Die zwei Freunde - C5 (1776)
    Va:1776
Johann Faust - D5 (1775)
    Mu:1775
Der Mädchentausch - C2
    Va:1789
Der Mißbrauch der Gewalt - C5
(1778)
    Va:1778

Der reisende Student o. Das
Donnerwetter - C2 - Sp (1776)
  Va:1773
Die schöne Wienerin - C5
(1786)
  Va:1776
Der Schreiner - C2 (1794)
  Va:1787
Der Schwätzer o. Die
bösartige Mutter - C5 (1773)
  Bn:1774   Dr:1780   Fr:1804
  Va:1773
Der Stolze - C5 (1774)
  Va:1774

**WEIDNER, A. F.**

Luftschlösser - C4
  Ha:1853   Va:1838

**WEIHRAUCH, AUGUST**
Berlin 1818-1883 Rudolstadt
Ref: Ko 2, ADB

Die Maschinenbauer - F3
  Fr:1862   Ha:1860   Mh:1865
Die Mottenburger - F2 - with
D. Kalisch
  Ha:1868
Vetter Flausing o. Nur flott
leben - F3
  Fr:1853   Ha:1852
Die weiblichen Seeleute - Vv2
  Ha:1857
Wenn Leute Geld haben - C3
  Da:1865   Fr:1850   Ha:1850

**WEIKARD, MARIANNE SOPHIE** see
Reitzenstein, Marianne Sophie

**WEILEN, JOSEPH von**
Tetin 1828-1889 Vienna
Ref: Brüm 19, Ko 2, ADB

Am Tage von Oudenarde - D1
(1865)
  Va:1865
An der Grenze - D3
  Va:1876
Dolores - D5 (1874)
  Da:1873   Fr:1874   Lg:1874
  Va:1874
Drahomira - T5 (1868-70)
  Mh:1868   Mu:1869   Va:1867
Edda o. Der Aufstand der
Friesen - D4 (1865)
  Bn:1865   Lg:1864   Va:1864
Graf Horn - D5 (1871)
  Lg:1871   Mh:1871   Va:1870

Heinrich von der Aue - D4
(1874)
  Va:1860
König Erich - T4 (1881)
  Lg:1881   Mu:1881   Va:1881
  Wm:1880
Der neue Achilles - D3 (1872)
  Bn:1872   Va:1871
Rosamunde - T5 (1868-70)
  Mu:1869   Va:1869   Wm:1869
Tristan - T5 (1860)
  Dr:1861   Fr:1859   Ha:1859
  Va:1859

**WEIMAR, A.**   see Götze,
Auguste

**WEISHAUPT**

Die Isolierten - D4
  Wm:1837

**WEISKERN, FRIEDRICH WILHELM**
Eisleben 1710-1768 Vienna
Ref: Goe 5, Ko 2, ADB

Pamela als Mädchen - C3 - It
(1758)
  Va:1763

**WEISS, KARL**   [Pseud.: C.
Karlweis]
Vienna 1850-1901 Vienna
Ref: Brüm 19, Ko 2

Bruder Hans - C4 (1886)
  Va:1889

**WEISS, O. S.**

Der neue Paganini - C1 - with
F. Mamroth
  Va:1883
Die Reise nach Sumatra - F4 -
with F. Mamroth
  Va:1883

**WEISSE, CHRISTIAN FELIX**
Annaberg 1726-1804 Leipzig
Ref: Brüm 18, Goe 4, Ko 2,
ADB

Amalia - C5 (1766)
  Bn:1771   Dr:1777   Ha:1767
  Va:1783   Wm:1772
Armut und Tugend - D1 - Fr
(1772)
  Bn:1772   Fr:1780   Va:1773
Crispus - T5 (1764)
  Ha:1768

Eduard III. - T5 (1759)
  Bn:1772  Ha:1768
Der Fanatismus o. Jean Calas
D5 (1780)
  Bn:1780
Die Freundschaft auf der
Probe - C5 (1768)
  Lg:1777  Va:1771
List über List - C5 (1768)
  Ha:1768
Die Matrone von Ephesus - C1
(1778)
  Bn:1771
Mustapha und Zeangir - T5
(1763)
  Va:1782
Die Poeten nach der Mode - C3
(1759)
  Bn:1771  Mh:1780  Wm:1772
Richard der Dritte - T5 - Eng
(1759)
  Bn:1771  Fr:1777  Ha:1767
  Lg:1774  Mh:1779  Va:1770
  Wm:1772
Rosemunde - T5 (1763)
  Ha:1768
Walder o. Der treuherzige
Räuber - C1 (1770)
  Bn:1771  Va:1776  Wm:1772
Weibergeklatsche - C1 (1778)
  Mh:1782

**WEISSENBACH, ALOYS**
Telfs 1766-1821 Salzburg
Ref: Brüm 18, Goe 6, Ko 2,
ADB

Die Barmekiden o. Die Egyp-
tier in Bagdad - D5 (1801)
  Dr:1800  Va:1799
Der Brautkranz - T5 (1810)
  Da:1813  Fr:1812  Va:1809
Der zehnte November - C1
  Va:1816

**WEISSENTHURN, JOHANNA FRANUL
von**
Coblenz 1772-1845 Vienna
Ref: Brüm 18, Goe 11, Ko Th,
ADB

Adelheid, Markgräfin von
Burgau - D4 (1810)
  Bn:1810  Da:1810  Dr:1807
  Fr:1809  Mh:1813  Mu:1822
  Va:1806  Wm:1813
Agnes von der Lille - D4
(1822)
  Dr:1819  Fr:1819  Ha:1819
  Mh:1825

Alles aus Freundschaft - C1
(1848)
  Bn:1839  Ha:1839  Va:1839
  Wm:1848
Beschämte Eifersucht - C3
(1810)
  Bn:1801  Da:1810  Dr:1801
  Fr:1804  Ha:1816  Lg:1805
  Mh:1802  Mu:1805  Va:1801
  Wm:1805
Die Bestürmung von Smolensk -
D4 (1810)
  Bn:1809  Dr:1809  Fr:1810
  Ha:1808  Lg:1811  Mh:1811
  Mu:1815  Va:1808  Wm:1810
Der Bevollmächtigte - C1
  Bn:1841  Fr:1841  Lg:1844
  Va:1840
Die bezahlte Schuld - D4
  Va:1845
Der Brautschleier - C1 (1836)
  Bn:1833  Dr:1833  Fr:1841
  Va:1832  Wm:1837
Die Burg Gölding - D5 (1829)
  Da:1827  Fr:1827  Ha:1827
  Va:1826
Clementine [Die Versöhnung] -
D3 - Fr (1810)
  Bn:1807  Da:1810  Dr:1806
  Fr:1821  Lg:1808  Mh:1811
  Mu:1816  Va:1806  Wm:1811
Deutsche Treue - D1 (1810)
  Va:1803
Die Ehescheuen - C1 (1810)
  Bn:1809  Da:1813  Dr:1809
  Fr:1811  Mh:1810  Va:1808
  Wm:1812
Die Engländerin - C1 (1826)
  Dr:1824  Va:1824
Die Erben - C4 (1810)
  Bn:1804  Da:1814  Dr:1803
  Ha:1804  Lg:1804  Mh:1804
  Mu:1805  Va:1804
Die erste Liebe - C3 (1810)
  Bn:1808  Da:1813  Dr:1808
  Mh:1813  Va:1809  Wm:1813
Der erste Schritt - D4 (1836)
  Bn:1833  Dr:1834  Fr:1841
  Ha:1833  Va:1833  Wm:1842
Es spukt - C2 (1817)
  Bn:1819  Da:1813  Dr:1821
  Fr:1826  Mh:1821  Mu:1816
  Va:1810  Wm:1818
Die Fremde - D5 (1848)
  Bn:1839  Dr:1840  Ha:1839
  Mu:1839  Va:1838
Das Frühstück - C1 (1810)
  Bn:1833  Da:1815  Dr:1837
Die Geprüften - C5 (1836)
  Dr:1834

Das Gut Sternberg - D4 (1821)
Bn:1817   Da:1817   Dr:1817
Ha:1823   Lg:1818   Mh:1820
Va:1816   Wm:1819
Dies Haus ist zu verkaufen -
C1 - Fr (1810)
Bn:1801   Dr:1802   Lg:1817
Hermann o. Die Befreiung
Deutschlands - D5 (1817)
Dr:1814   Fr:1815   Ha:1817
Mh:1814   Va:1813
Johann, Herzog von Finnland -
D5 (1817)
Bn:1817   Da:1813   Dr:1821
Fr:1813   Lg:1821   Mh:1814
Va:1811   Wm:1815
Kindliche Liebe - D5 (1810)
Dr:1802   Fr:1806   Ha:1805
Mh:1802   Va:1802
Das Konzilium - C1 (1822)
Bn:1817   Da:1822   Va:1817
Das letzte Mittel - C4 (1826)
Bn:1820   Da:1826   Dr:1820
Fr:1820   Ha:1822   Lg:1820
Mh:1821   Mu:1829   Va:1820
Wm:1821
Liebe und Entsagung - D3
(1810)
Dr:1801   Ha:1805   Mh:1802
Va:1801
Des Malers Meisterstück - C2
(1836)
Bn:1832   Dr:1831   Fr:1845
Ha:1839   Lg:1831   Mu:1832
Va:1831   Wm:1855
Ein Mann hilft dem andern -
C1 (1823)
Bn:1822   Da:1822   Dr:1826
Fr:1823   Ha:1822   Lg:1829
Mh:1823   Mu:1823   Va:1822
Wm:1822
Das Manuskript - C5 (1832)
Bn:1827   Da:1827   Dr:1827
Fr:1827   Ha:1827   Mh:1832
Va:1826
Das Mißverständnis - C1
(1810)
Dr:1805   Ha:1805   Lg:1812
Va:1804
Das Nachspiel - C1 - Fr
(1810)
Dr:1811   Ha:1804   Lg:1814
Va:1800
Pauline - D5 (1832)
Bn:1825   Ha:1826   Lg:1835
Mh:1831   Va:1826
Die Pilgerin - D4 (1829)
Bn:1823   Dr:1822   Ha:1822
Mu:1822

Die Radikalkur - C3 (1810)
Bn:1815   Da:1810   Dr:1806
Fr:1805   Ha:1805   Mh:1826
Mu:1805   Va:1805   Wm:1813
Die Reise nach Amerika - D1
(1826)
Dr:1824   Va:1824
Die Reise nach Paris - C4
Va:1828
Der Reukauf - C2 (1810)
Ha:1806
Ruprecht, Graf zu Horneck -
T5 (1822)
Fr:1821   Va:1820
Die Schwestern St. Janvier -
D5 (1822)
Va:1822
Sie hilft sich selbst - C4
(1848)
Va:1842
Die stille Braut - D1 (1848)
Va:1842
Das System - C1
Va:1842
Totila, König der Gothen - D5
(1810)
Bn:1805   Dr:1805   Ha:1805
Va:1804
Der Traum - C1 (1826)
Dr:1824   Va:1824
Der Wald bei Hermannstadt -
D4 - Fr (1810)
Bn:1808   Da:1811   Dr:1807
Ha:1807   Lg:1817   Mh:1823
Mu:1816   Va:1807   Wm:1809
Welche ist die Braut? - C5
(1817)
Bn:1814   Da:1817   Dr:1815
Fr:1815   Ha:1830   Lg:1816
Mh:1820   Va:1813   Wm:1817
Welcher ist der Bräutigam? -
C4 (1821)
Bn:1816   Da:1817   Dr:1816
Fr:1818   Ha:1820   Lg:1818
Va:1816   Wm:1816
Wer Herzen behält, hat nichts
verloren - D3 (1810)
Va:1806

**WELISCH, JOHANN**
Ref: Goe 5

Der Kerkermeister von Norwich
- D4 (1776)
Va:1793

**WELTEN, OSKAR**
Lemberg 1844-1894 Mödling
Ref: Brüm 19, Ko 2, ADB

Eine Heirat auf Probe - C3
(1872)
  Va:1879

**WERDER, KARL FRIEDRICH**
Berlin 1806-1893 Berlin
Ref: Brüm 19, Ko 2, ADB

Christoph Columbus - T5
(1858)
  Bn:1842  Dr:1848

**WERNER, ELISABETH**

Aberglaube - C
  Mu:1880

**WERNER, MARIA**  see Olfers,
Maria von

**WERNER, P.** [Pauline Raupach?]

Frage und Antwort - F1
  Bn:1838

**WERNER, ZACHARIAS**
Königsberg 1768-1823 Vienna
Ref: Brüm 18, Goe 6, ADB, OC

Attila, König der Hunnen - T
(1808)
  Dr:1813  Fr:1832
Martin Luther o. Die Weihe
der Kraft - D5 (1807)
  Bn:1806  Fr:1847  Ha:1842
  Wm:1857
Die Templer auf Cypern - D5
(1803)
  Bn:1807  Va:1811
Der vierundzwanzigste Februar
- T1 (1815)
  Bn:1815  Dr:1815  Fr:1819
  Lg:1815  Wm:1810
Wanda, Königin der Sarmaten -
T5 (1810)
  Wm:1808

**WERTHEIMER, JOSEF von**
Vienna 1800-1887 Vienna
Ref: Brüm 19, Ko 2

Der Bucklige - D5 - Eng
(1838)
  Va:1833
Der Hirtensohn - D1 (1838)
  Va:1839

**WERTHER, JULIUS von**
Roßla 1838-1910 Pertisau
Ref: Brüm 19, Ko 2

Der Fürst von Isolabella - D
(1876)
  Mu:1875
Das Grabdenkmal - D (1873)
  Mu:1875
Der Kriegsplan - C (1876)
  Mh:1878  Mu:1881
Mazarin - T (1871)
  Mu:1871
Pombal - D5 (1871)
  Lg:1873  Mh:1872
Weite Gewissen - D4 (1879)
  Lg:1880

**WERTHER, KARL LUDWIG**
[Pseud.: Karl Lampe]
Thuringia 1809-1861 Dresden
Ref: Brüm 19, Ko 2

Susanna und Daniel - D4
(1855)
  Bn:1853

**WERTHES, FRIEDRICH AUGUST
CLEMENS**
Buttenhausen 1748-1817
Stuttgart
Ref: Brüm 18, Goe 4/1, Ko 2,
ADB

Bayard o. Der Ritter ohne
Furcht und Tadel - D5
  Dr:1786  Va:1786
Rudolph von Habspurg - D5
(1775)
  Va:1785
Die zwei schlaflosen Nächte -
C5 - It
  Va:1785

**WETZEL, FRIEDRICH WILHELM**
Mönchberg 1738-after 1800
Ref: Goe 4/1

Der König o. Das Abenteuer -
C3 (1785)
  Dr:1788

**WEYLAND, PHILIPP CHRISTOPH**
Buchsweiler 1765-1843
Ref: Goe 6, Ko 2

Die Spiele des Zufalls - C3 -
Fr
  Wm:1810
Die überraschung - C3
  Wm:1806

**WEZEL, JOHANN KARL**
Sondershausen 1747-1819
Sondershausen
Ref: Brüm 18, Goe 4/1, Ko 2,
ADB, OC

Der erste Dank - C1 (1782)
   Mh:1783
Ertappt, ertappt! - C1 (1778)
   Bn:1779  Mh:1783
Die komische Familie - C5
(1782)
   Dr:1787
Rache für Rache - C4 (1778)
   Bn:1779  Fr:1779  Mh:1780
Wildheit und Großmut - C2
(1782)
   Bn:1779

**WICHERT, ERNST ALEXANDER**
Insterburg 1831-1902 Berlin
Ref: Brüm 19, Ko 2, OC

Biegen oder brechen - C4
(1874)
   Lg:1871  Mu:1871  Va:1875
Das eiserne Kreuz - D1 (1870)
   Fr:1871  Mu:1870
Die Fabrik von Niederbronn -
D5 (1872)
   Lg:1872  Mh:1872
Der Freund des Fürsten - C4
(1878)
   Bn:1879  Mu:1879  Va:1880
   Wm:1879
Der geheime Sekretair - C3
(1880)
   Bn:1880
Ihr Taufschein - C1 (1867)
   Bn:1865
Licht und Schatten - D (1861)
   Ha:1806
Der Mann der Freundin - C1
   Bn:1889
Der Narr des Glückes - C5
(1867)
   Bn:1870  Da:1872  Mu:1870
   Va:1869
Peter Munk - D4 (1881)
   Lg:1883
Post festum - C1 (1888)
   Bn:1889  Da:1889  Wm:1889
Die Realisten - C4 (1873)
   Bn:1874  Mu:1873  Va:1874
Ein Schritt vom Wege - C4
(1870)
   Bn:1872  Da:1874  Fr:1872
   Mu:1872  Va:1872  Wm:1873

**WICKENBURG-ALMASY, WILHELMINE**
**von**
Ofen 1845-1890 Gries
Ref: Brüm 19, Ko 2, ADB

Das Dokument - D3
   Bn:1882  Fr:1882

**WIDMANN, CHRISTIAN ADOLF**
Maichingen 1818-1878 Berlin
Ref: Brüm 19, Ko 2, ADB

Sarah Hassfurter - D (1858)
   Mu:1859

**WIEDEMANN**

Der verfolgte Witwer - F3
   Da:1846

**WIELAND, LUDWIG FRIEDRICH**
Weimar 1777-1819 Jena
Ref: Goe 6, Ko 2

Die Überraschung - C3
   Dr:1805
Die Unvermählte - C3
   Dr:1807  Lg:1807
Will niemand Schauspieler
werden? - C3
   Dr:1813

**WIENER, MORRIS** [i.e. Moritz
Bergomanter]
Berlin 1812-1903 Baltimore
Ref: Brüm 19, Ko 2

Die Waise von Lucca - T5
(1844)
   Bn:1845

**WIESNER**

Ines de Castro - D5
   Va:1840

**WILBRANDT, ADOLF**
Rostock 1837-1911 Rostock
Ref: Brüm 19, Ko 2, OC

Arria und Messalina - T5
(1874)
   Fr:1881  Lg:1876  Va:1874
Assunta Leoni - D5 (1883)
   Bn:1884  Va:1884
Auf den Brettern - D3
   Lg:1877  Mu:1878  Va:1878
Durch die Zeitung - C1 (1874)
   Mu:1870  Va:1872

Frieden im Krieg - D4
  Lg:1881
Gracchus der Volkstribun - T5
(1873)
  Fr:1873  Lg:1876  Mh:1873
  Mu:1872  Va:1872  Wm:1872
Graf Hammerstein - D5 (1870)
  Bn:1870  Da:1886  Fr:1871
  Lg:1870  Mh:1870  Mu:1871
  Wm:1873
Johann Ohlerich - C!
  Va:1884
Johannes Erdmann - D4
  Va:1881
Jugendliebe - C1 (1872)
  Bn:1871  Da:1871  Fr:1871
  Mh:1871  Mu:1872  Va:1871
  Wm:1871
Ein Kampf ums Dasein - C3
(1874)
  Mu:1873  Va:1873
Kriemhild - T3 (1877)
  Bn:1882  Lg:1882  Va:1880
Der Lootsenkommandeur - D
  Mu:1890
Die Maler - C3 (1872)
  Bn:1872  Da:1877  Fr:1879
  Ha:1878  Lg:1874  Mh:1874
  Mu:1871  Va:1871  Wm:1873
Das Märchen vom Untersberg -
D3
  Va:1884
Marianne - C
  Mu:1890
Der Meister von Palmyra - T
(1889)
  Mu:1889
Nathalie - D5
  Va:1878
Nero - T5 (1872)
  Va:1875
Die Reise nach Riva - C3
(1877)
  Va:1877
Suchet, so werdet ihr finden
- D5
  Va:1873
Die Tochter des Herrn
Fabricius - D3 (1883)
  Fr:1880  Lg:1881  Mu:1879
  Va:1880  Wm:1890
Der Turm in der Stadtmauer -
C3 (1878)
  Va:1878
Unerreichbar - C1 (1870)
  Bn:1869  Da:1874  Fr:1872
  Lg:1870  Mu:1869  Va:1869
  Wm:1870
Der Unterstaatssekretär - C4
  Va:1890

Die Verlobten - C
  Mu:1868
Die Vermählten - S3 (1872)
  Bn:1871  Fr:1871  Mu:1868
  Va:1871
Die Wahrheit lügt
  Mu:1870  Va:1874
Die Wege des Glücks - C5
(1876)
  Va:1876

**WILDENBRUCH, ERNST von**
Beirut 1845-1909 Berlin
Ref: Brüm 19, Ko 2, OC

Auf der hohen Schule - D5
  Wm:1875
Christoph Marlow - T4 (1885)
  Bn:1884  Mu:1884
Der Fürst von Verona - T5
(1887)
  Bn:1887
Harold - T5 (1882)
  Bn:1882  Fr:1884  Lg:1882
  Mu:1882  Va:1884  Wm:1882
Die Haubenlerche - D (1891)
  Fr:1890
Die Karolinger - T5 (1882)
  Bn:1883  Da:1884  Lg:1884
  Mu:1889  Va:1882  Wm:1887
Der König von Kandia - 4
  Fr:1883  Wm:1884
Der Menonit - T4 (1882)
  Bn:1888  Da:1882  Fr:1881
  Lg:1883  Mu:1882  Wm:1882
Das neue Gebot - D4 (1886)
  Fr:1886  Lg:1886  Wm:1888
Opfer um Opfer - D5 (1883)
  Bn:1882  Fr:1882  Wm:1883
Die Quitzows - D4 (1888)
  Bn:1888  Fr:1889
Väter und Söhne - D5 (1882)
  Fr:1882  Lg:1886  Va:1883

**WILHELMI, ALEXANDER** [Pseud.
of Alexander Viktor Zech-
meister]
Ofen 1817-1877 Meran
Ref: Ko 2, ADB

Abwarten! - C1 (1853-60)
  Dr:1853  Fr:1853
Eine Anzeige - C1 (1853-60)
  Dr:1859
Der Chevalier und der treue
Diener - C
  Ha:1844
Durch's Fernrohr - C1 (1853-
60)
  Bn:1858  Dr:1858  Va:1858

Einer muß heiraten - C1
(1853-60)
    Bn:1850    Da:1851    Dr:1850
    Fr:1850    Ha:1850    Mu:1872
    Va:1851
Er hat Recht - C1 (1853-60)
    Dr:1857  Fr:1865  Va:1857
Fest im Entschlusse - C1
(1853-60)
    Dr:1851  Fr:1851  Va:1851
Ein gutes Herz - C2 (1853-60)
    Dr:1854
Der letzte Trumpf - C1 (1853-
60)
    Fr:1855  Va:1857
Mit den Wölfen muß man heulen
- C1 (1853-60)
    Da:1858  Dr:1856  Ha:1858
    Va:1857
Eine schöne Schwester - C3
(1853-60)
    Bn:1853  Dr:1852
Zurück! - D4 (1853-60)
    Dr:1861

**WILKEN, HEINRICH**
Thorn 1835-1886 Berlin
Ref: Brüm 19, Ko 2

Auf eigenen Füßen - F - with
E. Pohl (1883)
    Fr:1878
Ehrliche Arbeit - FP
    Fr:1876
Elzevir - F1 (1868)
    Ha:1868  Lg:1868  Va:1872
Gesellschaftliche Pflichten -
F4 - with O. Justinus (1881)
    Lg:1883
Im Charakter - F1
    Fr:1872
Die neue Magdalena - D4
    Va:1873

**WILLFRIED, HERMINE**  see
Villinger, Hermine

**WILLIG, E.**  see Geyer, Ludwig
Heinrich

**WIMPFEN, Baron**  [Pseud.: F.
Walther]

Die Amerikanerin - D5
    Bn:1852
Form und Gehalt - C4
    Bn:1854

**WINKLER, KARL GOTTLIEB
THEODOR**  see Hell, Theodor

**WINTER, A.**

Ein anonymer Kuß - C1 - Fr
    Ha:1868  Lg:1868
Ballschuhe - C1
    Ha:1868
Die Ehestifterin - F1 - Fr
    Ha:1868
Unsere braven Landleute - D4
- Fr
    Ha:1867

**WINTERFELD, ADOLF WILHELM
ERNST**  [Pseud.: Adolphi]
Alt-Ruppin 1824-1889 Berlin
Ref: Brüm 19, Ko 2, ADB

Frauentränen - C1 - Fr (1859)
    Da:1860  Dr:1858  Fr:1863
    Ha:1861  Wm:1859
Guter Name - D3
    Bn:1877
Der Hauptmann von Kapernaum -
F3
    Bn:1875
Ich esse bei meiner Mutter -
C1 - Fr
    Fr:1857
Neckereien - C1
    Bn:1874
Der Winkelschreiber - C3 -
Lat (1868)
    Bn:1860  Fr:1861  Ha:1860
    Lg:1868  Mh:1863  Va:1861

**WITTLINGER, HELENE**

Der Storch hats gebracht - D1
    Fr:1882

**WITTMANN, HUGO**
Ulm 1839-1923 Vienna
Ref: Brüm 19, Ko 2

Wilddiebe - C4 - with
T. Herzl (1891)
    Fr:1889  Va:1889

**WITZLEBEN, KARL AUGUST von**
see Tromlitz, A. von

**WODOMERIUS, ERNST**  [Pseud. of
Gustav Adolf Heeringen]
Mehlra 1800-1851 Coburg
Ref: Goe 10, Ko 2

Iwan - T4 (1836)
    Ha:1832

**WOHLMUTH, LEONHARD**
Hohenzell 1823-1889 Bayreuth
Ref: Brüm 19, Ko 2

Ännchen von Tharau - D (1864)
   Mu:1887
Deutsche Treue - D (1869)
   Mu:1873
Mozart - D3 (1856)
   Fr:1854

**WOLF**

Der Selbstgefällige - C1
   Wm:1805
Die Witwe und der Mops - F1
   Wm:1814

**WOLFART, KARL CHRISTIAN**
Hanau 1778-1832 Berlin
Ref: Brüm 18, Goe 6, Ko 2,
ADB

Kaiser Nero o. Die Katakomben
- T5 (1810)
   Mh:1818   Mu:1822   Va:1812

**WOLFF, JULIUS**
Quedlinburg 1834-1910 Berlin
Ref: Brüm 19, Ko 2, OC

Der Fiskus - C4
   Wm:1882
Junggesellensteuer - C4
(1877)
   Fr:1881   Lg:1882   Mu:1878

**WOLFF, OSKAR LUDWIG BERNHARD**
Altona 1799-1851 Jena
Ref: Brüm 18, Goe 13, Ko 2,
OC

Walter Scott - C2
   Wm:1826

**WOLFF, PIUS ALEXANDER**
[Pseud.: von Leitershofen]
Augsburg 1782-1828 Weimar
Ref: Brüm 18, Goe 11, Ko 2,
ADB

Bankrott aus Liebe - F1
   Wm:1805
Cäsario - C5 (1823)
   Bn:1810   Da:1811   Dr:1810
   Fr:1810   Lg:1813   Mh:1813
   Va:1810   Wm:1810

Die drei Gefangenen - C5 - Fr
   Bn:1804   Da:1810   Dr:1804
   Fr:1823   Lg:1804   Mh:1805
   Va:1825   Wm:1804
Der Hund des Aubry - F1
(1822)
   Bn:1818   Da:1819   Dr:1818
   Lg:1818   Mu:1822
Der Kammerdiener [Baron
Schiffelinski]- F4 (1832)
   Bn:1828   Da:1859   Dr:1836
   Fr:1856   Ha:1851   Lg:1832
   Mh:1832   Wm:1829
Der Mann von fünfzig Jahren -
C2 (1830)
   Bn:1828   Da:1830   Dr:1828
   Ha:1828   Lg:1830   Mh:1830
   Mu:1834   Va:1828   Wm:1829
Mathilde o. Der letzt Wille
einer Engländerin - D3 - Fr
   Bn:1829   Va:1828
Pflicht um Pflicht - D1
(1817)
   Bn:1816   Da:1821   Dr:1817
   Fr:1830   Ha:1827   Lg:1814
   Mh:1825   Wm:1814
Schwere Wahl - C3 - Sp
   Bn:1822   Ha:1822
Der Selbstgefällige - C1
   Wm:1805
Die Steckenpferde - C5 (1829)
   Bn:1825   Da:1829   Dr:1825
   Lg:1825   Mh:1829   Mu:1825
   Va:1825   Wm:1826
Treue siegt in Liebesnetzen -
D1 (1828)
   Bn:1817
Der Vermittler - C5 - Fr
   Wm:1806

**WOLFSOHN, WILHELM** [Pseud.:
Carl Maien]
Odessa 1820-1865 Dresden
Ref: Brüm 19, Ko 2, ADB

Nur eine Seele - D5 (1857-59)
   Da:1864   Dr:1857   Fr:1861
   Lg:1865
Die Osternacht - D5 (1857-59)
   Dr:1858
Zar und Bürger - D5 (1857-59)
   Dr:1854

**WOLLHEIM, ANTON EDMUND**
Hamburg 1810-1884 Berlin
Ref: Brüm 19, Ko 2, ADB

Andrea - D4
    Dr:1838
Der Barbier von Lerchenfeld -
D4
    Ha:1845
Dom Sebastian - D5
    Bn:1843
Der fliegende Holländer - F3
    Ha:1840
Der letzte Maure - T
    Ha:1845
Meisels Wanderungen - F
    Ha:1847
Raphael Sanzio - D5 (1856)
    Da:1850   Dr:1849   Fr:1850
    Va:1848   Wm:1849
Rosen im Norden - Z4
    Ha:1849
Der Sohn der Elfen - D
    Ha:1843
Tillys Tod - D
    Ha:1842

**WOLLOMITZER, JOSEF**

Kritik der reinen Vernunft -
F1
    Va:1880

**WOLZOGEN, ERNST von**
Breslau 1855-1934 Munich
Ref: Brüm 19, Ko 2, OC

Die Verschwörung von Nérac -
C3
    Wm:1881

**WOLZOGEN, KARL AUGUST ALFRED**
Frankfurt/M 1823-1883 San
Remo
Ref: Brüm 19, Ko 2, ADB

Die glückliche Braut - C1
(1870)
    Fr:1871
Sakuntala - D5 (1869)
    Mu:1875   Va:1874

**WÖRLE, KARL HEINRICH THEODOR**
[Pseud.: Oswald Stein]
Metzlos 1830-?
Ref: Brüm 19, Ko 2

Stilicho - T5 (1864)
    Da:1865

**WORTTIL**

Ein Kuß - C1
    Lg:1866

**WULFF, FRIEDRICH WILIBALD**
Hamburg 1837-1898 Ginsterfeld
Ref: Brüm 19, Ko 2, ADB

Madame Bonnard - D5
    Fr:1874   Lg:1874

**WÖRKERT, LUDWIG FRIEDRICH**
[Pseud.: Ludwig Rein]
Leisnig 1800-1876 Leisnig
Ref: Brüm 19, Goe 13, Ko 2

Die Prüfungen - T1 (1821)
    Lg:1821

**WYKANDER, OSKAR**

Siri - C1
    Lg:1879

**ZAHLHAS, JOHANN BAPTIST**
Vienna 1787-1870 Vienna
Ref: Brüm 18, Goe 11, Ko 2,
ADB

Der Bruder - T4 (1824)
    Fr:1820
Heinrich von Anjou - T5
(1819)
    Bn:1816   Dr:1817   Fr:1816
    Lg:1816   Mh:1821   Mu:1815
    Va:1815
Das Leben ein Traum - D5 - Sp
(1818)
    Lg:1818
Ludwig XIV. und sein Hof - C4
    Fr:1849   Ha:1846   Lg:1847
Marie-Louise von Orleans - D5
(1824)
    Ha:1840
Ein Tag Karl Stuarts II. - C4
    Bn:1839   Dr:1840   Fr:1840
    Ha:1839   Mu:1839
Die weiße Frau - T5
    Lg:1819   Mu:1821

**ZECHMEISTER, ALEXANDER VIKTOR**
see Wilhelmi, Alexander

**ZEDLITZ, JOSEPH CHRISTIAN von**
Johannisberg 1790-1862 Vienna
Ref: Brüm 18, Goe 8, Ko 2,
ADB, OC

Cabinets-Intriguen - C3
(1836)
    Ha:1837

Herr und Sklave - T2 (1834)
     Da:1838   Dr:1833   Fr:1830
     Ha:1839   Lg:1827   Mh:1829
     Mu:1841   Wm:1833
Kerker und Krone - D5 (1834)
     Bn:1836   Fr:1837   Ha:1836
     Mh:1836   Mu:1849   Va:1834
     Wm:1837
Liebe findet ihre Wege - C4
(1827)
     Va:1825
Der Stern von Sevilla - T5 -
Sp (1830)
     Bn:1829   Da:1830   Dr:1829
     Fr:1837   Ha:1827   Lg:1833
     Mu:1830   Va:1855   Wm:1830
Turturell - T5 (1821)
     Va:1819
Zwei Nächte zu Valladolid -
T5 (1825)
     Da:1825   Mu:1823   Va:1823
     Wm:1827

**ZELL, F.**  [Pseud. of Camillo
Walzel]
Magdeburg 1829-1895 Vienna
Ref: Brüm 19, Ko 2

Die Büste - C2 - Fr
     Bn:1878   Da:1879   Fr:1880
     Lg:1879   Mu:1878   Va:1878
Seit Gravelotte - D1
     Fr:1873   Va:1872
Der Raubmörder - C1 - Fr
     Fr:1875   Va:1874
Vom Touristenkränzchen - F1
     Va:1878
Ein zweiter Tallyrand - C2 -
Fr
     Va:1879

**ZIEGLER, FRIEDRICH WILHELM**
Braunschweig 1759 [1756?]-
1827 Preßburg
Ref: Brüm 18, Goe 5, Ko 2,
ADB

Barbarei und Größe - T4
(1793)
     Da:1794   Va:1793   Wm:1795
Benvenuto Cellini o. Das Bild
der Porzia - C4 (1824)
     Bn:1831
Der Erbprinz o. Das große Geheimnis - D4 (1801)
     Va:1800
Ernst und Scherz o. Das
seltene Duell - C3 (1817)
     Va:1809

Eulalia Meinau - T4 (1791)
     Bn:1791
Die Freunde - D4 (1797)
     Bn:1796   Dr:1796   Fr:1799
     Va:1796
Fürstengröße - D5 (1793)
     Bn:1793   Fr:1792   Ha:1792
     Mh:1792   Va:1791
Das Gastrecht - D5 (1800)
     Da:1812   Dr:1800   Mh:1813
     Mu:1816   Va:1799
Die Großmama - C4 (1817)
     Da:1815   Dr:1810   Fr:1819
     Mu:1815
Der Hausdoktor - C3 (1802)
     Dr:1819   Fr:1820   Mh:1800
     Va:1797   Wm:1811
Das Inkognito o. Der König
auf Reisen - C4 (1793)
     Bn:1793   Da:1814   Dr:1792
     Ha:1792   Mh:1793   Va:1792
     Wm:1795
Jolantha, Königin von Jerusa-
lem - T4 (1799)
     Bn:1797   Da:1814   Fr:1807
     Va:1797
Der Liebhaber im Harnisch -
C4 (1799)
     Va:1798
Liebhaber und Nebenbuhler in
einer Person - C4 (1791)
     Bn:1792   Dr:1791   Fr:1792
     Mh:1792   Va:1790   Wm:1793
Der Lorbeerkranz o. Die Macht
der Gesetze - D5 (1799)
     Da:1810   Dr:1798   Fr:1808
     Ha:1820   Mh:1800   Mu:1816
     Va:1798   Wm:1799
Die Macht der Liebe - T4 - Fr
(1817)
     Fr:1811   Va:1811
Der Machtspruch - T5 (1807)
     Bn:1813   Da:1810   Dr:1807
     Fr:1807   Lg:1807   Mh:1808
     Mu:1823   Va:1807   Wm:1809
Mathilde, Gräfin von Giesbach
o. Das Faustrecht - T5 (1791)
     Dr:1792   Mh:1790   Mu:1790
     Va:1790   Wm:1792
Die Mohrin - D4 (1802)
     Bn:1802   Da:1821   Fr:1819
     Mh:1820   Mu:1822   Va:1801
Parteienwut - D5 (1817)
     Bn:1815   Da:1816   Dr:1816
     Fr:1811   Lg:1816   Mh:1817
     Mu:1816   Va:1815   Wm:1817
Das Petschaft - D5 (1800)
     Dr:1799   Mu:1816   Va:1798

Die Pilger - D5 (1792)
  Dr:1793   Mh:1792   Va:1791
Repressalien - D4 (1802)
  Da:1802   Mh:1802   Va:1801
Das Scheibenschießen o. Die
Liebe von Jugend auf - C4
(1824)
  Va:1820
Die Schirmherren [Der Schirm-
herr] von Lissabon - D5
(1817)
  Fr:1812
Seelengröße o. Der Landsturm
in Tyrol - D5 (1799)
  Va:1799
Der seltene Mann [Ehemann] -
D4 (1824)
  Lg:1802   Va:1801
Der seltene Onkel - C4 (1792)
  Dr:1791   Fr:1793   Mh:1792
  Va:1791   Wm:1793
Die seltsame Heirat - C4
(1824)
  Da:1820   Lg:1819   Mh:1822
  Va:1819
Stumme Liebe - C1 (1802)
  Va:1799
Der Tag der Erlösung - D4
(1799)
  Fr:1799   Mh:1800   Va:1798
Thekla, die Wienerin - D5
(1817)
  Va:1809
Vaterstand - C4 (1802)
  Va:1802
Die vier Temperamente - C3
(1821)
  Bn:1820   Da:1821   Dr:1819
  Fr:1819   Ha:1820   Lg:1819
  Mh:1827   Va:1819   Wm:1820
Vierzehn Tage nach dem
Schusse - C1 (1824)
  Bn:1820   Da:1821   Dr:1819
  Fr:1819   Ha:1820   Lg:1819
  Va:1819
Weiberehre - D5 (1793)
  Da:1813   Fr:1808   Lg:1793
  Mh:1796   Va:1792
Weiberlaunen und Männer-
schwäche - C5 (1797)
  Dr:1793   Va:1792
Weltton und Herzensgüte - D4
(1799)
  Bn:1827   Da:1812   Dr:1794
  Fr:1796   Ha:1798   Lg:1794
  Mh:1797   Va:1793   Wm:1797

### ZIERRATH

Cromwells Sohn o. Eine
Restauration - D5 - Fr
  Wm:1845
Die Tanzstunde in der Dach-
stube - F1 - Fr
  Ha:1852

### ZIMMERMANN, J. F. S.

Damen und Husaren - C3
  Bn:1834

### ZSCHOKKE, HEINRICH
Magdeburg 1771-1848 Aarau
Ref: Brüm 18, Goe 10, Ko 2,
ADB, OC

Aballino - T5 (1795)
  Bn:1795   Da:1810   Dr:1796
  Fr:1795   Ha:1796   Lg:1795
  Mh:1797   Mu:1798   Va:1808
  Wm:1795
Die eiserne Larve - T5 (1804)
  Bn:1804   Ha:1820   Mh:1808
Das entdeckte Verbrechen
  Va:1799
Der Geizige - C5 - Fr (1805)
  Bn:1805   Da:1810   Dr:1819
  Fr:1806   Ha:1821   Lg:1818
  Mh:1806   Mu:1812   Va:1807
  Wm:1805
Georg Rothbart - C3 - Fr
(1805)
  Bn:1806
Die Heirat wider Willen - F1
Fr (1805)
  Bn:1807
Hippolyt und Roswida - D4
(1803)
  Mu:1807   Va:1803
Julius von Sassen - T4 (1796)
  Fr:1807   Ha:1802   Mh:1825
Der Marschall von Sachsen -
D4 (1804)
  Fr:1804   Mu:1804   Wm:1804
Der Wunderarzt - C3 - Fr
(1805)
  Mh:1806   Wm:1805
Die Zauberin Sidonia - D4
(1798)
  Bn:1796   Da:1811   Fr:1806
  Ha:1817   Wm:1799

### ZUSCHAUER, FREIMUND   see
Rellstab, Ludwig

### ZWENGSAHN, KARL   see Langen-
schwarz, Leopold

# Title Index

## About the Compiler

VERONICA C. RICHEL is Associate Professor of German at the University of Vermont. Her books include *Luise Gottsched: A Reconsideration* and *Miss Sara Sampson, Erlauterungen und Dokumente*. Her articles have appeared in *Germanic Notes* and *Neuphilologische Mitteilungen*.